**Power
Yachts**

Power Yachts

Rosemary and Colin Mudie

ADLARD COLES LIMITED
GRANADA PUBLISHING
London Toronto Sydney New York

Published by Granada Publishing in
Adlard Coles Limited 1977

Granada Publishing Limited
Frogmore, St Albans, Herts AL2 2NF
and
3 Upper James Street, London W1R 4BP
1221 Avenue of the Americas, New York, NY 10020 USA
117 York Street, Sydney, NSW 2000, Australia
100 Skyway Avenue, Toronto, Ontario, Canada M9W 3A6
Trio City, Coventry Street, Johannesburg, 2001, South Africa

Copyright © 1977 Rosemary and Colin Mudie

ISBN 0 229 98663 3

Filmset in 'Monophoto' Univers 10 on 12 pt by
Richard Clay (The Chaucer Press), Ltd, Bungay, Suffolk

For Max

Contents

CHAPTER 1
The Way of a Ship in the Sea

General

Two thousand years ago (was it in the middle of the Sinai desert?) some sage declared that one of the biggest mysteries in the world was the way of a ship in the sea. Two thousand years more of daily use of oceans and a modicum of scientific research have passed and still there are many of us who cling to the same views. We look at ships and are eager to see mysteries instead of the often commonplace explanations. There are many, many mysteries left at a somewhat esoteric level, but by and large the greater part of the understanding of the way of a ship in the sea comes from looking for simple and logical explanations. We are perhaps still unable to translate our knowledge into the hard and rigid language of science,

but this is more of a problem for interpreters than for practitioners.

Consider first then our ship, motor boat or motor yacht, sitting quietly at rest in flat water in complete equilibrium with the watery world all around. Then we start the engines and let in our ahead clutches to apply the propulsive power. Three things happen — at least three, that is, for the unexpected is always with us. However, the three main effects of applying the power are:

1. The thrust from the propulsive unit produces a couple about the centre of buoyancy of the boat. This can only be balanced by a change of hull trim. With a normal inboard engine arrangement the propeller thrust acts along the shaft line producing a couple to push the bows down,

Fig. 1   First the launching — some boats just do not seem to want to go to sea.

Fig. 2 *The launching of* Avila, *leaving behind the residue of two years of building.*

Fig. 3 *. . . sitting quietly in the sea.*

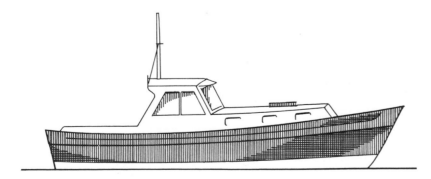

and the normal outboard engine would produce the opposite effect to push the bows up.

2. The forward thrust pushes the hull through the water.

3. The water pushed aside by the bows sets up a wave system along the length of the hull. The arrangement of crests and hollows can also affect the basic buoyant trim of the hull. Some unbalanced power-thrust systems, such as a single propeller, can also affect athwartships trim from the simple effect of the torque.

The wave system divides itself into two distinct forms. From the bow and stern spring divergent waves running away diagonally from the craft and along the length of the hull; this develops a neat system of so-called transverse waves which travel at right angles to the hull and, of course, at the same speed. These transverse waves are a major factor in the performance of the craft in that the energy absorbed in creating them is the biggest factor in wave-making resistance at speed, and the attitude in which they leave the craft sitting is critical in considering the extra power required to drive her faster. The length between crests of a symmetrical standard wave form of the type set up around a craft is $\left(\dfrac{V}{1\cdot 34}\right)^2$ and it is no coincidence that this can be rearranged, for waves, to take the form $\dfrac{V}{\sqrt{L}} = 1\cdot 34$ and that the normal maximum speed for a boat is the same formula.

The ship moves forward accompanied by its train of waves, and the distance between the wave crests is proportional to the speed of the boat. It is also proportional to the square root of the waterline length of the craft, which therefore allows all craft to be compared on a relative speed basis. If V, the speed, divided by $\sqrt{L}$, the waterline length, is the same for two craft of different dimensions, they are operating the same kind of wave-making systems and are therefore open to comparison.

When V is measured in knots and L in feet it so happens that when $\dfrac{V}{\sqrt{L}}$ is unity the wave system has come down to two crests separated, of course, by a hollow. Up to this speed the craft is quite easily driven and is supported in a reasonably even manner by a number of wave crests which are comparatively small. At $\dfrac{V}{\sqrt{L}}$ of 1 the

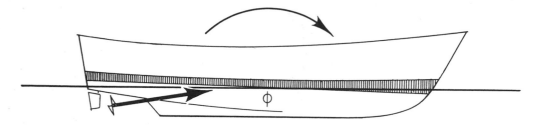

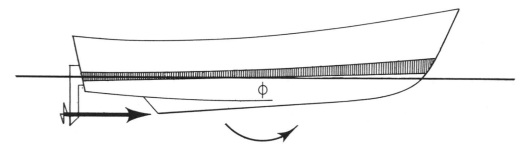

Fig. 4   The thrust of a well angled propeller shaft will push the bows down.

Fig. 5   The thrust from an outboard unit will push the bows up.

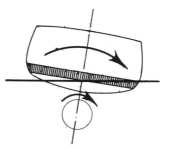

Fig. 6   The propeller torque will cause the craft to heel.

Fig. 7   The basic wave system set up around the hull.

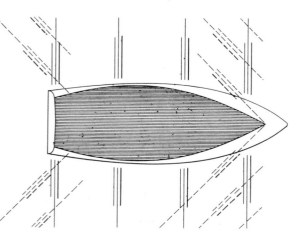

hull is nicely supported by a wave at each end. This also fits very happily the most convenient shape for making boats and some are especially designed round the wave form. This is the most efficient and economical speed at which to drive a boat.

Above $\dfrac{V}{\sqrt{L}}$ of 1 the wave system starts to get longer than the boat and the support for the bow moves aft and the support for the stern also moves aft, tending to drop the aft end into the trough. The maximum practical speed at which the wave system still gives enough support for the vessel to travel in a reasonably respectable

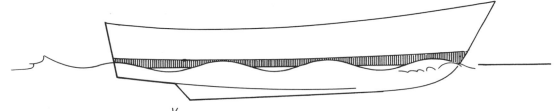

Fig. 8 The transverse wave system at $\frac{V}{\sqrt{L}}$ of about 0·75, say about 4½ knots for 36 ft waterline craft.

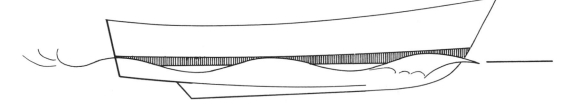

Fig. 9 The transverse wave system at $\frac{V}{\sqrt{L}}$ of about 0·9, say about 5½ knots for 36 ft waterline craft.

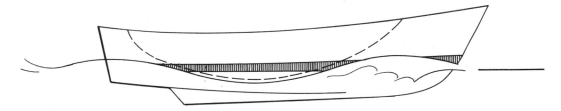

Fig. 10 The transverse wave system at $\frac{V}{\sqrt{L}}$ of about 1·2, say about 7¼ knots for 36 ft waterline craft. Note how the buttock line (shown by dotted line) can be designed to follow the wave form.

posture is somewhere between a $\frac{V}{\sqrt{L}}$ of 1·3 to 1·5, depending upon the hull form. Obviously the capacity of the shape of the vessel to make use of the stern wave makes a difference to the effective *L* which might be used instead of the nominal length measured by a ruler off the profile.

It is possible to use the coefficient of water-plane area, which indirectly indicates the fullness of the ends, as a factor to convert *L* to a more accurate figure for estimating the wave system,

but once the principle is understood it is really not worth the trouble.

When the boat is powered to go faster than this the stern wave falls right aft of the stern and the hull is left climbing the bow wave. Quite a proportion of the combination of the buoyant lift from the bow wave and the thrust up the propeller shaft is directed now to push the hull upwards bodily. The buoyant lift is not a single force as shown in Fig. 12 but is spread all over the hull bottom and is approximately proportional to the depth below the surface. The water flow is,

The Way of a Ship in the Sea **5**

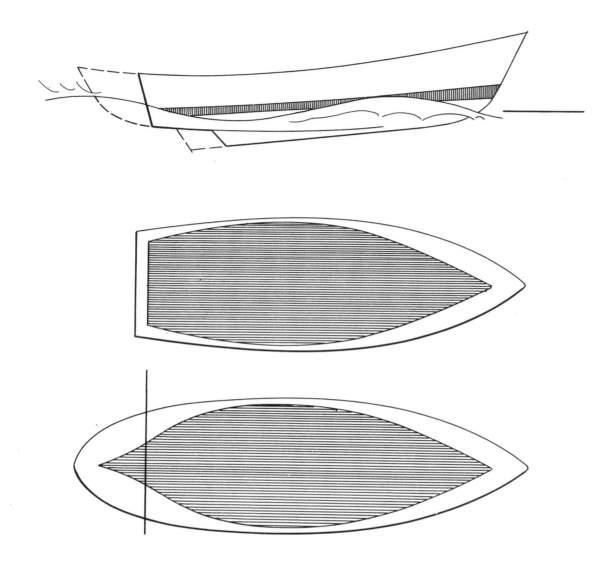

Fig. 11 The effective waterline length in setting up wave systems is not necessarily the measured length of the hull. The two forms shown will have the same wave systems with different nominal dimensions.

apart from the lift of the waves, practically horizontal and can be considered the equivalent of the boat standing still in moving water. This of course acts on all surfaces presented to it. On a surface inclined upwards, such as the bow lines of a boat, the resultant force is lift. On a surface inclined downwards, like the stern shapes of some sailing craft, the resultant force is downwards. The whole system has, as the usual natural law, to achieve an equilibrium and the situation looks like the example illustrated in Fig. 14.

With further speed the situation just gets worse and worse. The bow lifts and the stern drops until, sometimes, the craft is overwhelmed by sea pouring in over the stern. Very occasionally cavitation might set in but this, although reducing the suction aft, can create an even worse hazard with violent and irregular motions. These effects are commonly seen when children pull their toy boats too fast on their strings, and are very commonly heard about when small craft are towed towards safety by ships. The towing ship travels at its very modest $\dfrac{V}{\sqrt{L}}$ but this

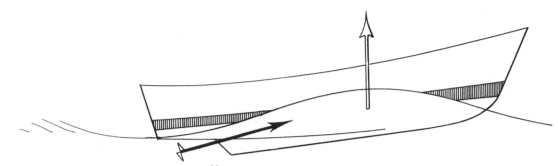

Fig. 12 When the yacht moves faster than $\frac{V}{\sqrt{L}}$ of 1·3 it is left supported by the first wave.

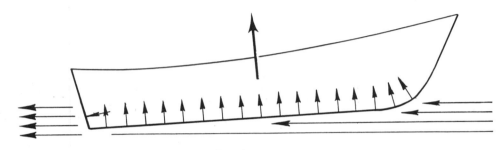

Fig. 13 If the hull surfaces are inclined to the water flow the hull will lift bodily.

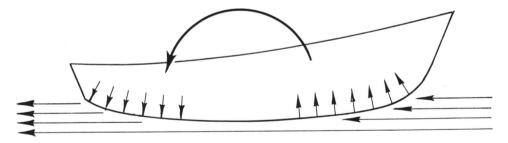

Fig. 14 If a substantial area is inclined away from the water flow then that end of the hull will sink until equilibrium is reached.

often represents a $\frac{V}{\sqrt{L}}$ well above that which is safe for the towed boat, which is then overwhelmed if it is not pulled to pieces. A 200 foot ship travelling at 15 knots has a $\frac{V}{\sqrt{L}}$ of just about 1 but the 20 foot boat it might tow would have to travel at a $\frac{V}{\sqrt{L}}$ of nearly 3½ to stay with her.

Fig. 12, however, just swallows its bow wave — really gets the buoyant lift right under the hull and aft of its centre of gravity (c.g.) so that the bow will drop and the craft remain supported both by the buoyancy of its hull and the pressure of the water.

Two possibilities can at once be seen: (1) the variation of lift possible by altering the angle at which the bottom is attacking the water; (2) the relief of drag by inducing a measure of cavitation or other form of breakaway in those parts where suction develops.

The simple wave system is, of course, above the slowest speeds often obscured by the spray flung off the top of the bow wave. Aft, the resurgent water appearing from under the boat and the jet thrust from the propellers also combine to obscure the system about and aft of the stern.

As the speed of the craft is increased even further the water pressures on the bottom increase and the proportional effect of the buoyancy reduces. The craft rises from the sea until it is virtually completely supported by the water pressure due to its speed, exactly as is a water skier who uses his personal buoyancy for support only in emergencies.

At slow speeds the craft is supported by its personal buoyancy and as this is equal to its displacement the slow speed hull is known as a displacement craft. At high speed the craft is supported principally from the action of planing across the top of the sea and this is therefore called a planing craft. Where the division comes is very hard to define exactly and there are increasing numbers of intermediate speed craft labelled semi-planing and semi-displacement craft. Many authorities give a speed of $\frac{V}{\sqrt{L}}$ of 3·5 as the bottom limit of true planing craft.

Heaving, Pitching and Rolling

Of all the terms in naval architecture which should be kept from the eyes and thoughts of a prospective owner, heave, pitch and roll must head the list. They are cold damp words to strike a chill in any heart warmed with thoughts of Riviera sunshine and not ready at great expense to be serious about the grey North Sea. However, as all boats nowadays are expected to be strong and safe, heaving, pitching and rolling cover a great part of what is thought to be seaworthiness.

Heaving is defined conveniently enough in the *Oxford Dictionary* as the 'force exerted by the swell of the sea on the course of a ship'. There is also another definition, but we will leave that out.

Since the swell of the sea is proportionally larger for the smaller craft, the effect of heave is probably more pronounced among yachts than

ships. A swell of the sea under your counter at the wrong moment is one of the main factors in broaching-to, and a swell of the sea just to weather of your bows can stop the swing of an underpowered craft through the wind. A convenient swell of the sea about amidships or aft has got many a reluctant overweight planing boat out of the sea to do its stuff. The heave is due entirely to the motion of the sea and is therefore only very broadly predictable. Wave heights and lengths and periods are theoretically averageable for different parts of the sea, but for a small craft it is often the waves inside the big waves which are important and these are rarely classified. The principal effect of heave, apart from inconveniencing the manoeuvres of the vessel, is to modify the natural pitching and rolling of the vessel. Pitch and roll are individual to each craft, and if a boat is set rolling or/and pitching in flat water it continues at the same rate damped only by the skin friction of the hull. In rough water it is modified, at any moment aided or opposed by the swell of the sea. The overall effect is further modified by the vessel's own wave train due to her own speed of advance through the seas, which can itself

Fig. 15 A hull form designed to do the minimum of heaving, pitching and rolling in rough water.

Fig. 16 Heave is the movement of the craft by the sea itself.

change from moment to moment in a seaway. This builds up a quite complicated system of factors to affect what a yacht hull is doing at any moment in the sea. The system is probably too complicated for any reasonable analysis except perhaps one day with a well briefed computer. However, the problem for the designer is much simplified. Only two criteria really need to be examined. First, is the motion acceptable to the humans on board? It is still fortunately the prime duty of a yacht to carry people and give them confident pleasure. This is approached principally through similarity with previous craft checked through reasonably simple calculations. The second criterion is that the natural period of the yacht in pitching and rolling should not be such as to cause a harmonic build-up of motion between the natural period of the yacht and the seas she is expected to encounter.

A yacht with a large fore and aft period (equivalent to a long pendulum motion) responds only slowly to a wave and therefore tends to plough straight into and through every sea in her path. This of course increases the hull resistance by including the full depth of the topsides in the bulk to be pushed along, thereby slowing the craft as well as making her unduly wet. However, if the yacht has a very short period, such as with all weight ridiculously concentrated amidships, she will lift quickly to the sea but will get in some more pitching off her own characteristics before she meets the next sea. We all know of boats like this of which it is remarked that they go up and down twice in the same hole.

The ideal is to produce a weight distribution fore and aft such that the hull lifts quickly and easily to the wave it encounters, and either damps out the motion quickly before the next wave comes along or is just lifting again when it does. The former is probably the best characteristic to aim for in a design and leads into the question of damping out a fore and aft periodic motion.

Natural skin friction is doing this all the time, but a quite heavy damping occurs if the fore and aft bodies are far from being symmetrical due to the

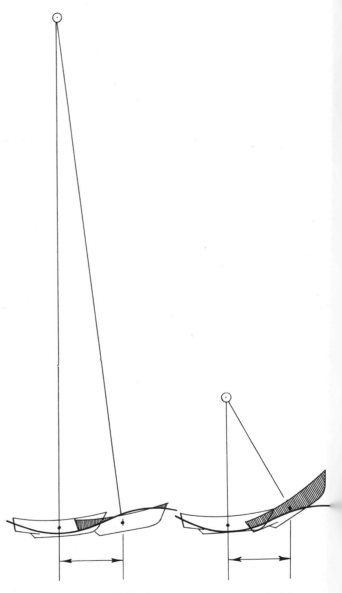

Fig. 17 The effect of the fore and aft pitching period in a seaway.

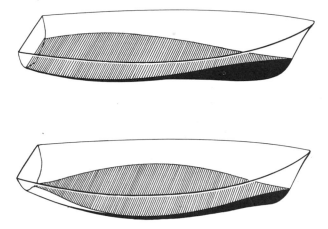

Fig. 18 The asymmetrical waterplane area will dampen a periodic pitching in a light craft.

effect of alternately immersing one end and the other as the yacht pitches.

Two generalisations can thus be offered. The first is that light craft with weights concentrated near amidships should perhaps be of fairly asymmetrical form fore and aft, and that heavy craft and those with weights well spread fore and aft should be more symmetrical fore and aft. This must be heavily qualified by adding that other features might considerably modify these requirements in a satisfactory yacht. Fortunately we have generations of experience of what is and what is not a good sea boat for most waters and therefore plenty of precedent, the designer's best friend, to call upon. Few yachts have their fore and aft metacentric height calculated, perhaps too few. It is a laborious calculation which doubtless will become routine computer work.

The athwartships calculations are much more commonly embarked upon because the roll of a yacht is rather more noticeable than its pitching, more alarming at times, and is part of the question of stability and therefore of basic safety. The period of encounter from the seas is slower when encountered beam-on compared with bow-on, and the yacht is very much smaller across its beam than fore and aft. The natural symmetry between the two sides also reduces the damping of the roll. Thus the natural period of roll has a much bigger chance to develop athwartships. A vessel of great stability that rolls quickly and sharply is probably very safe but often feels unsafe, whereas a vessel of modest stability that rolls wide and slowly often appears to respond and work with the sea in a confident manner. Here the designer has to know the type of motion which the owner or owners will feel happiest with (for tastes differ very widely in this respect) and ally it with a suitable stability and rolling period. Many an uncomfortable craft has been made more seaworthy by such apparent madnesses as hoisting anchors to the masthead or pumping out the ballast or freshwater tanks.

The effect of wind on a vessel is nearly always to steady it and to damp rolling. Sometimes small vessels are to be seen sporting large funnels and these are little more than aluminium steadying sails. The real thing of canvas, sticks and string is of course quite common on slower craft designed for open water use. All make use of the principle that energy is required, even on a windless day, to wave a large flat area through the air, and this energy can only come from that available to start the yacht rolling in the first place.

The natural skin friction of the hull has the same effect and this is often augmented by underwater fins and bilge keels. If the yacht is rolling *in* the sea with the motion stemming principally from its periodic characteristics, then skin friction and keels will reduce the roll. However, if the yacht is merely rolling *with* the sea, then the skin and keels will not be travelling across the waterflow and the motion will not be affected.

Roll damping fins are now quite common. These are little controllable underwater wings on each side of the yacht which can be quickly angled to give lift or downthrust. They are controlled directly from the angle of heel and are set to work with quite astonishing effect in direct opposition to the rolling. Their only real defect is that they rely on the forward speed of the craft for effect, while most marine emergencies cause a vessel to be slowed or even stopped at the time when freedom from rolling would be best appreciated.

Roll damping tank systems give their benefits whether the vessel is under way or not, but they are, at this time, very tricky in their operation. In essence these systems consist of a half-filled tank fitted right outboard on each side of the craft. The tanks are connected by a pipe and the water is allowed to swill from tank to tank as the vessel rolls. The trick is so to control the water flow by means of the skin friction of the connecting pipe and a control valve as to get the through flow out of phase with the natural roll. The effect is rather as if the whole crew rushed to whichever rail was rising as the yacht rolled.

Another simple arrangement to reduce rolling in open waters has been called the 'Flopper Stopper'. This requires two large poles to be rigged either side of the yacht rather in the manner of fishermen's trolling rods; miniature paravanes are suspended from these into the sea. These are designed to drop easily through the water when their pole drops as the yacht rolls but to require some force to pull up again. By using long poles the leverage effect can be great and the actual size of the paravanes very small, so that their effect on the speed of the parent craft is small.

The Helm Effect

At first sight the steering of a vessel might seem to be brought about by using a rudder blade to create drag on one side of the vessel, thereby causing that side to slow down and the whole craft to rotate. To a slight extent this might occur but it is a patently unreasonable explanation for the whole phenomenon of steering. If pure drag were the cause then an oar blade or bucket used amidships might be expected to be at least as effective as a partially inclined rudder blade, and of course they are not. Consider also the relatively tiny rudders which were and are used to control large sailing ships. The drag of such a rudder broadside-on to the water is only a fraction of the difference of drag between the two sides of the craft when it is heeled over and yet a few spokes of helm can change its direction. Look at the racing power boat which sometimes to save drag uses but a single tiny rudder well out of the propeller jet stream to control enormous power.

There are many theories of steering but perhaps the most likely is to consider the rudder as a trim tab for the main parent hull. When the trim tab is moved to one side it creates a modest sideways pressure which pushes the aft end of the hull in the opposite direction, perhaps almost imperceptibly. The main hull is then at an angle to the waterflow coming from (relatively) ahead. This builds up the pressure on one side of the bows compared with the other and the bow swings away until the hull reaches a position of equilibrium athwart the water stream. The propulsive thrust, however, remains acting along the length of the hull and the process is continuous and hence the vessel turns. The bigger the movement of the trim tab/rudder the bigger the initial movement of the parent hull and the faster the turning and the sharper the corner.

The whole process can be observed in a vessel at anchor in a tideway. When the helm is put over the stern of the vessel moves first until the tide catches the bows and pushes hard against the restraint of the anchor cable. Again the whole process can be observed in narrow water manoeuvring, when care has to be taken to allow for

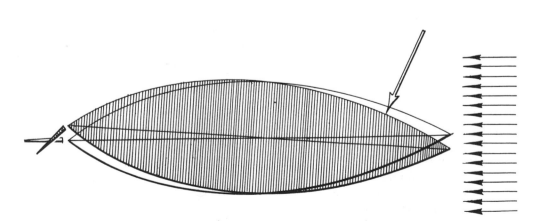

Fig. 19 The rudder acts principally as a trim tab to make the hull steer itself.

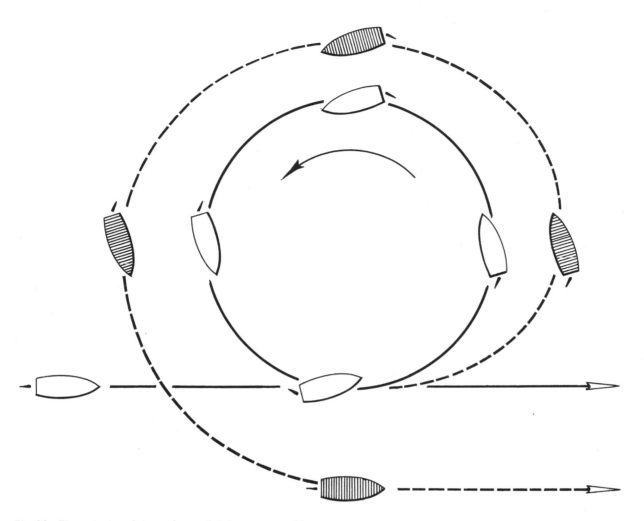

Fig. 20 The attitudes of the craft are slightly exaggerated in these turning circles. The shaded vessel is a fast planing craft and shows the effect of skidding on cornering.

the athwartships movement of the stern and the whole craft manoeuvred as if it were pivoted about some point nearly amidships.

Of course you cannot, floating free in nice slidy water, corner without skidding. In a moderate speed displacement craft this skidding is really of little consequence and is noticeable only as a matter of interest when making full power turning trials. In a fast raceboat, however, skidding can be a major factor in cornering. The craft can change her pointing direction probably quite quickly but her momentum will carry her in the direction she was travelling for some distance. Little centreboards and keels are used to give some raceboats a better grip on the water when turning, for, apart from the directional insecurity, travelling sideways can ruin the propulsive effi-

ciency of the propeller, which cavitates and protests until the craft skids nearly to a stop.

This skidding is due to the effects of the centrifugal forces acting on a turning vessel. On a slow speed craft the effect is nearly balanced by a further modest change of hull direction which brings more water pressure to bear on the outboard side. However, the centrifugal force acts as if through the centre of gravity of the ship and the counter pressures act approximately as if through the centre of the lateral plane (c.l.r.). As the c.g. is usually above the c.l.r. a heeling moment is produced to heel the vessel outward in the turn. The rudders produce a small opposite force but in most displacement vessels a heel outboard is normal.

In a fast planing hull, however, a different set of

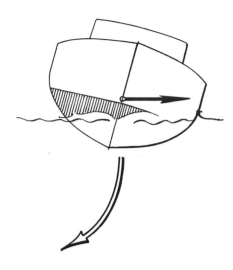

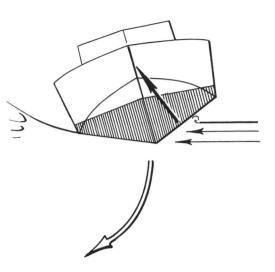

Fig. 21 The forces acting on a displacement craft (shown here turning to starboard) incline her outboard.

Fig. 22 A planing craft, also shown here turning to starboard, has a more powerful set of forces to incline her inboard on a turn.

circumstances apply, for the centrifugal skidding is equivalent to the craft planing sideways. The outboard bottom experiences an increased planing pressure and the inboard bottom a reduction, and so the craft heels but this time in the opposite direction. The effect of the rudders is also helping and so a planing craft will heel inboard when turning.

The effects of propeller torque must also be taken into account and a single high-powered screw turning in the same direction as a large single engine can of its own torque give a craft an angle of heel on the straight and narrow. This must be added to the effect of the steering on trim. Fortunately we have not yet run much into problems of precession from these large engines. The gyroscopic effect of large masses turning fast might well become a factor to take into account in an exaggerated installation.

Steering can also be accomplished by the application of thrust forces independent of the movement of the hull of the vessel itself. A sailing vessel can be steered to some modest effect by variation of the sails set to catch the breeze. A power vessel, manoeuvring, often makes more use of the jet thrust from its propellers than the pure steering effect of its rudder. A twin propeller craft can simply use the offset of each shaft-centred propeller thrust for control, and the single-engined craft can use the rudder as a deflector vane in the jet thrust from its screw to remarkable effect.

Some of the new propulsion units in fact do away with the rudder altogether. The outboard engine and the outdrive unit and the various tunnelled water jet units are all virtually rudderless. The technique of close quarter handling of such craft is different from that of those with rudders in that they are virtually out of control when the propeller is not turning.

The prodigal availability of the modern power unit makes multiple installations attractive and some vessels, usually cargo ships and tankers but occasionally yachts, fit a complete little engine and propeller unit athwartships right through the bow. This bow thruster unit can then be used to push the front of the ship bodily in one direction or the other. It is now therefore quite feasible for that old dream of the manoeuvring seaman to come true — to go broadside-on dead into the eye of the wind.

Yawing and Broaching

A combination of rolling, pitching and heaving and the effect of the hull characteristics can and do combine to make a craft depart from her

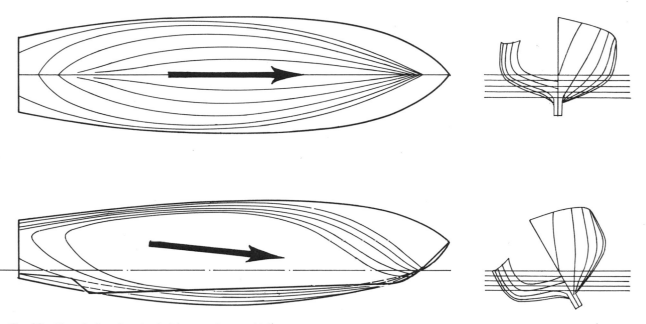

Fig. 23 *Most hulls when heeled have a shape which steers them strongly in a different direction from the way they are heading.*

proper course. In itself such yawing is of little account and, if steering is your pleasure, gives interest and the exercise of skill to enjoy during a passage. Yawing is usually at its most pronounced with a quartering sea, and when the seas become large the innocuous yaw can develop into the relatively dangerous broach. Here the swing becomes uncontrollable and the vessel swings broadside-on to the seas in a trough. The accompanying roll leaves her at her most vulnerable to an initial capsize or to being inundated by the next crest.

In a light craft broaching is rarely more than a momentary annoyance in that the forces involved are small and the craft is more flung with the seas and tossed ahead by the following wave crest. In a bigger and heavier craft less able to respond the effect can be catastrophic. Broaching is therefore one of the greatest hazards to the motor yacht and its prevention requires consideration in the design as well as care by the seaman.

The basic mechanics of broaching are relatively simple. The yacht's bow rises over the wave crest and drops into the trough. The yacht runs down the front of the wave and buries the bow in the back of the next wave. The bow is held but the stern is still carried by the preceding wave and propelled by the engines. Unless careful control can be maintained over the direction of the craft the stern will swing to one side or other down the slope, until she finishes with some force broadside-on in the trough.

The two most obvious methods of reducing the broaching hazard are:

1. To shape the bow so that it digs in as little as possible and the stern so that it has as little buoyancy as possible to be caught and lifted. This would be allied with a distribution of weights so that the bow would be able to respond quickly as it hit the sea.

2. To shape the hull so that she tends to steer straight.

There is a limit to how far one can pursue the first possibility for we would like a fat scow-like bow and fine stern for anti-broaching, and the same shape the other way round for performance and going into the wind and sea. The second possibility is less obvious in a motor yacht except in terms of adding skegs and lateral area which, although excellent in reducing the possibility of a broach, can increase its violence when it does occur. However, a yaw really becomes uncontrollable once the vessel takes up an angle of heel, when two things happen. The natural shape of the hull, fair and symmetrical when upright, becomes often quite banana-shaped with a strong, often uncontrollable, built-in self-steering

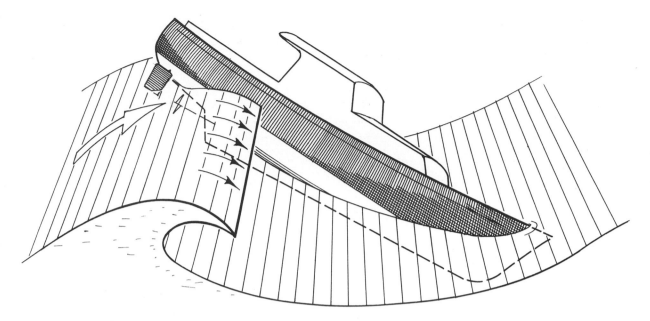

Fig. 24 The mechanics of broaching: the bow is braked strongly by immersion and the stern is carried forward both by the propellers and by the following wave crest. At the same time control is reduced by the rudders lifting out of solid water.

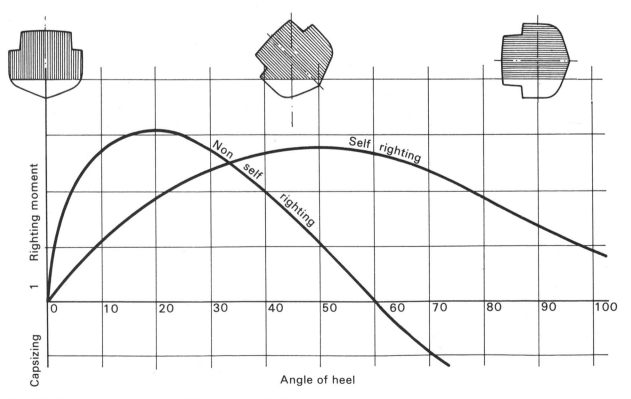

Fig. 25 Comparative righting or stability characteristics for a stable river craft and a self-righting sea boat.

effect. The yacht also rises bodily when heeled, often raising one if not both rudders into the surface spindrift where they have virtually no effect.

The best self-steering hull forms have long straight buttock lines aft and the problem then becomes one of allying these with a bow form of matching fullness and at the same time getting the rudder or rudders nice and deep without too much keel or skeg right aft.

Broaching is also affected by the speed at which the yacht is running in the sea, for the faster she is travelling the further she is likely to plunge her bow into the sea ahead and fling her stern after it. In a high-powered vessel the steering value of the engines in these conditions can be considerable, and if the engine throttle or speed controls are easily and readily to hand many an incipient broach can be stopped by a burst of speed or by pulling back one of a pair of engines. Eventually, however, the vessel will become virtually wind propelled in the worst conditions and the only safe attitude for her is facing the other way into the wind and sea. If she must go on downwind then a drogue to keep the stern into the wind becomes a necessity of life.

Stability and Self-Righting

Stability, to the yacht owner, usually means that when he steps on his yacht it does not give to his weight and when at sea or at anchor does not roll too much. The effect of rolling is of course tightly tied up with real stability, but the initial feeling as the owner steps on board is principally a function of the waterplane area and the height of the metacentre. A yacht with narrow form must, it would seem obvious, respond more to the owner's avoirdupois than an otherwise similar craft of wide waterline beam. This initial stability can give some guidance to what the yacht may be like in gentle service but is often misleading when the complete picture of the change of stability as the yacht heels is considered. We should also mention the dynamic stability that occurs during planing, and many a deep vee hull which might roll itself silly on moorings will become a happily stable craft as soon as the planing action establishes itself under the bottom.

The range of stability required is usually evident from its type and from the service expected of the yacht. It is rare that a river launch meets upsetting conditions and therefore there is little need for her to be self-righting through the full 360° of heel angles. An open water craft used off shallow beaches has, on the other hand, little use for a heavy initial stability but a considerable interest in self-righting at excessive angles.

When a vessel is called self-righting without qualification it infers that in whatever attitude she is placed she will return to her normal upright trim. It is a condition required for some lifesaving craft and means that she can capsize and return without detriment provided her crew are still aboard. This means basically that the vessel has to be designed to be unstable when upside down. This often means whittling away at the stability when the vessel is in the near-capsize condition

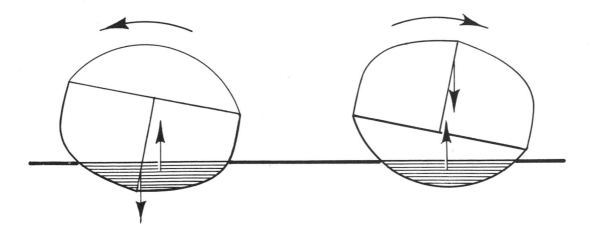

Fig. 26   The forces which bring a self-righting lifeboat of the old type upright from a normal heel and from a complete capsize.

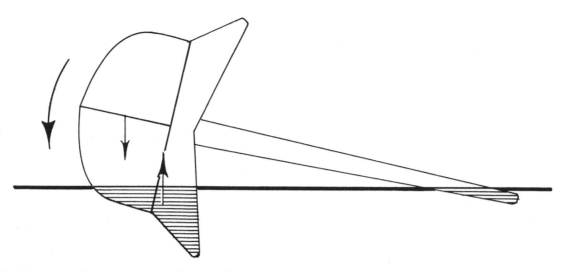

Fig. 27   The use of wing sponsons, after the style of the proa Cheers, *to make a craft self-righting.*

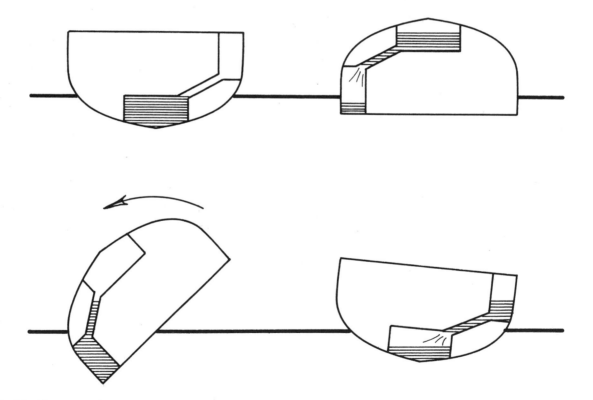

Fig. 28   The action of a self-righting ballast tank.

and it is true to say that the self-righting craft is sometimes more likely to capsize in the first place.

Self-righting is usually achieved by one or both of two methods. In the first, buoyancy is provided well up on the hull, usually at the ends as in the manner of old-fashioned lifesaving craft. This provides enough lift to the capsized hull to bring the centre of gravity above the buoyancy and hence provide a returning moment to the hull. The other is to provide a water ballast tank which drains quickly into side tanks to provide enough righting moment to get the hull returning to the point where its natural stability can take over the righting process.

An entry in the 1968 single-handed transatlantic sailing race, the proa *Cheers* designed by Richard Newick showed a further thought on self-righting. She herself has a flotation hump on the windward hull and solves elegantly the particular righting problems of a proa. However, the principle involved might easily be extended to more conventional craft. It is simply the provision of a buoyant blister above and outboard on each side of the hull coupled with a strong buoyant mast or masts to prevent complete capsize. The blister is so placed as to leave the centre of gravity of the hull with a righting moment through the full range of heel until the masts are in full action as a final defence against the complete capsize.

Staying Afloat

It would seem a sensible requirement of a yacht that no matter what disaster overtook her machinery or the normal integrity of her hull, she should stay afloat. Old-time ships built of wood very often did, to become derelicts which were once a considerable hazard about the oceans. The advent of steel construction and heavy engines made vessels basically unbuoyant — they sank when full of water. Now that in many ways hulls and machinery are becoming lighter it is possible again to consider seriously whether the basic vessel can be made buoyant. The arrival of plastics foams allows us to fill unused parts of the hull with almost pure buoyancy, and at 50 to 60 lb of buoyancy per cubic foot of foam it does not take too much to add up to floating the machinery. Hulls are usually just self-floating in wood or glass reinforced plastics. Perhaps the principal question is whether one does in fact want to go to the trouble. Very few craft are actually sunk at sea and the greater part of those that do sink are perhaps so antiquated as to have no real business in deep water. For these one suspects that a first-rate lifesaving set of dinghies, radios and flares would be for the general good all round.

The traditional answer to staying afloat in trouble is in the use of watertight bulkheads and some of the classification societies still require the fitting of collision bulkheads close to the ends of the vessel. These can be and are still used and fitted, but as yachts become smaller and more complex any really valuable system of watertight compartments, as far as staying afloat is concerned, becomes increasingly impracticable. Doors between compartments are the more necessary as the accommodation reaches an increasingly high density; and systems pipes and conduits have to run throughout and would require a trained crew to operate a battery of cocks to make watertight in an emergency. The principal use of many so-called watertight bulkheads seen in motor craft is to prevent the engine room spillage and smell extending through the owners' accommodation, or to stop a surge of bilge water to one end or other of the craft in a seaway.

It is a somewhat macabre process working out the effect of flooding in a yacht. To consider all the fine machinery and joinery work only for their underwater value requires a bit of a mental leap

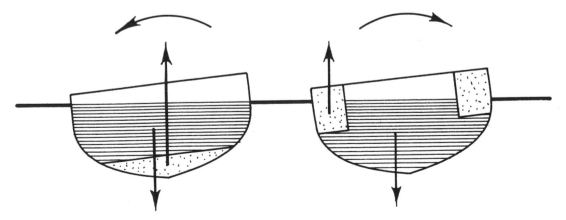

Fig. 29 Buoyancy placed too low can produce a capsizing moment in a craft full of water.

Fig. 30 Buoyancy placed in the right place can keep the craft stable and upright in a disaster.

but is essential if the poor owner is not to be further embarrassed in his emergency. The buoyancy has to be arranged so that the yacht will if possible settle level in the water and as little as possible. The vessel even full of water has to be stable and able to cope with the free surface effects of the sea rolling from compartment to compartment. To keep the yacht level and stable the buoyancy material needs to be distributed all around the deck edge, and to keep it floating high it should be distributed through the bilges. As always in designing, a compromise is required with the buoyancy spread well about the hull and above the centre of gravity. In effect it should be placed at about half the height of the topsides throughout the length and high up in the ends.

cipally by gravity and a few modest fastenings. A good thrust from a buoyancy block would perhaps lift the deck, and if the buoyancy can escape you might as well not have bothered in the first place.

Apart from foam buoyancy there are other buoyancy materials available. One of the traditional materials is cork, although this is so surpassed by the artificial foam blocks and foamed in place buoyancy that it is now rarely seen. The same really applies to ping-pong balls, the record breaker's friend, for many vulnerable craft have been stuffed with these lightweight balls for security. Air bags are also to be seen. If they are kept inflated there is a chafe and maintenance problem and if they are kept uninflated ready for automatic inflation then someone has

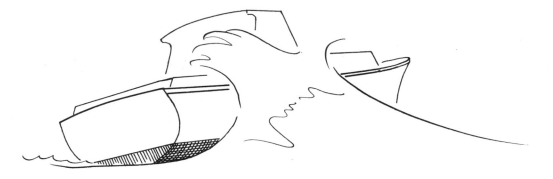

Fig. 31   *The sea hits craft only infrequently and usually in the grand manner.*

In making the calculations or estimations for buoyancy the effect of any excessively self-buoyant hull or fitting features must be taken into effect. Bilge tanks can often provide a capsizing moment to be taken into effect. Yachts are sometimes overwhelmed by seas when they are lying momentarily on their sides. The buoyancy arrangements have to be such that she rights herself as she fills rather than capsizes.

Another modest and obvious point about foam buoyancy which is occasionally overlooked is that it is only of value while it is held in place. This not only refers to such elementary problems as happen to the capsized sailing dinghy whose buoyancy bags are not secured and float away happily by themselves. In the greater loading of the buoyancy at work in a sizable vessel the securing of decks and structures above the buoyancy has to be taken into account. Many elderly yachts are decked like pot lids held in place prin-

to put the automatic inflation into operation. The principal disadvantage of the foams lies in their weight, surprisingly enough. They weigh usually between 3 and 10 lb a cubic foot and therefore enough buoyancy to float an engine weighing a ton can amount to nearly 400 lb.

Freeboard and Dryness

There are many rules and even regulations offering guidance on how high your craft should stick out of the water. In fact the real answer is that it should be just high enough and no more. Any height over the minimum is just another offering to the vagaries of the breezes of heaven to catch and carry the craft contrary to the whims and controls of her driver. If a boat were designed solely for crossing a patch of water without consideration of why and with whom, the right height would be just enough to stop the water coming in for the crossing of that particular patch. A deep sea boat might well like high bows to stop her plunging her forepart into sea after sea, but on an inland river 90 per cent of their height would never be used except to part the bulrushes. If a boat were designed solely to be inhabited by humans without regard to where, one might expect to find her sticking up very nearly the height of a house. In fact one often does in a yacht, for there is little pleasure in bending.

Another factor is in the so-called dryness of the hull. Nobody really prefers to be made wet repeatedly and the dryness of the passage of the vessel is as much, if not more, of a factor in a yacht as in any other craft. Some yachtsmen it is true prefer a short sharp wet journey to get the full taste of the salty seamanship, but the yacht designer should be able to offer the alternatives of wet and dry, for to offer only the former will greatly reduce his clientèle. Dryness is materially affected by freeboard: the higher the wall the harder it is to throw water over it. If the freeboard is altogether too low then the craft will undoubtedly be wet no matter what else is done, for she will stick her nose under the seas she meets and fling them back around her luckless complement.

Given then that the height of the bow is well chosen, the height of the stern must also be chosen with the same care. Here the demands of the accommodation are often less exacting and the proper profile to suit the required buoyancy for the form can be selected. It is extraordinary how well this usually is designed. Running in a big sea the crests will often appear ready to spill over the dry deck except for a modest few final inches of freeboard.

Freeboard amidships has basically to be such as to allow the vessel to roll to her natural extent without immersing the decks. The next demand on amidships freeboard is that it must cover the accommodation, which is often at its most critical here in terms of headroom. A big sheer sweeping well down from bow and stern is often considered the hallmark of a good sea boat. It certainly looks handsome, but the philosophy behind it is at least suspect in terms of yachting. The bold sheer stems originally from two requirements. Perhaps the strongest of these is the practical problem of bending sizable scantling timber to frame and plank a hull. Wood is difficult enough to bend round the flat of a plank but

almost impossible to bend sideways. A wooden hull built without too much sophistication of plank shaping therefore has to have a strong sheer. The ordinary Scandinavian rowing boat could be quoted here as an instance. The second factor is that within living memory the commercial craft of yacht size which had to be seaworthy to ply their trade required a low freeboard amidships to pull their fishing nets on board.

Dryness in a hull is a much more elusive factor than the pure height of the walls that you build to keep the sea out. Two things occur at sea to disturb the water and provoke it to fly. First the sea can take a swipe at your craft, and second your craft can take a swipe at the sea. There is little the designer can do about such things as wind-driven spindrift and rain, from which the best protection is foul-weather gear or a good window.

When a sea hits a hull, a comparatively rare event, it is usually a fair and square hit covering a good area of topsides. A thick stream washes about the hull and a fair amount of it tries to climb to the rail and spill over. It is comparatively solid water and only to be discouraged by a good overhang or flare. It is best, in terms of dryness, to let this flow and drain with as little other obstruction as possible so that it passes quickly and without getting broken up too much into spray.

The real wetter, however, occurs when the hull hits the sea. This is a very common occurrence and is not always marked by a slamming or thumping. Every time the hull pitches the bow is pushed down hard on to the sea. This accelerates and squirts a comparatively small stream of water into the air. If the hull is well designed for dryness this is flung low, but if not it is flung high, to be caught by the wind and blown back, usually straight into the face of the helmsman. The effect of a hull plunging is also to send a small thin skin of water rushing up the hull surface, often in a forward direction. This is clear water and almost invisible to the eye until it hits a rubber or spray rail when it erupts into a fine spray. If this too is badly aimed then it will fly high to be caught and carried by the wind.

The most important factor in dryness is therefore the shape of the hull in way of wind and water when she is moving in her appointed seaway. The shape of the topsides outside this area has very little value for dryness.

We noticed this once when returning from a

race in a fast power boat. Our craft, for strength, had topsides which swept round into an excessive tumblehome along her full length; a form which one might expect to be particularly wet when travelling at non-planing speeds. It was a rough day and we were sitting on deck eating our sandwiches at about ten knots when we came upon and passed a vessel of similar size and fishing boat style. She was enveloped in clouds of spray and her crew wore oilskins in the wheelhouse. Our vessel would probably have been equally wet if we had been at racing speed, but at the same speed as the fishing boat the spray was flung low by our planing bottom shape and we travelled dry and comfortable.

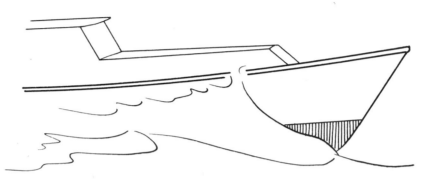

Fig. 32   Boats hit each sea in turn as they move forward.

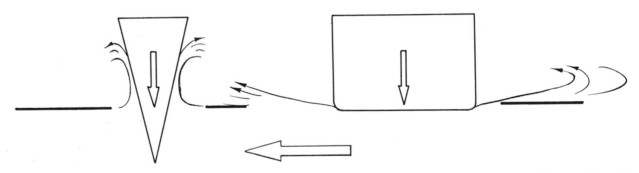

Fig. 33   A fine bow dipping makes a vertical spray without much momentum.

Fig. 34   The barge bow squirts spray out sideways with great pressure as it hits the sea.

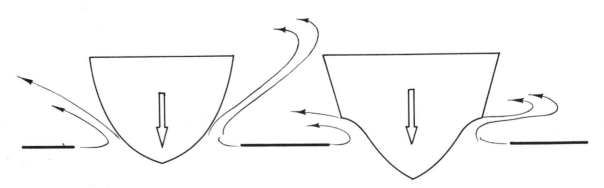

Fig. 35   An intermediate rounded forefoot gets the worst of both worlds by squirting its spray high enough to be caught by the wind and driven back on board.

Fig. 36   If the vessel could be guaranteed to run only in small seas then the entry should be fine with a knuckle immediately over it to drop the spray so that the wind cannot carry it on board.

CHAPTER 2
The Seamanship of Power Yachts

The Principles

When thinking of seamanship it is difficult to dissociate the very word from those fantastic feats of skill and endurance epitomised and immortalised by the big square rigged sailing clippers racing half across the world each voyage. Or, on a more homely level, from the fisherman working his tiny craft in all weathers. Because both inshore and offshore craft were historically propelled by extravagant contraptions involving ropes and canvas draped around wooden sticks to catch the wind, seamanship is often closely, and wrongly, attached to the fine skills necessary to work and maintain a wind ship. A sailor used to be required to be able to maintain and use ropes, including repairing and making the end attachments. To be rated 'able' he had to be able to hand a sail, reef a sail and steer. A modern power yacht would find very little employment for these talents — even steering is often automatic — but the need for seamanship on the sea is just as great as ever it was.

Seamanship is principally an attitude towards the problems of a ship and the sea which is basically one of preparedness. In fact, the same qualities that make a good businessman are often found in the outstanding sailor. Life, present and future, must as far as is possible be under control, with every foreseeable contingency provided for. Risks, when taken, must be controlled risks with favourable odds and all the problems assessed in a strict order of immediate importance.

First in powerboat seamanship must come, as it did in the windjammers, the care and maintenance of the power unit. This does not mean that the seamanlike owner of a motor yacht must spend all day head down over a smelly engine with his hands covered in black fat. Rather, it means that the engines must be known to receive first-class maintenance and be known to be almost one hundred per cent reliable. If this cannot be guaranteed then the power seaman must know that he can repair the engine and make it go again at sea all by himself. If neither of these possibilities applies then the power seaman looks for another source of propulsion in his locker. Oars, sails, outboard, or a second main engine would each help to keep his vessel under control. It might be considered seamanship to install a powerful radio set and a good set of anchors and ground tackle, but this is second-line seamanship, unless you also happen to own a tugboat.

Next, the power seaman might do well to sit back and consider the integrity of his vessel for the voyaging proposed. Most boats are reasonably well designed for their particular station in life and intended maritime location — not least because designers and builders find disasters bad for business. Often — too often — boats are hopefully used out of context and the odds against trouble must fall sharply. The craft must be secure for the worst conditions likely or unlikely to be encountered.

It is possible to make an unsuitable craft more suitable by alterations and adaptation, even by nailing wood and canvas over the hull openings. In terms of seamanship, however, these are desperate measures as they indicate that the vessel was never intended for the service for which it is to be used. This in turn means that many other factors are probably unsuitable. Elderly craft also suffer from old age, and fatigue attacks all sorts of insignificant items which might cause trouble. Unless, like Alfred's axe, they have had ten new heads and four new handles since the date on

Fig. 37 (left) Traditional seamanship involved contending with such complexities as this — the Portuguese sailing training ship Sagres.

Fig. 38 Controls of a modern power yacht are in their way equally complex and call for skills of a different nature — but it is still seamanship. Motor sailer Green Lady.

Fig. 39 No-one would dispute the seamanlike qualities of this control position. RNLI 44 ft lifeboat.

their certificate, they must be put to more gentle work than they were designed for.

Perhaps under the same heading comes the act of inspecting the craft itself, item by item, before putting to sea. This is not necessarily a technical inspection, but a simple and thorough check that everything is in its place: hatches and portholes shut and latched, warps and chains stowed away but ready for use, fans and safety devices switched on, gear stowed away in the cabins, lifejackets to hand, and lifebuoy ready. This is not being unduly pernickety, for quite small items can lead to the most exaggerated nastiness — even if it is only a jar of marmalade loose in the owner's wife's berth.

We have all heard of the most singular disasters which spring from a tiny lack of care and which are warnings to us all. A brand new twin screw

Fig. 40a and b Anchor and electric windlass each has its own hatch.

Fig. 41 *The anchor, warp, warp drum and mooring cleat are all inside the hatch in the foredeck leaving a nice clean and clear foredeck.*

Fig. 42 *Anchor clear of deck — neat but not entirely neighbourly at close quarters.*

fast motor yacht had just completed trials and been handed over to her proud owner. He, as is natural, could not wait to try the craft and cast off and put to sea. Crossing the bar at the mouth of the harbour the yacht took a jump at a sea and tossed off a mooring warp which had been left on the foredeck. This promptly wrapped itself round one propeller. For a moment all was chaotic as the yacht spun round in circles in the rough water. The helmsman realised what had happened and flung the engines into reverse, both to straighten her up and to try to clear the rope. At once the loose end caught round the other propeller and the power of both engines smartly wound the two shafts together until the stern gear was bent, the engines stopped and the shaft glands tore loose. In an instant, from a fine new powerful motor yacht the craft had become no more than a barge stopped in the water and in grave danger of sinking. She was towed home, but a pennyworth of forethought would have saved the whole debâcle.

The Mechanical Seaman

It cannot be too often emphasised that just as the sticks-and-string seaman required a comprehensive ability to look after his lofty power unit, so the power seaman must look after his propulsion outfit. In their own interests engine manufacturers

always supply maintenance schedules for their engines, but these have to be considered as covering only the exact needs of the engine machinery rather than the complete picture of its operation.

First one might consider the fuel, the lifeblood of the power boat. It is elementary to ensure that there is enough and that it is sufficiently clean. Fuel from large storage tanks often acquires a fair amount of condensation water. When a newly filled tank in the yacht has had time to settle, this water content should be drawn off. How often this should be done is a matter of individual circumstances, but it would be reasonable, for instance, to check tanks before starting a run. Engine manufacturers usually incorporate their own fuel filter, but in some marine usages this may be too small. It is normal to set another large filter in the line from tank to engine, and this should be inspected at regular intervals. The best type for yacht use is the duplex which by movement of a cock allows the choice of a pair of filters. This allows filters to be cleaned while the yacht is under way, but as filter cleaning is not much of a yachting sport to most it allows an owner to change the filters in use under way and have them cleaned at the dock. Fuel should also be kept fairly cool and this can be easily checked by a touch of the hand on the fuel supply pipe to the engine. If the pipe feels hot then the machinery might be run more easily until it cools a little.

The end product of fuel is exhaust, and the seaman might look at it for two reasons. The first is to see that it is not escaping into the hull, where even small amounts of exhaust gas can, if nothing more, cloud the judgement of the crew. Second, the state of the exhaust itself is a first-rate indication of the state of the engine. Exhaust should be clear and regular. Smoking exhaust can indicate a mechanical problem such as engine wear, or it can indicate incorrect fuel metering, which would affect the engine consumption, or that the engine is being worked too hard or too lightly. In short, that something is not exactly perfect and that therefore the ship is no longer one hundred per cent seaworthy.

The other fuel for an engine is the air supply, and an occasional check that the supply ducts and vents are not obstructed is routine. A simple check to see that the engines are not starving for air is simply to open the engine room door or engine case and note whether any change in rpm occurs. Also, this air supply should not be too hot. If the engine room air temperature rises, from, say, running on a hot day, then the engine will not perform so well. Should the temperature rise on a normal day with the yacht loaded normally, then here again is an indication that something is going wrong with the engine.

Lubricating oil level and grease check points are all given by the engine manufacturer as a matter of simple routine maintenance. The power seaman, however, would make certain that he had enough spare oil and grease with him and that he knew the working pressure and normal temperatures; any minor variation again giving him a warning of possible trouble ahead, while major variations would give warning of a more imminent nature.

The most elementary check on the cooling water system is a glance over the side after the engines start running to see that the water is hosing out nicely from its normal outlet — either from a shipside outlet or as part of the exhaust effluent. In both cases the water flow should be generous and any reduction in flow taken as a sign of possible trouble. Another simple check is to lay a hand on the cooling-water inlet to the engine — this will feel distinctly cold if water is passing through and warm if it is not. The running limits of the water temperature for the installation should of course be known, and any running outside this range treated with the utmost

suspicion. The seacocks to the engine cooling system normally incorporate a weed trap, and the power seaman pays particular attention to this after and during running in dirty and weedy waters and after any other action which might bung up the water inlet filter, such as taking the ground on a mud bank. Similarly, the shaft glands and bearings should be running at no more than hand held temperatures. If these rise unduly then the yacht can be run more slowly or the gland slacked back to allow a water leak through it, to keep things cool until the yacht reaches dock.

Other equipment — generating sets, steering gear, etc. — are perhaps not of such importance as the power unit but they should also have such first principle overseeing. It does not require a skilled mechanic on board to make sure that the machinery has a reasonable chance of remaining reliable.

Perhaps one should not omit the batteries from the vigilance of our seaman for, when all is said and done, the engines usually remain lumps of metal until the battery starts to crank the starting motor. Every opportunity for topping up the power in the batteries should be taken. A tiny petrol generating set which could be set to work to charge up flat batteries would be a very seamanlike shot to have in the locker of a power yacht.

Rope Seamanship

Some yachts live in docks where they are attached by permanent metal arms with hooks that engage in eyes and without a piece of rope in sight. Fenders are increasingly being attached to hulls by short lengths of rope with a keyhole latch at the end which fits into a special hull fitting without need for knot, hitch or bend. Anchor chains can be metered out from the hull housing for the anchor and clamped from the bridge without benefit of being 'made up' on mooring bitts. Who is to say that we are the worse seamen for it? However, the great majority of craft still attract a fair amount of rope or string about them and the power seaman ought to know how to use them, know how strong they are and know how to attach them in various circumstances.

The choice of rope for a yacht is governed by three factors. Is it strong enough, does it wear or last long enough, and is it sufficiently comfortable in the hand if it has to be pulled upon? The properties of most normal ropes are well documented but one can take as a general rule that one and a quarter inch circumference is the smallest rope that anyone should be asked to pull hard on by hand, and that one and a half inch circumference might be taken as a normal minimum.

The sticks-and-string seaman knows a great many knots to cater for many circumstances of his knot-attached ropebound vessel. The power seaman can cover his eventualities with a great many less, but they are none the less important. It is a principle of seamen's knots that they are self-locking and that they can be undone as easily as they are done up, if necessary under load.

First he must be able to make a rope fast to a cleat. The trick here is to keep the rope from jamming itself and to ensure that if you want to let a bit of rope out under load that it can be 'checked' or slipped easily. Making fast to a bollard can be done in the same way if it is a double bollard. A simple and elegant attachment can be made by dropping a clove hitch over a single post, or, if it is a loaded mooring coming on to a sampson post, whether it is rope warp or chain, the principle of first getting a couple of turns on to take the strain, followed by a locking hitch, would be the same. This locking hitch can be repeated until you feel completely secure.

Very often it is helpful to have an eye or loop in the end of a warp, for throwing ashore to somebody helping you moor up, for instance. The bowline is by far the best knot to use here — very little practice will make it quite simple, although the story of the rabbit who came out of his hole, went around the tree and back down his hole has been known to help.

There are various complicated knots for tying ropes together to make them longer. However, the fisherman's knot is almost absurdly simple and effective for tying ropes of different sizes without worry. One should also know how to tie down various bits of loose equipment when going to sea, and the perennial reef knot and the equally perennial clove hitch ought to be used. The marline hitch is another of general use in lashing up a great mass of things in one go. It is often useful to be able to attach a rope to another so as to share its load.

A lot of time and trouble will be avoided if the power seaman can throw a rope. In turn this requires a rope to be carefully coiled the right way.

All else is probably vanity, but ropework is a delightful hobby with marine associations of the strongest. The traditional smell of rope, though not perhaps that of the synthetics, is pleasant in itself and the thought and skilful design of knots, bends and hitches a source of wonder for a nice sunny morning under way. Books on the art of knottage are also full of splendidly improbable knots, such as the elephant knot for lifting elephant. Splicing, whipping, worming and parcelling have nearly all been overtaken by little bits of plastics or metal, but we once used a gun tackle and a Spanish windlass to move an engine back into proper alignment with its shaft during a race, and you never can tell when a bit of old-fashioned seamanship will come up trumps.

The Manoeuvring Seaman

It is a never-failing source of amazement to sit near the mouth of the Hamble River towards the end of a sailing day. Sailing yacht after sailing yacht comes sailing up to heave to, lower sails and start up engine. In a minute the yacht is transposed from being a completely manoeuvrable sailing yacht, sensitive to modest alterations of helm and capable of sailing forward, backward, sideways or stopping still, into the most unhandy kind of power yacht imaginable. The windage of the rigging is high and the power of the engine unusually low. The propeller is often tiny and stuck right out on one side, and reverse is frequently more of a gesture than a practical change in the direction of the craft. Yet sailing boat owners presumably feel a great deal safer in narrow waters under such inefficient power than they do under the power unit for which the craft was designed. It is not just to save the labour of tacking should the wind be ahead, but rather an awareness of the damage they might do both to themselves and other vessels should they get out of control. Under sail a sudden gust from heaven can upset a manoeuvre unless very quickly appreciated. In power craft it might mean the equivalent of the sudden application of full power at an unexpected moment. In addition, the sails have a large influence on the direction of the craft and several adjustments are required to get the yacht under control again. Under power, however, as long as there is way on the craft the rudder usually provides ample control of direction.

A pure power yacht carries much the same characteristics as the auxiliary sail boat with her sails stowed, only perhaps not quite so exaggerated. A propeller or two stuck right at the back provides propulsion in a right unhandy manner. The saving grace is that once way is on the hull the exact source of the shove is not really of much importance. When way is off, however, it becomes of great importance which end you start pushing, and how, and it is in the initial manoeuvring that a realisation of the effect of propellers is of most importance.

A propeller has three main influences on the behaviour of the craft. First, there is the thrust of the propeller shaft. If this is not aimed directly at the centre of gravity there will be a couple tending to swing the craft. A vertical couple is usually of too small account to show in the trim of the yacht, but a horizontal couple often provides a substantial effect, particularly at low speed. Some twin engined vessels, for instance, are unable to set off in a straight line under one engine only and have to make a complete circle before they get enough speed to straighten up. The second influence is in the way that propellers have a tendency to act as a paddle wheel, rolling the ship off in the direction of rotation. The third effect is that a propeller stopped dead and not rotating can act as a brake. All three effects, if appreciated, can be used to the advantage of the helmsman in manoeuvring the yacht. In fact, the modern high-powered twin engined craft is probably one of the most manoeuvrable yet to be seen, apart from some of the more exotic propulsion outfits sometimes fitted on ferries.

A boat hull can be steered by no less than four separate actions.

1. There are many versions of the simple theory of steering, but the effect is most easily envisaged if the rudder is taken to be a form of trim tab which has the principal effect of altering the attitude of the hull to the water flow. When the rudder turns, the hull is turned by it to a modest angle across the water flow. This puts a considerable force of water to the cheeks of one side of the bow and the vessel turns. This theory certainly has to apply to large ships or else the size

Fig. 43   The ability to get back home quickly when the weather looks like this is a part of good seamanship. The boat is a Hunt Hiliner Sportsman.

of their rudders would have to be enormously greater.

2. The hull can be paddled into a different attitude. On small boats with large rudders it is possible by fairly violent pulls at the tiller to paddle a hull, stopped in the water, to point in a different direction. This effect is rarely of account in any size of vessel where it matters, but pride should not stop one using an oar even in a substantial vessel if it saves the day.

3. The effect of wind on the superstructure can result in the yacht trying to take up a certain attitude to the wind. Whether the yacht tries to point herself upwind, downwind, or across the wind is individual to each craft and very easily found out.

4. The water jet from the propellers can also be used to turn the craft. In a single engined vessel the jet stream can usually be deflected by the rudder to one side or the other, producing a steering effect independent of movement of the hull forward or backward. With twin propellers and rudders the effect is still present but largely supplanted by the twisting effect of having one engine ahead and one astern. This can be quite powerful and it is possible nearly always to turn the yacht completely around in circles without moving from the spot. In addition, the paddling effect of a propeller running slowly can also be used for its turning moment on the hull, although it is usually fairly modest. In a powerful twin screw launch with both propellers turning the same way the paddling effect is substantial if full power is applied suddenly in reverse when running fast forward. Generations now of young boat drivers have taken advantage of this feature to stage the most spectacular 'come alongsides'. The launch is aimed at fast speed almost straight at the landing stage. At the last moment the engines are slammed into reverse and the launch swings broadside to stop exactly alongside. Of course, for some ten minutes afterwards there are palpitations, both as the launch is battered by its own wash and on account of the general injections of adrenalin all round. The engines do not last long either, but it is pretty to see done well.

The effect of propellers on manoeuvres can be listed as follows:

1. The single centreline propeller of left-handed rotation will tend to swing the stern of the boat to port when going ahead.

2. A single centreline propeller of right-handed rotation will tend to swing the stern to starboard when going ahead.

3. Twin propellers of the same rotation will show the same characteristics as a single propeller of the same rotation.

4. Twin propellers of opposite but outward turning rotation will handle without any bias effect.

5. Twin propellers of opposite but inward turning rotation may give marginally better top speed but generally prove to be highly erratic in effect during low speed manoeuvring.

Given an appreciation of the various forces which can turn the yacht against your will, manoeuvring a power yacht in and out of tight corners becomes only a matter of practice. Little runabouts can often be driven like motor cars, with one essential difference — you use reverse instead of brakes. In some craft the steering wheel is of less importance than it looks for manoeuvring. In twin engined fast craft it is often best left amidships and the steering done with the throttles and gear levers — much more effective and positive and half as much effort as spinning the wheel.

Rough Water

A power boat in rough water misses the stabilising effect on motion of the sails of a sailing yacht. The latter may be sliding along on its ear at such an angle as to make life on her very difficult, but the wind on the sails stops her rolling, or reduces the rolling, and the wind system set up about her sails has a slightly inhibiting effect on pitching. The power yacht is occasionally seen with steadying sails — either temporary ones of canvas or permanent ones of metal disguised as funnels of disproportionate size. If the naval architecture of the ship is right the motion, roll or pitch should not be too uncomfortable. Mechanical stabilisers have often transformed seagoing into yachting.

The greatest source of rough water damage to power yachts comes in over running. That is, driving too hard for too long in worsening conditions. It is often difficult to decide exactly when the weather is bad enough to justify taking gale precautions. Often, in a well-designed hull, the helmsman or skipper sitting in his fully enclosed

Fig. 44 What the seaman is up against. One of the late
Harold Hayles's excellent pictures taken when he was coxswain of the Yarmouth, Isle of Wight, lifeboat.

Fig. 45 Perhaps the smallest seamanlike power boat — an 8
footer with small outboard.

Fig. 46 Capability of manoeuvring in a seaway is another aspect of seamanship.

office can only rely on the appearance of the sea and the wind force given by his electronic instruments. Most craft eventually show clearly enough that they are being pushed too far and then action must be taken at once before things get worse. The principal signs of over running come from the motion of the craft. If she is thumping her forefoot enough to jar your teeth, or dragging up a sea as high as the bulwarks, then it is time that the safety of the yacht were given attention.

The classic advice to all small craft caught at sea by bad weather is to get the maximum amount of searoom under your lee as quickly as possible. This advice often has to be considerably modified for power craft. First, the amount of fuel in the tanks is of paramount importance. If the yacht is being flung about, then the amount of fuel available from the tanks in terms of safety should in some cases be taken as less about 10 per cent of the tank capacity. If there is a large amount of fuel available, ample to keep the engines turning at about half power for the length of the gale expected and to get the yacht home afterwards, then there is no doubt that the safest action would be to get into a position to ride the weather out at sea. Most power yachts are safest, it seems, just plugging ahead slowly into the sea — just slowly enough to ensure very good steer-

age way. Occasionally, perhaps to save fuel, it might be necessary to ride to a sea anchor streamed from the bows. Very few yachts, however, will lie streamed dead downwind from the sea anchor. Most tend to lie partly across the wind with the sea anchor warp leading off about 45° from the bow. If possible, the engines should be kept running if this condition becomes necessary, as the yacht is rather vulnerable and a burst of engine power might become essential to avoid a dangerous degree of roll building up. When lying to a sea anchor the yacht will in effect be travelling backwards through the water and a surprising speed can build up. It is usually essential to reduce the speed of a boat through the water in bad weather as the disturbance of its passage can cause waves to break heavily about it and on board. If the sea anchor is inadequate, and most are for really bad conditions, then the yacht must be slowed down by trailing warps, and in fact anything from dinghies to furniture can be tied on the ends as long as they produce enough effect. The loading on these warps to sea anchors, etc. can be very heavy and they must be both strong enough and properly secured to the hull. It is not ridiculous to pass them completely around the deckworks if the cleats and bollards are on the mean side. Oil is also used to inhibit the breaking of waves around a boat. There are various reports as to the effect ranging from the miraculous to the negligible. We have never used it ourselves, but in severe conditions no doubt one would use every possible means towards safety.

If for some reason, say to conserve fuel, the engines have to be stopped then it is no use expecting to be able to steer the boat backwards downwind behind the sea anchor for more than a very short period. It is bad enough steering a boat astern on the rudders in harbour. If the boat can be turned downwind before the engines are stopped and before the sea becomes too bad, it is not too dangerous. If this is not possible then the transference of the sea anchor from bow to stern must be taken as a major physical and mental operation to be executed with the utmost care. Once the operation is complete it is as essential as ever to keep speed down by trailing warps and everything else behind. The harder the blow and the greater the seas the more likely the warps are to chafe and break, and their condition and welfare must form the greatest point of vigilance after the steering. Eventually, however, the wind will decline and the sea drop and it will be time to get under way again. The crew will be tired and the possibility of putting one of the warps round the propeller looms large.

If the fuel capacity is insufficient to think of sitting out the gale at sea, then the whole voyage should have been planned on the basis of being able to get into harbour before any seriously bad weather built up. However, no-one is perfect and the possibility of being caught out is quite real. The first refuge to look for is shelter to windward. A nicely protected harbour not more than an hour or so upwind is the proper place to make for whether you were bound there or not. A nice harbour downwind should only be considered if it has an entrance as open and easy as Spithead, and if not it should be avoided like the plague. If the yacht can make for an easy harbour protected from most directions of wind then it should do so, and if it cannot then it must make quick and ample precautions for riding out by running before the wind. Sometimes a power yacht with modest draught can creep into shallow water for protection, but the shallows too must be sheltered and not open enough to allow shallow water waves to build up into surf.

In less extreme conditions, when you decide to make the best of the weather and plug on, then the golden rule is really to slow the yacht down until she is thoroughly comfortable. Many, many power yachts are proper pigs to take downwind as they try and broach to in even a modest following sea. The bow dips into a sea and the following sea catches and lifts a fat and buoyant stern and tries to overtake the bow with it. The condition is usually alarming before it is dangerous. There seems to be little possible cure for a 'broacher' without substantially rebuilding the hull. The only course of action available is to tack downwind like a sailing yacht, putting her as near to course as is reasonable without bringing on the broaching and then altering course to bring the wind on the opposite quarter on alternate legs about the proper course.

Fast motor boats have their own problems in rough water — particularly going into the sea, when they often bang and pound. In a well-designed fast power boat it is only a question of slowly reducing speed until the motion becomes bearable again — this might mean only a modest reduction in planing speed or reducing right down to displacement speed. A bad fast boat is often only bearable if she is going at a good planing speed. If this is too hard for her then there is no intermediate speed until you come down almost to stop. However, most fast boats these days are really remarkably good sea boats.

Driving a fast boat in rough waters is a beautiful skill. To see one of the masters, like Jim Wynne or Peter Twiss, make the best of such a job is an education even if viewed only in a film of a race. To ride with one of them and feel the craft driven to its maximum on the knife edge between disaster and performance is to realise to the full that powerboat racing is not just a matter of opening up the engines and hoping that neither you nor anything else of value will fly off before you finish. Peter Twiss in particular has, perhaps from his flying days, a very neat line in judgement of the take-off, so chosen that the bottom touches and is partly cushioned on the next wave top before plunging on to the next again for another full dose of propulsion from the propellers.

Navigation

Most of the actual mechanics of navigation are common to all craft which use the sea. Most small power craft are usually more concerned with pilotage, the plotting of position from shore marks and the planning of courses around and about obstacles, rather than with the purer navigation of finding a path across the trackless oceans. The average power craft is of a size and speed sufficient to make the navigation required extremely simple. A comparable sailing yacht rarely travels at the same speed and in the same direction for more than a few hours at a time. The power yacht can reckon to travel with a regularity of great convenience. It is possible to estimate the length of a passage and to apply, accurately, a single correction for tide. It is possible to plan a passage so that the important landfall occurs conveniently with, say, lighthouses lit up. It is possible to regulate speed to make use of any of the maritime aids to seamen, such as fair tides and high water at the bar. It is all basically so easy as to be often treated casually, which, like most aspects of seamanship, is all right while you are getting away with it.

Some problems, however, are peculiar to power craft. A simple one is the limiting of range by fuel capacity and the limiting of ports to those with fuelling points. The supply of fuel is a dominant part of the life of a power boat and voyages have to be planned, if tank capacity is small, not only between fuel pumps but with an

Fig. 47   Seamanlike protection taken to great lengths in the tyre fenders of a crew boat in the Gulf of Mexico.

eye to an alternative supply in case the first has dried up or the yacht is forced elsewhere. It is important for the navigator to know the fuel consumption of the craft in various circumstances. Most yachts, if they have fuel consumption accurately metered on trials at all, have figures only for the nice sunny day with the yacht new and light and clean. If fuel consumption is a factor in the voyaging proposed then the navigator ought to allow a substantial margin, as much as 30 per cent, of fuel in hand beyond the expected consumption. It is possible to compose polar diagrams showing fuel consumption variations depending on wind strength and direction and bottom condition, but these are extraordinarily rarely seen and most owners rely on a record of fuel used on major voyages together with a note of the sea conditions.

A problem which occurs in all landfalls but which is often more difficult in motor yachts is which way to turn. If you cannot recognise a landmark, are you approaching too far one way or the other? It is a common dodge to build in a deliberate bias on the course set so that the landfall is certain to be to one side of the objective thus making the next move obvious. Sailing craft with the possibility of differing conditions of wind and weather to affect their speed always make their allowance on the safe side so that, if possible, they are up-tide if the wind fails, or to windward so that they can free their sheets. The motor yacht with its superior speed and reliability has a freer choice.

The three factors on which all navigation is based are speed, distance gone and direction. Speed can be estimated relatively accurately from the engine revolutions, weather and load, on the basis of trial speeds or experience. However, the electronic speedometer devices are now accurate and cheap and, as the same basic unit is required for a reading of distance gone, most motor yachts rely upon an electronic speedometer. The old-fashioned towing log is still to be seen but it is a right old bore to use and always a potential danger to the propellers.

The days of hand-flung lead lines for trying the depth of water have also, fortunately, been overtaken by electronics. The equipment is reliable, inexpensive and of very great help to the modern mariner. Given that the engines work properly, the next most important items to be given the best protection are the propellers. Even if the hull

is fitted with skegs, taking the ground unexpectedly puts the propellers to hazard. The depth meter is also useful in position finding, and a single bearing and a depth figure can give quite a useful fix if there is any shape to the local sea bed.

Direction finding radio navigation has, on this

Fig. 48 Transom platform is useful for bathing but rather vulnerable when docking.

Fig. 49 It is important and seamanlike to plot paths all round the boat including one to and from the sea itself.

side of the Atlantic, practically replaced all other kinds except reading the names off buoys as you pass. Frequently you will see someone on deck being told to keep quiet while the navigator is getting a radio fix on a lighthouse beacon, when what the poor lookout is trying to shout down is that the same lighthouse is now in full sight and has been for some time.

An accurate compass is essential, but very often the compass is placed conveniently in front of the helmsman close to masses of electric wires, all carrying variable and unpredictable currents to tip the needle just a little this way or that. A main compass for reference should be sited in some part of the ship where it is at least three feet from anything that might affect it. A main compass with an electric repeater at the dash panel is a convenient arrangement. In any case, any vessel which is likely to lose sight of land, even if only in thick fog, ought to carry two compasses against the day when one gets smashed.

The pilotage of a fast power boat need be no different from that of any other craft provided that it is slowed down or stopped from time to time to allow the normal processes to be taken in some peace and quiet. Somehow, stopping a fast boat just to navigate always seems ridiculous and unreasonable at the time. The best drill is to pretend from the start that you are a racing power boat unable even to pause to check a mark, and any chart work is only to be done before the passage. Every racing navigator has his own pet ideas on procedure but basically it is arranged as follows:

1. All the chart work is done in good time before the start and the courses, distances and even probable elapsed time noted on cards. Other major items of importance are also transferred to cards — the configuration of important buoys, a sketch of the landfall characteristics and run of tides.

2. These cards are set up somewhere safe — under glass in front of the helmsman or in the navigator's pocket.

3. Under way all the information required is therefore instantly available. Incidentally, the printing on the cards should be large — say at least half an inch high — to ensure that it can be seen if the yacht is pounding hard into a hard sea.

CHAPTER 3
The Traditional Ways of Construction

General

By 'traditional' we refer to the methods of constructing craft in wood before the invention of waterproof glues. This ancient art is still with us in fact, but its future can only be that of a history to the new skills which already engulf yachting. Most boatbuilders today could still build a boat by the old methods and some still do, only replacing the white lead bedding between members with a modern glue as a gesture to progress. Furthermore, perhaps half the boats afloat today have been built by traditional methods.

It is perhaps only now when these traditional ways of building are being superseded all around us that we can stand back and really appreciate

Fig. 50 An elegant example of traditional wooden construction. The hull for the 61 ft 6 in motor yacht Giftie — essentially a round bilge form with chines grafted on aft to improve performance at the upper end of the speed range.

Fig. 51 An earlier stage in the building of the Giftie hull shown left.

what an incredibly skilful craft it was. With its multitude of special names for components, tools and work, boatbuilding is almost a language to be learned before you can comprehend what is really going on. Just as one should learn to speak space language before talking to astronauts about more than superficialities, so one finds boatbuilding living in a sea of oddly attractive jargon. The likeness goes even further, for ships were the spacecraft of their day and attracted the same brands of people to their construction and usage as do the moonships. It was no series of accidents or casual developments which resulted in wooden ships being built as they were, but the result of hundreds of years of consideration by the best brains of the day. The wooden ship became one of man's masterworks in its time: a structure more highly stressed than any other known, yet formed of comparatively small bits of wood, and it still had to float and, even further, sail. With a certain amount of stagnation creeping in with the formation of admiralties controlling navies in the seventeenth century, development continued, for wood ships, right up to the industrial revolution of the nineteenth century. The technocrats then went into iron and steel construction and the small ship and boat became the sole outlet of the great tradition. The yacht, power or sail, then became the principal development factor leading the wood builder into delightful excesses of skilful craftsmanship building. The constructional members of a yacht, rarely ever revealed to the eyes of guests or crew, became as accurately made and as beautifully finished as the best palace furniture.

When one is brought up to these standards it is difficult to appreciate them fully, but sometimes they become revealed. A wooden rudder trunk in a yacht built by that masterbuilder of his time, Fife of Fairlie, when cut to install wheel steering, was thought to be one piece of wood until the butt was planed to reveal that it was actually four pieces of wood joined with four internal splines. Soon after that we saw a schooner being built in one of the remoter West Indian islands. Here trees with the bark on them were being used for frames of broadly the right shape and the whole vessel was pulled together to some state of equilibrium with the fastenings. Both were examples of traditional construction and resulted in the minor miracle of a boat making her way through the water. One was undoubtedly better built than the

other but left the nagging thought as to whether it was just an indulgence to build as well as a Fife.

Boatbuilding Materials (Traditional Wood)

There are many requirements for the wood used in traditional building. It is difficult to put one requirement above another, but perhaps the most basic is that it should be reasonably tough to withstand pulling into shape and reasonably close-grained to let the fastenings hold it in place. Then it must be fairly stable, that is it must not shrink or swell very much when exposed to the sun or immersed in the sea. This condition is always improved by a proper drying or seasoning process, but stability must be a characteristic of the timber. Next, perhaps, it must be reasonably resistant to rot. There is no point in constructing a fine vessel for a life of only a few months. Perhaps last, but not least, it should be a timber which is easy to work and which, straight-grained and knot-free, bends sweetly into the curved form of the hull. In different parts of the hull different requirements occur. For instance, the rubbing strakes must be good against abrasion, and underwater parts should be unattractive to shipworm and the marine borers. It helps if the inside linings and furniture are easy to clean, and the spars are of a wood which has a good whip in it.

The principal factor in the choice of timber for the various parts of a wooden craft lies in availability both in suitable sizes and in suitable degrees of preparation. To a quite considerable extent these factors have influenced both the type of craft and the type of construction used all over the world. Where oak forests grow, as once in Britain, it is convenient and reasonable to use the bends and convolutions of the oak tree for 'grown' frames and knees. This in turn allows the vessels to adopt a fairly complicated hull form, and the weight of material employed requires a craft of moderate to heavy displacement. The Scandinavian countries are rich in straight-growing pine trees, giving a supply of lightweight and durable boards. Scandinavian craft are traditionally therefore of a form which can be achieved with long straight planks, and of light displacement. The teak forests of Burma give

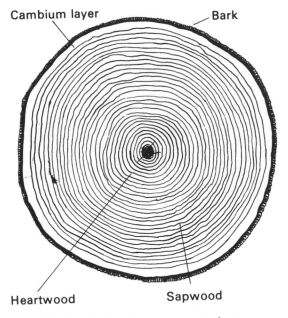

Fig. 52 *Section showing the arrangement of a tree.*

a supply of heavyweight material and the balsa forests of South America give rise to ultra-lightweight displacement working boats. Only in the temperate parts of the world where there is a choice of growing timber and in those countries where nearly all timber has to be imported can the differing properties of various timbers be properly appreciated.

The terms hardwood and softwood are used to differentiate between different classes of timber. It is confusing that both soft and hard classes of timber can vary between the physically hard and physically soft and that the terms really are of value only to botanists.

A fantastic range and variety of timbers are now used for boatbuilding and many hitherto little-known types come on to the market each year. The properties of any of these can be checked with the Timber Research and Development Association, who provide useful information and advice. The names of many of these woods are themselves evocative and interesting. Among the hardwoods are ones like afrormosia, afzelia, agba, balsa, bolondo, freijo, gaboon, greenheart, iroko, black locust, makore, obeche, sapele and utile, as well as the more comfortably familiar sounding elm, oak, mahogany and teak. Among the soft-woods are kauri and parana pine, with all the other pines, and fir, larch and spruce to help swell

the litany. How felicitously they roll off the tongue in contrast to all the plastics names we are now so familiar with.

The Preparation of Wood

A newly felled tree contains as much as a quarter of its weight in water. This water gradually evaporates from the cell cavities where it is stored, allowing the wood to shrink. The wood eventually reaches a general equality with the humidity of its surroundings, but will throughout its future life still shrink or swell according to its moisture content, which will vary, if only slowly, with any variation in its surroundings. The initial process of drying out is the seasoning process. Great care has to be taken to ensure first that the process is not too fast, for the sudden withdrawal of the water from the cells can cause them to collapse. Second, it must be done as evenly as possible so that the inevitable shrinkage occurs smoothly without causing local stressing inside

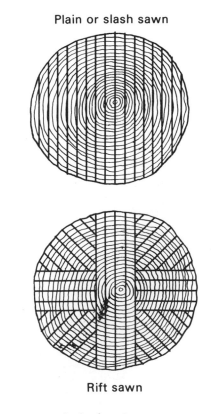

Fig. 53 *Basic methods of sawing up trees.*

the material to split it. There are two main methods employed. For both, the tree is sawn into planks which are carefully stacked, with air spaces all through. In air seasoning the stack is left for natural drying out to occur. In kiln drying the planks are stacked in a brick room fitted with heating pipes and a circulating fan. Frequently both methods are used, with the initial seasoning done in the air followed by kiln drying. The air process alone can take years while the kiln takes only weeks. The disadvantage of the air drying is that the final moisture content can be as high as 20 per cent. The normal content required for boat use is between 10 and 15 per cent, which means that the builder has to restack the timber under cover in his shed for a final seasoning period. The shrinkage that occurs between the felling of the tree and its final use for the construction of a boat is of the order of half an inch per foot of plank width.

The sawing of the log into planks is known as the breaking down and is important in that it establishes which way the grain will run in the planks. After seasoning the timber is 'converted' into the actual planks and pieces required for use. It is important for economy that this conversion will produce the maximum amount of useful planks, etc. from each log, but it is equally important for the vessel that each plank be sawn so that the grain direction will be of service rather than of hindrance to the movement and life of the craft. The shrinking and swelling of wood occurs to the greatest extent parallel to the outside of the trunk, or in other words along the lines of the growth rings. If these change direction too much in the section of a plank it will distort with different moisture contents. Also, the softer material between the growth rings or grain of the timber is easier to stretch or compress than that of the grain. A plank therefore will bend more easily into place if the grain is running down the length of its section rather than across it. A plank to be used in way of hard wear, such as on a deck, is better with a good run of edge grain along its face to make that wear more even.

One clever West Country boatbuilder who

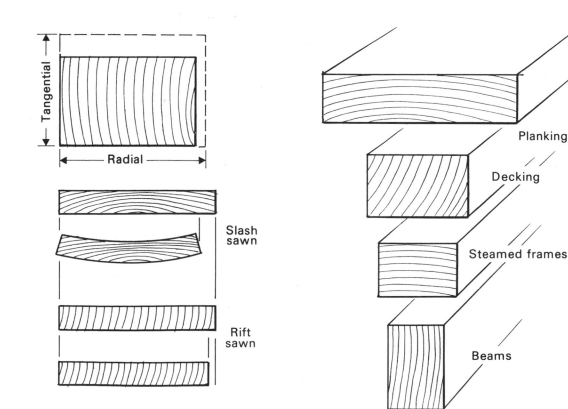

Fig. 54   Effect of drying out of timber.

Fig. 55   Grain direction required for different usages.

specialises in racing craft has even told us that he starts a new craft by choosing the tree. He follows the tree through the seasoning with care and then planks his craft 'with the bottom end of the tree pointing aft'. The proper choice of timber is often, in fact nearly always, neglected by both designer and builder in these days when it is ordered by telephone ready sawn rather than chosen in the forest.

The Boatbuilders' Metals

Metal was once a precious material for the boatbuilder, who found that an iron nail was many times better at holding his craft together than a wooden nail. Copper rivets were also found to be an improvement on leather thongs for holding planks together. In fact, in times of old and derring-do the first things to be saved from a shipwreck, after the souls on board and the essentials of life, were the nails, often before the gold in her hold. The ship was carefully unpicked, sometimes even burnt, to preserve and release the fastenings. The common iron nail has been in its time an international currency every bit as good as cigarettes and watches.

Practically the first metals to fall into the hands of boatbuilders were iron and copper, and fortunately these are excellent seafaring metals which have been in use ever since. The various alloys and other improved versions have been produced principally to make them stronger and to reduce the electrolytic corrosion problems that occur when different metals are used in common contact with the sea. Iron has a tendency to rust and requires to be uncomfortably hot when riveted. However, it is an excellent material for nails which can be protected with tar and hidden in the ship's planking, and it is a good cheap material from which to make rather soft nut-and-screw bolts for fastening the principal members of the hull together. It is also the blacksmith's metal and is used for all manner of miscellaneous fittings.

Copper is, or can be made to be, quite soft and can be riveted cold. The pounding of the riveting hammer compresses the metal and draws the planking together and at the same time the copper is hardening. The brasses and bronzes mix copper with zinc and tin respectively to increase strength and other properties. Gunmetal has a dash of both and is principally used for castings.

Iron, aluminium, manganese, nickel and silicon are also used in various alloys and the so-called aluminium bronzes use only aluminium and copper.

Iron is, alas, almost completely replaced by steel, for commercial reasons. Common or garden mild steel needs a proper protective coating of zinc, cadmium or plastics before it is really usable for boats, but the so-called stainless steels are increasingly used, both for their attractive appearance when polished and for their general freedom from some forms of corrosion. Steel is made stainless by the addition of chromium and is made in various degrees and types. The three principal types are: a low-carbon steel suitable for fabrication; a high-carbon steel which can be tempered, such as is used for knives; and a nickel steel which is perhaps the most commonly used type.

Aluminium is hardly a traditional material for the boatbuilder although boats have been built of aluminium for some time. For marine use it has to be reasonably free from corrosion in a salt atmosphere, which requires, it seems, some magnesium in the alloy — somewhere between two and four per cent is the usual amount.

The Language of Boatbuilding

All arts and sciences develop their own vocabulary over the years and it is one of the attractions of boatbuilding to us romantics that it possesses an apparently inexhaustible supply of words particular and peculiar to the construction of boats. One learns them with pride and appreciates them with relish. If the subject is boats, conversation with a traditional boatbuilder is difficult without knowing this language. There is something of the closed society about those who speak it, rather like gipsies or the Welsh.

The words of this language, however, are in fact basically extremely simple and straightforward in origin. It is in part the language that all old-time woodworkers used about the practice of their craft and in part a straightforward description of the function of parts of a ship. As always in English, some basic words are derived from Old English and Norse, but the retranslation into a modern idiom throws a clear and somewhat unexpected light on to the construction of craft — a light which is quite welcome at this moment when the straightforward approach of the traditional construction is a little obscured by modern possibilities.

Keel, for instance, is from the Middle English *kele* or Old Norse word *kjolr*; but the keelson running over the frames is the keel's swain, where *swain* is from Old Norse and Middle English words for lad, as in boatswain. The rungs are the bottom frames laid across the keel and obviously resemble exactly the single-string ladders which used to be common in boatyards. The word string is still used for the long length of wood which holds the steps of a staircase or the rungs of a ladder, and in boats the stringer is the member which ties the rungs or the frames together. Futtocks are the foot hooks between the rungs and the rising

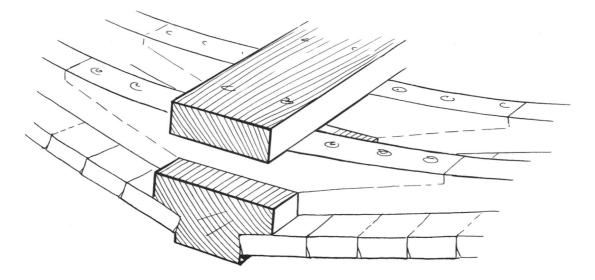

Fig. 56   The keel and the keel's swain.

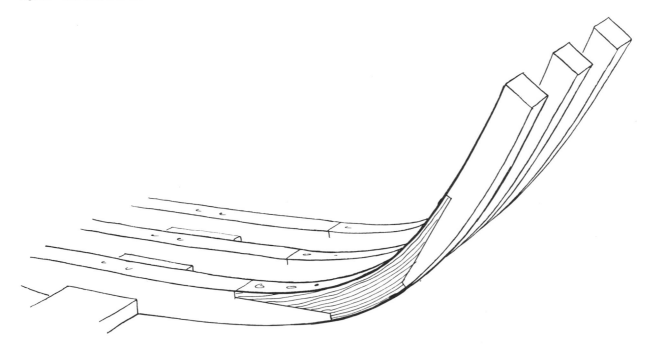

Fig. 57   Foot hooks or futtock frames.

frames which support the topsides. The sleepers are members which rest on the frames beside the keelson.

In the same sense the foregripe is the member which grips or holds the stem and apron to the keel; and the apron, of course, is no more than something worn in front for protection. The garboard strakes are the gather board strakes, perhaps from the Dutch *gaar*, which means gather, for they gather or grasp the frames and centreline structure together. *Wale* is an Old English word for a stripe or ridge and therefore the raised plank is called a wale, and that under the gunport openings is of course the gunwale. The shelf is the member on which the beam ends are supported and they are held tightly in place by a wooden clamp fitted underneath. The transom is a transverse or cross swain, using the term lad to mean a

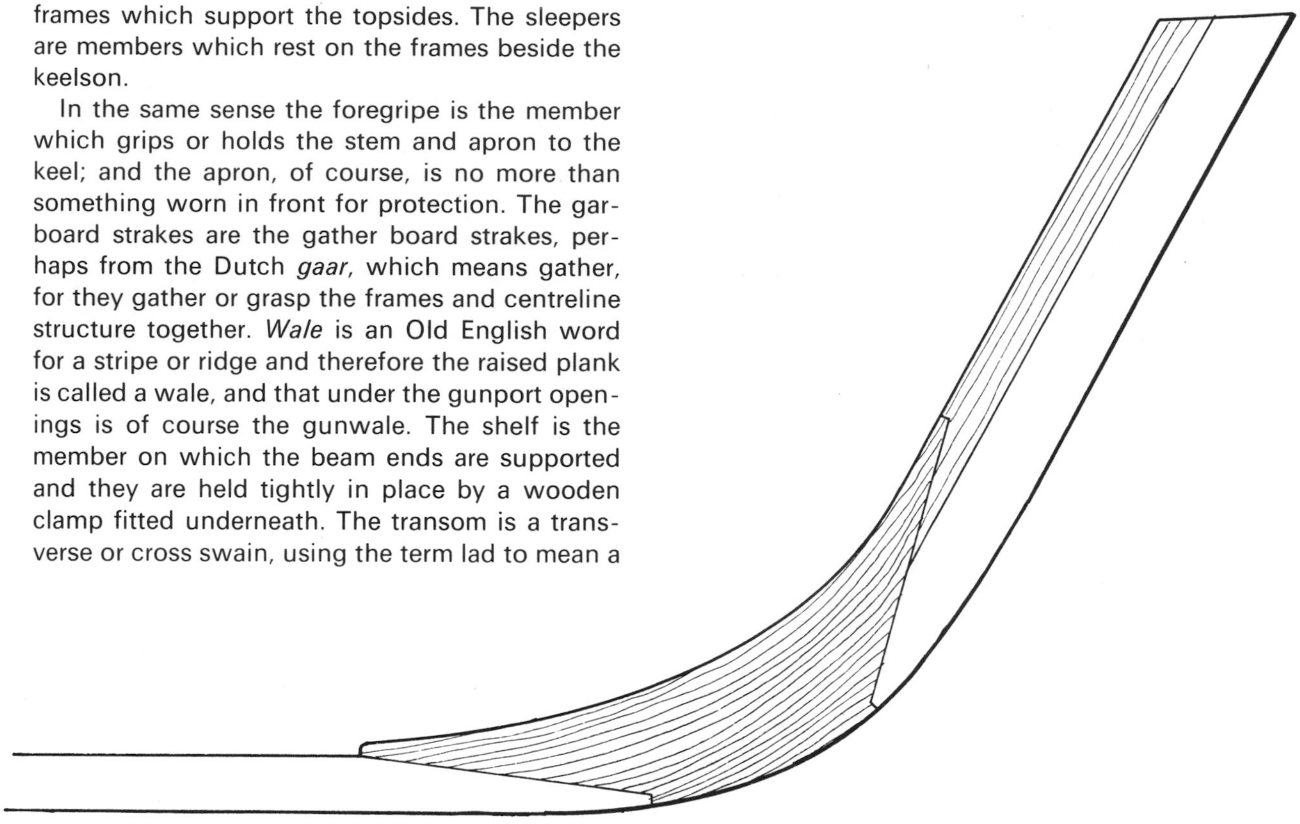

Fig. 58   The apron and foregripe.

Fig. 59   Beam shelf and clamp.

minor member, and the fashion pieces are those which have to be carefully fashioned to receive or fit to the planking at transom or bulkheads. The planking is held with trunnels which are no more than tree or wooden nails, which was a word for a hard pin before it became metal, and it is caulked directly from the Old French *cauquer* — to press. The mast stands on its step and is held properly at the deck by its mast partners. In many ancient books on boatbuilding the word coaming is happily spelled 'come in'. And what could be more logical than that the surrounds of the hatches, which were the only deck openings, should be known as 'come ins'?

Boatbuilding Tools

The traditional tools of boatbuilding, the adze, the axe, drag knife, awle, etc. were really, with modest variations, only the basic woodworking tools before the introduction of machinery. When ships became iron and the wood ship and boatbuilding industry became tiny, the boatbuilder was left high and dry beside the general advance of technology. Machines were used to cut the trees into planks and the planks into the

rectangular timber used to build houses and make crates. There was neither the volume of trade nor the money to develop at that time the machine to convert timber into the complex, continually changing form required by the boatbuilder, who had, perforce, to use the same tools employed for centuries before.

The heavy work was done by saw and axe whereas the adze was really a kind of portable power planer. The modern machine planer with rotating blades supplies perhaps some 800 adze cut equivalents a minute, while a skilled builder could supply up to, say, 100 adze cuts a minute. The long handle gave considerable power and in skilled hands the adze could produce a finish close to that of the plane. The drag knife was principally used for shaping planks. The knife could be dragged into the wood with great control from the two widely spaced handles, which were cranked forward of the blade to give leverage for splitting the plank along the grain. By a judicious choice of splitting and knifing a plank could quickly be cut to the required shape.

The greatest tool in a boatbuilder's bag, however, was and still is the cramp, in one form or another. Most of the parts of a hull have to be bent or twisted or squeezed, first into place for fitting and then into place for fastening. It may also be a long walk from the hull to the bench

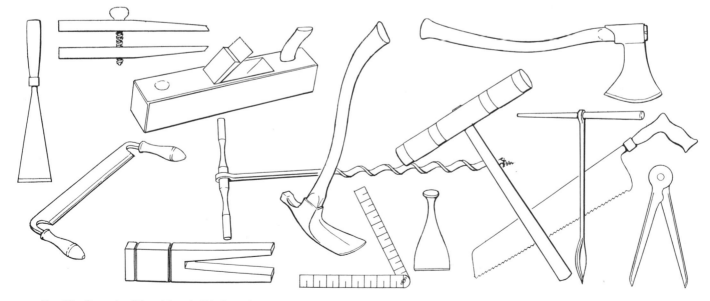

Fig. 60 *Some traditional boatbuilder's tools.*

and the boatbuilder much prefers to cramp the piece he is working on to the nearest bit of structure.

Traditional Framed Construction

A framed construction is essentially one where the shape of the craft is determined by a fairly solid internal structure which is then skinned with planking. The frames are sizable lumps of wood cut to the required shape from timber chosen so that the curves of the tree match the curve of the ship. It was sometimes the practice to erect all the frames in place and to let them finish their seasoning together for as long as seven years before planking and completing the ship. The principal member, however, in all ships is the keel, and this was of itself considered so important that the length of the vessel was usually given as the length of her keel. The laying of a keel on the building blocks or ways was the formal start of a new craft and accompanied by religious ceremonies. The traditional stories of craft being built with a single golden rivet in the keel for luck follow the same line of thought. To the front of the keel were added the various parts which comprised the stem assembly and to the rear of the keel was built a sternpost and transom structure. Across it were laid the ribs of the skeleton craft and from these rose the futtocks and side frames to establish the shape. The ribs were further

Fig. 61 The massive size of the wood frames used in traditional framed construction looks dramatically different from modern construction. (Photograph courtesy Edward Allcard.)

Fig. 62 This delicate and apparently haphazard tracery of frames is the result of the fast work required to get the hot timbers bent before they cool.

secured by a centreline keelson and by stringers and sleepers, and these in turn were secured by further additional ribs called floors. The careful diminution of the structural stresses by a pyramid of reinforcements is striking.

The tops of the frames were connected across the craft with beams at the appropriate deck levels and the corner stresses relieved with sizable wooden knees. Around the outside of the frames long timbers called wales tied the frames in their correct positions.

The principal structure of the vessel was then broadly complete and in due course the spaces between the wales were shuttered up with planking and the whole made watertight by poking twisted yarns soaked in tar into the gaps. The decks were similarly constructed and the vessel completed with a myriad of finishing touches to reduce the stress points, combat the entry of water, and for decoration. It is worth noting that the principal secondary function of the wales is to stop the ramming of caulking between the seams of the planking from just pushing the planking further apart.

Steamed Frame Construction

A steamed frame construction is usually used for lighter craft, although the combination of steamed frames and grown frames is sometimes seen where a reduction of weight or an economy in material suggests it. It is essentially a construction where the shape of the craft is established by an auxiliary structure which is not part of the completed craft. It takes a number of forms. In the most common, a set of frame-shaped moulds is placed on the keel and stem around which the stringers and other longitudinals are wrapped, together with a number of auxiliary and temporary stringers which are called ribbands. Around this cage the steam-bent frames are wrapped straight from the boiling steampot and allowed to cool and set to the required shape. Around these bent frames in turn are wrapped the skin planks, which are through-fastened to each frame. When the moulds and ribbands are removed the various parts ease and stretch until they are in equilibrium with each other like a basket and the ship is ready for caulking. Steamed frames supply comparatively little athwartships stiffening to the vessel and their principal function is to strap the planks together so that the planking itself becomes a structural member. Also, as a cross-strapping to the planking it prevents the caulking from just making the ship bigger.

Another common method of using steamed frames is to plank the vessel around the moulds and then to drop the frames into the hull to be bent and partially secured in place in one operation. This is limited to small craft both by the size of timber which can be handled in this way and

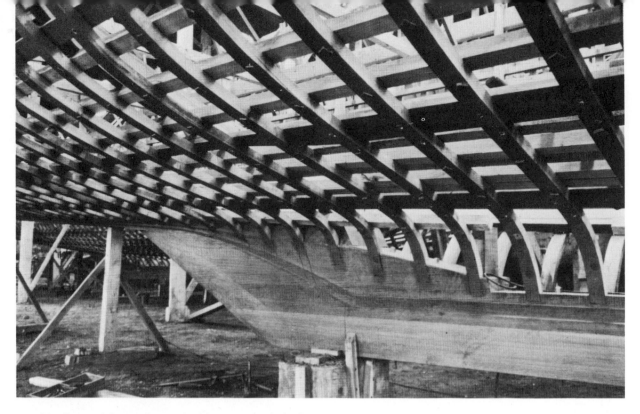

Fig. 63 Steamed frames fastened with temporary bolts for
the ribbands before planking.

Fig. 64 Clincher makes for a very light construction and it is
tempting to use it for different hull forms.

the speed required in fastening the frame down so that it takes up exactly the right shape before it cools and sets.

Clincher Planking Construction

There are many variations and cross-breedings between the various types of construction, and clincher planking is to be seen and has been used in many different circumstances. Essentially, however, it is a frameless construction where the planking, overlapping and through-fastened to its neighbours, directly determines the shape of the craft. It is possible and practical to build a clincher craft without frames or moulds by forming the planks as required for the shape desired. It is, when properly done, a beautiful construction both to the eye and in terms of constructional strength for light weight. It is often modified with a widely spaced sawn plank frame or two, or even a complete set of steamed frames, in order to reduce the cross or splitting loading on the plank fastenings where the timber is vulnerable to this stressing. The origin of the construction can be noted in the order of planking where the garboards are fitted first and the planks added one after the other up to the required gunwale height. There is a very good case for lapping the planking the other way and it is quite practical to do so in these days when every plank shape can be drawn before construction. However, no practical builder creating a shape as he builds would seriously consider starting with a couple of planks flying free in the air as a sheerline only to work back to the disciplined shape of garboard which must fit to the keel.

Craft Practice

Water is an insidious enemy and wood is an unstable defence. The structural stresses of a hull are substantial and a secondary defence system has also to be organised against rot and corrosion. The maritime woodworker therefore has to be more than just crafty in his work if seamen are to go over the deep waters with confidence. The traditional boatbuilder was and is one of the most sophisticated craftsmen. The craft practices employed in building complex vessels from a thousand individual parts of unstable material are often

beautiful to the eye and intriguing to the mind. They have the fascination of, say, the defensive systems of old fortifications where enemies were repulsed with a show of force, trapped with ingenuity and at all times kept at a disadvantage if they penetrated the outer walls. Harrison's celebrated four chronometers are another analogy which springs to mind, where the pleasure of tracing Harrison's methods of compensating, one by one, for the variations which affect time are comparable to the defence and traps used by the boatbuilder against the sea.

Unfortunately this beautiful craft is dying. Its wiles are no longer necessary now that we are able to stop making ships from matchsticks. One might, however, stop and admire them for sheer pleasure and also from them draw analogies and examples to apply to the new materials.

The classic joint of boatbuilding is the scarph and its variations to suit differing circumstances. A straightforward angled butt joint relies completely on its fastenings for strength and therefore a certain amount of straightforward pushing surface has to be worked in. The joint in some circumstances, notably in stems, has to take a tension load and therefore a cunning hook system is also incorporated. When fastenings became more reliable the ends of the scarph could be slightly tapered so that the action of tightening the fastenings up put a certain pressure loading into the scarph — pre-stressing in fact — so that the variations of humidity had less effect on the value of the joint. A stem scarph, even if bonetight on moorings, is apt to work a little when the bows push their way through the seas. The alternate opening and closing works as a tiny pump of great pressure which can force water into the structure as well as let it into the interior. This is stopped in a delightfully simple way. A hole is drilled right through the entry path of water and filled with a soft wood dowel. The moment water appears on the scene the dowel swells tight and seals the joint.

One of the first principles of wood construction is to avoid any triangulation of structure around another piece of wood. This is the type of arrangement which cannot possibly cope with the inevitable variations in size of the timber as it gets wet or dry. This means that it is more usual to construct by adding wood members one above the other. To stop them moving, one to another, various configurations are employed of which the

Fig. 65 A delightful example of traditional construction — one of the sail training ship Danmark's boats.

simplest is a block of wood let into the surface of both members, called a tabling. If the adjacent parts are likely to be pulled apart then an equally simple device, called a dovetail plate, is often employed. In both cases the fastening assumes a secondary role and the main stresses are assumed by the tabling and the dovetail plates.

Another classic example of the boatbuilders' art is the housed dovetail joint used to join beams to carlins and carlins in their turn to the end beams. Here the first job of the beam end joint is to carry

directly the full weight carried by the beam. This is done by housing or recessing its full dimensions into the supporting member. The second requirement is that it should not pull apart, especially if it is under a caulked deck. This requirement is achieved by adding a dovetail end to the beam.

Other examples might be in, say, a splined rudder trunk, the main fore and aft end structure of a sizable wooden yacht, and the traditional structure around an intermediate deck in a wood ship.

Fig. 66 Simple scarph joint which may be forced apart under longitudinal loads.

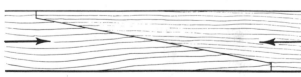

Fig. 67 Butted scarph used for compression load.

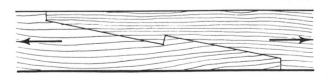

Fig. 68 Hook scarph used for tension loads.

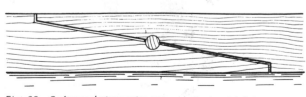

Fig. 69 Softwood stopwater prevents leaks at joints.

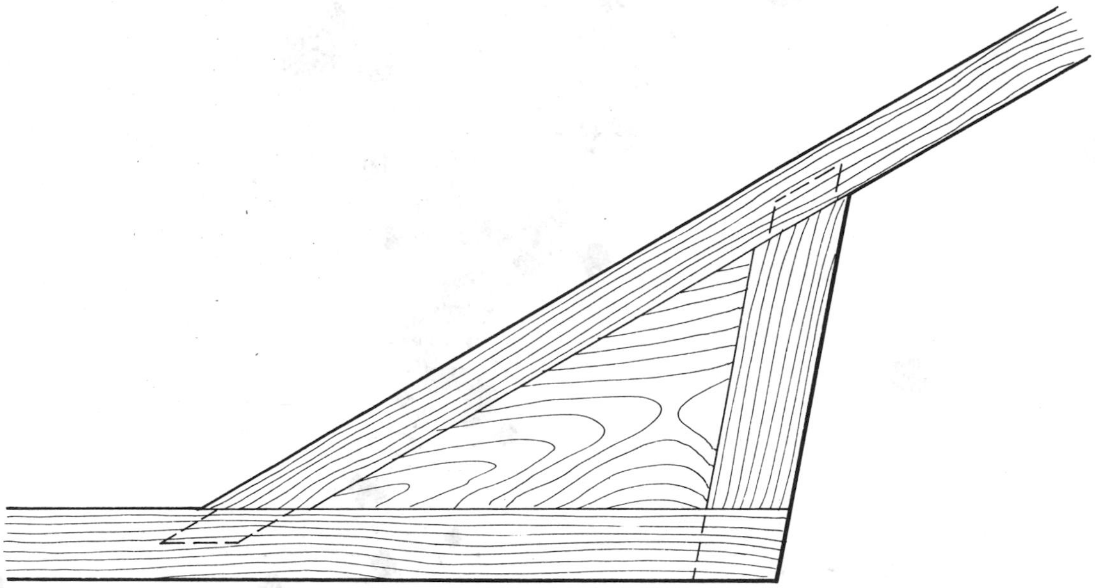

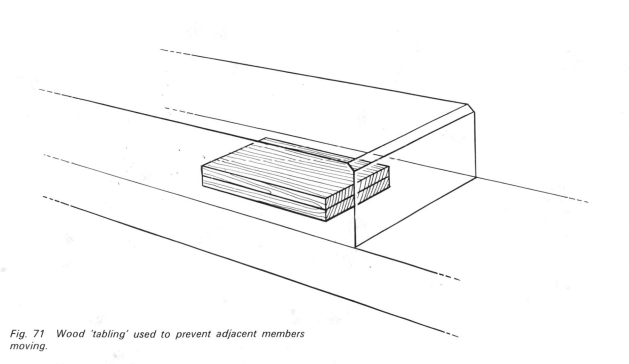

Fig. 70   In a triangulated structure like this the swelling and shrinking of the wood cannot occur without at least one joint splitting.

Fig. 71   Wood 'tabling' used to prevent adjacent members moving.

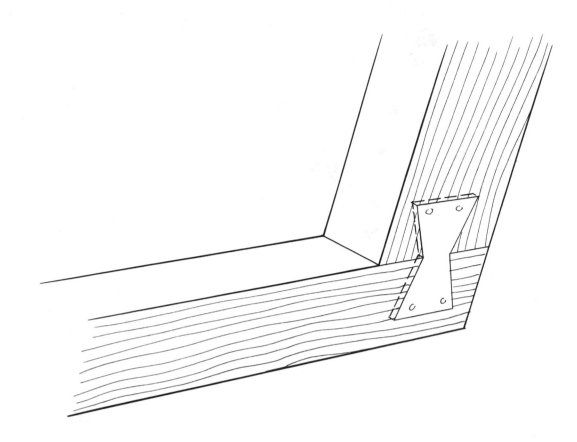

Fig. 72   Wood or metal dovetail plate used to prevent timbers
pulling apart.

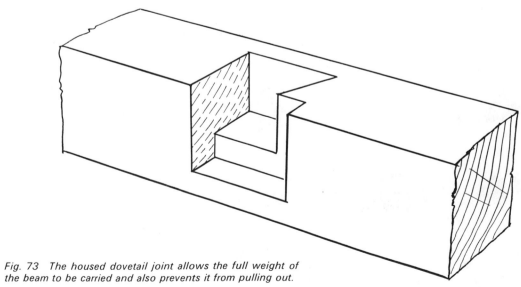

Fig. 73   The housed dovetail joint allows the full weight of
the beam to be carried and also prevents it from pulling out.

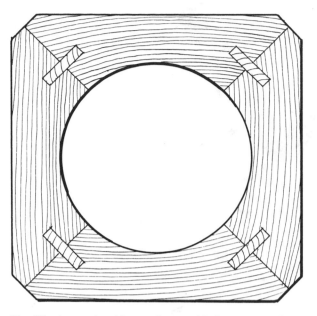

Fig. 74 A wood rudder trunk assembly by a master boat-builder.

Traditional Metal Construction

The Industrial Revolution greatly increased the pure physical dimensions of the foundries and the appliances for working metal, and at the same time increased the amount of metal available. It became possible to buy long lengths of rolled angle-bar and to forge complete shipside frames in a single operation. The long lengths of sheet and bar could also be used to build a more efficient framework for a ship to be clad, first with wood and later with iron or steel plating. An iron ship was easier to build, stronger when built and often with less weight of construction materials. In addition, with a very much thinner shipside construction there was appreciably more room on board. Although the iron vessel is slightly less sympathetic than wood for a vessel for pleasure, both the composite and full metal constructions were and are used for yachts.

A full composite construction is virtually a metal vessel planked with wood, and an intermediate degree of composite is probably more usual for yachts. Here the framing and floors are made of metal and the main structure and planking in wood. The great skill of this construction lay in the forging of the frames. These usually had to be heated in a long thin furnace to a white-hot workable temperature and then fully shaped, both to form and bevel, before being cooled. Once

shaped they could not be put back in the furnace and could have only modest corrections when mounted up on the building ways.

The initial composite constructions followed essentially the form and style of previous wooden constructions for, of course, they had essentially similar problems to overcome. Athwartships framing was still used to strap the planking together against the caulkers' mallets, and the ship was held together by bolt fastenings. It was natural, therefore, that when iron plating came to clad the framework it was used initially as a substitute for wood. The style of construction designed and eminently suitable for wood then became, somewhat illogically, generally used for all metal vessels.

The all-metal vessel depended on the skill of her platers in addition to the blacksmiths for her form. The plates had to be rolled and hammered into the shape of the ship before they were riveted into place. The ability of the plater to keep each plate eyesweet with its neighbours made or marred the reputation of the shipyard.

Books and books have been written on the explicable and calculable problems of riveting metal to metal. It is a well-documented science which is also declining in value to boatbuilding.

Iron is, of course, a soft material compared with steel and the advent of steel in general use superseded it almost overnight. Steel construction, however, followed almost directly along the lines of iron construction and in turn of composite construction, itself stemming directly from wood construction. One should mention the quite extraordinary skills in making metal craft developed by some workers, especially for small craft and yachts in Holland. The Dutch appeared to be the first to realise that the new material had quite different properties from wood and could be, with advantage, used quite differently.

Intermediate Constructions

Between the classic traditional constructions and the modern homogeneous craft lie several attempts at improvement to suit the changing requirements of this century and its mechanised craft. It is probable that two individual and quite separate influences provided the greatest stimulus to experiment. First was the arrival of the fast motor boat. This not only moved or worked as it bounded across the sea, thereby making it more difficult for the caulking to stay in place, but the big rise in the pure water pressure loading on the bottom coupled with the need for light weight also made caulking outdated. At the same time the ocean liners were being required to carry reasonable lifesaving boats in considerable quantities. These were carried high on the ship through tropical sunshine and winter storms for year after year and had to remain watertight to meet the regulations.

One of the answers to both requirements was the use of multiple planking. This was either a second layer of planking applied fore and aft so that the seams of one skin were at midbreadth of the plank of the other layer. More usually the skins were planked diagonally to give in a much cruder manner the same strength and weight advantages now used for moulded construction. To stop water percolating through the pinholes at the junctions of skins in diagonal construction a layer of oiled cloth, usually calico, was introduced between the two skins. The bottom was then unified into a homogeneous skin by an elaborate system of copper clench nails. Sometimes three or more skins might be used in a highly stressed craft, but two were usual. The tough resilient bottom thus constructed was common in both speedboats and lifeboats. The principal disadvantage lay in the almost absurd difficulty of repair in case of damage or decay. The unpicking of the planking had to be extensive to make good even the smallest hole, and the general disturbance of the bottom that occurred during such a repair often devalued the whole craft.

Another attempt at holding the planking together to form a constructional skin integral in itself is the famous Saunders Roe sewn planking. Here, for light weight and high pressures, a copper wire was threaded through holes in adjacent planks to stitch them one to another, as if they were sewn or perhaps as if they were held together with leather thongs like some of the craft of antiquity.

Perhaps we could also put in this section two planking methods still in use. The first is to fit a stringer batten to the framing so that it will act as a butt strap for the outer planking seam. Two plank edges at a time are screw-fastened direct to the seam batten stringer, in effect using the wood

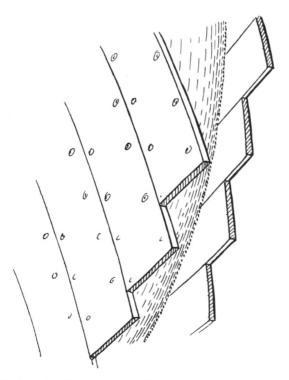

Fig. 75   *Double diagonal planking.*

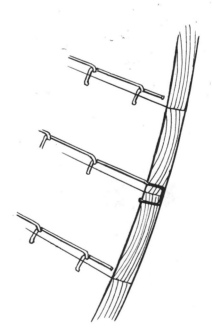

Fig. 76   *Sewn planking.*

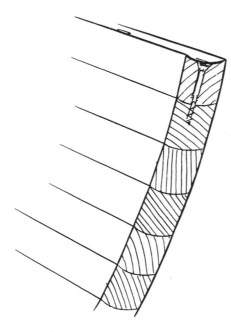

Fig. 77 Strip planking.

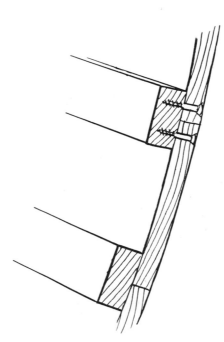

Fig. 78 Seam batten planking.

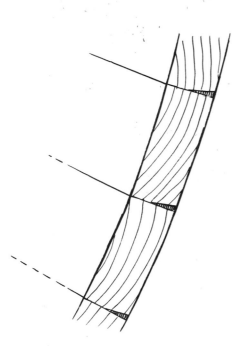

Fig. 79 Carvel planking.

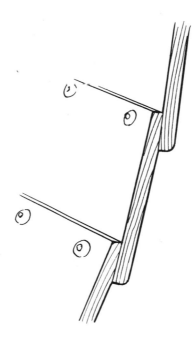

Fig. 80 Clincher planking.

batten instead of Saunders Roe's copper wire. The other method, called strip planking, has been and perhaps is still much favoured by amateur builders and makes a considerable step towards the desirable homogeneous construction. For amateurs it also avoids the problem of the physical acquisition and handling and shaping of large planks. Here the planking is formed of almost square sectioned wood which is then through-fastened internally edge to edge with the plank beneath it. Various tricks of section, principally the use of radii, make the planking easier to apply. Such a method requires moderately heavy planking to make it strong and practical.

CHAPTER 4
Modern Construction

General

The whole essence of modern construction can be summed up in the words 'one-piece'. From the careful and cunning weaving of seaworthiness from a hundred parts, the building of boats jumped in one step into the single indivisible one-piece hull. The cares of watertightness disappeared in a flash to be replaced by the more up-to-date bogies of chemistry, metallurgy and 'plasticology'.

In its many different forms the one-piece hull was introduced to boating during the ten-year period from 1945. The welded metal hull, the all-glued wooden hull and the reinforced plastics hull all arrived during this time and at first were treated as mere extensions of existing weapons in the eternal battle. Welding replaced riveting, glue was used as a rather better bedding compound than white lead for woodwork and even the reinforced plastics were slightly tortuously arranged to give a fair imitation of structures that Nelson would have recognised. The new constructions were not immediately seen as the atom bombs they were in the age-long struggles to stop water percolating into the boat and to keep a paint finish on the outside.

Now that we are beginning to be aware of the proper extent of the revolution it is perhaps a little frightening. We are now freed from the benign disciplines of the sweet form taken up by wood when bent or cut to follow grain grown free for years; freed too from the simplicity of the sheet of metal rolled to a constant thickness, or the framing which has to be formed from a bar of mechanically constant section. We can now decide what characteristics are actually required from materials, and methods can be tailored to suit. What does the boat designer do then, poor thing? Cling to memories of the past and advance with the utmost caution towards the sunset of unlimited possibility?

Technical requirements

The modern power yacht is an exceptional creature compared with any other vehicle used by man. The fast power boat is subject to constantly repeated loadings in excess, by a considerable margin, of anything else in normal use on our planet. The impact loadings of a fast boat doing a belly-flop can be of the order of $10g$ and loadings of a half this order can occur every three or four seconds throughout the passage time. One should perhaps be ashamed that such a state of affairs is allowed to go on, but while it does the skin, structure and fittings, not to mention the crew, of a fast open water power boat take, by any modern standards, an exceptional beating. Military aircraft and rockets and racing cars and even fast tanks do not provide anything like the material test facilities offered by the fast power boat. Even moderate-speed power boats can, in some sea conditions, take quite a hammering. Boating is still, despite its expansion in recent years, a small industry compared with others and one which cannot afford to spend much money on research. It does therefore rely to a substantial extent on the research results that filter down to it from the giant automobile and aircraft and building industries. They do not have our problems and until they do, and turn their vast facilities to light the way, the yacht designer can only proceed somewhere between reproducing the characteristics of antique wood constructions and the well-known 'suck it and see' principles. Somewhere, that is, between what one well-known designer used to call the 'tightly controlled guess' and the 'controlled guess'.

It is difficult to persuade the academics who should be sitting under their 'dreaming towers' contemplating the solutions to our problems that we even have any. They cannot, it seems, reconcile the rough characters up to their knees in wood shavings, that they recall from their boyhood visits to seaside boatyards with any demands of high technology. The same attitude is also frequently to be found among those who deal with the new materials. A white coat and some whiffy smells with chemical names are often apparently thought to be as much technology as the boating trade will be able to take in, and the development is all allowed to curdle in the pot. The technology of glass reinforced plastics is a suitable example where, apart from some advances in craft practice, development was practically moribund for years as far as the eye could see until further plastics constructions hove on the horizon and the metals also began to fight back.

The principal problems of the moment are structural. The simplest is the strength of double curvature forms of irregular shape. It is a first principle of the use of sheet material that it gains strength through shape and it is possible in many instances to calculate an approximation of a particular area of hull form. The most difficult is to estimate the structural requirements of a whole hull when regarded as a pure curved sheet envelope. We are used to a certain amount of movement in a wooden hull and this is regarded as an acceptable standard for comfort to both the eye of the beholder (most important) and the operation of the craft, but we do not have any conclusive ideas whatever on whether more movement or less would be better or worse. We are also fairly short of knowledge on the effects of stress concentrations and energy absorption in general. About fatigue and electrochemical corrosion we are all a little apprehensive, especially about the effects of the ultraviolet end of sunlight. We need better fire resistance in some materials and better chemical resistance against normal household substances from others. We would like to know how to assess materials more accurately both on the workshop floor and for a general condition survey of plastics craft. These are, however, aspects of craft usage which improve every

year as the technology advances and knowledge becomes more widely disseminated. The principal problems of the boat designer in his often highly competitive professional environment are those of structural design and the future. At one time all boats, amateur or professional, were built in much the same manner and it was possible to predict with confidence that a builder had every chance of keeping his constructional methods up to date. Now, when a production line is put down for a five year run with enormous capital investment, the process used has to be extremely carefully considered. The introduction by a rival of an even newer process, say, cutting labour costs in two, could easily put a blight on the whole enterprise.

Sheet Plywood

Everybody knows what is meant by plywood, for it is used throughout our lives. Although often known as 'three ply' it comes, depending on thickness and quality, in many forms and with many different numbers of plies. The veneers are usually sliced circumferentially from the log, and adjacent layers usually have the grain running at right angles to each other. When plywood is of marine grade it is made from timber with that quality of durability and freedom from rot which is desirable for any boatbuilding material and is bonded with marine grade resin glue. In different countries differing standards are used to check the quality of marine grade plywood.

It is widely known that there are different grades and varieties of plywood and many a specification proudly announces that a boat is built of marine plywood throughout, some even giving chapter and verse of the British or American standard that is met by the particular sheeting used. It is tempting to relax from that point believing that rigorous standards are busy preventing the use of anything but ideal materials for the job in hand. Unfortunately this is not altogether the case. For instance, the well-known BS 1088 standard refers only to the average requirements for this boatbuilding plywood and requires only modest standards of veneers, a modest degree of adhesion between the veneers and of rot resistance in the materials. It does require the use of a good marine type glue in the make-up, standards for the core materials, and a reasonable arrangement of the veneer joints, but not, you will note, anything at all to do with the actual strength of the finished product. The label marine ply, in fact, forms only an irreducible minimum standard in the process of the proper selection of the plywoods for boatbuilding. In fact as the plywood will normally be working at higher stress levels than in straightforward wood construction there is even greater reason for care in selection.

Plywood factory-made to marine standards is one of the most popular materials of which boats are built and has been used for very many years in craft of all sizes. Though it is less used these days for hull construction it is still a fair bet that some plywood will be found in any boat of any size built today. It is an unique material which fits like a dream into the world of the conventional boatbuilder. It looks rather like wood and works rather like wood and can be finished in exactly the same manner as the rest of a wooden vessel. There is no other way of spanning great areas of hull and joinerwork in wood without the builder using considerable skill, selected matched materials and a great many separate bits of wood which have to be attached to each other.

An old builder friend of Mr Francis Herreshoff is once reported to have said about plywood, 'Mr Herreshoff, a man must be a ***** fool to slice up some nice stock and glue it together so half of it is crossgrained.' That same builder was probably engaged at the time in laying a skin of carvel planking at right angles to the frames, And who, one might ask, was then being crossgrained? This story, however, illustrates one of the most important principles in the use of plywood; that is in the matching of this cross grain and the structural need for which it is to be used. The material is in general rather heavy and, being in sheet form, has to be used over an extensive framework or in generous thicknesses to obtain reasonable rigidity. Careful matching of the main and secondary grain directions to the loading is necessary to get the best from plywood.

Again, because it is a sheet material which is capable of only the most modest double curvature, boats designed for plywood skins have to be shaped so that the ply will wrap around the moulds or frames. Considerable ingenuity is necessary in the design if the finished vessel is going to avoid the rather boxy appearance which has come to be associated with plywood. Plywood is also a factory produced product manu-

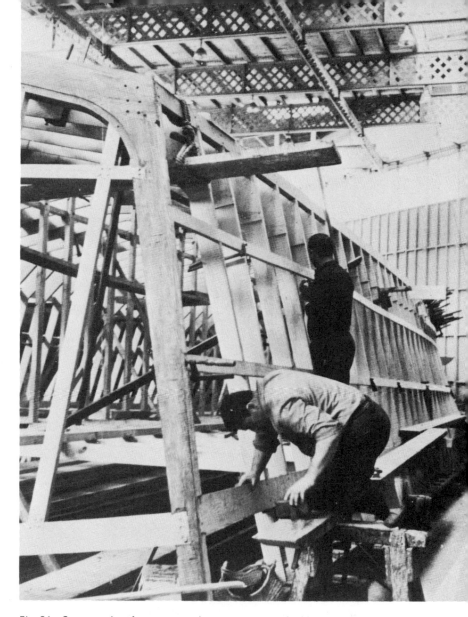

Fig. 81 Some modern fast motor yachts are constructed with an elaborate set of frames with corners reinforced with plywood brackets. In this manner a basic rigid load-carrying framework is built up in which the skin carries only panel rather than structural stresses. A motor yacht being built at Viudes yard, Barcelona, for Italy.

factured to overall dimensions probably calculated rather more on the size of the lorry which will carry it away than on the size of the craft for which it is intended. This tends to make plywood more popular for the smaller boats, although most manufacturers of plywood are prepared to scarph together lengths to suit the builder if required.

Many plywood craft are still built on a full set of frames. These, as our crossgrained builder pointed out, are no longer required to hold the planking together against the wedging apart of the planks by the caulking. They have only really any value as devices to reduce the panel loading on the skin. In a fast boat there is a

Fig. 82 Another view of the boat shown in Fig. 81.

directional value in the shock loading which makes athwartships framing on the stressed bottom skin somewhat similar to sticks broken across the knee. Where such framing is used the bottom skin has to be unnecessarily thick to cater for the stress points. This directional loading was amply proved and illustrated by some of the early entries in the present phase of powerboat racing. These

Fig. 83 This multi strake construction makes best use of marine plywood's characteristics. The bottom is applied in three strakes a side like an inverted clincher planking. In this boat, built in Italy, two of the strakes have been fitted and the third has still to go on.

were the ones which used to be fished out by cranes at intermediate points along the course with bottoms cracked at each and every frame. We used to call the *Daily Express* powerboat race a 'predicted log' contest because it was possible, or so we maintained, to predict which boats were going to 'hit logs'.

We invented a multi-strake plywood construction for fast, i.e. highly stressed, power boats back in 1959. Nothing is new under the sun and we will probably find that it was the construction used by Noah, but we devised our version especially for plywood and fast power boats with an eye to great simplicity of construction. Many hundreds of boats have been built by this method, all over the world and by all manner of boatbuilders, and so to describe it might well illustrate the manner in which we think plywood is best used for power boats.

Essentially it is a frameless construction with the plywood used as the major part of the structure and not just as a means of keeping the water out. It is of course essential to such a form of construction that the material (that is, marine grade plywood) can be relied upon to be to the same standard within reasonable limits no matter from which dealer it is purchased. It is after all one of the advantages of plywood construction that the material is of a known standard and is bought ready to use. In particular this gives the amateur constructor a flying start without the considerable logistics required in assembling, drying, cutting and laminating timber at home.

The main constructional members in our multi-strake building are four longitudinals which run almost the full length of the hull. These, assembled in moulds with keel, chines, and shelves or gunwales, form the framework about which the plywood skin is fitted. Great care is taken in this form of construction to ease out any stress points so that the hull will, when it has to, distort under load in a smooth and gentle manner. The few athwartships members in these hulls are kept clear of the skin and so are all furniture and heavy fittings. Engines, tanks and soles are carried from the longitudinals. Where a watertight bulkhead is required this is specially considered and provision made so that it is not too hard a member against the skin.

It is a feature of the structural design that the bottom is applied in three strakes a side as for inverted clincher planking. This allows both the

Fig. 84 The same boat as in Fig. 83 with hull finished and coamings and deck beams in place.

Fig. 85 Interior view of the hull being fitted out, after removing moulds.

Fig. 86 The 15 ft Mustang, *a build-her-yourself design, sponsored by* Yachting World, *built by the multi-strake method. (*Yachting World *photograph.)*

doubling of the material under the longitudinals as a stress relief and also the designing of some shape into the bottom. Compared with the conventional straightforward application of a single sheet from chine to keel, the amount of shape which is possible is sufficient to make quite a significant improvement in the seakeeping qualities of the boat. An additional advantage is to reduce the working size of the sheets being applied, thereby making it possible to build larger vessels with quite modest facilities.

Moulded Plywood

The term moulded plywood construction, whether called hot or cold, refers to wood veneers or very thin planking laminated straight over a mould shaped to the form required. The resulting sheet of plywood is happily and conveniently exactly to the complex and curvaceous shape required. In practice, thin planks of the order of two or three millimetres and thicker are most commonly used, rather than true veneers. Another major difference from factory made plywood is that the pressure brought to bear on the glue joints of the cold moulded process is of the order of 2 or 3 lb per sq. inch rather than the 100 lb per sq. inch of the factory presses. The difference is really one of the chemistry of the glue and drying time rather than any critical difference in the strength of the final joint.

The moulds used for this process usually have to be quite elaborate to provide sufficient guidance and support for the first skins. It is not uncommon to 'shutter' the moulds over completely so that the mould itself, in any other century, could be given a good caulking and put out for launching. The first skin, probably laid diagonally, is planked up in the usual way but with the planks secured to the mould with temporary fastenings, usually staples set through a wood sliver to aid removal. The next skin, probably laid diagonally the other way, is then glued and temporarily fastened plank by plank over the first skin. This process generally starts in the centre of the hull and the fastenings for the inner skin are removed in the way of each new plank being applied. This process, known as 'wallpapering' to some of Wilf Souter's experts on the subject, continues until the required thickness of hull is achieved. Sometimes, for fancy craft, the outer skin is laid up fore and aft to look just like the planking of yesteryear.

In the hot moulded process each layer is only held in place by comparatively few fastenings and glueing pressure is then applied by collapsing, with a vacuum able to support some 27 inches of mercury, a large rubber bag draped over the mould. At the same time the whole mould is put into a large oven to be heated to a temperature of about 100° C to suit the glue. Each layer of wood

Fig. 88 Another shapely cold moulding — the 40 ft News of the World raceboat also built by Souters.

Fig. 87 Cold moulding the twin tunnel 80 ft hull of the motor sailer Green Lady at Souters of Cowes. Fixing a mahogany veneer over the mould with staples and battens. Successive veneers are bound together with synthetic resin to make a strong light hull.

Fig. 89 News of the World conference. Wilf Souter (left), Colin Mudie and Tony Needell (right) inspect progress during the building of the hull for the News of the World raceboat.

is treated separately in this manner and the finished hot moulded hull can be distinguished from a cold moulded hull by the absence of the million pinpricks which show, mainly in the interior, in the latter.

The main advantage of the moulded plywood processes, apart from the absence of seams, is that the designer can begin to engineer the properties of the skin plies to his liking. The outer skins often have to be of a good tough wood to stand up to thumps and abrasion, or of a suitable matched grain for varnishing. Beauty, however, can remain skin deep and the intermediate skins, which do little real work except to pad out the moment of section, or, in other words, to push the face skins into the best place to do their duty stresswise, can be of quite weak but light material.

To a certain extent hull stress points can be strengthened by judicious use of intermediate veneers of different material but it remains a disadvantage of moulded ply that the planking is consistent layer by layer and any wholesale variations in strength characteristics are not easy to achieve within the skin.

The main framing of the hull is often laid in the mould before planking so that it is directly connected to the skin in one go. The hull taken off the mould is virtually complete and ready for fitting out. Such a hull is at this time likely to be lighter than any other construction of comparable strength and durability, even taking into account lightweight foam sandwich constructions.

Glass Reinforced Plastics (GRP)

There are probably more boats built in this form of construction at the present time than any other. It is difficult to know exactly why, other than that it was the right material in the right place at the right time. It was the first of the really homogeneous hull constructions to be put before the public. It allows the designer a certain amount of freedom of shape. It certainly compares well with the antique constructions in terms of maintenance and comfort on board. Perhaps as important as anything is that it is a construction which requires factory rather than boatyard conditions and, being particularly suitable for quantity production, fell straight into the lap of industry rather than into that of the undercapitalised,

romantically inclined, friendly, neighbourhood boatyard.

Very respectable craft are constructed by this means, let there be no doubt about that, but the note of hesitancy, the lack of wholehearted approval which must be apparent, is due to a feeling of frustration about glass reinforced plastics. The material is good but not quite good enough, and frequently not as good as it could be. If you judge it by the standards of the antique constructions, or by comparable constructions available about 1950 or even 1955, it is an excellent method of producing slightly heavy boats which are perhaps a tiny bit dead in their movements. Glass fibre development then appears to have ceased. True, there is some minor research going on into cheaper alternative reinforcements, and some improvements have taken place in resins and the glass components, but the industry would appear to believe that to erect a wall strong enough to keep the water out is all that is required. A boat is a living, moving, object and the engineering of the skin laminate and of the structural members can have a big part to play in giving the hull the right kind of life, and we do not refer to longevity.

Unfortunately, boatbuilding remains, despite the prodigious number of craft involved, only a modest part of the market for glass reinforced plastics. As an industry we are rarely able to commission any great amount of original research. We have to wait until the need occurs in some greater industry and the results filter down to us. Boat hulls are by far and away the most highly stressed, loaded and worked structures made of glass reinforced plastics and there is as yet only a comparatively tiny background of structural technology for the designer to work on. What there is is founded on two basic and quite reasonable starting points. The first is that the panel strength shall be calculated so that it will not burst on maximum impact, and the second is that the main strength of the hull should approximate to that of the comparable antiquely constructed wooden craft — it being known to be good enough. A third and also reasonable factor is sometimes considered: this is that the amount of bending that occurs should not be enough to alarm the occupants.

Plainly there is a great deal more to the structure of a boat than this and we could do with millions more spent on research into the strength of double curvature forms, hull resilience and energy absorption. Indeed, we would like this for all the modern constructions but in a material where there is the prospect of engineering the laminate to our needs it is essential.

Equally essential is some know-how on improvements to the reinforcements of the resin. Perhaps glass is far and away the best, but if it *has* reached its zenith then we should all now be looking elsewhere.

The words glass reinforced plastics are so well dug into the brain that it is difficult really to give more than lip service to materials other than glass being used to reinforce plastics. There are, of course, others, of which the doyen must be carbon fibre, now settling down into more or less everyday use as stiffening for more humble composites. Carbon fibres had a few heady years when their presence afloat could almost be felt by an awed crew, and the owner of a carbon fibre reinforced anything might almost have been expected to wear a twist of it in his buttonhole as an indication of both his scientific and financial standing.

Carbon fibres are derived from acrylic fibre through a complex process of baking and stretching, and have a high specific strength and stiffness. The latter is the biggest attraction for boatbuilding where a deck panel or, say, a mast, normally has to be built much thicker than is required for pure strength in order to cut down the flexibility. Carbon fibre comes in different grades but the stiffer versions might have a Young's modulus of 60×10^6 lb per sq. inch compared with something like 11×10^6 lb per sq. inch of the low alkali glass usually used for boat laminates. The problems in its use generally stem from the relatively poor adhesion to the resin, either polyester or epoxy, and its increasingly different characteristics during the distortion of the composite. The carbon fibre is coated to improve the mechanical bond and one process even covers the carbon fibres with little silicon carbide whiskers to hold them fast in the resin.

One should also mention boron fibres in the high class end of the resin reinforcing market, and even take a look at jute for the other end. Glass is quite costly by the time it is reduced into fibres, rovings, mats, cloths, etc. and of course it is logical to look round for other reinforcements which might be less expensive and indeed might not have the high tensile strength of the glass which may not always be required in a particular

Fig. 90   Hot moulded motor boat hull under construction at Fairey Marine with the oven yawning ready in the background.

Fig. 91   Lifting the hot moulded hull off the plug at Fairey Marine.

moulding area, or, for instance, in the centre of a laminated sandwich. Jute, hessian, sackcloth — call it what you like — has among other materials been extensively tested, but for boats is too vulnerable to deterioration if the weather gets at it.

The strength of reinforced plastics construction is that it does allow a one-piece hull to be manufactured with the hull thickness geographically

Fig. 92 *GRP construction at Tylers. The wooden plug for a 56 ft Keith Nelson motor launch.*

Fig. 93 *Next stage in the preparation of the plug shown in Fig. 92.*

Fig. 94 *Half mould for the 56 footer with plug in the background.*

varied as required. It is a thin material which allows all the extra space to be used inside the craft and it is fairly easy to maintain. The disadvantages are the slight increase in weight, the smell and the individual integrity required from each man of the building crew working the material. Another disadvantage of glass reinforced plastics is really quite unfair to the material. There is a certain feeling that it is invulnerable and GRP boats get treated with a great deal less care than, for instance, do wooden boats or even metal ones. It is a little vulnerable to chafe, but not really more so than other materials and a feeling of disappointment when chafe occurs is just one more manifestation of the cruelty of life where nothing is actually ever perfect.

The most usual resins employed for reinforced plastics are the polyesters, more correctly called unsaturated polyester resins. These are thermosetting. A continued application of heat causes an irreversible chemical change in the material, turning it into a hard, infusible product. Polyester resins are 'cured' in a variety of ways, mostly involving mixing with a catalyst and accelerator. Different kinds of polyesters are used for various properties such as increased flexibility or heat resistance. All polyesters will burn but can be made fire-resistant to some extent by the addition of chlorine compounds or HET resin.

The glass reinforcement is normally the so-called 'E' glass which is a low alkali borosilicate. The 'A' grade which is sometimes used is a lime-soda glass with an 8 to 15 per cent alkali content. The high alkali glass is supposed to be more susceptible to moisture and chemical attack and makes up into laminates which may have 10 per cent less strength than the comparable 'E' glass laminate, possibly due to a reduced bond between the glass and the resin.

A conventional glass reinforced resin hull is made in a mould which in turn is usually made from a pattern or plug. Thus the first step in production is to build a full size wooden or plaster hull finished exactly as the final vessel. This plug is, by a nice convention which requires boats to be of a perfect finish, highly polished to a really smooth and high gloss. A parting agent is sprayed over this plug and the mould is formed over it. It is usual for convenience in larger craft for the mould to be in two or more parts. The two major parts are usually split along the centreline of the hull. Each part is therefore laid up independently on the plug and a good joining flange formed in it at the same time. When all the mould parts can be assembled, still over the plug, they are reinforced with a heavy framework of steel or wood. The mould is then ready for making the final hull and given a final polish.

A releasing agent is sprayed on the mould, followed by the first coat of resin. This is called the gel coat and is the visible outer skin of the yacht. Sometimes a different resin is used which will stand up better to the knocks an outer skin has to take. This gel coat is quite thin, in fact as thin as possible, and as it is the most highly stressed skin of the laminate it is sometimes supported by a very thin layer of glass tissue. The subsequent laminations usually take one or all of the following forms. The best reinforcement is glass cloth which is usually reserved for the outer and most highly stressed lamination. Next come woven rovings which often form the bulk of the layers of a good quality hull. Glass mat is often used just to fill the large inequalities of the coarse woven rovings, and also on its own account. A layer of resin is sprayed or painted on and the cloth, rovings or mat, carefully tailored to the shape required and rolled down until completely impregnated with the resin. This complete impregnation is quite critical as unsupported resin is brittle and air pockets left in the laminate make it substantially weaker.

There are, of course, other methods of GRP construction, and techniques vary from builder to builder. It is possible to get reinforcing cloth already impregnated with the required resin, or to spray resin and glass strands together out of a gun to the required thickness. The resin can also be vacuum-sucked or pressure-injected through glass and/or other reinforcement in a mould.

Whatever method of construction is used the time in the mould is most important. Due to the tension set up in the drying laminate there can be a certain amount of movement or distortion in the moulding during the curing period. The times involved can vary very much with the chemical components and temperature. A moulding may have set hard enough to remove from the mould in as little as a few hours but may not reach a nearly fully cured state for a week, or a completely cured state for three months. The time which the moulding is allowed to stay in the mould is therefore a factor in the fairness of the hull. A hull destined for a boat show can with advantage

Fig. 95   The first of the 56 ft Keith Nelson motor launches leaving the mould at Tylers.

Fig. 96   Hull fluting of the Maclan 22 illustrates the flexibility of shape allowed by GRP construction.

Fig. 97   The GRP Marauder 46 is to be built by an injection system in a one-piece moulding with frames, stringers, tanks and bulkhead formed integrally and at the same time as the main skins.

spend a month in the mould before being surrounded with hot arc lamps. Movement while drying can also drag flat GRP surfaces away from the mould to cause a pre-release distortion of the moulding. For this reason the most satisfactory GRP work incorporates fine fat curves in all directions. Edges and corners are hard to lay up properly and may also give difficulty.

A GRP moulding which has to have large flat areas can often conveniently use pre-formed sheet made in a press. In fact it is possible to build whole hulls with factory-supplied GRP sheet similar to the way in which one might make a plywood boat.

Essentially, however, what is needed in all cases of reinforced plastics construction is to get the right types and amounts of resin and reinforcements put together by the right operators under the proper conditions to obtain a moulding whose integrity can be relied upon.

One of the incidental disadvantages of the freedom of form which GRP construction brings is the lack of discipline in shape. It is not only a freedom to be ugly but also a freedom to be unfair, if anything the greater sin. Two particular constructional methods appeal to us because they seem to allow the materials to form their own fairness.

First is the 'sock boat'. A light framework, possibly of cardboard, is made to outline the main shape of the boat, defining the keel, chines and gunwales. Over this is drawn a sock of slightly elastic material, which with a little judicious pinning springs from keel to chine, and chine to gunwale in lovely fair catenaries. A quick spray of resin and hey presto! an elegant and fair boatshaped moulding is all ready for sprayed or handlaid up GRP reinforcement to any required strength.

The other method of construction uses a mixture of long GRP rods woven up with rovings and lightweight open weave glass fibre cloth. The rods are rigid enough to span the distance between moulds without sag and to curve sweetly around the hull curves. A simple set of wooden moulds will then be sufficient to establish the shape which can be 'planked' up with great wide sheets of the stuff which is capable of a fair amount of double curvature. After impregnation with resin the subsequent reinforcements can go ahead on the basis of a nice fair basic moulding.

Sandwich Construction

It is probably fair to say that most of the current crop of plastics materials used for the construction of boat hulls are quite strong but rather elastic. The tensile strengths of steel and GRP, for instance, are approximately 56,000 lb per sq. inch and 32,000 lb per sq. inch, a ratio of about 2:1; whereas their respective moduli of elasticity are 29 million lb per sq. inch and 1·4 million lb per sq. inch, a ratio of 20:1. It is therefore obvious that if a GRP hull were made only twice as thick as a steel one it would be strong enough against tearing but very flexible. In a straightforward GRP lamination therefore the principal criterion for the scantlings is the question of stiffness. With this satisfied the resultant hull will be overstrong in some particulars and, with all the material required to achieve the necessary thickness, be overheavy.

There is therefore a great attraction in trying to achieve stiffness by other means than just pouring on extra material at great expense and this usually leads to some form of sandwich construction. The material thickness required for tensile strength only is split and separated by another lighter material until the required stiffness is brought about. The meat is therefore on the outside of the bread in this sandwich.

In a satisfactory sandwich construction three points are important. The first is a good bond between the layers. Second is that the material in the middle of the sandwich is stiff enough in its own right to withstand a modest amount of distortion during the overall flexing of the structure. Third is that the skin laminates are of themselves strong enough to withstand the puncturing type of loads of normal everyday boating life, such as coming alongside or hitting small flotsam.

The customary filling materials are the various types of rigid plastics foam or wood. Ordinary strip wood planking left with penny gaps to key the resin makes an extremely satisfactory sandwich construction for relatively inexpensive yachts which can be one-off in shape. End-grain blocks of balsa wood are commonly used both for race boats and for production boats to make sandwich stiffening for decks and coachroofs and also for hull panel areas. The end-grain arrangement is particularly satisfactory in making a reasonably strong connection between the two outer high-stress skins.

The principal problem of the sandwich is delamination. The difference in strength and elasticity between the skins can build stress concentrations, not at the glued surface of the filling material but just inside it. The comparatively weak material tears and the delamination greatly reduces the strength of the hull. A good quality, reasonably dense, foam well bonded to the face skins will often be sufficient in itself, but there are many fancy systems of construction which go to great trouble to make direct strong connections between them. This is usually achieved by applying the foam in strips with GRP brought between them to form webs between the skins, enclosing the foam in pockets.

The foam plastics most commonly used are probably polyurethane or PVC of some 4 to 6 lb per cu. foot, although every day seems to find another chemical in usable foam form. Plastics balls of various types and sizes are also used as fillers and spacers. The aluminium honeycomb produced for the same purpose for the aircraft industry can also be given an honourable mention as a sandwich filling for extra special work. It requires considerable care in its use if only to avoid filling the hollow honeycomb up with expensive and heavy joining or coating resins.

A close relation to the sandwich constructions involves the use of rather more dense foam as a substitute for, say, wood, for the main structural members of the craft and then lightly cladding it with a finishing skin of GRP. Polypropylene foam is commonly used in this manner. It can be foamed as lightly as 2 lb per cu. foot but generally the bottom limit is about 5·5 lb, and it can be as dense as 45 lb and therefore covers all the normal wood weights. Compared with wood it is grainless and rot-free, comes in machine made dimensions, and has a surface finish, oil-free and rough enough to give a good mechanical bond to polyesters. The free choice of foaming densities allows a more exact engineering of the design than might be possible with wood, and the heat-softening properties compare well with all the problems of steam bending or laminating timber.

Sheet Forming

Any sheet of material which is watertight and workable is potentially a boat. It might, like a coracle, require a separate internal framework

Fig. 98   The tooling for vacuum forming is skilled and careful, as befits the shaping of the progenitor of a production run which may be numbered in thousands. Here the moulds for the inner and outer skins of the Durafloat 10 footer are completed at G. Perry & Sons Ltd.

or it might be stiff enough in its own right, or after treatment, to stand on its own. The first sheets of really useful material were, of course, of metal rolled to a constant thinness. A sheet of metal can be folded into an approximate boat form, as in the famous Grimston system, or it can be beaten by skilful panel beaters to take up the shape of a boat. More recently, oddly enough, brute force has taken over from skill and a whole range of aluminium boats are made by a stretch-forming technique, and various prototypes have been made by explosion forming. In stretch forming the sheet of aluminium is clamped into a frame of a large and powerful machine which proceeds to pull the sheet bodily over a boat-shaped former. The metal gives way to the shape, perforce, and in a very short time indeed there lies a perfect boat-shaped sheet of metal ready for trimming. An even shorter time is required for explosive forming, in which the sheet is blasted down over the former by an explosion set off in a chamber above it. More recently there has been some success in vacuum forming aluminium, but this process is more normally used for plastics.

The plastics used for vacuum forming are thermoplastic, which means no more than that they go soft when heated. A sheet of such material is clamped into a frame and heated by a great battery of heaters all individually controlled or even

Fig. 99a   Notice the immense strength and the elaborate air chambers required for this vacuum forming mould.

Fig. 99b   Two stages in the production of a mould for a single skin low density polythene paddling pool dinghy for vacuum forming in Chile.

programmed. For simple and thin mouldings heating on one side is normal but bigger mouldings may require banks of heaters on both sides. Individual control over the heaters is necessary to vary the distribution of heat, and therefore plasticity, over the sheet to suit the moulding. The hotter the area the more it will stretch, and so the final thickness is kept under control. When the sheet is warm it begins to sag into a shallow bag and is then inflated by compressed air to form a plastic bubble just bigger than the finished moulding. This allows the mould to be raised inside the bubble which is then collapsed over it by the air being sucked out from underneath. The mould is constructed with a system of air galleries and vent holes to allow the vacuum to suck the sheet into every nook and wrinkle of the mould, allowing mouldings of great complexity and detail to be made. After a few minutes' cooling, which may be helped along with a blast of cold air to reset the plastics, the moulding can be removed, the whole operation for a twelve foot boat, for instance, taking some six minutes. Many boats these days are still not rectangular and the excess sheet area can be used to mould at the same time any little tiddly bits which may be required.

Vacuum forming is used industrially for any number of thermoplastic sheet materials, but for boats either low or high density polyethylenes and ABS are most common, with polycarbonates beginning to make an appearance. The polyethylenes are perhaps the cheapest and are used most often for inexpensive single skin dinghies. The material looks like washing-up bowls and is slightly unconvincing to anyone seeking an eyeful of traditional craftsmanship. However, it is surprisingly durable and a little paddling pool boat we designed for a South American firm has stood up to a incredible amount of varied use in our family. The principal disadvantages lie in the problems of securing fittings. Polyethylene is usually joined by heat welding but this tends to leave local stresses, and the polyethylene boats are usually equipped with a substructure of wood or pipework to carry the loads, even of rowlocks and outboards.

ABS is what you might call a rather better quality material. It is usually formed in thick single skins, or in thinner skins which are often used as the surfaces for foam sandwich boats. Another variation is to vacuum-form sheet which itself is

Fig. 100 Vacuum moulding machine with platen area of 18 ft × 5 ft used for the production of Durafloat dinghies. Heaters soften thermoplastic sheet which is then blown into a blister and sucked down on to the mould — shaping a single skin in a matter of seconds.

Fig. 101 Inner and outer skins are clamped into a double mould and a foam filling poured in. Pressures built up by the foaming process in this sandwich construction are high and very strong foaming jigs are required.

Fig. 102 Vacuum formed thermoplastics give the designer freedom to choose the shape he prefers for rigidity, strength and ideal characteristics in use. The Durafloat 3·60 — a 12 ft general purpose dinghy suitable for sailing, rowing and outboard power.

made with a foam core, and this appears to be satisfactory although rather limited in the degree of shape which can be formed. ABS can be joined with solvent welding and is therefore more easily reinforced at stress points, and so has a bigger structural potential than the polyethylenes, so far as one can predict. It is still rather softer than one would like and requires fairly elaborate design to absorb large stresses satisfactorily. It is expensive as a material and therefore is more commonly found in boats with a sandwich core of foam, which of course is also desirable in terms of spare flotation buoyancy.

Both ABS and the polyethylenes need protection against ultraviolet rays from the sun. This is normally done by incorporating a filter in the mix before the material is rolled out into sheet, or by an acrylic coating (although the latter does not as yet appear entirely practical for large or deep mouldings). An ABS or polyethylene boat is therefore best covered from the tropical sun when not in use in order to keep it looking its best.

Like other plastics the thermoplastics are a bit short of stiffness and are best moulded with plenty of shape. It is one of the advantages of vacuum forming that a great deal of shape detail can be formed as easily as none.

Cast Construction

There are so many new and different types of construction about that it is difficult to keep them in tidy groups. The word cast is used to cover those groups of hulls which receive their shape by the filling of a cavity mould. Therefore we are free to include sinter forming and injection moulding with the cast foam constructions. In fact, only metal casting will be absent because so far as we know very little metal casting of hulls has been done.

Injection formed plastics are very much part of daily life, and the size of the injection formings increases every year. There is already an eleven foot injection moulded sailing boat on the market and although the tooling costs are high there is no technical reason why larger mouldings may not be made.

Sinter is a name given to the hot rocks precipitated from hot springs and formed by precipitation of the minerals. In sinter forming or rotational casting material is put into a hollow mould which is heated and rotated in all directions, say at about 40 rpm on the minor axis and 12 rpm on the major axis. The material is deposited by centrifugal force on to the mould faces, where it is crusted by heat to produce a large hollow casting with comparatively thin walls. There are moulding frames as large as 14 feet in length by about 9 feet in diameter, which give two quite sizable dinghy hulls back to back. Size is limited more by factory area and machine size than anything else and the maximum dimensions increase annually. Extra stiffeners or reinforcements can be placed in the mould before the process starts and be cast into the finished hulls. By insulating, completely or to some degree, whole areas of the moulding can be left clear of skin or with a thinner skin than standard, giving a useful degree of flexibility to the process. Time for each cycle of production for a large moulding would be about 30 minutes, or 15 minutes per hull. Though originally used with metals, this process was first used for boats with low density polyethylene, but it is now possible to work in high density polyethylene, polycarbonate, polystyrene, and PVC — a fine bunch of names to trip off the tongue. As whole car bodies may be made by rotational casting it is a perfectly practical way to make boats, with, as ever, the economics having the final say as to whether it is ever done in any numbers.

On the other hand, there have already been thousands of cast foam boats built. We like to think that we have a special interest in the pioneering of the foam plastics boat in that we believe our *Small World* to have been one of the first, and in fact she held the long distance record for voyaging in foam plastics as well as the duration record for flying as a balloon car. She was built in 1958 of polystyrene foam reinforced with epoxy-impregnated Terylene and survived the rigours of her 3000 mile, four week, air/sea voyage very handsomely.

Cast polystyrene boats had the merit of being cheap, light and, usually, well designed. They were suitable for car-top craft, for instance, but suffered badly from their surface softness. There were terrible stories about how they cracked and split into two, or crumbled away into a whole windborne flock of polystyrene seed if given the slightest misuse. It is doubtful if they were anything like as vulnerable as this, but some manufacturers were offering 'do-it-yourself' GRP skinning kits for their polystyrene boats in very

short order. Probably these soft-skinned boats represent an intermediate step towards the hard-skinned foam craft to be built from self-skinning foams. In theory these may be the craft of the future, for the possibilities look very exciting. As a group they are called structural foams and are defined as 'expanded plastics material having integral skins'. There are several different methods of producing the integral skin, but that used for the urethane foam group relies on the foaming mixture being cooled and set on the surface by the heat-conducting metal-skinned mould. This means that the skin is of a density very close to that of the basic resin material and that the density merges gradually into that of the foam core, eliminating the interlaminar stress problems of the fabricated sandwich constructions. If that were not enough, it seems likely that the actual skin thickness can be controlled by local temperature variations of the mould, allowing sophisticated structural design. Enough, you may think, but it is also possible to foam into and around most kinds of stiffeners and reinforcements, anything from the conventional glass mat to steel plates. Thus the inside and outside of a boat can be ready for fitting out immediately it comes out of the mould. The process is automatic and uses little hand labour and there is no foreseeable limit on size except in relation to the cost of the moulds and the marketable number of craft. The boat would be self-buoyant of course and as well insulated as an ice bucket. This paragon of possibility holds out the prospect of a whole new world of boatbuilding which is distinctly interesting.

Concrete Construction

Concrete is an unsympathetic name to give anything to do with boats. The word is somehow inevitably connected with the land, from the concrete jungles of its use to the grit of its composition. It may be better regarded in hot climates where the sun shines daily, but concrete in the northern parts of the world relates to a grimy, often badly architectured, material apparently unskilfully used for cheap city blocks. You may have the impression already that one way and another we are not too enthusiastic about concrete for boats.

Oddly enough, however, it is possible that the current wave of concrete construction represents

Fig. 103 Seacrete of Wroxham were UK pioneers in ferrocement production boats. 34 ft Seacrete diesel motor boat
for Maidline Cruisers Ltd.

one of the most significant advances in the structure of hulls. In its present form it is probably
destined for the unlimited markets of amateur
construction and possibly some further commercial applications. This fate is settled for it, or so
we feel, because of the high, semi-skilled labour
content in the assembly. It may also be settled for
it because of the unfortunately truthful and unattractive name it is saddled with. To step from your
Rolls-Royce on to your concrete yacht does not
sound a hedonistic step to boast about in a gentlemen's club.

Consider, however, what the construction
represents. A properly and simply engineerable
structure, stressed, pre-stressed or even post-
stressed to the designer's fancy, clad in a cheap
and compatible skin. The simplicity is breathtak-
ing and makes GRP construction look very unsophisticated indeed; not since the coracle or cur-
ragh has it been so possible to design the structure
of a vehicle so exactly to its task rather than to suit a

whole smokescreen of minor problems such as
keeping the water out.

The most common method of building in concrete these days is that named ferrocement by the
famous Italian reinforced concrete expert Professor
Nervi as long ago as 1943. For this, three types of
structural material are used in addition to the concrete or cement. First, is steel waterpiping for the
principal outlines of the finished work and the main
framing in general. Next are wire rods which are
used to fill the gaps between the main framing at a
spacing of about two to four inches and thereby
completely establish the shape of the craft. To the
ethereal boat form thus established are attached
layers of chicken wire (it does not seem quite right
to talk of chicken wire in the same breath, so to
speak, as Fife or Souter) until the required thickness is produced. It is the addition of the wire mesh
to the normal reinforcing rods which makes the
ferrocement of boat construction so much more
resilient and strong than the reinforced concrete of

the house builder. The rods are welded to the pipes and the chicken wire mesh wired on to the rods. The chicken wire is disposed equally inside and out around the framing but pushed through from the inside to achieve a reasonably flat or smooth exterior. Metal frames are welded in for windows, and tubes for shafts and rudders, and wood blocks fitted where holes will be required for seacocks, etc. Lugs are welded on the inside to take bulkheads and other fittings for furnishings and the whole is ready for skinning.

Whether the skin material is concrete or cement is a fairly useless argument. It certainly uses cement mixed with sand which, to our way of thinking, still leans towards cement rather than concrete. With this are often mixed special additives of varying degrees of secrecy to improve the working characteristics and reduce the water absorption of the material. This mixture is ladled on to the inside of the hull and pushed through the wire mesh to be met by a skilled plasterer who smooths and fairs it to a very acceptable degree of finish. The inside will also be made as smooth as possible but naturally the best efforts will be reserved for the outside. The hull is then at its most vulnerable when the full weight of the wet cement is hung on the framing and before it hardens to support itself. The drying must be carefully supervised, with protection from too hot sun, drying winds or driving rain, for a period of up to a month. It may even be necessary to organise a constant spray mist to keep the skin at the best humidity to allow it to dry out to its full strength and waterproofness.

The world is divided in this age of leisure into increasingly less time at professional work and increasingly more time at amateur work. While the professional boatbuilder is all the time looking for construction processes with less labour content, the amateur has an increasing amount available to him. Concrete or cement construction is essentially labour intensive and would therefore seem eminently suitable for amateurs and for emergent nations (for work boats, for instance). Side advantages might make it attractive in some professional applications, such as cheaper materials, the ability to change the shape of each boat and easy repairs and general sturdiness for commercial craft. For yachts, however, the saving in materials costs, even an overall saving on the hull cost, represents a minute fraction of the overall cost of most craft.

As a construction for amateurs concrete may well appear to have several advantages. It appears a much less onerous construction in terms of sheer skill. Nearly everyone feels capable of working with chicken wire and nearly everyone not only feels capable of mixing a nice puddle of cement with a shovel or mixer but positively enjoys the prospect. One problem is that of assessing the hull once it is completed, and this as much as anything can cast a blight on the second-hand value of an amateur built concrete hull.

Aluminium

Aluminium is a pleasant and sympathetic material for metal. It is not unpleasant to look at in its natural state of sheet or extruded section and can be finished in a number of different ways to give a bright, smart and individual surface. It is light for its strength, which is always an attraction to the boat designer, softer to work than most other metals, non-magnetic and non-sparking. In addition it has very poor thermal conductivity properties (one third that of steel) which means that aluminium tends to be cool to the touch in hot climates. Alumium is a product of a large industry and is therefore more likely to be of carefully controlled consistence of quality and available in a number of forms to suit the application. It has a great many virtues to set against its major disadvantage of stronger than usual liability to electrochemical corrosion.

Pure aluminium is of itself highly resistant to corrosion in air and water because of the tough film of aluminium oxide that forms quickly on its surface. Chemically pure aluminium is not only difficult to achieve, however, but is generally not strong enough, and the normal 'aluminium' is an alloy of one kind or another. Those alloys which contain any parts of copper or some other element become very liable to electrochemical corrosion between the copper and aluminium when placed in salt water. Marine grade aluminium alloys contain between 2 and 4 per cent of magnesium and of themselves are virtually free from corrosion in salt water. The problems start when aluminium is put in contact with other metals during the construction or service of the craft. The galvanic series table, Fig. 110 (p. 79), shows the relative potential destructiveness of other metals placed either directly against aluminium or in contact with it through salt water.

If slightly elaborate precautions are taken to insulate and provide electrochemical protection for an aluminium hull there is no doubt that it makes a satisfactory construction material. The problems are greatly reduced if aluminium is used for deckworks only, or for day boats which are normally kept out of the water or used in fairly clean fresh water. Many so-called fresh waters are, however, brimming with effluents which can corrode even faster than salt.

Aluminium for boat construction is usually in the form of sheet for the skinning and angles and extruded sections for the framework. Very rarely are castings used because of the ease and cheapness of construction of fabrications by welding. The framework can include a forest of vertical frames covered in a rash of stringers, making a completely self-supporting edifice to be plated with sheet. Alternatively, a simple fore and aft framing can be used or, in some very small craft, the skin is used unsupported. The basic construction unit for the framework is the angle bar, but special extruded forms are increasingly used for deck edges, chines and keels. These are formed to simplify the attachment of frames and skin and make for both an elegant construction and a handsome appearance.

The sheet skin is often just used as a flat sheet wrapped about a framework designed on one of the conical projection systems. Aluminium is, however, comparatively easily worked into double curvature forms and it is probably in this way that the best use is made of its properties. Double or complex curvature can be formed by rolling and by hammering with rubber mallets, sometimes also with a moderate application of heat by blowtorch. Large sheets can be formed before assembly on a production line basis in a number of ways. Pressing, drop forming and hydraulic forming are all used. Stretch forming, where the sheet is wrapped around a form and then physically stretched until it takes up and retains the moulded form beneath it, is also used — again for production line craft which allow for a considerable investment in tooling.

There are several methods available for attaching the various parts and the usual two guiding principles for boat constructions apply as strongly as ever. These are that all parts must be arranged to give complete drainage. (In aluminium this

Fig. 104 *Aluminium construction of the 25 ft* Khalidia *built by Enfield Marine to a Don Shead design.*

Fig. 105 *Aluminium passenger ferry under construction at Striker Boats in Brisbane, Australia.*

may mean drilling or punching holes in hat section girders and even leaving a weld line a little short to leave a tiny drainage crack.) The other is in the avoidance of triangulated structure where any change in the physical conditions, a change of temperature perhaps, must mean that one part of the triangle is put into stress. This includes the avoidance of so-called triaxial points where stresses are produced both during the welding process and accentuated by any stressing of the hull.

The traditional method of fastening is riveting and this is still used, although largely superseded, especially for hulls, by welding. Riveting is common where it is impracticable to introduce the welding torch and where the use of dissimilar materials makes desirable the tiny amount of movement which is possible in a rivet joint. Riveting is also common in very light construction such as superstructures. Rivets have to be of a compatible material to the sheet they are fastening especially if to be used under water.

Modern techniques of welding allow it to be used for thin sheets and it has, or ought to have, taken over from riveting for all sizes of aluminium craft as the main fastening process. There are two principal welding processes available. The first and perhaps more common is the metal electrode inert gas method and the second the tungsten electrode inert gas method. In both methods the

Fig. 106 Flying Fish, *designed by Peter Du Cane and built by Vospers, had a welded aluminium hull and twin Daytona installation totalling 1350 hp.*

aluminium at the weld line is melted by heat from an electric arc struck between the welding electrode and the aluminium. The weld area is protected from oxidation during the process by a shield of inert gas, usually argon, although helium is sometimes used in the United States. In the metal electrode system the aluminium filler wire forms the electrode itself, and in the tungsten electrode system the aluminium filler is in rod form and hand fed to a tungsten electrode. The latter produces a much smoother bead than the former and can often eliminate the need for grinding to make an acceptable finish.

Hand work is becoming more and more expensive, and automatic travelling welding torches are becoming increasingly used in production set-ups. Here the electrodes take the form of wheels which can travel along a pre-set path welding either continuously or intermittently as they go. The great problem with welding is the distortion of the sheet by the heat produced from the process. The distortion can be reduced by spot or tack welding and then welding each small section individually. A large lump of heat-absorbing metal may also be applied behind the weld so that the heat is practically limited to the weld area. Pulse arc welding is also used to reduce the distortion of thin materials. The energy put through the torch is pulsed rather than continuous to reduce the total amount of energy applied and therefore the heat generated. In the future perhaps electron-beam welding might be applied to boat construction purely on the grounds of the lack of distortion involved.

Where it is only required to attach thin sheets of aluminium or other material, such as linings perhaps, it is possible to staple them in place or to use metal wire as a stitching. The metal commonly used for the staples or stitching is stainless steel. The 'seam' is strong enough but rarely acceptable to the eye of the owner and should be covered with some kind of trim.

Adhesive bonding is increasingly becoming used with aluminium construction. It has been used, of course, for years to stick linings and insulations in place, but modern development of the epoxy adhesives now make it practicable to stick structural parts together. The joints are strong enough in themselves but care must be taken to design them so that the whole surface of the adhesive takes the loading equally. If a 'peeling' or other offset loading is applied to a glued joint the full strain is taken by the edge line of epoxy alone. When, or if, this fails the load transfers to the next line and the process known as peeling occurs.

Aluminium is perhaps 25 per cent more expensive as a method of construction due to the cost of the material, but it is said by its advocates to repay this extra cost in reduction of maintenance in as little as three years. However, any comparison of costs depends on the current state of material supplies and should be looked at anew on each occasion. As a material aluminium is particularly suitable as a successor to wood for craftsmen in wood, in that it requires the good fitting piece by piece which is more a characteristic of wood craftsmanship than of steel craftsmanship. Like wood, it is also light and clean and can be worked with similar tools, while the whole process is similarly open to inspection and repair without detriment to the finished craft.

Perhaps one of the most attractive properties of aluminium competition craft is that large chunks of hull may be cut off and replaced without, as it were, prejudice to its structural probity. Hulls can therefore be altered, repaired, advanced and developed at a modest cost compared with that of a new boat every year.

Steel

Steel, by now a traditional material for building boats, turns up again as a modern construction. It is strong, reliable, cheap (relatively) and weldable, and the problems of rust corrosion are receding. For craft which can be regarded as small ships rather than large power boats it remains the almost universal material for the hull. However, for smaller craft it has never been really popular, perhaps not as popular as it deserves to be. Give a dog a bad name, and steel has it for boats of, say, less than 50 feet. Steel hulls are thought to be noisy at sea and it is true they can be. They are thought to run with condensation in the most modest of atmospheric conditions, and this can also be so. They are also thought to be heavy, but perhaps the worst fear is that the steel may rust and that sooner or later large chunks of the structure and plating will have to be renewed at considerable expense.

In steel construction as in many other things you get what you pay for, and the terrible tales are almost always traceable to cheap construction and false economies in maintenance. Good quality materials, good quality craftsmanship, even good quality design, all cost just a little bit more than the cheapest, and all are essential to the building of a satisfactory steel craft. It is quite easy for anyone with a supply of steel and a few hours of practice at welding to assemble a good-looking object that looks entirely like a boat. A few coats of paint and a launching party and she is off to break someone's heart and pocketbook.

Rusting is certainly the greatest bogy, for it removes structural material which can only be bodily replaced. Unprotected mild steel plate rusts away at the rate of about five-thousandths of an inch a year from both surfaces, which could reduce a quarter of an inch of plate to about half in twelve years. The low alloy steels, such as Cor Ten, put up a much better performance both in and out of sea water – probably rusting at somewhere about a quarter of the rate. Even the rust from a low alloy steel is much less permeable than that of mild steel, giving some protection to the metal beneath it as well as keeping more free from paint blisters. The extra cost of the high strength low rusting steels is only marginal when set against the initial cost of a complete craft reasonably well fitted out. If anyone ever did work out the complete cost of a boat over its complete life the saving in maintenance and repairs would probably show quite a big advantage in the initial outlay.

Steel comes from the mill covered in a thick, hard coat of mill scale which has to be removed before any proper protective coating can be applied. In shipyards the plate is allowed to weather where the action of wetting and drying and the variations in temperature combine to flake off the scale. This may take as long as two years and may be satisfactory in the construction of a large ship but does not fall either into the time scale of building a small craft or in the resultant standards of coating required. Small craft are therefore usually built of plate which has been either chemically or electrolytically pickled by the steelworks to remove scale and rust. The chemical pickling process consists of immersion in an acid bath and the electrolytic pickling consists of immersion in an electrolyte with the plate either anodic or cathodic depending on the process. Alternatively, scale and rust may be removed after assembly of the hull by sand or grit blasting. It is

Fig. 107   *Steel boats do not have to be of vast size. This delightful little steel dory was built in Holland by Beenhaaker of Kinderdux.*

Fig. 108   *The inflatable is one form of modern construction which has been developed principally since the Second World War and which is now used for many kinds of boating, from paddling pool craft to inshore rescue boats and taking in powerboat racing along the way. This ten man 16 ft C-Craft has four separate air compartments, rigid keel and is rated for 60 hp.*

possible to clean a hull by hand with grinder and wire brush, but it is extremely laborious and unlikely to be sufficiently thorough to avoid the prospect of more rust.

The clean and tidy steel can be coated in a number of ways of which spraying with hot zinc is one of the most effective starts for a sandblasted hull. The various new plastics based coatings also seem to be extremely effective and, with a good start in life, a proper paint finish on a steel hull will need only modest maintenance for a long time.

Steel is not an attractive material to live with unlike, for instance, wood. Steel craft are therefore usually fairly expensively lined inside in way of the accommodation and this takes care of a great deal of the condensation. Foamed insulation applied directly to the steel structure is increasingly being used to combat the noise of the hull, condensation and heat and cold.

For small craft, say of less than 50 feet, steel still remains a heavy construction, although this can be greatly mitigated by the skilful use of small scantling materials. Welding is the universal method of construction and the skill of the welder with thin plate is one of the criteria on how light the work will be. The heating of the metal during the welding process causes distortion, leading to the characteristic 'hungry horse' appearance of a welded ship with thin plating. For a yacht finish this washboard effect can be hidden with cement but that too adds weight. The sequence of welding and the avoidance of weld butts and triangulation are all extremely important in the production of a thin steel plate hull with any pretensions to appearance. It can be done, but the skill ought to be better appreciated.

CHAPTER 5
Decay, Rot and Corrosion

General

This is a chapter which perhaps should have uncut pages and a death's head emblem warning yacht owners that the matter within is not for those of a nervous disposition. It might give the impression, and it might occasionally be true, that while you are relaxing on deck with your long drink in the sun the forces of evil are hard at work undermining your security. With a last fiendish flourish the electrochemical forces are about to eat a hole in the plating, or gribble to remove the last piece of stem, to leave nothing but your accountant trying to work off the depreciation against tax.

Just after the Second World War there was a great deal of discussion in the yachting press of this country as to why the post-war yacht rotted more easily than the pre-war yacht. Various ideas were bandied about, ranging from inferior timber to inferior workmanship. George Gill, a member of the well known designing firm of Laurent Giles and Partners, finally wrote the authoritative words on the subject, words which we have treasured ever since. 'Before the war,' he wrote, 'a gentleman did not let his yacht rot.'

The modern yacht is, if anything, less prone to deterioration than its predecessors. Modern glues, resin coatings and plastics parts reduce the contact between your yacht and the forces of decay. Hulls of GRP and other plastics are basically less vulnerable, while better deckings on all craft reduce the destructive deck leaks which often cause more trouble than honest sea water pouring through the seams into your bilges. However, all craft are still vulnerable to neglect and the principal anti-rot defence you can give to a new boat is a good owner.

The Forces of Corrosion

Ashes to ashes and dust to dust. It is a fact of life that most inanimate things ultimately return to their natural state. It is also a fact that the greater part of the component materials of our modern life are not natural. That is, they are not just found lying around and picked up more or less ready for use. Most metals, for instance, are produced by forceful methods from their natural ores and, given half a chance and the right conditions, will have a good try to revert. Away from the happy stability of their natural form metals are vulnerable in various degrees to those reversionary processes of nature which are called corrosion.

Corrosion is essentially a destructive process, or at least the destructive processes are the only ones we complain about. It is the corrosion that turns fine steel ships into rusting hulks and strong bronze keel bolts into copper sponges that we have to worry about, rather than that which turns copper-clad domes and roofs an attractive green. The destruction of the metal is principally an electrochemical process. For most forms of corrosion in metals it seems that an electric current of some kind must be about. This, in boats, generally takes the usual path from a point of high potential to a point of low potential through the structure, and completes its circuit by using the sea or the sea-damp atmosphere. The current is carried through the metal by electrons and through the sea or air by dissolved ions. The point of high potential is known as the cathode and that of low potential is called the anode. (*Cathode*, incidentally, comes from the Greek for 'way down', and *anode* from the Greek for 'way up'; facts which, alas, only cause confusion.)

The principal reaction at the anode is the dis-

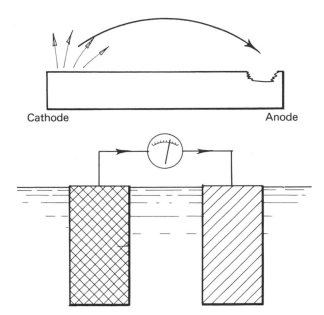

Fig. 109   A galvanic cell has a current flow from the cathode to the anode which may be separate components or which may be different parts of the same piece.

solution of the metal in the form of ions and the principal reaction of the cathode is the production of hydrogen. The whole cycle, or circuit, is called a galvanic cell. Any metal immersed in sea water will settle to a particular level of electrical potential which is peculiar to it. If two different metals are immersed they will have different potentials. If they are then connected, a current will pass, a galvanic cell be started and corrosion begin. The direction of the current shows which metal forms the anode and which the cathode, and this relationship will always apply provided there are no other factors involved. If the various metals are listed in order of their natural electric potential in sea water then the table lists in effect a galvanic series. Current will always flow in such a manner that any metal will corrode in the presence of another higher up the table (see Fig 110).

The degree of corrosion is proportional to the potential difference between the metals, illustrated by their distance apart in the galvanic series. Also, the higher the position in the table the smaller the actual physical effect of the corrosion. At the top of the table are the grander metals which are appropriately called noble or cathodic, while those at the bottom are known as base or anodic. Gold, which is prized for its freedom from corrosion, heads the list of nobles

and, it is worth noting, is one of the few metals found in its natural state.

Many factors influence the degree of corrosion. If a metal sheet were infinitely large and infinitely smooth and infinitely cold, in other words with its various atoms evenly and quietly spaced over its surface, there would be no better reason for one ion to start off on the process of corrosion than any other and therefore the galvanic cell could not establish itself. At any temperature, however, the ions will be vibrating in the heat. The surface can never even approach perfect smoothness and must be bounded by edges. The ions at bumps and edges are more tenuously connected than those in the middle of a plane area and therefore more likely to go into solution to start the process of corrosion. The processes of working the metal, such as bending, can also affect the internal

---

GALVANIC SERIES IN SEAWATER

CATHODIC OR MORE NOBLE — PROTECTED END
Gold
Stainless steel (EN 58 J) Passive
Monel
Silver
Titanium
Stainless steel (EN 58 J) Active
Nickel
Cupro-nickel (70:30)
Cupro-nickel (90:10)
Gun metal
Copper:nickel:iron (90:5:5)
Aluminium bronze (BSS 2032)
Naval brass
Copper
High tensile brass
Admiralty brass
Lead
Mild steel, Wrought and Cast iron
Cadmium plate
Aluminium alloys
Zinc and galvanised iron
Magnesium alloys
Magnesium

ANODIC OR LESS NOBLE — CORRODED END

Fig. 110   Galvanic series table.

energy of the metals and affect their vulnerability to chemical decay.

In materials of mixed composition neighbouring atoms can be of different metals and little local actions can be set up between them, as for instance when the zinc corrodes away from brass leaving the spongy copper representation of the original fastening. In materials of unmixed composition the potential can vary between areas of different stress loading and galvanic cells be set up. Again it is usually the more highly stressed area which becomes anodic and corrodes more easily. Differing temperatures between ends of the same bar can have the same effect and, of course, the hot end becomes anodic and corrodes.

The corrosion process sometimes forms a skin which then basically protects the metal from further corrosion, as in the oxidised skin on aluminium and, indeed, on iron. This, however, is never perfect and the tiniest pinhole through the protective products of corrosion has the effect of concentrating the electric current wonderfully and a deep pit is formed. The surface below the skin is increased in its anodic value and corrosion proceeds apace. Pitting can be the most tiresome type of corrosion in that a comparatively modest amount of current removes a comparatively modest amount of metal but in so doing either holes the vessel directly or injures its mechanical strength.

Pitting is also found on propeller blades when cavitation is present. This is thought to be principally a form of mechanical erosion of the metal by the sudden and violent collapse of vapour cavities caused by pressure changes and vibrations on the blades. There is, however, an element of electrochemical decay often present in that the scouring of the surface stops any protective film forming in the normal way to give some protection.

Of course, the destructive currents can be supplied from an outside source as well and an ordinary common or garden ship's system, perhaps earthing itself through a metal bar in contact with the sea, will set up a cathode at its point of entry and an anode to corrode away where it leaves the metal for the sea.

The commonest methods of protection against corrosion take the form of adding protective skins to the metal. Aluminium is often protected with a thin sandwich skin of pure aluminium. Iron is dipped in another metal of low melting point like zinc, and various metals are given protective coats of brass or copper followed by nickel and a thin coat of chromium for decoration. Steel is often sand blasted to remove the scale which forms during its mill processing as well as the rust, and sprayed with zinc. New coatings, principally the epoxies, are also used, as well as the time honoured and simple red lead followed by layer after layer of paint.

It is more difficult to give protection when different metals are present in the same area of boat. Some moving parts like propeller shafts and rudder stocks work in bearings where a protective skin would have a short life. Here an effort is usually made either to counter or divert the destructive current to some part of less importance. This provision of cathodic protection usually takes one or other of two forms.

The first and simplest is to provide a lump or

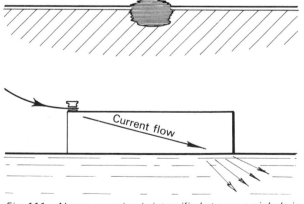

Fig. 111 Above: corrosion is intensified at even a pinhole in a protective coating. Below: current tends to take the longest path through a conductor.

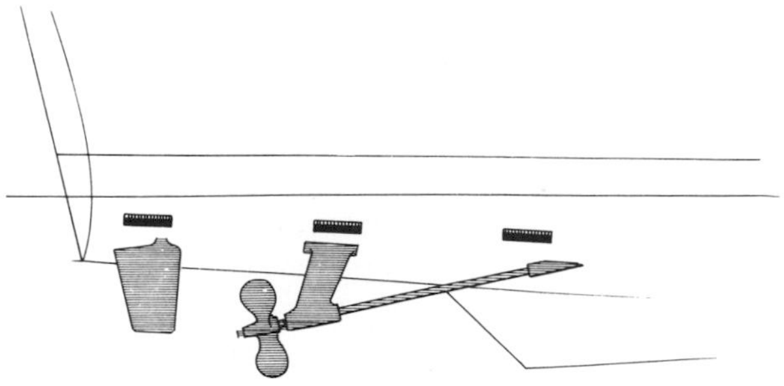

Fig. 112 Cathodic protection is usually achieved by placing more desirable anodes as close as possible to the vulnerable parts.

lumps of a cheap metal further down the galvanic series than that used for the important parts requiring protection. Both the original anode and cathode are now put in the position of becoming cathodes and the corrosion is directed to the new anode which thus sacrifices itself on behalf of its nobler comrades. Zinc is the metal most commonly used and the sacrificial anodes of especially pure zinc are usually fastened to the hull within reasonable distance of, say, propellers, rudders and shafts, if these require protection. If the vessel is being left on moorings for any length of time, then zinc anodes are often lowered over the side to afford protection which can be checked without the cost of slipping.

The second method is, in effect, carefully to measure the current passing among the various galvanic cells working away unseen to destroy your beautiful yacht and to counter them with an applied current equal and opposite. This has to be done with great care as the basic current can vary quite largely with a change of temperature or if the ship is moving rather than stopped, causing the sea to become turbulent rather than smooth. If regulation is not automatic then it is easy to overcompensate, with equally tiresome results.

It can form an instructive afternoon to borrow a micro ammeter and use it to measure the destructive currents running between the various underwater parts of the yacht, particularly one of conventional construction. The introduction of plastics seacocks and underwater fittings has done a great deal of hidden good for the yacht owner, but the increasing use of electrics of substantial power leaves even bigger pitfalls for the unwary.

Fungi

'God save thee, ancient Mariner!
From the fiends that plague thee thus!'
— Coleridge.

In ancient times, before metals became complicated and common, the principal enemies of the wooden ship were the terrible shipworm, the voracious gribble and the frightful fungi. Fortunately these horrors, like the vampire bat or werewolf, are not really pressing problems of the civilised world any longer, having been replaced and superseded by more scientific and advanced troubles. They are not problems in the new forms of construction, having been largely outgeneralled and, in fact, almost completely repulsed by that old world tonic and general specific — money.

It is probably logical to describe first the attack of fungi as affected timber was often used in construction and, most commonly, dry rot would be well established before the ship was even planked, never mind launched and put to work. Fungi are living plants which like any other living plants need food, moisture, air and warmth to grow. They differ from garden flowers, for instance, principally in living only on organic material and therefore they need plant or animal tissue on which to grow. Like any other plant they multiply by the distribution of seeds which are carried by the fungus growing outside the tissue it is living upon. These seeds or spores are tiny and easily carried by the smallest draught of air as they voyage away from their parents. When they land on, for instance, wood which is damp enough they drop anchor and start mining into the wood for food. The cells of fungi take the form of long thin threads which are capable of penetrating the cells of wood for food and also of penetrating porous material in their search for further food.

There are two main types of destructive fungi which attack wooden craft.

1. The so-called brown rots where the fungi attack only the cellulose of the wood. Cellulose, however, is the principal structural component of wood and may perhaps be considered as the principal factor in its bulk.

2. The so-called white rots where not only the cellulose is eaten but also the lignin, which is the substance which holds the wood together and might be considered as making the greatest contribution to the mechanical strength of the wood.

The principal fungoid enemy of the wooden hull is undoubtedly that which produces dry rot. This is so named because the wood at an advanced state of fungal attack becomes dry and cracked and crumbly, looking with its brown staining as if it were charred. The name is confusing, however, as moisture is an essential component of an attack of dry rot. A normal boatbuilding timber is usually required to have not more than 15 per cent moisture content these days but timber normally needs to have a 20 per cent moisture content before it becomes liable to attack and as much as 40 per cent moisture to give ideal home conditions for fungi. Dry rot is an extremely tiresome fungus in that once it is established it does not need the continued presence of water in order to live and develop. When each plant requires fresh wood to eat it sends out strands which can penetrate through almost any porous material if it smells fresh wood on the other side. These strands cunningly carry their own water supply and damp down the new wood to the right moisture content before attacking it.

The best defence against dry rot is a plentiful supply of ventilation to keep the wood dry and an absence of leaks to stop the wood getting wet. This, in fact, only controls one of the essentials for fungus life. It is scarcely practical to reduce the supply of oxygen or warmth, leaving only the food supply (the wood itself) as an alternative control factor. This can be poisoned by impregnating the wood with a so-called preservative before it is assembled into the form of the craft. Once dry rot has settled it is difficult to eradicate. In houses it is thought necessary to remove and burn all wood within as much as a twelve-foot radius of the affected parts. Such wholesale treatment would make most craft look silly, but as much wood as is practicable should be burnt and the rest treated with preservative. There are also resins which can be used to impregnate the attacked wood and these are worth investigating where removal seems too drastic a remedy.

Wet rot is found only in the presence of water and, unlike dry rot, will not travel to dry wood. If a piece of wood is soaking with water but partially dried on its skin by ventilation then wet rot can establish itself to rot the centre of the wood, leaving an apparently unblemished skin. Salt water can act as a preservative for timber, and wood completely immersed is generally fairly secure against fungi. However, there are comparatively few parts of a ship which do not have one face at least open to fresh water, if only in the form of condensation. The effect of an occasional salt dip is generally only to keep the wood nice and damp for any passing spores.

Marine Borers

A greater hazard for wood in contact with the sea, however, is the marine borer. These pests come in

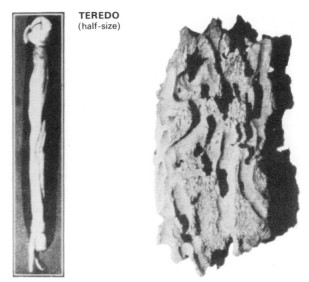

TEREDO (half-size)

WOOD ATTACKED BY TEREDO

Fig. 113 Not a sight that any yachtsman wants to see — the teredo and its horrible home.

two distinct styles. The more dramatic is the shipworm, or teredo worm, which is no true worm but a mollusc of the same type as the oyster. The other common borer is a small member of the lobster crustacean family called the gribble.

The tiny larvae of the shipworm settle on the surface of your yacht and if they find clear access to wood they stop and burrow. The larvae are perhaps half a millimetre in size and therefore only need a small space, and leave only small holes behind them. However, once in the wood the larva starts to burrow and to grow. It can grow to some 7·5 millimetres in diameter and to a considerable length, and it grows with two shells mounted on its head. These grind continuously at the wood to provide food for the teredo which tunnels ever deeper into the wood. The teredo occupies the whole of the tunnel, leaving a pair of tiny tubes sticking out of the entry hole to circulate water to its gills and to send more larvae into the world to live in other planks and other ships. The entry holes are almost invisible to the eye and therefore an attack of the worm is difficult to spot, although the structural worth of the wood may fall to an almost negligible value. It is small comfort to know that this hungry marauder has always been with us. We have some fossil wood complete with fossil shipworm — all of forty million years old.

The gribble, however, rarely burrows more than

10 millimetres into the wood, and an extensive attack by gribble will so weaken the surface of the timber that it wastes and erodes away in an apparent and alarming manner. The gribble looks like a little woodlouse and rarely becomes larger than 2 or 3 millimetres in length or more than 2 millimetres in breadth or diameter — whichever is the right way to dimension a crustacean. An attack of the gribble looks as if your yacht is actually being chewed away.

The best defence against marine borers is a continuous surface coating over the hull without even a pinprick of access through to the wood inside. This may be achieved with paint, but this is always open to an accidental scratch to the wood. The most reliable skinning used to be copper sheathing and is now probably in one of the resin-impregnated nylon or glass cloths.

If the wood is not skinned for protection then the type of wood should be chosen for its resistance to attack. The soft woods in general have little resistance to borers and only a moderate resistance to decay. Some of the hard woods, such as teak and greenheart, are extremely resistant to both marine borers and to decay. A hull built of teak is well known to be extremely durable without further protection whatsoever. This durability is thought to be due to the presence of natural preservatives, such as resin, and natural toxic defences such as aromatic oils, against the destructive wild life. It is noticeable that the majority of the durable timbers tend to be on the hard and heavy side, but western red cedar, which is one of the lighter weight woods and certainly one of the softest, is as durable as any.

The majority of patent preservative mixtures used for boatbuilding timbers are based upon the use of a solvent, a volatile oil or spirit, to carry well into the wood a chemical poisonous to fungi and marine borers. Some water soluble preservatives are occasionally used for interior joinerwork, and oily protections such as creosote or tar are rarely used nowadays for yachts or small craft as they are extremely difficult to coat with a satisfactory finish.

When in ancient times constructional difficulties made it almost impossible to carry ventilation completely about the structure of a wooden ship, the builders could only make allowance for the inevitable processes of deterioration by increasing the size of each part. A certain amount of protection was added by the use of tar, and various attempts were made to divert the hungry molluscs by fitting an external sheathing of tempting timber to the hull, rather on the principle of preferential corrosion for metals. In recent times structural design has been able to advance and it is quite reasonable to expect proper ventilation through the structure and the incidence of dry rot in reasonably maintained craft has fallen quite low.

Fatigue and Soaking

Fatigue and soaking — another depressing group of words familiar to all who put to sea in competition craft. The component parts of the boat also suffer from fatigue and soaking and, not being living organisms, have very little if any regenerative and recuperative power.

When subjected to a sufficient number of cyclical stresses at a high enough load, metals and other materials will suffer from fatigue. Cyclical stresses and high loads are almost a definition of seafaring craft, structure and components, and therefore fatigue is a possible line of destructive attack to be considered by the designer, builder and owner. To make the situation worse material, given the stressed cyclical treatment in corrosive conditions (say salt water), will fatigue much more quickly. Special treatment such as heat (the annealing of copper pipes for instance) will delay the advent of fatigue in metals in open air but a salt atmosphere will still hasten it along.

The combined action of fatigue and corrosion is called corrosion fatigue and is fairly easily recognised. As with normal fatigue the cracks are

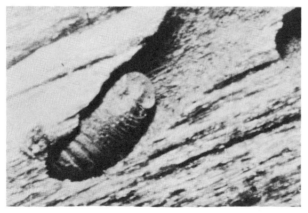

Fig. 114   The gribble (limnoria) in its burrow.

transgranular and normal to the direction of stress but, unlike normal fatigue which has a single crack, there are usually a number of them. The actual fracture itself will also have two distinct zones, one smooth which is the area of true corrosion fatigue, and the other rough and fibrous, equivalent to the normal failure of a notched specimen under load. The higher the stress level the sooner, obviously, failure occurs and therefore the smaller the smooth area of the cracked surface. It goes without saying that fatigue is a phenomenon which only occurs in a tension stress situation. It seems that it is the extent of the stress range which is important rather than the maximum figures which may be reached. A cyclical loading, therefore, which alternates tension with compression is likely to prove more onerous in pure arithmetic than one which stays in the tension zone. A graph of the number of stress cycles to failure against the actual load figures starts out quite steeply but flattens out at a value which is called the limiting range of stress. Below this figure, which varies for different metals differently treated, as far as anyone can tell you can work your metal right into infinity without any fear of failure. A great deal of engineering, however, has on pure economics to work on an anticipated lifespan.

Wood if thoroughly soaked loses strength but the effect on the fastenings of a quite modest degree of salt water in wood is of much greater concern. The wood in fact becomes a matrix to hold the electrolyte for a galvanic action affecting the fastenings. At the cathodes a caustic alkali is produced and, around a fastening for instance, cannot easily escape or diffuse. No wood is immune from the effects of a high alkali concentration, the only difference being that the more dense woods are better because they have more bulk and substance to be overcome. At the anodic ends the metal salts produced are, in the cases of copper and zinc, those which are actually used for wood preservatives, and everything benefits. The iron compounds, however, degrade wood and cause softening. Denser wood, or rather the less permeable wood as the amount of soakage is a factor, is likely to be more durable in this situation. A great deal can be done by careful choice of the fastening materials and by giving them, individually, some kind of insulating coating. Bitumen, for example, is commonly used for iron fastenings.

The actual soakage by volume of GRP is small but can have a significant effect on its flexural strength although the tensile strength remains approximately the same. This accentuates the difference between wet or dry fatigue failure to the point where the failure strength of wet GRP in fatigue can be as little as half its nominal strength.

Creep and Degradation of the Thermoplastics

With a chapter subheading of this cheerfulness what can we do but launch directly into the subject taking, say, ABS as a typical example. Thermoplastics have something of a memory, to use a fashionable term. They remember as if it were yesterday the machine in which they were born and yearn, it seems, to return to the pristine shape in which they were formed. A sheet of thermoformed material therefore has something of a tendency to return to the flat sheet form, whatever lovely boat shape or so forth it might have been sucked or blown into during manufacture. Given time, therefore, it is likely to show some tiny inclination in this direction, but we hasten to say that this is no more than the merest creep which you may not even notice. There is no question of your dinghy suddenly going pop into a flat sheet form as you are rowing to the yacht club.

The sun is probably the worst enemy of thermoplastics. Heat, if extreme, can excite moulding memories and the action of ultraviolet rays causes a surface degradation of the material. The longer wavelengths and visible light have no proven aging degradation effect. It is believed that other weathering factors play only quite a secondary part. Low temperatures make the material brittle but these are extremes and not normally found in pleasure yachting.

ABS, to continue our example, is composed of three constituents with the handsome names of acrylonitrile, styrene and butadiene. These combine into two principal factions in the finished material, one rigid and one elastic. The rigid materials form a basic framework among which are evenly distributed spherical particles of the elastic material. The number and size of the spherical particles does, in fact, determine the strength and elasticity of the manufactured ABS and can vary to meet different requirements. The elastic group is very susceptible to ultraviolet rays and the rigid group is very resistant. It is a bit like politics.

When exposed to the sun the particles which are elastic and close to the surface deteriorate, whereas those further inside are protected and screened by the surrounding material. Thus a brittle, chalky layer is gradually formed on the surface. This develops quickly at first but gradually stabilises as the chalky layer itself provides a protective coat and little action follows. The depth of the attack is quickly shown by the scratch of a fingernail. The deterioration in strength of the sheet thus attacked is quite modest but it gives the surface a dry, powdery appearance which is not very attractive. It can be polished off but this opens up the next layer of material to similar attack.

The actual type and make-up of any particular ABS can affect the rate of this kind of aging and the method of manufacture can also have a considerable effect. In injection moulding, for instance, the movement of the material at the mould face causes the rubbery particles to be buried and covered with the rigid matrix material so that they are much better protected from the deadly rays. There is no similar process in extrusion moulding and it is unfortunate that this is how sheet material for boats is usually produced.

It is possible to give some protection by adding up to one per cent of pigment into the mixture. Black and, oddly enough, white, pigment seem to produce the best results. There is a wide variety of suitable protective pigments of which the most common are ferric oxide, carbon black, titanium dioxide and zinc oxide. Further protection can be given by surface films which are themselves an ultraviolet filter, such as some of the acrylic coatings, although these are often difficult to match with a deep draw vacuum forming process. The object at all times is to shield those vulnerable elastic particles on or close to the skin of the material.

Deterioration of GRP

Voids, blisters, leaching, wrinkling and embrittlement are just a few of the attractions we offer for this subsection. Actually it might come as some relief to set these few words against the almost creepy feeling that GRP endures for ever. Wooden boats fade away in anything from ten to a hundred years but here we are thirty years into the resin-glass age without any appreciable deterioration in well built and well maintained GRP boats. On the one hand there are scores of factories turning out fifty new boats a week and on the other a quite occasional seafaring disaster in which the loss of a boat is reported. So what is going to happen to all our GRP craft in the years to come? There is even a moderately desperate thought that there is nothing to scrap a GRP yacht for; the only way to remove it from the scene is to burn it. The result is a great deal of black smoke for which no-one will thank you and a small heap of quite unusable glass chock-a-block with carbon and other impurities. Unless we are careful, badly made and ill-looked-after GRP craft will rest like dismal hulks around the shore and the rest will cram the marinas and anchorages, and boatbuilding and yacht design will be dead. Nature, which is so benevolent in other departments, really will have to get weaving on the genes for the GRP-relishing bug reported so graphically a few years ago.

Basically, most GRP moulded craft these days are quite sound and are certainly so designed and intended. Such modest defects as occur can usually be traced to human error either in the mixing of the formulations or in the extensive handwork in the lay-up. It is easy to tell a well-finished moulding from a roughly made one by the internal and external finish, but it is nothing like so easy to tell one which includes defects. Some problems, such as blistering, can take as long as two years to develop. The first method of assessment of a GRP moulding however is probably that of giving it a good tap with a mallet. As with pinging a wine glass, a good clear response indicates a good moulding, whereas a bad one sounds muffled. If a bit breaks off as well it may only indicate a gel coat problem.

Voids and air bubbles cannot be completely eliminated in moulding and it is reasonable to accept them at up to 2 to 3 per cent of the laminate volume. They are most easily seen by visual inspection of the surfaces or by reflected or transmitted light, or an electronic flaw detector may be used. They are due to poor wetting out by the moulder, air entrapment between the plies of glass material, to volatiles released from the resin during cure, or to excessive air inclusion in the resin, perhaps from overmixing. Surface bubbles only affect the appearance of the moulding and can easily be made good. Small internal bubbles only affect the strength if they are grouped.

Blisters are an obvious indication of actual delamination caused by entrapped air or volatiles, or may be due to entrapped water. This latter starts as a small pimple as water permeates through the gel coat and gathers in a tiny cavity behind it. Osmotic pressure, especially in fresh water, builds this up into a blister. Water, of course, should not get through the gel coat to this degree and such blistering usually indicates that the gel is overloaded with pigment paste or fillers.

Surface crazing is structurally unimportant and is nearly always associated with a rather resin-rich area. It can be due to high stress concentrations or possibly the use of the wrong resin, or even a subsequent attack from some other chemicals. Crazing inside the laminate is a sign of undercure due to climatic conditions during the moulding or to some chemical problem such as an undue concentration of catalyst. When seen in an unpigmented lamination it shows as a kind of hazy translucence or may in a bad case be seen as a definite white pattern like a watermark.

Undercuring on the surface can lead to the gel coat being too soft, causing the leaching of material from the surface by wind and weather. This is a serious condition and can lead to the effective destruction of the craft if it is not stopped. Another surface condition is known as patterning, where the form of the glass fibre reinforcement becomes visible or traceable inside the moulding. This is merely the effect of the final curing of the moulding with the glass still amply covered with a proper glossy resin coat. It is entirely unimportant structurally and can, with woven rovings for instance, even add a certain textural distinction to the hull colour. However, it is not usually intentional on the part of the moulder and can sometimes be seen developing at boat shows when the hull is set up for all to admire surrounded by hot lights.

Delamination is relatively rare. It implies that the bond between adjacent layers was never made properly in the first place, or that the bond has failed due to interlaminar stress such as can be caused by forcing or springing a moulding into place with a great deal of pressure. Internal dry patches are just due to bad construction, probably because the moulder did not bother to do the job, perhaps where it did not matter structurally, or it may be due to the use on a vertical surface of a resin without sufficient thixotropic qualities so that it just dripped away.

Undercured gel coat can also lead to wrinkling on the surface. This is a serious condition due to its greatly reduced water resistance. A gel coat which is too brittle can lead to stress cracking where fine surface cracks develop from behind the gel coat.

The gel coat or a paint-protected surface can also be affected by the alkali conditions related to cathodic protection, particularly if they are not too well bonded in place. Cathodic protection on GRP craft has to be carefully and professionally gauged because of the destructive effect which can be caused by overlarge zinc plates for the cathodic protection of, say, propellers.

Perhaps the saddest case of GRP deterioration we ever saw in the making was owner induced. We came upon a GRP yacht carefully beached on the hard for cleaning — with the owner and his family energetically attacking the gel coat with scrapers.

Erosion and Weathering

Erosion is, like concrete, one of those words which you do not expect to come across in the context of yachting, whereas weathering sounds completely natural and the word weathered is frequently used as a compliment especially when referring to retired sea captains. Sand is the principal element in abrasive erosion and weathering, and unfortunately the sea is largely bounded and contained by the stuff. In the air it can be blown with some violence for extended periods against your beautiful boat, wearing away at the paint surfaces or the GRP gel coat. Given time it can open up the protective coatings to allow the air to get at steel or the damp to wick away through the GRP. In its own right it will grind the softer grain from between the harder to leave wood with the ridged grey rough/smooth finish which is much prized in a different context. Below water the sand floating in the sea may scour the bottom surfaces to a degree but before that will be causing trouble through the cooling-water system and wear in the shaft bearings. Once water can enter below a paint surface then alternate swelling and drying from day to day will accelerate the weathering process and so the first protective steps should be fast ones. There is not much to do except to keep a proper coating on all surfaces and to arrange as much sand trapping as possible in the engine systems. Engine cooling water can be discharged in part through the stern gland to protect that part of the shaft from abrasion but a close eye should be kept on the shaft bracket bearings.

In a flow of fast moving or turbulent water mechanical damage can be produced on a surface not only by solids such as sand, but by the action of the liquid itself or of air bubbles trapped in it. This mechanical damage can result in the breakdown of protecting oxide films on the surface of metal. The exposed metal is continuously oxidised and removed — a process which might be assisted by any air involved in the action. Although this is a problem largely documented for flow in pipes it is to be found at times on underwater fittings of fast boats. For pipes it is enough to reduce the speed of the waterflow, but for fast boats it is necessary to take great care to avoid turbulence-generating edges and corners which may lead to impingement attack on fittings further aft.

The sun is as destructive an element in weathering as any and in the tropics more than any. Coatings find it difficult to cope with the high temperatures the sun produces both in the coating itself and in what it is coating. Oil-based paints and varnishes, for instance, are baked dry by the sun and become flaky, and a first-rate varnish finish may require renewing monthly. Part of the sunborne deterioration lies in the energy conveyed all about by ultraviolet light and this particular aspect has become extremely important with the plastics materials now used. Ultraviolet rays are basically invisible, with a wavelength range from the visible violets down to the X-rays. Used in moderation they are thought to be beneficial to the human race and good for treating tuberculosis, bronchitis and rickets; they are also said to have strong germicidal properties. In many plastics, however, the u.v. energy produces chemical change in the material. Unprotected polypropylene rope, for instance, is said to have its strength reduced to nothing in two years if left in open sunlight.

Stainless Steels

At first sight this chapter on corrosion might seem an odd place to find a few words about stainless steels. A short acquaintanceship with the material afloat and all will be clear, for the overwhelming interest is not so much in how it does not corrode but how it does — sometimes in a spectacular and dangerous manner.

Stainless steel is an attractive and somehow 'authoritative' name to give for a whole group of what are more properly called corrosion-resistant steels. These in general contain chromium and those in the particular group which are used afloat also contain nickel and are austenitic or in other words non-magnetic. The most common alloys are:

AISI 302 (EN 58 A) with 18 per cent chromium and 8 per cent nickel and popularly known as 18–8. As it takes a super finish it is often used for parts which do not need too much working or welding.

AISI 304 (EN 58 E) has the nickel increased to 10 per cent to improve the working and welding at the expense of some finish.

AISI 316 (EN 58 J) has 18 per cent chromium, 8 or 10 per cent nickel with the addition of 3 per cent molybdenum and is the stainless steel which is most often used afloat for its improved anti-corrosion potential and full weldability. It does not take quite such a good finish as the others and is, of course, the most expensive of them.

Stainless steel deck fittings can therefore quite legitimately develop rust spots and, to a degree, the shinier the fitting the worse you may expect the rust to be when it develops. This rusting of the odd deck fitting is merely tiresome and the stains usually look a great deal worse than the actual corrosion due to the rust weeping away from it.

The great problems occur with what is called oxygen-deprivation corrosion which can happen on any stainless steel surface in the presence of electrolyte and deprived of free access to oxygen. This group can include underwater fastenings inside the material of the hull, shafts in way of bearings, underwater hull fittings bedded against the hull surface, propellers fitted to shaft tapers, and so on. This is a very disturbing and worrying circumstance when the use of stainless steel is so popular for every part of a boat and fashionable because it is considered as a generous measure against corrosion actually happening at all. The corrosion occurs at the interface between the stainless steel and its surroundings where the oxide film on the face of the steel is attacked and cannot renew itself from any surrounding atmosphere. Thus stainless steel fastenings below water may have heads in perfect condition and nothing much left of the shank and thread. Such attack does not seem to be universal and there have been a great many cases where it has not occurred. Hoping that it will not, however, is no way to go to sea.

This has been an extremely depressing chapter. It infers clearly that the only way to be certain that your beautiful boat is not deteriorating is not to build it at all. As someone once said, the only way to stop aircraft crashing is to keep them on the ground, preferably with concrete wheels.

CHAPTER 6
Naval Architecture – The Artistic Science

General

It is at once the strength and weakness of the art and science of yacht designing that the essentials of making a craft float and perform to a degree are supremely simple. Most children have mastered the principles before they are three through observation of rubber duck and bath sponge. Even a desert Arab who had never seen the sea would know the value of propelling a boat forward rather than sideways and arranging the craft so that the water, in general, was kept outside.

The weakness of the science is that quite passable results can be obtained without too much application of it. All over the world craft are being built without benefit of formal design by builders who have never realised that even Archimedes' principle might be involved. Every castaway on a desert island feels competent, if the materials are to hand, to make himself a boat. A close imitation of a previous vessel is both safe and miracle enough. Boats are themselves such attractive objects that the very beauty of the vessel and of the sea around it can cloak what is, by scientific standards, a really quite indifferent product.

On the other hand the very fact that most people, without tutoring, can make a reasonable stab at designing a boat has kept it from becoming a formal science and largely out of the hands of the academics. It appears to be a fact of life that once a subject becomes buttoned up in such detail that given five years of lectures you know it all, then that subject dies. It is the same as the old story of the donkey who was being trained to live without food. Room to investigate, expand and improve is the life of a designer. It is the great strength of yacht designing that there is, beyond the simple and easy part, a great limbo of the unknown where we can all poke away at the problems that interest us to our hearts' content.

It is, of course, impracticable to attempt to do more than outline the normal design procedures of a design office in a small part of a single book. On the other hand they have developed over centuries and are as much a craft in some respects as any fancy work with the adze or drag knife. They are to our mind a reasonable factor in any attempt to understand boats. Understanding improves the enjoyment whether you want to build, design, drive or just paint boats sitting on the beach.

Boats rarely start from any flight of fancy on the designer's part. The back of the envelope sketch of tradition is much more likely to be the work of the owner or his friend, if only for the fact that the designer is stuck with a responsibility for his work. The designer in fact is usually presented with instructions on what is to be the outcome. This might be as little as 'like the *Saucy Sue* but with an extra cabin and five knots faster' or might come from several pages of closely detailed requirements. From these he sketches an outline design which covers all or as much as possible of the design requirements. The amount of work which goes into this stage depends very largely on the problems which the requirements produce. For instance, if the proposed new craft were similar to an existing vessel then a great part of the properties of the final work could be safely assumed. If, on the other hand, there were no immediate precedent and the new craft had several unusual features then a great deal of work would be involved in making certain that the craft as sketched was a working proposition. That is the essence of the preliminary sketch, improvements and changes might well occur during the final design work but the sketch produced for

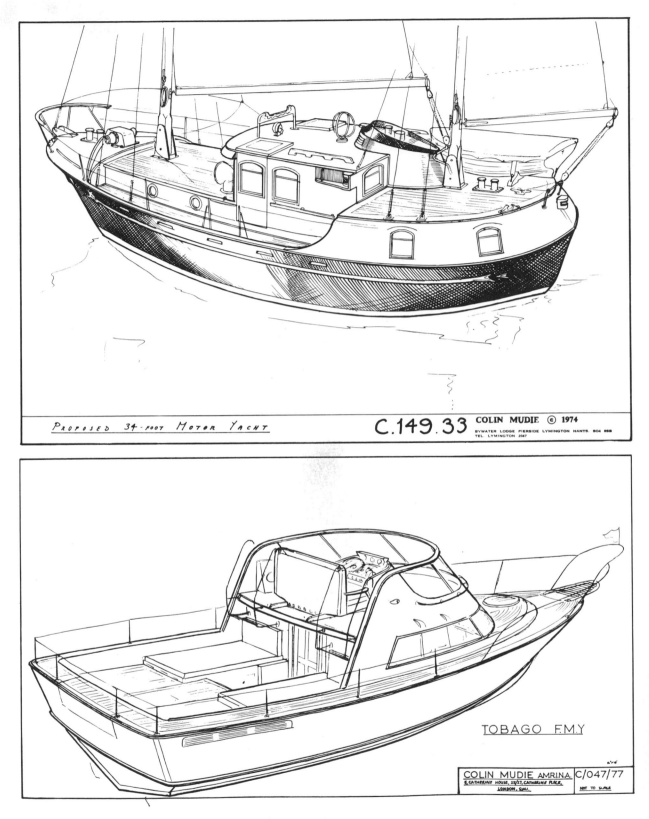

PROPOSED 34-FOOT MOTOR YACHT

C.149.33 COLIN MUDIE © 1974

BYWATER LODGE PIERSIDE LYMINGTON HANTS. SO4 8SB
TEL. LYMINGTON 2047

TOBAGO F.M.Y

COLIN MUDIE AMRINA C/047/77

5, CATHERINE HOUSE, 25/27, CATHERINE PLACE,
LONDON, SW1.

NOT TO SCALE

*Fig. 115a, b, c, d   The preliminary sketches set out for general
agreement the kind of vessel to be designed.*

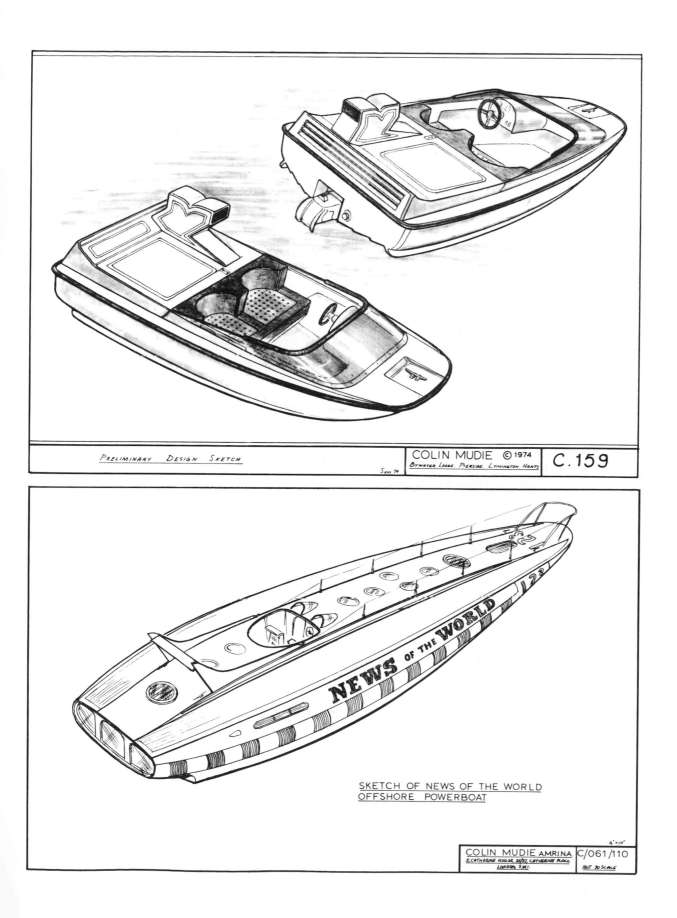

PRELIMINARY DESIGN SKETCH

Sem 74

COLIN MUDIE © 1974
BYWATER LODGE, PIERSIDE, LYMINGTON, HANTS

C.159

SKETCH OF NEWS OF THE WORLD
OFFSHORE POWERBOAT

COLIN MUDIE AMRINA
S.CATHERINE HOUSE, 25/27, CATHERINE PLACE
LONDON, S.W.I.

C/061/110

NOT TO SCALE

the potential builder must represent a workable vessel for his approval. This stage might be repeated several times but eventually the designer has before him a sketch of an approved vessel to design. Of course, by this time the boat is really half designed and the final procedures of naval architecture now outlined will perhaps have already been used half a dozen times to reach the approved sketch. It might be more accurate to say that by now the design is half established rather than that the boat is half designed, for the greater part by far of the design work lies ahead.

Air and Water

Boats and ships are extremely odd in the vehicular world in that they operate in two different fluids at once. The upper part is stuck up into air and the lower part down into water. The junction between the two fluids is nominally fixed but very easily gets confused and even loose, as any seaman will confirm as he empties his seaboots. In extreme conditions of seafaring, like typhoons and hurricanes, the junction can become extremely confused but generally by then matters will have moved more into the theological plane rather than naval architectural discussion.

Both air and water are fluids and a fluid is that which flows. It has no shape of its own and in fact the smallest shear stresses if applied for long enough can make any required alteration to its distribution. A fluid which is at rest therefore is without shear stress. Under stress the resistance of the fluid is to the rate of change of shape rather than to the change of shape itself. Fluids are divided into liquids and gases. The apparent difference between the two is that the former are roughly a thousand times more dense than gases and what is more have generally speaking a definable size of their own. Liquids maintain their size and adopt the shape of their containers while gases expand indefinitely unless completely contained or may even be compressed into small containers.

The molecular theory is not without interest. In a solid it is thought that the molecules oscillate tightly in positions fixed relatively one to another. When heat is added to the point where the solid turns liquid the additional energy is such as to allow the molecules to break the rigid pattern and each is free to fizz around within the limits of mutual attraction and the face of the solid container. The addition of more heat allows them to break completely free and to travel where they will in the form of gas.

The molecular attraction within a liquid means that it will stand a tiny bit of tension and this causes an apparent shear resistance between adjacent layers which is what is understood by viscosity.

Both the gases of the air and the liquid of the sea are constantly reacting to the various pressures on the world from the heat of the sun to the pull of the planets. The fluids' rush to find equilibrium is felt by seamen as their wind and weather, seas and currents. Their craft sits tossing at the mutual boundary, both being disturbed by and disturbing both. Air being the less dense is the faster moving and easier to pass through. Water being the more dense gives better support but can build up a cruel loading when it comes to a contest.

Fluids under ideal conditions move smoothly and easily. The lines of stream are then such that every particle passing a given point treads exactly along the same path and this is called laminar flow. Laminar flow can exist on the surface of a boat hull, especially forward and especially on a very smooth finish. When external conditions of temperature, pressure or speed cause the breakdown of this laminar flow the streamlines themselves break up into eddies and the flow is called turbulent. Between the two there is an area of transition.

Water can also be a gas under certain conditions. If the pressure under normal sea conditions is reduced to less than one third of a pound per square inch the water will vaporise, usually to our dismay. Such reductions of pressure are usually found only on the blades of rudders and fast moving propellers. The water vapour leaves the equivalent of holes in the sea in the immediate area and the whole process is appropriately called cavitation.

The average cubic foot of sea weighs some 64 lb. Every foot you go below the surface has to support the weight of water above it and therefore the water pressures on each square foot of hull and tank bulkhead increases by 64 lb for every foot of depth. Air, on the other hand, weighs only 0·08 lb for the same quantity, and therefore the pressures on the above water boat can be considered as constant, although the

Fig. 116 A Hunt Hiliner Sportsman runabout among 'fluids rushing to find equilibrium'.

winds of heaven when they get going can blow like the very devil and the windage of a quite normal craft can be a surprise. Even end-on, with windage at its minimum, the average 30 foot power boat might have an apparent area of about 70 sq. feet. A light breeze will propel this area with some 70 lb of thrust. A moderate breeze will double this, and an ordinary common or garden gale will knock nearly 400 lb, which would be enough to drive her along at some 6 knots. A 60 or 70 mile an hour wind, force 11, would build up around 1000 lb of thrust, end-on, which, if the sea were flat and the hurricane steady, would be enough to get her on the plane.

The mass of air varies with temperature and therefore the northern yachtsman is commonly dealing with more energy for the same wind speed than the southern yachtsman. A fact which, unregarded, has given rise to some basic misapprehensions about the comparative calls on seaworthiness of northern boats compared with their sunshine critics.

The Static Balance

A boat hull is initially considered in terms of what might be called its static balance. That is, the balance and characteristics of the form lying, most unnaturally and unusefully, quite still in the water. This is principally for convenience since the many variations of floating line produced for instance by wind and weather, sea and speed, would produce an infinity of calculables. The static and still condition is an obvious and useful mean position from which to start.

In the very beginning, the designer will have

Fig. 117 The calculations start by considering the vessel at rest in quiet conditions.

Fig. 118 *The bustle stern of the current ocean racers is not a new invention, for here it is in an elderly steam yacht with the same type of hull for the same high prismatic reasons.*

chosen the type of hull form he thinks best and he will have established some idea of the weight of vessel he expects to finish with. Whether this is established by the full and laborious calculation of the expected weight of each component or whether it is to any degree what one designer calls a 'controlled guess', there will be a definite volume of underwater form required for the craft. By using the prismatic coefficient normal for the hull form being drawn to establish the correct master section on the lines plan, the designer can usually expect to get within spitting distance of the right figures on the first drawing. The underwater volume then can be established by any of a number of mechanical methods.

It is worth noticing in passing that Froude's theories made the attainment of a high prismatic coefficent, for instance, a desirable achievement

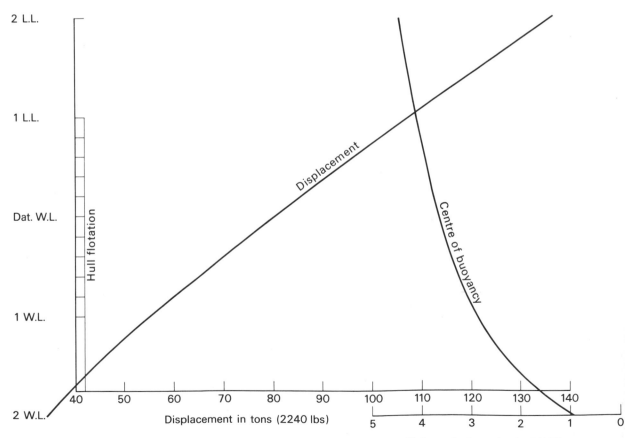

Fig. 119 *The displacement curves for a motor yacht.*

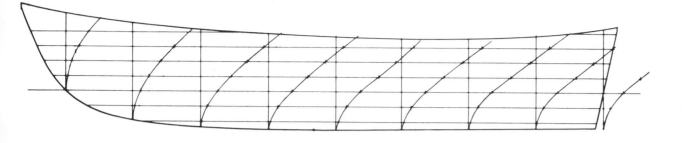

Fig. 120   A set of Bonjean curves for a 10 ft dinghy, a type probably subject to the greatest range of differing loadings.

for performance in some parts of the speed range of the hull. There are also several ideas abroad about the most desirable form of the curve of displacements. These arguments often have some validity but normally only in relation to a certain and exact state of hull performance which might in some cases be of importance. They usually reflect the wave form expected along the hull.

The mechanical calculations for displacement also produce the position of the centre of buoyancy fore and aft. This has to coincide within small limits with the expected centre of gravity of the construction. Few vessels have the same weight from hour to hour, because fuel and stores are used and crews come and go. It is therefore of great interest to know how the craft will float throughout the range of possible variations. The most useful calculation device here is the Bonjean curves, which are no more than graphs of the immersed area of each hull section. These are most conveniently set up on a scale profile of the hull when any trim can be marked and the sectional areas to that line read off and popped straight into a standard calculation. The waterplane area will give the nominal 'immersion' figure in tons per inch and the moment to trim one inch can also be derived from the displacement and waterplane area calculations. Thus one can make a quite reasonable estimate of the trim of the yacht in any given condition and confirm it direct from the Bonjean curves. A useful guide for the owner is a graphical representation of the fore and aft movement of the centre of buoyancy with the vertical movement of the datum waterline with, on the same graph, the estimated positions of the centre of gravity of the boat in different load conditions. The inspection of the righting lever at various angles of heel is also a normal feature of the static balance. This can be

done purely by calculation but it is very commonly performed and most easily explained by using cardboard cut-outs. The difficulty is that the waterline at rest represents the correct volume of hull but as soon as the yacht heels she either lifts or sinks a little on her bilges and her new waterline does not, unfortunately, coincide any longer with the centreline of the datum waterline.

The underwater sections of the hull are traced off the lines plan on to thin card and are then cut out carefully and glued together in their exact relationship to each other. By balancing this model across a knife blade it is possible to establish fairly easily and quite accurately both the vertical and athwartships position of the centre of buoyancy (c.b.) — this latter of course on the centreline in this case.

The same is then repeated at various formal angles of heel such as 15°, 30°, 45°, etc. Only here the nominal waterline is carefully cut back parallel to the original until the heeled sections are exactly the same weight as the original upright sections, inferring that they both show the same displacement. The c.b. found for the new position is carefully marked and plotted back onto the lines, when a series of horizontal distances between these centres of buoyancy and the c.g. of the hull can be plotted, giving the righting lever characteristics of the hull. These should be continued until at least the deck edge is in the water — when stability begins to disappear in a power boat — and perhaps until the deckworks are entering the water or such a point is reached that the sea would in any case pour into the hull. These righting levers should be treated with some suspicion for they can lead to false confidence if the dynamic characteristics — such as the way the yacht rolls — are not considered as well.

A graph showing the righting levers compared

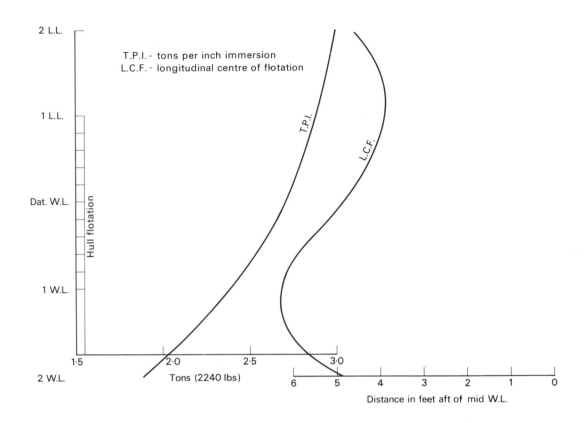

Fig. 121a, b   The hydrostatic curves for a motor yacht illustrate only the geometric particulars of the actual hull form.

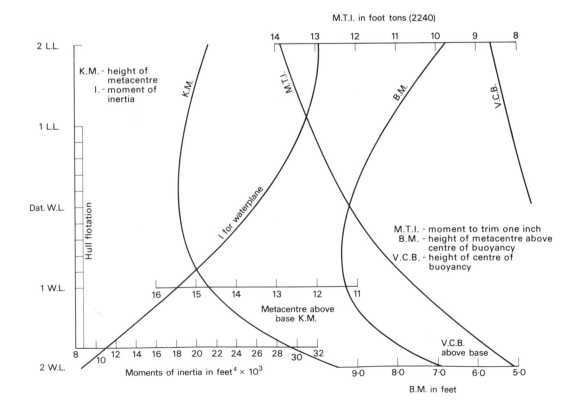

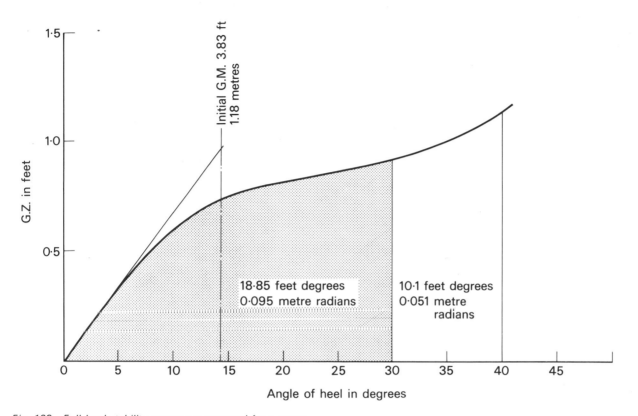

Fig. 122 Full load stability curves are prepared for a motor yacht with the final design work but are only a calculated assessment and have to be checked by a metacentric trial after launching.

with the angle of heel in a static stability analysis in fact defines the amount of energy involved in rolling the craft. Approval organisations usually define their stability requirements in terms of the area under the curve up to a nominal angle of heel for which 30° seems to be favourite plus a required amount up to say 40° or any lesser angle at which water could enter the hull. This excess is regarded as a reserve of stability and is required to take account of the dynamical factors which occur at sea. The ghost of HMS *Captain*, the Victorian warship which capsized despite apparently satisfactory paper stability, is felt strongly to this very day.

The righting lever, as you will see, is zero when the yacht is upright but should she roll even an infinitely small amount the righting moment appears at once to push her back. At this infinitely small amount of heel the hull is in fact rolling about a vertical pivot which is called the metacentre. The height of the metacentre above the centre of gravity of the hull is called the

metacentric height and is a most important factor in the comfort and safety of the vessel.

The choice of the correct metacentric height is largely based on experience. In order that the hull be stiff a large metacentric height should be chosen. In any case the height must be enough to resist the inclination of the boat by external forces such as wind and weather and by internal forces such as the crew all moving to one side together. On the other hand, a vessel with a very large metacentric height comes back to the upright very suddenly and with such violence as to make the vessel uncomfortable to be on board. The traditional advice to hoist an anchor to the masthead of an uncomfortable vessel in a seaway is a practical method of reducing the metacentric height.

The largest metacentric heights ever occurred in river gunboats where the combination of flat water and the need for a steady gun platform allowed the use of a metacentric height of about twelve feet. This is fantastic when you compare it with the normal range which runs from just under a foot to three or four feet in sailing ships. It always sounds alarming to hear that the metacentric height of the great Queen liners was of the order of twelve inches. The stability of such a large ship, one feels, ought to depend on a figure of hundreds if not thousands of feet. The answer is, however, that it is 80,000 tons or so times one foot.

The height to be chosen for a power yacht is again a matter of experience which might be modified to suit the inclinations of the owner. Some feel a sense of security in a hull which, if ever heeled, whips up quickly again, while others prefer the gentle, soft motion of a ship which appears to give and take with the sea. The fast, chine power boat often suffers badly from excessive stability when running slowly and some are intolerable if anchored off in a seaway. The problem is usually excessive metacentric height, or rather one should say that the problem would be alleviated if the metacentric height were reduced. Once, on some little 25 footers, we deliberately mounted the water tanks high on the bulkheads of the cabin. Not only did this give the most inexpensive running water system but the boats were markedly good sea boats.

Rarely considered for small yachts but of almost equal importance is the fore and aft metacentric height. In power yachts pitching is as much a factor to consider, both for safety and comfort, as rolling.

One further item of static balance which should be considered is that of windage. This is of principal importance in two conditions; the most commonly felt being in slow running up to moorings and the other in very fast craft running in a high wind. For both it is a case of balancing the silhouette of the above water profile against that of the underwater profile A certain amount of 'lead' as in a sailing craft is desirable but the correct amount can vary substantially from, say, as little as 1 or 2 per cent in a fine bowed, blunt tailed hull, to as much as 10 per cent for a blunt bowed, fine ended craft. The shape of the deckworks also has a large influence. In fast planing craft, of course, one must take the silhouettes in running condition when there is likely to be only a narrow triangle of hull stuck in the water and that right aft. However, it takes such a strong wind ever to become a relative beam wind of a 40 or 50 knot boat that the whole should be considered from only some 15° or 20° on the bow where the silhouette looks a great deal more reasonable.

Resistance and Movement

The real difficulties of the designer's life start when the power boat fires up its engines and the craft starts away through the water. She is then subject to a shoal of factors all varying one to another from moment to moment in a manner calculated to confuse a computer. This is when boats become as complex in their behaviour as humans and equally endearing, or maybe the reverse. The simplest of them all is the straightforward resistance of the hull to motion, or rather the resistance of the sea to the pushing hull.

The resistance of a hull form moving in the sea and air can be separated into the following components for both media, namely skin friction, wave making, and compression wave making. For that part above water everything can be ignored in practical terms except wave making, and even that can be simplified and approximated to the wind resistance of the frontal area. Below water both the first two components are especially important but the third, compression wave making, refers only to the state when the whole vessel is either completely immersed in the sea or in the air. The former just does not bear thinking about and the craft would have to be travelling at hundreds of miles an hour for the other to become a problem.

Skin friction can be considered a thoroughly

Fig. 123   *Fortunately the relative winds on a fast power boat are rarely from the beam where balance might be difficult to achieve at speed.*

up-to-date problem. A great deal of the work of the naval architect, with test tanks as tools, has been to reduce the resistance of hull form to a minimum. This has had the effect of increasing the proportional effect of skin friction and therefore the importance of good surface finishes. A difference in bottom polishes may make a significant difference to the performance of a modern boat while the old-fashioned commercially minded fisherman on the next slip is happily busy tarring his barnacles.

Skin friction is in fact better thought of as fluid friction, for the friction occurs between the layers of fluid and not between the hard surface of the vessel and the water. The craft carries along with her a thin skin of water lying motionless against her surface. This layer of water slips a little against the next and so on until, a measurable distance off the hull, the water nominally at rest is reached. The friction resistance of the hull is due to the viscous drag between the layers or stream bands of water and this viscous drag itself is due to breaking the molecular attractions between water molecules; the total amount of friction depending on the area of hull in the water, the density of the water (constant for practical purposes) and the surface roughness of the hull, the overall figure rising with the square of the speed.

While looking at friction it is worth noting that the total friction caused by the passage of the hull is not exactly and only dependent on the hull area. The straightforward area measurement needs a modest correction to take account of the continuity of flow around the curved form requiring the water to travel further and therefore faster. Experts argue happily as to what the extent of this form effect should be but it is not too far off a 10 per cent increase for an average hull. In addition the wake from a hull which is also using up energy is partly due to the readjustment of the streamlines as they join again and also partly to the skin friction of the hull.

Wave-making resistance refers to the work done in raising bow and stern waves, and so on bodily out of the sea, and also incidentally forms a blanket for minor factors which are either unimportant or unappreciated. The hull pushes forward and pressurises the sea. At atmospheric pressure this cannot be kept at surface level and therefore volumes of sea are lifted against gravity until the balance is obtained. The total amount of wave-making resistance does therefore depend

upon the density of the water (constant), the force of gravity (constant), the shape and size of the craft, and its speed.

Surface waves formed by the passage of a hull are very nearly trochoidal in form like open sea waves and have a constant speed length ratio of $1{\cdot}3\sqrt{L}$, where speed is measured in knots and L in feet of waterline length — close enough to the

Fig. 124   The three wave system to be seen along the length of this oil rig tender shows that she is running at $\frac{V}{\sqrt{L}}$ of about 0·7 and therefore that she is making about 6 knots.

Fig. 125   This powerful tug designed by Cove, Hatfield & Co Ltd shows the distorted wave formation typical of a short hull which because of its duty is relatively overpowered. Note how the hull is relatively unsupported amidships and that therefore great stability has been designed into the ends.

$1.4\sqrt{L}$ figure which governs the displacement speed of boats to be significant.

At low speeds friction resistance is by far the bigger of the two components. At a speed length ratio $\left(\dfrac{V}{\sqrt{L}}\right)$ of 0·8 (say about $5\frac{1}{2}$ knots for a 50 foot waterline craft) the wave-making component starts to grow. At $\dfrac{V}{\sqrt{L}}$ of 1·0 (7 knots for the 50 footer) the two factors are about equal. Wave making grows apace until at a $\dfrac{V}{\sqrt{L}}$ of 1·4 (the maximum normal hull speed and about 10 knots for our 50 footer) wave-making resistance is three or four times greater than frictional resistance. If the hull form can be driven faster wave making increases still further and then starts to settle back to much the same figure and gets confused by the planing action setting up under the bottom.

Skin friction can only be controlled by the designer by attempting to enclose the necessary flotation volume with all its distribution requirements inside the most efficient envelope area for volume. In this respect the closer the hull approaches a segment of a sphere the more efficient it becomes. In addition every square inch of the deadwoods and such fittings as bilge keels must be paying its way and answering some specific need. With modern hull building materials and techniques it is now quite practical to consider a hull form which will trap air forward, carry it right under water and release it aft. This air lubrication of the bottom will cut skin friction although it must be used with some care to avoid ventilating the propellers and rudders to ruin their performance.

Wave-making resistance has in the past proved a more fruitful hunt and a great deal of tank testing has drawn up some basic parameters for

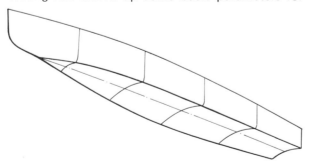

Fig. 126 *Sketch of the air lubricated hull form model tested by Sir John Thornycroft as an alternative to the Royal Navy's first torpedo boat at the turn of the century.*

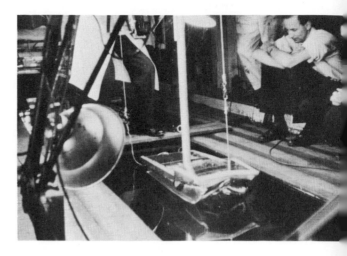

Fig. 127 *A transparent model is tank tested to allow a sight of what is actually happening in the air lubricated tunnels in the hull form.*

guidance. For instance the correct angle of entry, where the bow slices forward into the undisturbed sea, affects the initiation of the entire wave-making system. When wave making is not an important factor of the performance, the bow can be quite blunt. At a speed length ratio $\left(\dfrac{V}{\sqrt{L}}\right)$ of 0·5, equivalent to a speed of $3\frac{1}{2}$ knots for the 50 foot waterline vessel, the bow can be as fat as 60° but for the maximum normal speeds for displacement craft the bow angle should be reduced to about 20°, which is very fine indeed. This bow angle is not necessarily the one drawn on the lines plan as the effect of hull trim has to be taken into account, especially at speed. Fine waterlines allow the wave-making system to start further aft but often some difficulty is found in getting back to the full hull form required to be wrapped around the hull contents. Hollow waterlines can help in this respect although they are often the start of a wet ship as the suddenly increased hull bulk helps the bow wave on to the deck. Another problem is finding enough buoyancy forward, both to restrict pitching and to keep the vessel running drier.

The form and sweetness of the hull obviously has some effect on wave making but it has also been found that the sheer bulkiness of the hull as expressed by the prismatic coefficient has an ideal amount for each relative speed. It is not obvious to the mind why this should vary from low for small speed to high for high speed but a prismatic coefficient of less than 0·55 gives best results for wave-making resistance for speed length ratios up to 1·0 (7 knots for the 50 foot waterline) rising as close to as much as 0·70 for speed/length ratios of twice that amount (14 knots for 50 foot waterline). Of course these are ideal figures for one particular set of circumstances and you should not set off at once to shoot your yacht designer if your prismatic coefficient is not ideal. He has probably gained more for you on some swing elsewhere than he has lost you on that particular roundabout.

The Dancing Boat

All marine vehicles dance on the waters. Large ships move with an elephantine movement which only becomes impressive or even attractive in heavy seas. Small craft have movements varying from the ponderous through the graceful as far as the frenetic. But all have this individual quality of movement of a largely rhythmic character to make them dance with the largely rhythmic movement of the sea. Even a racing power boat doing its ridiculous belly-flops in rough water is responding to the sea with its own particular qualities of movement.

Human and animal dancers have muscles all over their bodies to influence their natural movements while boats have only the prop thrust and the incitement of the sea. Their quality of motion is therefore almost completely dependent on the distribution of weights within the volume of the vessel modified by the hydrodynamic values of the underbody form and the aerodynamics of the top.

Set a boat rolling in flat water and she will roll to a constant period like any other pendulum. The rolling is damped by the movement of the hull in the water, and the speed of damping depends on skin friction, keels, bilge keels and so on, plus the effect of the hull form. The rate at which, and the amount the hull has to be lifted and lowered bodily as it rolls up and down on its bilges can obviously have a big damping effect or, in some cases, if it should match the period of the hull weights, can reinforce the rolling. There is the occasional boat in most anchorages which is a real roller and which mysteriously keeps at it even in flat water. This phenomenon is more common to sailing boats than motor boats but illustrates the effect of hull shape on movement other than that of moving forward.

Set a boat pitching in flat water and a similar set of factors will apply, with the one important difference that the hull form fore and aft is unlikely to be symmetrical. The centre of movement between the ends is unlikely to be the same as that of the vessel and the lunge forward is likely to be greater than the lunge aft. The affect of pitching is therefore likely to be reasonably quickly damped.

At sea the craft is affected by the period of motion of the waves. The athwartships rolling motion due to the hull pendulum seems to be reasonably quickly damped out and the hull physically moves usually to the rather longer period of the waves she is encountering. Pitching is also quickly damped until the wave length approaches that of the ship when it starts to augment the natural period of the hull to produce a motion which can build up past the frightening to the violent. The same can occur with a beam sea and the only action open is to alter the direction of

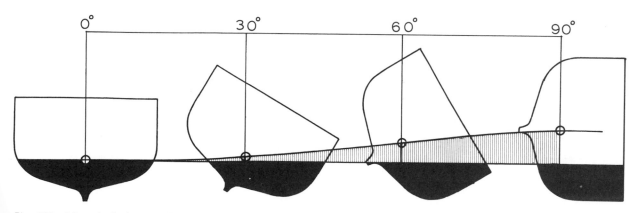

Fig. 128   Many hulls have to be lifted bodily in the water when rolling, greatly increasing the energy need.

the vessel to try and alter the period of encounter. Specific areas of water are subject to prevailing wave conditions and it is possible to design a boat to avoid the dangerous synchronous rolling or pitching periods of these conditions, perhaps to their detriment in alien conditions. This is not sufficiently understood by people who operate craft or see them operating in seas different from those for which they were designed.

The hull at sea is largely considered on rolling and pitching, but she is also heaving with the lift of the sea and yawing or being moved in a direction not along her fore and aft axis. One can see that the resultant array of factors of movement is rather out of hand as far as any comprehensive analysis is concerned. Practical experience, the designer's *vade mecum*, is normally the final component of design in this department.

Heaving has a modest value on the comfort of those on board. It is principally affected by the ratio of the waterplane to the weight of the hull or in other words the area the lifting sea can get at compared with what it has to do in lifting. More important perhaps is that it forms an additional component of the accelerations to which the hull and equipment of the craft are subjected.

Yawing appears to be the result of the couple set up by combined pitching and rolling as modified by the distribution of the hull volume in the water at the time. It has the principal danger that it is the beginning of broaching. If the yawing couple coincides with an angle of heel which makes the underwater form a strong self-steering component, the bow digging deep and the rudder losing effect as the stern rises, then the vessel will broach. To counter these the designer can lower the centre of gravity to reduce the heeling component, reduce the stern buoyancy to keep the rudders in action and reduce the depth of the forefoot to cut down any tripping. The fitting of a keel or bilge keels is a well-known palliative which makes the basic initial sideways movement a little more difficult to initiate. It is however perhaps the least factor in importance in reducing broaching even if it is the easiest to apply to an existing hull form. It must sometimes also extend the violence of the final broach by setting up a rolling couple in the final sideways lurch.

A tank full to its top acts very much as a fixed weight, but this is its most unusual condition. In a tank which is not full the liquid is free to move to match the angle of heel or pitch of the vessel. The extent to which its centre of gravity can move often depends, with the shape of the tank, on the amount of liquid in it. In addition, the liquid can set up a rhythmic motion of its own which will have a period which does not have to match that of the vessel. The effect of such tanks has to be taken into account in stability calculations and also considered with the rolling and pitching and so on. Tanks are fitted with baffles to inhibit the build-up of rhythmic movements of the contents while, on the other hand, this same rhythmic movement can be controlled and used specifically to reduce rolling in what are called stabilising tanks.

The superstructure can be of great value in reducing rolling by making use of its windage. The sailing vessel with wind abeam is greatly freed from rolling and this improved motion is one of the most pleasant benefits of the motor sailer. Many a large funnel on a motor yacht does its best work as a metal sail. Fast boats nowadays shoot along at speeds where light aircraft take off and therefore the aerodynamic value of the deckworks can have a significant effect on the movement of the hull. Many, with a modest change of heart of the race rulemakers, would soon be more like low-flying aircraft than high-bouncing boats.

Inside the overall picture of the craft battling with the seas is another of every component battling with its surroundings. Every movement of the parent craft involves the acceleration or deceleration of all its components. Combined they form the characteristics of motion of the whole craft but each has its own purely local problems. A fast planing boat banging away through rough water has been known to be subject to decelerations (thumps) of the order of $20g$. This means that every part effectively weighs twenty times more for as long as the deceleration lasts. The extent of the maximum loading will vary through the length and breadth of the vessel, and the direction is not necessarily even close to the vertical. In non-planing craft the loadings will not be anything like the excesses which current racing power boats put up with, but a doubling of effective weight is normal. Centrifugal motion can be significant in a rolling or pitching situation and Newton's laws of motion are amply demonstrated in any seaway. If you should be so foolish as to let half a dozen eggs free in the cabin of a small boat in a seaway they will take off like birds and fly in a flock before your very eyes. Humphrey Barton tells the sad story of how his porridge once flew away, to land in his companion's sleeping bag. 'It was,' he remarked in his usual laconic style, 'bad luck for both of us.'

Planing

Planing is rather like tobogganing over the top of crusty snow rather than plodding knee deep through soft snow. If you really want to get around your patch of water fast it is obviously a most desirable achievement, given that the safety and comfort of the boat are up to scratch. Many people who use the sea for pleasure are not interested in speed as such and, in truth, are delighted to prolong their absence from their landbound cares. However, speed is becoming a recognised part of seamanship and the ability to move fast would occasionally be welcome to the most hidebound seaman.

At rest all boats are cradled and supported by the natural static water pressures about them. As soon as the hull moves and water has to flow

around it the varying lengths and patterns of the flow produce their own local changes of pressure. At slow speeds these are negligible but as speed increases the local pressure changes increase while the static pressures stay the same. The local pressures keep on increasing until they eventually have a much bigger significant value than the original static pressures and they become the controlling influence on the action and performance of the craft.

The best shape for the normal speeds of slow craft is roughly pointed at each end. This means rather more pointed in terms of bulk than, say, the waterline plan. It is reasonable to understand that as this shape accelerates there will be a build-up of pressure under the front part and a decrease of pressure under the after part. It is therefore no occasion for surprise that the front of the boat tends to lift out of the sea and the back to sink into it until eventually the whole thing becomes ridiculous and sinks stern first. The planing craft is shaped to provide what is in effect only the forward body. The result is a positive pressure over all, or at least the greater part, of the bottom and this as speed increases gives lift

Fig. 129 As soon as the hull moves out of the displacement speed range the first reaction is for the bow to rise and the stern to sink a little. This is Dimarcha, *Peter Du Cane's own yacht, showing to perfection his own distinctive design styling.*

Fig. 130a, b *These two pictures of the Levi designed ultra-fast* Barbarina *illustrate perfectly the difference between buoyant support and full planing.*

which raises the boat bodily in the sea thereby reducing resistance and so on, allowing much greater speeds to be reached. Should power for very high speed be provided then the boat will continue to lift until the craft is virtually borne on the surface of the sea. At this stage the amount of water the hull displaces is negligible and therefore the buoyant lift reaction also negligible. The great majority of planing craft however operate at intermediate speeds where lift from planing and that from buoyancy are still comparable.

The planing boat has to start its forward movement as a displacement hull with a basic planing action establishing itself at a comparatively modest speed. If it were not for the effects of wave making on trim there would be a comparatively smooth and even changeover through the speed range from buoyant support to planing support. As it happens, however, the trim of the hull is heavily affected by the wave train it forms about itself when moving. It also happens that planing hulls are pretty good wave makers at slow speed. At the natural limit of displacement speed when the last stern wave falls astern of the hull the planing hull has to be powered not just to rise a little further out of the water but to drive it right up the back of the bow wave. An unusual amount of power is required at this stage until the centre of gravity reaches the top of the wave and the bow can drop into a more normal attitude. The boat then reverts to what might be considered its normal speed power relationship and appears to roar off as if released from some trap. This is usually taken as the start of real planing and the intermediate stage between the displacement speed and full planing is called the semi-planing range.

The full displacement speed and the semi-planing speeds are accompanied by heavy wave making but when full planing is established the wave making is progressively reduced until a really fast craft can streak past making less wash than a rowing dinghy.

These quite distinct areas of performance require distinctly different ideal hull shapes and the final choice of form is likely to depend on the amount of power available for its propulsion. The ideal displacement hull for best efficiency will have a rather long waterline, modest beam and fine ends. In the semi-planing range a fine bow will still be required so that it does not attract too much lift and for the contrary reason a wide flat

Fig. 131   A planing hull form travelling at semi-planing speeds in shallow water can pull up a quite considerable wave train.

stern is required. This form helps to reduce the hull trim as it perpetually climbs the bow wave. The bow rises but the stern also rises, with the result that the semi-planing boat often looks as if it is riding on the icing on a cake. The planing hull basically likes beam for efficiency and there is no doubt that the nearly flat bottom gives a better efficiency than the deep vee type. The snag lies here in the ideal proportions of the immersed planing surfaces. A flat-bottomed planing craft shows, to passing fish, a roughly rectangular surface which reduces in length as the boat goes faster and drives itself further out of the water. The ideal proportions of such a form are therefore tied fairly closely to a particular speed. The deep vee shows its passing fish a triangular set of planing

Fig. 132   The typical trim and 'cake top' appearance of some semi-planing hulls at speed.

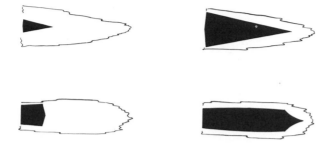

Fig. 133 The fish's eye view of the rectangular and the triangular planing forms at different speeds.

surfaces and as it goes faster or more slowly the proportions of this triangle will remain much the same although its size will vary. The difference is probably illustrated by considering each type at its ultimate seafaring speed. The flat bottom planing surface will be reduced to a thin line across the transom – plainly unlikely to be efficient; whereas the deep vee will have reduced itself to a dot – plainly highly unstable but maintaining the original proportions of beam to length of planing surfaces.

Fig. 134 This Admiralty 25 ft fast motor boat shows the narrow, almost flat bottomed hull form necessary to get a rather underpowered hull through the semi-planing range into full planing.

Each desirable hull form has to take into account those other ranges of speed through which it has to pass to get to its maximum. The rather low-powered planing craft will therefore probably have to have a long thin shape in order to power its way through the semi-planing stages. A little more power may let the hull blast its way through the lesser speeds to achieve planing when a beamy flat hull may be necessary for a sufficient maximum speed performance. Given even more power there may be enough to spare in the interests of a better range of efficient operation and a softer ride and the bottom can be given a deeper vee. With yet further power available then the actual working area of the bottom is getting quite small and the beam can be whittled away in the interests of windage, minimum deceleration when plunging into a sea and overall weight.

The normal maximum speed for displacement running of $\frac{V}{\sqrt{L}}$ of 1·4 is approximately 10 knots for a 50 foot waterline craft. Planing is sufficiently established by $\frac{V}{\sqrt{L}}$ of 2 (14 knots) for the vessel to be run in the semi-planing condition. She will have climbed her bow wave, be over her resistance hump and away as a true planing vessel at $\frac{V}{\sqrt{L}}$ of about 3·5, or 25 knots. Her performance will improve on a reasonably predictable relationship from then but it is usually accepted that at $\frac{V}{\sqrt{L}}$s of the order of 10, say 70 knots, life gets a little unpredictable. This is due to the modest amount of boat in the water compared with the large amount of it travelling through the air. The effects of the air flow over the hull start to become really significant and bring the vessel into the semi-flying machine category.

Originally, planing had to be achieved with heavy machinery of modest output and therefore every ounce of planing efficiency was required from the hull form. Now there is enough to spare for some balance and comfort in the hull allowing speeds, not increased of themselves to any great degree, but extending performance into rougher sea conditions. The original long, thin, flat-bottomed craft have almost universally given way to craft which even look a great deal more like boats and certainly behave more like them. The most dramatic modern development is the deep vee form with steep deadrise for the full

Fig. 135 *The characteristic full bow and fine stern of the classical warped bottom hull seen here in the Scott Paine designed 41 ft 6 in seaplane tender.*

Fig. 136 *The full deep forefoot is one of the best anti-slamming shapes for a fast boat. In this hull the chines and forefoot grow out of a basically lifting buttock form designed to give the quickest possible lift to the bow when run into a sea before the wind.*

length of the hull — a type made viable by Ray Hunt with his introduction of a series of small longitudinal steps or spray rails. This form offers a basic and simple balance of hull volumes that allows it to operate successfully at a wide range of speeds and loadings with a notable decline in rough water thumping.

The development of balance is particularly important for rough water boats where the hull is given movement from outside sources. When there is little buoyant reaction left the slightest heave of the ocean will send a fast boat spinning into the air, to be kept under control only by its own dynamic and aerodynamic characteristics. A nicely rounded chine section forward will efficiently return a flat sea bow wave but when it is swung like a hammer from the transom will jar down with an impact like a car crash.

There are many followers of the monohedron theory of planing boat hull design where it is held that the greater length of the hull should be shaped like an upside-down roof top. This is undoubtedly a reasonable shape for many conditions but, like most arch simplifications, clouds the principal problems and therefore the line of advance. The monohedron adherents are often to be heard talking disparagingly of the warped bottom shape. Give a dog a bad name indeed, for it is clear that there is more to this hull form than the term appears to indicate. The form is so called for the way each side of the bottom warps from a near-vertical bow to a near-horizontal stern. To achieve the necessary balance in this shape it becomes necessary to keep the maximum beam well forward, with the result that in small boats there is often not enough buoyancy left in the stern to carry sterndrive engines or large cockpit loads. It is somehow only natural to use the whole of the bottom of the boat as planing area although there is no real evidence that this is in any way necessary except perhaps in the most heavily laden under powered craft. The 'long wheelbase' planing of a level running boat with a full hull length of support surface in contact with the sea gives comfortable running at a modest cost in speed. The rest, however, are often to be seen proceeding happily at such an angle that they are in fact using only a very small area of planing surface and all at the very far end. This situation in relation to hull balance is to say the least peculiar. Even the accepted levels of bottom loadings and certainly the accepted views on the ideal propor-

Fig. 137 Long wheelbase planing gives the greatest comfort at a slight loss of top speed. Notice also the spray rails doing their stuff and the tiny amount of wave making.

tions of planing surfaces would make some more careful consideration of their placing worthwhile.

The basic planing balance is that between the centre of gravity of the hull and the centre of pressure of the planing surfaces as modified only by the direction of the propeller thrust. The intensity of pressure on the bottom, usually of the order of 100 lb per sq. foot, gives great stability both fore and aft and athwartships as long as the centre of hull weights remains somewhere above the planing area. Should the craft drive out of the water to the point where the centre of hull weight gets ahead of the planing area the bow will drop sharply, resistance increase, speed drop momentarily and then increase to repeat the whole process. This porpoising can build up rhythmically to become disastrous in a flat-bottomed boat, although it is used by some soft riding raceboats as a means of spending more time in the air (where they go faster) and less time in the sea.

The position of the centre of hull weights is basically difficult to alter but it is possible metaphorically to saw the back end off the planing surfaces to keep the ultimate working area further forward than usual. Another approach is to use two or more separate planing surfaces well spread as steps so that hull weight is suspended, as it were, between them.

The Strength of Boats

The traditional manner of arriving at the proper dimensions of the various parts of the craft so that each and all are strong enough is to use another previous example as a reference point. If she was strong enough then make her like that, or thicken up this part where some weakness has shown, or have a stab at going a bit thinner where no problems have been found. It would be idle to pretend that this method is now outdated and that every new design is stressed through and through like a warplane design. In fact one West of England designer, some time retired now, was once heard instructing the yard on the scantlings for a new working craft in the following somewhat forthright manner. 'Make her,' he said, 'not neat, nor nice, but strong as the very devil.'

The size of the various parts of a hull of traditional type, performance and construction, really need only be the subject of a quick confirmatory check-up, for well-documented precedents and practices are freely come by. In addition to the designer's own records, the various classification societies and other official bodies issue tables and rules covering established constructional customs. These can safely be taken as representing a conservative approach to the rigours of the deep water and, above all things, safe. Such classification is now offered by these societies for glass fibre reinforced plastics, as well as for the more traditional woods and steels. The classification societies, being conservative or perhaps even without money available for research, tend to use the substitution method of assessing the strength of unusual constructions. In this manner a direct comparison is made between the strength of the known and of the unknown. A substitute glass fibre reinforced plastics calculation would, for instance, produce a GRP boat dimensioned so as to reproduce as nearly as possible the characteristics of the comparable wood construction. This on first sight seems an admirable approach until you start asking which characteristics have been used in the comparison. Wood, for instance, has quite different properties along or across the grain while GRP shows only a modest difference. Wood is stiff for its weight whereas GRP or aluminium are quite different. Aluminium and steel can absorb a considerable distortion without fracturing although they might remain permanently bent; wood is not like that and GRP is again different. Whatever properties are compared in a substitution calculation must ignore other different properties and even if it were possible to calculate a grand amalgam of properties and split them down the middle you would still be likely to be seriously wrong somewhere. The only safe way to consider a new material is to design it to suit its own properties. In practice it is not too silly to slide a substantial factor of safety into the scantlings of slowish craft not too sensitive to weight. Fast planing craft are, however, to be taken seriously and it is necessary to work out, even approximately, the loadings and stresses to which its component parts will be subjected. Planing craft like to be light and there is a serious performance penalty for an overweight hull. Again, the planing craft is often handled in what can only be called an unbecoming manner, sometimes leaping out of the sea altogether, introducing complications not really envisaged by the classification societies.

Before embarking on a stressing exercise on a new hull it is first necessary to consider the factors involved. The strength requirements of a hull are normally based on the following:

1. Steady state loadings — the pressures and loadings involved when the vessel is running steadily in a flat sea at maximum speed.
2. Periodic forces from regular vibrations — such as the regular pulsing of the engines or propellers.
3. Irregular forces — ranging from the slamming when driven hard in a bad sea to the impact when the vessel is badly docked.

To consider displacement craft first, these will be subject to the following loads:

Hydrostatic pressure. This is due entirely to the head of water over each part of the hull and will act at right angles to the hull surface throughout. Hydrostatic pressure has to be modified as necessary to allow for the height of waves formed about the hull at speed. These are usually estimated by experience, but take, generally speaking, about half the height of the topsides.

Velocity pressure. This is the additional pressure on the hull due to speed through the water. In practice this applies only to the forward parts of the hull and even in quite a fast craft is quite modest.

The sum of the hydrostatic and the velocity pressures is known as the *maximum hull pressure.*

In a well designed and equipped non-planing vessel the loading from vibration is small and so is the slamming. However, the requirements of *docking pressure* and even an allowance for *debris pressure* must be made. Docking pressure is usually assumed as being equal to the whole weight of the vessel applied at about 20° from the bow. Any more direct approach, like bow-on, could well be considered as more of a disaster than a normal bit of yachting and so need not enter the calculations unless required by the owner. Any impact further aft will be alleviated by the slipping of the hull along the dock.

Debris pressure is more difficult to assess. Certainly an allowance should be made and if the style of the yacht should permit should be calculated on the basis of running with the full weight of the craft on to a right angle edged solid at any point on the forebody. In the great majority of craft this is a quite impossible requirement and the designer should then be thinking in terms of watertight bulkheads or built-in buoyancy.

Vibration from propellers or machinery can of itself produce a panel loading equivalent in size to the normal static loading, particularly in the adjacent areas. This, however, is normally amply catered for inside the factors of safety.

These loadings refer to the individual skin panels and hull areas but in addition the main longitudinal strength of the vessel has to be checked. For this the hull is regarded as a beam alternately sagging between wave crests at either extremity or hogging over the back of a wave amidships. In addition to the weights of the

Fig. 138 The driftwood cast up along this American West Coast beach shows that debris impact loading has to be taken very seriously in the design of all kinds of boats.

individual items which provide the load on the beam, allowance has to be made for the momentum which each will be experiencing as the vessel moves. This can be assessed from the expected pitching moment of the hull and may treble the overall loading. On top of this a factor of safety has to be allowed which may be as little as three for a soft riding vessel upwards to as much as ten for a stout thumper.

In planing craft all the loadings which apply to non-planing craft still obtain but they have been overwhelmed in magnitude by what are politely called the high speed impact loadings. Less politely these are well known as slamming.

A certain amount of research has taken place on both sides of the Atlantic into the extent and distribution of high speed impact loadings. Some has been government research done with science and recorded results of detail, and other urgent research has taken place in offshore powerboat races where the results were perhaps more indelibly imprinted on designers and crews.

Government high speed vessels of about 70 feet in length have been run in waves of 4 to 6 feet in height at speeds of up to 35 knots. Not an excessive condition you might think, but impact pressures of between 30 or 40 lb per sq. inch

(5000 lb per sq. foot) were recorded at the worst affected parts of the skin. Bow accelerations reached 12g, which means for instance that the effective weight of, say, the anchor would be thirteen times that at rest. The extent of such loadings varied of course throughout the vessel and driving a boat that hard may be thought to be unreasonable. On the other hand even the most considerate Sunday afternoon family boat driver has occasionally to get home fast and always to get home safely.

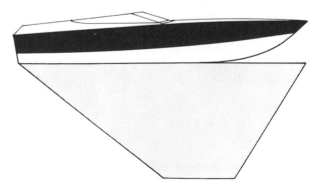

Fig. 139 Approximate distribution of sea impact loadings along the length of a fast power boat.

CHAPTER 7
Design – The Scientific Art

General

Naval architecture is a fairly rigid technical discipline which is rather more akin to ship engineering than to the art of the architect. It is primarily concerned with the actions and problems of the vessel versus the elements. Design is different and can be said to be concerned primarily with the actions and problems of people – in this context of people versus the boat. A good naval architect will certainly be a good designer as well, although the good designer may well require a naval architect to work out the final craft. Naval architecture can be well enough achieved by the exercise of rote and precept. Design can be taught to a degree but good design involves a great deal more personal judgement on line, colour and balance. Good design also involves

the almost continual exercise of critical evaluation and the occasional exercise of original thought.

The first requirement of design is, like any other art, still that overplayed necessity of conveying a message. In this case the designed boat has to convey the message to even the most ignorant eye on the yacht club balcony which explains its style and purpose. A fast boat should look fast, the luxurious yacht should look that way, the houseboat ought to be homely and the sea boat seaworthy. Identity can be concealed if the joke is a good one. The tarred fishing boat that will on demand pop out of the sea and fizz off at 40 knots is an excellent joke, whereas the polished speed boat that will only wind up to rowing speed is not.

Appearance is an important part of design but so-called 'styling' is only the first impression part

Fig. 140   A fast boat should look fast and the raceboat lines of Uno Embassy *with a motor racer paint scheme, could not be taken for any other kind of boat.*

Fig. 141   The Keith Nelson 75 ft patrol boat is also for high speed use in open water and is designed to present a proper authoritarian aspect.

of the designer's work. The first impression will soon fade if design throughout the craft is not of an equivalent standard.

The next object of design is to improve the human condition of the craft. It is often difficult to get back to the first principle of boating which is quite clearly that boats are not really of any importance by themselves and of themselves. Boats are for people and boats have to be adapted for people, not the other way about. We have had a fine series of running arguments with various specialists on the lines that boats are built for people to use and not just to not rot, or to not sink, or to not sail slowly. Many an ideal boat has been born with the single disadvantage that nobody actually wanted it. So the boat has to be arranged for the convenience of its crew and a balance decided between their life on board and any desirable characteristics which can also be worked into the design.

Fairness of form lies somewhere between the naval architecture and the design. Certainly eye-sweetness lies in the designer's eye and equally certainly the naval architect is better aware of those areas of hull where the correctness of shape is essential and those other areas where fancy can be free. Wood construction, as we have said before, forced fair curves on to the surfaces of boats as a benign discipline and only now are we discovering the extent to which we can depart from them.

Last but not least is the living and working comfort of the crew where design can ease the frame, comfort the eye and delight the senses when well applied, but this perhaps is better considered in a separate chapter.

The Aesthetics of Yacht Design

Aesthetics are an extremely tricky subject. Anyone who ventures opinions on such a subject is doing little more than opening up a soft underbelly for the critics' knives. Every piece we have ever read on the subject has more or less left us with the dry heaves. Examples carefully given to illustrate good or bad are often, by the time the book has actually completed the leisurely process of publishing, both out of fashion and may be transposed with equal effect on the weighty words of the text. We have no reason at all to suppose that this short piece will do other than have our fellow designers and probably everyone else rolling on the carpet. If this is so then please regard it as a little light relief halfway through the volume. There seem to us to be some quite basic foundations necessary to any application of design.

First must be the overriding effect of quality. Care and skill with every department of design will show for ever and be appreciated. Fife was the acknowledged master of the curved form

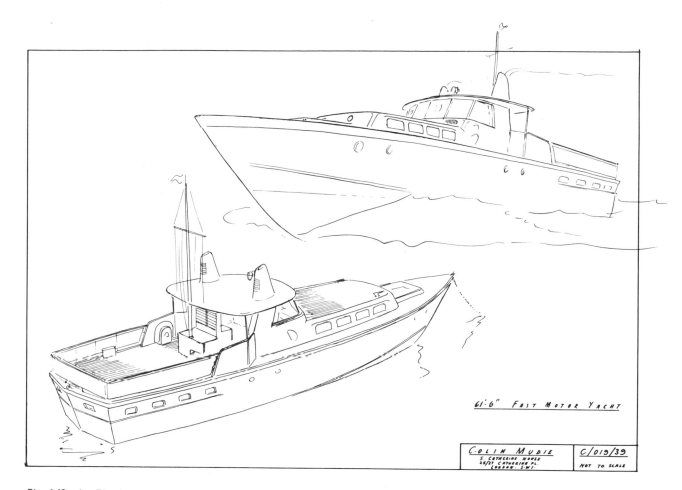

61:6" FAST MOTOR YACHT

COLIN MUDIE
S. Catherine House
25/27 Catherine Pl.
London. S.W.1

C/019/39
NOT TO SCALE

Fig. 142a, b   The 61 ft 6 in fast motor yacht Giftie *sketched before the final drawings were started, and the finished product photographed on trials.*

built boats which fifty years later still astonish with their beauty although unfashionable in every particular. A boat whose appearance is flung together may have the happy accident of good design but the odds are against it. Not long ago we stood at a harbour mouth to admire a steady and prolonged stream of craft leaving for a day afloat. It was very noticeable that the principal differences between the expensive and inexpensive boats at twenty paces lay almost entirely in this question of the quality of design. Oddly enough the cheaper the boat, generally speaking, the worse the design. This is odd because the cheap boat sells in hundreds to the tens of the more expensive and the cost of good design would be spread to such a degree as to make only an imperceptible difference to the total price. It has to happen, just as it did with cheap cars which once were cursed with the most unfair curves but which now sport a fairness of form such as previously distinguished only the hand-made jobs.

Involvement is also high in the order of priorities in any discussion of boating aesthetics. The opposite of involvement is condescension which is an arch sin in design. The moment a designer starts to say to himself, 'This is the sort of thing that *they* want,' rather than 'This is the sort of thing that I would want were I them,' the whole project is lost. It is easy to spot the odd occasions where even very good designers have indulged in some work they did not really believe in, and it is difficult to imagine that it came from the same drawing board. Good design comes from a passionate involvement of the designer's interest.

Next might come the vexed question of timing. It is quite possible to stand back and observe trends of design and, like any other market analyst, to project into the future with considerable confidence. The designer, whose work comes first in the chain which leads to a production boat, may look too far into the future and this is every bit as silly as following the fleet. A design for a builder who will usually have a five year production cycle for each design has to be well placed in the fashion time scale. The boat should be a modest novelty in its first year, bang up to date in its second year and gradually fade over the next three until its replacement is a natural event. It is as silly for that builder to be ahead of his market as it would be to be astern of it. One yacht broker in the heyday of the steam yachts made his fortune by buying vessels with long thin Victorian smoke stacks and replacing these with the short dumpy funnels currently fashionable. A clear case of adjusting design to the desirable time scale.

Fig. 143   It is not as easy as it looks to get a reverse sheer as right as it is on Triton II, *a 16 knot, 55 footer built by Vospers in 1946 and a design far from looking its age after thirty years.*

Fig. 144   A teak top to a coachroof opens up the feeling of deck space.

Scale is another of the basic factors, both the physical scale of the craft itself and scale in the application of design with a capital D. It is possible for a state of overkill to apply in design as in everything else and in its way it is probably worse than simple artless neglect of design. The function of a boat remains primarily that of being a boat and not a display board for the designer to shout his wares. The other kind of scale is a practical problem, that of giving a boat an appearance suitable for its size. As a practical problem it is the one which most often upsets the amateur designer, and the professional is also occasionally to be seen with scale egg on his face. Next time you see a boat looking uncomfortable in appearance half close your eyes and imagine it as a boat of quite a different size and as often as not it will look very much better.

One of the current problems of design is the prevalence of the model and the 'visual'. A model is nearly always looked at and estimated by admiring it on a table when the human eyes around it are hovering in a relative position which will never be used again except by some passing seagull whose views do not really matter. Have a look, for instance, at aerial photographs of the latest liners and bigger yachts. A model is also attractive in itself to a misleading degree and the combination of both factors can result in considerable disappointment when the craft is afloat. Visuals, or artist's impressions as they used to be known, can also mislead badly on questions of size and space and the visual importance of different aspects. Models and visuals may ignore the

effects of distance and dirt, although for a yacht which is expected to be clean and polished throughout its life this is not the disadvantage that it is in other departments of the designers' trade.

Stratagems of Appearance

Many a pretty boat is spoilt by a glance or two at her crew. Not so much the ugly sight of the worthless ruffians themselves but their quite disproportionate effect on their surroundings. Many a tiddly little boat with a natty bow pulpit, for instance, looks smart and handsome until a hulking great human inches his way insecurely along her sidedecks holding tiny handrails between finger and thumb. Even the occasional large craft suffers from deck space and distance which leaves the midget human without a handhold for those precarious miles which open up around a deck in rough water. The first trick of appearance in a ship, craft or boat is to get the human scale right. It is easy enough. A new design must be a close development of a previous one or have humans drawn in all over the plans to keep their normal dimensions a constant factor in the designer's eye. This is such a simple and basic trick that it is too often ignored.

Most designs are first drawn on paper and the great majority are accepted on the basis of this two-dimensional representation. The difficulty lies in the quite exceptional difference which can occur between the two-dimensional and the three-dimensional representation of the same vessel. The most important lies in the skill of the draughtsman to give each line the importance which it will actually deserve in three dimensions. Draughtsman's windows for instance are usually shown white whereas the actual windows afloat will be dark against the coamings. The profile on the centreline shows up clear and bold on paper but in fact is more of a shifting line which alters from every aspect and is never so well defined as it is on paper. Lifelines and stanchions also assume an importance on paper drawings which they never achieve on the actual briny. Rigging disappears to the eye in fact but never on paper where the thinnest shroud has often to be drawn as a line very little thinner than that used to show a principal eye-catching line like the gunwale.

More subtle than the draughting pen is the

Fig. 145 *The upper chine effectively masks the rather uncompromising chine line of this Shetland 570.*

Fig. 146 *Strong sunlight slanting past a hull emphasises every perfection of form.*

confusing effect of perspective. The actual area which the human eye can scan without moving its muscles is extremely small. A practical experiment will show that a triangle of about a quarter of an inch at a distance of about 10 feet is as large as you can inspect properly without feeling the eyeballs swivelling in their sockets. When looking at a drawing and at the actual ship the eyes send back quite different signals to the aesthetic computer. Perspective is based on parabolas. If you do not believe it try standing on the edge of a long straight road and slowly look from full left to full right. Architects' perspective as usually taught is based on straight lines, but they only get away with this simplification because their usual vista for a perspective drawing is so far away that the particular arms of parabolas they should be using have become as near straight as makes no matter. It also helps that the human eye, being lazy, consciously looks for familiar shapes and will accept a close approximation of straight as straight (even if it ought to be parabolic).

The principal effect all this has on the translation from two to three dimensions is to droop off the ends of sheerlines and coachroof lines. On a boat of about 40 feet in length this perspective effect is worth as much as three inches on the sheer. Therefore to achieve a straight sheer to the eye the designer has to draw a normal sheer of about three inches, a normal sheer has to be three inches deeper on paper than its appearance in fact, and reverse sheers have to be treated with desperate caution. The actual straight-line sheer will look like a pleasant reverse sheer, three inches of paper reverse will look quite extreme and a good rounded reverse sheer which is pleasant to the eye on paper will look quite extraordinary in actuality.

The sheerline is one of the principal curves to meet the eye and is one of the most tricky to get right. The correction for perspective ought to vary with the curvature of the deck plan and indeed it is common to add a bit of 'compensating sheer' at the bows to make up for the increased droop due to the swing away from the eye. Even if this trick is managed with all the skill and experience of the draughtsman it still has to be translated into fact. Many yards have boatbuilders with good eyes who automatically make a perfect sheerline, but even their skill is next to useless if the boat (or plug for GRP) is built in too small a shed or too close to one wall. If you want a good-looking boat specify firmly that she is to be built in a big enough shed and with clear eye access all round. A good, critical, eye is still the most accurate hull fairing instrument available.

The good old lazy eye of the beholder on the contrary can be tricked into acceptance of 'appearance contrary to the facts' with boats quite as well as any advice given about dressing up ladies of unfashionable form. Stripes of paint in one direction or another can be quite as slimming or as fattening as any dressmaker's fancy. One modestly useful trick is to put main deck teak planking on top of coachroofs, thereby classifying the coachroof area to the eye as an extension of the main deck with a consequent gain in the feeling of spaciousness. Another now popular is to use dark glass in the windows which gives them a slight air of mystery and distance, and therefore gives the boat additional size in a quite indirect manner.

Another simple and effective deceit to practise is in regard to chine lines. The average run of chine does nothing for the appearance of a boat. It starts well half way up the bow adding strength to the forward profile but then it sags off just when it gets to its strongest shadow area, flopping into the sea at some unbecoming point along the length of the hull. We originally put two chines into some boat or other for good naval architectural reasons but the effect on appearance has been a bonus. Now the eye can follow a good strong upper chine line all the way from the bow to the transom with the actual working chine left to follow its fancy underneath.

When all is said, however, the best trick you can use with the appearance of a boat is fair curves. These will enhance the most nondescript vessel where unfair curves will spoil everything they are wrapped around. A fair curve is a simple thing which is obvious to the eye but which is perhaps the better described on paper with a reference to the theory of curvature. Any fairly curved line can be described and defined by some mathematical expression or other. The curvature of a curve is defined as the rate of turning of its tangent and this rate of turning has to be regular for a circle or to increase or decrease in some regular manner for any other fair curve. It is also worth noting that each curve has a single point of maximum curvature. In a complex solid form like a boat hull it is possible to combine several curves, but in any one direction there should be but one curve and that curve should have but one point of maximum curvature. There is sometimes a special case where, like half an ellipse, two curves can be placed end to end with their points of maximum curvature very well spaced towards if not actually at the opposing ends and their minimum curvature coinciding at the joint. Any other arrangement inevitably implies bumps and a hull surface that will equally inevitably offend the eye.

A by-product of a solid surface sitting in the sun is its shadow and the shadows on the surface of a hull are the positive evidence to the eye of its fairness of form. The topsides of a new design should be critically examined for their shadow pattern with soft shadows in fair sweeps as the ideal. Fife, for instance, was rarely if ever found to put tumblehome on his yachts and this may well have been because of the hard definite shadows. Reflected light, on the other hand, shows up all the minor unfairnesses of a hull, as the stand lighting at many a boat show will prove. A strong light sliding in at an angle on to a polished curved surface magnifies every slight imperfection of form by what seems like a million times. The proud manufacturer who displays his boat to the world on a plinth surrounded by floodlights and who remains proud of its finish really has something to boast about.

The Lines Plan

A great deal of the art of naval architecture is traditionally enshrined in the delicate and intricate process known as drawing the Lines Plan. The inter-relationship between curved sections in different planes, the definition of a solid multicurvature shape on flat paper, has fascinated naval architects ever since the paper planning of ships or boats was attempted. In many senses this fascination with the geometry of paperwork took attention off the value of the actual shapes being defined. Early books on the design of sailing ships are much more concerned with the proper procedure for the draughtsman than the pros and cons of the differing types of hull and their use. Several theories of ship design are to be seen outlined in detail but without exception they refer to a convenient geometrical system of constructing lines. The development of sailing warships began to drag from the time of the establishment of design departments in the various admiralties of the world. The design, that is, of

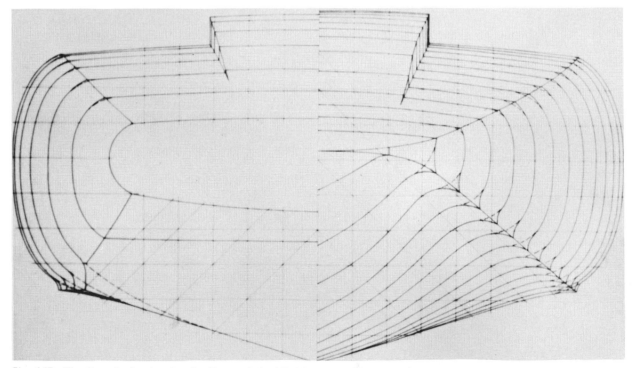

Fig. 147 The lines body plan for the News of the World *power boat.*

their sailing properties, for a great deal of valuable work was done on lesser subjects.

Much the same situation still applies today. The pleasing and satisfying process of constructing a lines plan by hand for a yacht is far too cumbersome. The investment of time, money and skill in putting a new shape on paper gives it an undue importance. If a lines plan when put through the subsequent calculations is not exactly as required then redrawing it is a major decision. If this second plan is not quite right then a further redrawing is becoming desperate. Three sets of lines or even more are not uncommon in the design of an important racing craft but they are certainly unusual in ordinary craft; and yet the only reason to put up with a design which is near enough right rather than go for the very best is only the time and expense involved in the cumbersome conjuring trick of reproducing a three-dimensional form in two dimensions. There is not even the excuse of preparing offsets for the construction moulds in these modern times of pantographic reproduction.

However, the computer analysis of modifications to a lines plan can quickly give the probable effects of variations, and this is a great saver of time and effort. True, many of the computer programs at present are for the rating rules, but as programs become more varied so the large computer becomes a more useful tool. The designer, however, is from start to finish dealing in a solid form. He should be able to carve it like butter to his fancy, pop it into a magic box and read off all the answers he requires on a nice little row of dials. If these are not immediately perfect then he removes the model, carves a bit more off, or smooths a bit more on, and pops it back. In short order he would conclude with the required technical factors built into a hull shape which he will know will please because he is holding it in his hand. Once the black magic is removed from the hallowed lines plan for a yacht we will be able to concentrate on the other largely unexplored factors of performance. We have all been brought up to believe that the fairness of lines is critical to performance (read any design competition judgement) and that a tiny variation of hull form will have a major effect on performance. Given reasonable hull forms, both maxims are untrue. It is essential that our yachts are fair of curve to please the eye. Any honest review of performance separated from considerations of rating rule will

show that the performance of most craft can be defined within quite narrow limits independent of their exact form, given always that the form is reasonable for the speed proposed. It is well known that in one team of sailing yachts racing for the Admiral's Cup one was said to be the same shape as one of the others going backwards. If it is true for such traditionally shape-conscious craft as ocean racing sail boats, then motor boats are unlikely to be more sensitive. Any reported effects of minor hull changes can nearly always be found to be attributable to other causes.

However, as we said just a little earlier, drawing a lines plan for a curvaceous craft is a conscious pleasure and one of the many benefits of our trade. The tools of the trade are pleasant. Weights and battens are large and important and satisfying to use. A good set of ship curves is worth having around just for the eye to light on from time to time. Sharp pencils and thin ink lines help to concentrate the faculties, and planimeters and scales lend a fashionable scientific tone. Even the desk-top computer is a positive source of pleasure these days and can be played like a musical instrument to produce numbers in harmony.

The Above Water Boat

The fanciful current technical description of what a boat is describes it as an 'interface vehicle'. Thus it travels along, hopefully, at the junction or interface of the two media – air and water. The water element is the more dense and therefore, quite properly, the naval architectural attention tends to focus on that part of the vehicle which is immersed in it rather than that which is immersed in air. The shaping of topsides, for instance, is decided principally on the basis of what continuation of the underwater form is required to be suitable when the rolling or dipping of the hull brings them in contact with water, or when the wave formation of forward movement alters the actual waterline. The topside area close to the waterline is also reasonably considered for what might be called interface problems. Water will all too readily jump from sea to air to become a problem of flying spume or driving spray. Air, to a lesser degree, can penetrate the surface of the sea to air lubricate the skin friction or play havoc with the propellers. Both actions can be influenced to a degree by the hull shape in the area of the interface.

Above this again every power boat is to some degree or other a wind ship, and there are some where even the name windjammer would not be out of place. Few are so heavily and so cunningly powered that they can completely ignore the draughts of heaven, and for all the rest a certain amount of sailing boat design work can improve life. Sailing craft, for instance, are so arranged that there is a balance between the centre of effort of the sails and the centre of resistance of the hull they are driving. In a power boat the sails are the hull and deckworks, and a similar relationship between them and the hull will make for a craft which is controllable at slow speed and high winds when, for instance, picking up a mooring or coming alongside. This kind of balance is absolutely essential for open sea boats. A large funnel will make a fine steadying sail for a motor craft but a certain amount of discretion with the deckworks is required if she is going to lie quietly on her mooring. A nicely shaped bit of windage can have a motor boat sheering all around and driving over her moorings as badly as a sailing boat with the mainsail set and the sheet hard in.

The above water hull still follows the rather austere form developed for boats, surprisingly enough, in Victorian times. A little decoration is beginning to creep back but the possibilities of shape are not much explored. Shapes of sterns have been perhaps the most circumscribed recently as a quick look at a model of an antique

sailing ship or a current Arab or Chinese vessel will show. With modern constructional materials and all this mechanical technology around it seems at least likely that we could make a great deal more enterprising use of the above water hull.

The architectural design of the upperworks has to combine that of the small house with that of the small motor bus. From the latter it derives its need for good all round vision for parking as well as for normal driving. A good view astern is next to essential when introducing your own expensive vessel between a pair of even more expensive vessels in, for instance, a tightly packed South of France yacht harbour. Good visibility in all the other directions is also important and the helmsman should be able actually to see the sea about a hull length ahead, except perhaps for that bit obscured by the very tip of the stem. He will not have a chance at all of seeing the anchor when it is being weighed and in a craft with heavily flared bows it will not be easy for anyone to see it at all. Good flare usually becomes a boat, but this should be modified if necessary to allow a preview of those nasty muddy problems that come up on the end of the anchor chain.

The deckwork architecture also has to take into account shelter and privacy. Many a shorebound architectural scheme turns out in fact to be a whirlwind generator where the lightest breeze soughing through its alleys gets charged and recharged with energy until old ladies are seen clinging for dear life to the lamp posts. A power

Fig. 148   Extensive deckworks and a funnel can do as much as a steadying sail for a power yacht in a breeze.

Fig. 149 A good flare nearly always sets off a hull and on Romantica, designed by Fred Parker, it has become a major factor in the appearance.

boat even at rest is anchored right in the open where any wind can get at her, and underway steams along making no mean wind speed herself. The wrong shape of deckwork can whip up wind speed and direction to make otherwise suitable deck areas quite unusable, and can drive rain and spray clear through watertight defences.

Privacy on board is increasingly a factor to consider when laying out deckworks. Basically it is essential for modern marine living to have some privacy available, but for many owners the chummy cottage life of the yacht harbour is a happy proportion of the yachting pleasure. The aft deck can then become a form of public *salon* where people are seen by their friends and seen to be seen by their friends.

Model Testing

It is tempting to put these few words on model testing back in the previous chapter under the general protective heading of Naval Architecture, for certainly a great deal of naval architecture is involved. However, the quite essential component of all but the most mundane model testing is the art of the interpretation of the resulting figures. The value of the process in development

and research can vary extensively with the skills and arts of both tester and designer.

First, it has to be understood that tank testing is a good second best to full-size tests. With the tank the costs of trials may in themselves be comparable to testing the full-size ship but the advantage lies in the economy and convenience. Obviously a model is much cheaper than a full-size vessel and equally obviously controlled conditions are more reliably found indoors with the tank. What is not quite so obvious is that really first-rate trials of finished ships are not only more accurate in themselves but that they are also essential to allow the testers to catch up with any gaps there might be between prediction and actuality. Yacht owners, with a fine new vessel before them and a saloon full of guests, are perhaps the most reluctant of all ship owners to go in for full trials, and the power yacht — and indeed the sailing yacht — is the poorer for it.

The first function of a model is visual. It is difficult to appreciate a paper shape properly after the eye has got used to it for even a short period and a model is a first-class visual shock. Models should however be treated warily for not only are they commonly viewed from quite the wrong eye distance and angle but they are in themselves attractive. A scale representation of almost anything takes on the qualities of a jewel and it is possible

Fig. 150   Typical head sea testing of a 106 ft yacht hull at the Wolfson Research Unit at Southampton University.

to find a model of a craft of unspeakable hideousness somehow looking attractive.

Next is to try the model afloat. The model of course is to a scale convenient to the tank tester's apparatus and is generally as large as possible to reduce the scale corrections in the results. If the model is to float or to be run in flat water, it is only necessary to get the scale weight and fore and aft centre of gravity right. If she is to be run in rough water or to do turning trials then the scale vertical centre of gravity has also to be got right in the model and, more difficult, the radius of gyration approximated to represent the probable distribution of weights in the hull.

A great deal of model testing has always been done by towing a model behind a launch or by hand from the bank of a river or even a public boating pond. The designer can then 'eye' the way the model rides and the wave formations which it kicks up in ease and comfort and with very little expense. It is not uncommon for a model to be roughly proved in this manner before it is taken to the tank for more precise performance predictions.

The test tanks, because of the multiplication required to translate their scale figures to real life, really go to town on accuracy. The carriages are miracles of the railway engineer's art as they whistle along precise tracks spanning the tank at carefully controlled speeds. The model is held by a towing post, itself held in a delicate linkage which translates resistance, up and down movement, and trim, into electronic circuitry which figures out actual results. The model itself is usually fitted with little studs at the bow to make certain that the water flow of the full size is faithfully reproduced, and some carry scale propellers and rudders which may or may not actually operate depending on the extensiveness of the test programme.

The simplest tests and most sought-after predictions are those of resistance and trim. Resistance gives the propulsive power required and therefore, through some standard assumptions of propeller efficiency, gives the engine horsepower which will be needed to achieve a required performance. Trim figures show how much the bow will be pushed down at low speeds, the area of the transitional speeds between non-planing and planing and the efficiency of the planing angle throughout the speed range. The rise, and occasionally fall, of the hull

throughout the speed range is also sometimes recorded and apart from being interesting in itself can help in the interpretation of other figures when trying to estimate the hull efficiency.

In most tanks rough water trials arrangements consist of a paddle at one end of the long thin tank setting up a controlled wave formation which proceeds to roll down the length of it. The model is then set at this lot rather like a dog being set at a pack of rats. By a quirk of the relative mathematics the dreaded synchronous seas are short and steep and high and the model bobs violently up and down in a quite unbecoming manner. This arrangement can only allow the effects of a head sea to be tried in the tank and unfortunately leaves largely unexplored the effects of beam seas and following seas. The head sea is of great interest to show how well the planing boat will thump, but the following sea is of equal interest to show how it dives and, to slower boats, for broaching problems. There are in the world large and splendid tanks where radio controlled models can be manoeuvred in all directions at once in seas of all sizes, but their operational costs are such that for yachts it would generally be cheaper to build real boats.

The spray that rises from a model, especially when it is running in rough water, looks very unrealistic and often is so. The difference would seem to be in the lack of scale in the water droplets which make up spray. Those for the model are exactly the same size as for real ships and consequently the trajectories they pursue as they leave the model hull are likely to be different and not to scale. Also a very thin water slick usually rises up the hull surface from the spray root in the bow area and very often rides forward up the hull before breaking off as spray. This water slick also does not scale down for models and can mislead the viewer, especially for rather fat forefoot boats and for estimating the effects of spray rails.

Power boats it is true make bad smells. Their engines puff out more or less obnoxious fumes all the time they are in operation, and these have to be discharged into the air surrounding the boat. If the owner, guests and crew are to travel reasonably unpickled and unpolluted the position at which the discharge occurs is important. A model of the above water hull can be put into a wind tunnel to check this aspect of open air living.

The hull carries with it at all times an envelope

Fig. 151a, b, c Wind tunnel trials of exhaust outlets at the British Hovercraft Research establishment, showing the great improvement from quite a modest change in the height of the outlets. The third picture shows the funnels as built on the yacht.

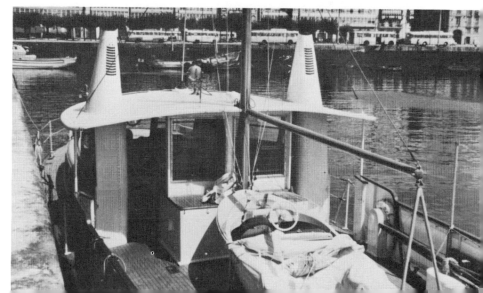

of confused air and the size of this envelope can even be calculated approximately depending on the relative wind speed. Any exhaust discharged into this disturbed air will recirculate all round the boat to some degree or other. The only safe place above water to make the discharge is by some kind of pipe sticking clear out of the disturbed air into the free blowing wind all round. The old-fashioned tall thin smokestack sticking straight up was ideal and although it was designed mainly to get a good draught running through the boilers the practical results and reasons are identical. In the wind tunnel it is easy to see that quite the most attractive solution to the exhaust problem is to send it up a reasonably high funnel. Inside the travelling air envelope transom exhaust outlets are probably best, for the passage of the boat tends to leave a good proportion of the fumes behind and only at slow speed do they tend to come on board badly and then the engines are only turning slowly. A strong following wind, however, reduces the relative speed and can make exhaust smoke tiresome. Side outlets are quite good in head and astern winds but half the smoke will be trying to come on board on whichever beam a side wind is blowing. Underwater exhaust is unfortunately not the complete answer either, for the smoke bubbles-up in the waves and wash to a degree. The amount of it is quite considerably less it is true but it tends to rise around the social areas of the deck and saloon and even up through hull skin fittings.

CHAPTER 8
The Problems of Arrangement

General

The arrangement of a yacht is based on the practical requirements of its owners for the life afloat as they see it, fitted into and around a styling and appearance which is largely fashionable. Whether the bow is upright or raking, or the funnel tall and thin or short and fat, in itself makes little difference to life afloat given that technically each is as good as the alternative. This of course is not quite true, for one of the most important requirements of a yacht is that the owner should be able to gaze upon her with pride and pleasure from the shore or from her tender. The whole has to have a harmonious grace, with whatever funnel is chosen finishing and complementing all the other parts. A yacht is a vessel for pleasure and this means the pleasure of her owner, so that if he or she cannot bear the sight of the vessel she is no yacht. The converse, however, strangely enough is allowed. If a yacht be sufficiently beautiful she can be as cantankerous and uncomfortable and unhandy as you can imagine but she will still find an owner prepared to love her, even if he does it through his telescope from the yacht club balcony. Here, however, we are talking of desperate cases, and the aim and object of any yacht design should be to produce a miracle of comfort and anticipation enshrined in striking beauty.

The fly in the yacht designer's ointment is the human frame. Yachts get bigger or smaller and

Fig. 152   A little bit of sitting headroom makes a difference even in a 12 footer – about the smallest size in which it is practicable.

Fig. 153 *Full headroom can be achieved in a 20 footer. In this Shetland 2 + 2 the extra headroom is concealed inside the bridge coamings.*

Fig. 154 *Each time you can add another full headroom layer of deckhouses to your yacht you gain another floor for your marine home. A magnificent Italian motor yacht built by C.R.N., Ancona.*

engines can have a wide range of powers and weights, but the physical dimensions of man distressingly stay the same within narrow limits. The occasional half-sized client or double-sized crew would make many of the arrangement problems disappear overnight. Children are a modest help in the matter and many a berth which has become inextricably and inexplicably smaller than it should be has been marked in as 'child's berth'. It is no use, however, trying to explain away inexcusable distances between handholds by saying, for instance, that you had giants in mind. Selective breeding might help but in the meantime we are stuck with a curiously inconvenient shape of occupant for our craft, an occupant who only folds very slightly for stowage and who bends only in a predetermined manner.

The most common requirement is for the animal to sit. This is a posture which can be disastrously uncomfortable through want of a little

care with the dimensions. It is worth noting that the sitting human requires more room for its legs the lower the seat becomes, and that it requires support for its back. Feet require quite a bit of space because they tend to fidget about; knees are fairly static; bottoms are really fixed; but shoulders require a great deal of room because of the way the body swings and because of the arms attached to them. Sitting headroom is important; in small yachts it might be the most important headroom factor in the accommodation because people can often get by without real discomfort if deprived of full headroom provided they can sit comfortably. This is because the human is usually already partly bent against the motion of the boat or because it is about to stand or sit or do something.

If the yacht is big enough to allow the owner to stride about his cabin then full headroom becomes of great importance and it is always

Fig. 155   The classic full headroom deckhouse of the workboat in this case placed as far aft as possible to leave maximum clear working deckspace.

Fig. 156 This American houseboat puts a very practical front porch over an elegant bow.

necessary to arrange enough headroom in any yacht for the pulling on of trousers. The two headroom standards can often be seen reflected in the apparent bulk of small motor yachts. The possibility of achieving the magic 'full headroom' by leaping the gap between 4 foot 6 inches and 6 foot makes yachts suddenly bulge 18 inches up into the air. The next leap upward comes when it suddenly becomes possible to jump a further 6 feet into the air and be a double decker.

The other great human requirement which has to be considered with care is sleep. Yacht owners can put up with surprisingly miserable quarters provided they can get their proper rest at nights or off watch. It is essential that the berth can be got into easily, that you do not fall out of it when the ship rolls and that your pillow does not fall out when the ship rolls. The berth has to be wide enough and long enough and the immediate surrounds free from sharp edged hazards. It should be possible to sit up in a berth sufficiently comfortably to drink the morning tea and to read the bedtime book. If there are any leaks in the decks they must not be over the owner's berth, and if there are any minor structural deficiencies they must not be in view from the owner's berth, for this is where the yacht is subject to the most intense and sometimes harsh scrutiny.

Tables have to be at a proper height and it must not be forgotten that they are sometimes used with fiddle rails. If these are just wrong in height the continual wrist movements can be very tiresome. Galley worktable heights and the right height dimensions for sinks, cookers and so on are well known from intensive ergonomic research by furniture manufacturers. One or two unexpected problems can arise in a yacht which may not have come the way of the researchers ashore. It is, for instance, essential to be able to get down and see into every locker, and drawers when pulled out for access must leave room for the legs of the operator. The swing of doors must leave room for the body to pass as well as work the handle, and hatches and companion ladders must allow the crew to depart without thumping their skulls.

The General Principles of Interior Layout

A yacht tends to pitch with its neutral point located on an axis between midships and a third of its length from aft. In this region there is the least motion in the yacht when she is pitching and tossing in a seaway. She will corkscrew and roll perhaps and thump according to her style but in all yachts there is one area of minimum motion. When a yacht is up to its antics in this manner there are usually and clearly several activities which take on a serious importance. The helmsman might be given a preference, or rather the bridge, as the brain of the vessel. The chart room is also important especially in pilotage waters and if the passage is a long one then the galley also has a claim. If the yacht normally carries guests who are sensitive to the motion then it would be a kindness to give them sheltered space just here, with perhaps also a toilet and a sleeping berth. In fact, by virtue of its weight and importance and the exigencies of propeller shafting, it is usual to find the engine in this favoured part. If the machinery is complicated and delicate then it has an overwhelming claim to the best part of the ship and the other departments should be grouped around roughly in order of their importance in the extreme conditions one hopes the yacht will not ever encounter.

The engine space is generally boxed off and sealed and lined to keep its smell and noise confined. Paths have to be plotted, however, for the engineer to visit them and for the removal of major lumps of machinery for replacement or repair. The exhausts also have to have a path plotted for them to the sea, a path which too often seems to snake down the length of the aft accommodation. Next we should look and see if the helmsman's position can be located close to one end or other of the engine space. Simple leads of controls, wires and pipes from bridge to engines are among the biggest blessings which one can give a craft.

When our human starts to walk about his craft, several critical levels occur where room is more desirable than others. The feet can accommodate without undue strain small differences of slope,

Fig. 157 The helmsman's space is important but not all are lucky enough to have as much room as this. Bridge on the 137 ft Romantica *designed by Fred Parker and built by Thornycrofts in 1968.*

Fig. 158 *The master bedroom in* Green Lady *has twin double beds. Her accommodation is furnished with standard furniture so that the whole scheme may easily be altered should her owner want a change of interior scene.*

Fig. 159 *In contrast to* Green Lady *the forward cabin in the 50 ft Al also sleeps two – but in the more traditional bunks – and the compartment can be divided off from the saloon with screens and doors.*

but they do not like to be cramped. Toe space when standing is important but the next critical zone does not occur until the hips come into view. Below the hips the legs of even the fattest person can work comfortably enough in a quite narrow space. The hips do not require a great deal more because it is apparently of little concern whether they have to be swung sideways to negotiate a gap. The barrel of chest with the broad span of shoulder above is, however, very critical of cramped quarters and at least two feet of width is required. The arms, too, should if possible have plenty of room to move about in. Space for the head needs to be greatest of all. The eyes need space to range in and they are, particularly at sea, more comfortable on a fairly long focus (and incidentally the comfort of the stomach ofen follows closely that of the eyes).

Sleeping quarters might come next in the general consideration for if the yacht is to make passages at night the berths should be as far as possible from the two major sources of noise and vibration — namely the engine room and the propellers. Perhaps it is a hangover from the sailing ship tradition which makes it common for the owner to find his quarters right aft over the propellers, although it might be due to a kindly host ensuring that his guests have the best. It is a common trick to use the galley and perhaps showers or toilet compartments as an extra insulation about the engine room.

In earlier times the galley of a yacht was almost invariably located in the forecastle and was presided over by a reasonably insignificant member of the crew. In fact, everything that the owner did not want to know about was pushed up into the crew quarters. In many cases it was even possible to search right through a ship for her engines and not find them until you tried the forecastle. Nowadays the galley is generally run either by the owner's wife or guest or by a chef of standing. For each the galley should be placed where the motion is not unreasonable, and it is necessary that the galley be a principal compartment placed high with a view of what is going on, or you will not get much cooking done.

In the owner's accommodation it is essential to see that each cabin has easy access to a shower and toilet. Preferably each cabin should have its own and it is embarrassing should it be necessary to tip your hat and say good evening to the company in the saloon every time you pass to the shower. Preferably, if there is space, there should be a particular toilet and shower compartment earmarked for, as it were, day time and day guest use. This should be within easy reach of saloon and deck so that it can also be used for showering after swimming.

Conditions for professional yacht crews have improved tremendously in the last few years and they, too, can now expect to have individual or double cabins, showers and some kind of private mess room. In some yachts, particularly in the Mediterranean, it is usual to place the crew cabin right aft so that he can act as a watchman when the yacht is moored stern on to the quay.

The Ergonomic Yachtsman

Ergonomics — The study of the performance of workers and of the external factors which influence output ... with a view to increasing ... well being and efficiency. *The Penguin Encyclopedia*.

One of the attractions of boating, it is sometimes said, is that personal performance and exercise are forced upon one. There is no setting out cold-bloodedly for exercise for its own sake as in jogging or squash. When action is required afloat its necessity is usually unarguable and immediate. When action is not required, the rhythmic movement of the boat or the absorption of the hull impact loadings is there to keep the muscles at work rather than let them relax into body fat. This gives a two layer system of personal movement to govern the ergonomics of life on the briny; 'well being' should be sought at every level for that is really what yachting is all about; 'efficiency' is only indisputably essential for a certain range of activities which are vital to the seamanship handling, including maintenance, of the vessel. For most yachtsmen and women life afloat has been deliberately chosen as a change from an increasingly efficient shore life. A bunk, to give an example, can be higher off the floor than a bed. This not only gains it more space but has the positive advantage of being consciously different from home. There is often a good case for allowing ergonomic inefficiencies to add to the character or ambience of the vessel, always providing they do not interfere with the basic serious business.

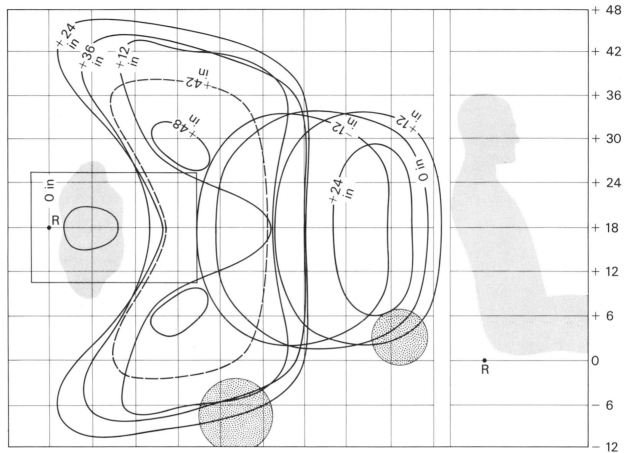

Fig. 160   The ergonomic envelope around a current standard Western sitting man in which arms and legs can operate in comfort. In other parts of the world and in other times this envelope will be different.

It is also worth noting how the wonders of the deep all around, in addition to the important nautical matters in hand, combine to mask quite serious ergonomic deficiencies. It is quite extraordinary how quickly the human computer gets used to and accepts the great majority of special and awkward movements which may be necessary in getting around a badly designed ship. It is therefore most important that the arrangements affecting the performance of the 'workers' — helmsman, engineer, navigator, cook and deckworkers — are correct from the very beginning. Three months after commissioning a whole battery of bad habits will otherwise be part of the yacht.

The Control Position

Except in big ships where helm orders are given to a coxswain often tucked away from the rough world outside, the helmsman is the controller of the operation of the ship. His problems, his need to assess, decide and take action, his responsibilities for craft and crew, will probably be greater than any others on board. Therefore it is important that he should have the best equipment for the job and that his control position should be properly laid out. Of course the problems of running a 4 knot canal boat have to be kept in proportion to those of, say, a high-speed coastguard cutter. The latter deserves a cockpit as carefully and expensively planned as that of an airliner, whereas the most elementary gear is ample for the former.

First and foremost the helmsman needs visibility, before in fact the helm itself. Preferably he should, without having to walk more than a step in any direction, be able to see the complete deck edge all round the yacht and forward to about one boat's length in front of the bow. This visibility, especially from forward to abeam each side,

Fig. 161 *The bridge of this Californian tuna clipper gives marvellous shade for work in a hot climate. The attractive shape and construction date back to the first steamships on the coast.*

Fig. 163 *Visibility — the fishing tower of a 32 ft fast sports fisherman.*

Fig. 162 *Seeing over the bows is a major consideration in motor boat driving at hump speed.*

Fig. 164 *High chairs for visibility — eminently practical solution to the problem of seeing over the cabin top in a Thames cruiser.*

Fig. 165 *The steering position of the 50 ft fishing vessel type yacht* Southern Flight *designed by Fred Parker for Neville Duke. This control position was specially laid out by her owner who as a world famous test pilot has a great deal of experience in the ergonomics of control.*

should not be obscured by any normal positions used by the others on board. Visibility in bad weather and in strong sunshine has also to be taken into account. For instance the further the windscreen gets from the eyeball the more opaque it becomes if there is rain or spray. An eye pressed close to the glass can see clearly between individual drops which without wipers present an impenetrable pattern at 3 feet. In the same way the cleared area given by a wiper becomes progressively less valuable the further away from the screen the helmsman is.

The controls: steering wheel, gear and speed and stop controls, should be well placed. The steering wheel must be at a comfortable height suitable for use for hours at a time. The engine controls need not be as comfortable to operate but must be arranged so that the steering wheel can be operated successfully at the same time. Gauges and switches should be clear in their marking and unmistakable. Grouping of gauges and switches can spoil what might be a handsome symmetry of installation but thereby becomes much easier to check. This last group should perhaps come under a heading of contact with the engines which is of the same level of importance as contact with the crew. An interior control position must have opening windows or a proved reliable public address system (with talkback). The actual manner of communication between helmsman and crew, especially when docking, can vary between a complete act from Wagner to auction room gestures, but communication there must be. An exterior position on the other hand needs some communication with the interior. The need is not so desperate since it is often possible to stop still in the water and nip below to shake the recalcitrant crew from their beds. In an emergency, however, the speed of contact between the helmsman and the rest might be critical.

The Deck Position

For the deck crew perhaps the most useful of all facilities is good safe access to the full perimeter of the vessel. There is nothing more potentially dangerous than the heroic style of seamanship, and nothing more calculated to provoke it than the sight of a rough bit of dockside about to impinge on an inaccessible and unguarded portion of shining topside. Many, many craft do get by with tiny side decks which have to be traversed one toe at a time but, even on flat river water disturbed only by the wash from passing swans, good all round deck space is worth buying a bigger boat for.

The proper amount and placing of handrails is the proper companion in importance to good deck space. The correct placing for these can readily be found by simulating a banana-skin slip — the handrail should be positioned exactly where your victim's hand first hits solid structure.

Liferails and stanchions, once frowned upon as 'not yachty', are nowadays to be found wherever there is a deck to be trod. Some are there to enhance the appearance of the little boat by disguising her scale. Unfortunately the presence of the crew tends to spoil such a picture and there is really no getting away from the basic safe heights. If the top rail or wire does not hit midthigh height or higher it might just as well be taken down to ankle height. Many craft with a proper set of liferails and stanchions around

the deck edge suffer from deckhouse coamings which are set too close to them. If the deckhouse does not itself have liferails then a proper catchment ditch must be arranged to catch the guest falling off the deckhouse. It is no use ever reckoning that any part of a yacht will not be walked on, especially if it is high up. It is also valueless to reflect that your fast departing guest should not have been up there.

Cleats, fairleads, winches, anchors and all the normal equipment of boat handling which has to be placed on the deck should, of course, be arranged with generous access and a generous dose of ergonomic consideration. The speed at which a warp can be made up or the efficiency of the pull which can be applied to the winch handle can each, for instance, have a big affect on the well being of the yacht in some critical circumstance.

The Maintenance Position

Other areas to be considered separately are those points of maintenance which have to be made as attractive as possible. These are on two levels: owner maintenance and yard maintenance. A few, but only a few, owners buy yachts for the pleasure of maintaining their machinery. Yachtsmen's minds are generally occupied with higher thoughts when afloat. Owners therefore have to be tactfully reminded of any necessary maintenance, usually by putting the items concerned either bang in their eye or where they will trip over them. After such a reminder the actual doing must be made obvious and easy, for it is tempting to be put off anything difficult or dirty when yachting. Yard maintenance, on the other hand, is normally done by a paid employee from a check list. The job will be done, but if it is easy and properly arranged it will be well done and the scene left clean.

The Roots of Comfort

Comfort on board a yacht, true comfort that is, comes from a deep feeling of security. The raging deep is all around us even if we are tied up tight to the dock at the shoreward end of the yacht harbour. Some people are secure enough within themselves, confident that no matter what emergency will leap upon them they will cope with it in a respectable manner. Others, however, require the constant reassurance of their eyes and senses that they are afloat in a well-found and eminently strong craft. No amount of statistics on the excessive strength of glass fibre, for instance, will really reassure the nervous guest who has just been woken by the sun shining through his yachting bedroom walls. No dissertations on the advantages of frameless construction will ever get over his or her fright at seeing the bottom of the wardrobe bending with the waves. A shipside lining and a wardrobe liner would in both these cases contribute more to real comfort than an extra electric blanket or hotwater bottle or icebox.

It is following the same line of thought to make all the fittings and furnishings and structure on which the eye can rest as it roves nervously about the vessel not only strong enough but seen to be so. A fairly simple top rail to a berthboard, for instance, can double or treble the apparent strength of the furniture while in fact allowing the actual construction to save weight. A slight increase in the scantlings of a door frame can have the same effect and leerails, bulkhead openings and handrails are all susceptible to the same treatment.

In larger yachts particularly it is possible to play games of double bluff. Here one deliberately makes the joinerwork and fittings of such delicacy and lightness that any nerve ups and says to itself at once that here must be security, because nobody would risk such workmanship if it were not. Such games must, however, be played with great boldness. Half-hearted fineness in a small craft just leaves a feeling of nonentity which rarely ever comforted anyone.

Security and comfort come from a host of little items which should be of themselves of such small importance as not to be noticed. Light switches for instance should be placed in obvious positions and door handles at familiar height. Even if the owner revels in the new sights, sensations and even dangers of yachting, there are ample major matters to master which are the more readily appreciated from a basic background of security.

All switches or circuit breakers should work in the same direction, and all seacocks and controls should have an indication of their function and normal position. Lavatories should have full working instructions (and be sound-proofed) in our ideal vessel. Give a thought, too, for the guest who grew a beard during a cruise. His skipper

thought that it was a gesture of freedom due to the bracing sea air but in truth that guest had plugged his electric shaver in on the first day and been too embarrassed to do it again. At the flick of the tiny switch in his hand there was a loud click and fizzle, a bang and rumble from the engine room, followed by the sound of mighty diesel engines working at a rate. When he switched off there was a fizzle, bang and rumble and they stopped. The astonished guest pictured an engineer sitting waiting for a signal from his plug to start cranking an engine up solely for his use and could never face doing it again.

In a large yacht the greatest single source of comfort and security comes from the professional crew. A first rate captain, first rate chef and first rate engineer, not necessarily putting them in order of importance, are luxuries almost beyond price. The whole of life on board the yacht, no matter how expensive and luxurious and automatic, depends upon the service from the crew. It is no surprise to find that in many yachts of new construction as much importance is given to designing the crew quarters as to the owner's accommodation.

Facilities

It is a simple and obvious requirement in a yacht designed to accommodate, say, six people, that the same six people should be provided with six

Fig. 166   Mediterranean living demands a different approach to the positioning of the galley and here the cooking/washing-up/storage/icebox corner opens to the cockpit. A variation of our 19 ft Mastiff design built by Cantiere Gino d'Este, Italy.

places to sleep. It is still a simple requirement, but often not quite so obvious, that the yacht has to provide facilities for all six throughout the other sixteen hours of the day. All six have to have facilities to wash, dress and some to shave, before breakfast, and all six will probably want to sit down to eat together. All six will want a saloon to lounge in together, perhaps with space for guests from other yachts. When the yacht gets under way all six will require space to sit or stand in comfort, and protection, probably because they like to keep together, close to the steering position. At the end of the day all six might want to take a shower before all six get into the yacht's tender to go ashore together for some fun. In fact when the occupants of the yacht go ashore it is often quite startling how they have come to identify themselves with their little maritime community. Cowes High Street during Cowes week is full of little bands of brothers wending their way to and fro with the host or captain striding in front like any Highland chieftain, followed by a fighting tail of guests or crew.

The same principle of room for all and all with room applies whether the yacht is designed for two or ten, but it is quite common to find that the yacht is designed for only four to be awake in and six to be asleep in. The pinch usually occurs

either at the dining table which is often too small, or in the wheelhouse which often only provides seats and shelter for too few. A shortage of washing facilities only amounts to a great deal of time lag in the life of the ship. Almost single handed this common shortage is responsible for the well-known marine saying:

'The speed of a crew of six is one-sixth the speed of a crew of one'

Some parts, of course, must be designed specifically to exclude a proportion of the yacht's complement. A galley which would allow all six to cook at once would simply not do, although the wise designer always tries to leave room for at least two and possibly three around the galley sink. A chart room should, for instance, only have room for the navigator to sit and practise his art in comfort, but should also provide some kind of gallery where the rest of the crew can crane to see the latest position and be briefed on the perils ahead. There is also a good case for making cabins only just big enough for their occupants — not only does it allow more cabins to be arranged inside the ship, always a popular point with owners, but the very smallness prevents the guests gathering in seditious groups for grumbling.

Fig. 167 Small yachts (this is the 22 ft Maclan) often combine sleeping and saloon accommodation in a dinette unit which converts to a double bed. Although everything is close to hand, with two bunks forward and the galley on the left, it does not seem cramped and being able easily to see out emphasises the effect of sufficient space.

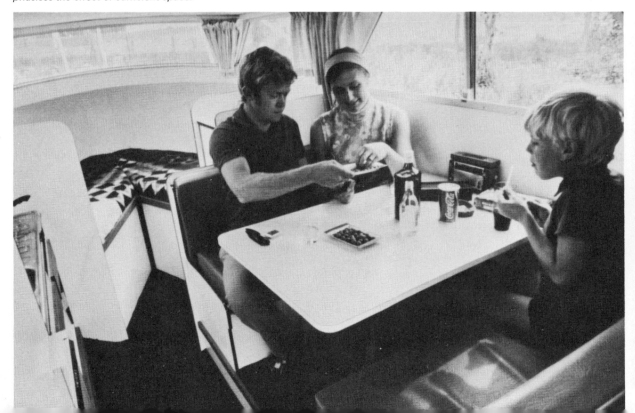

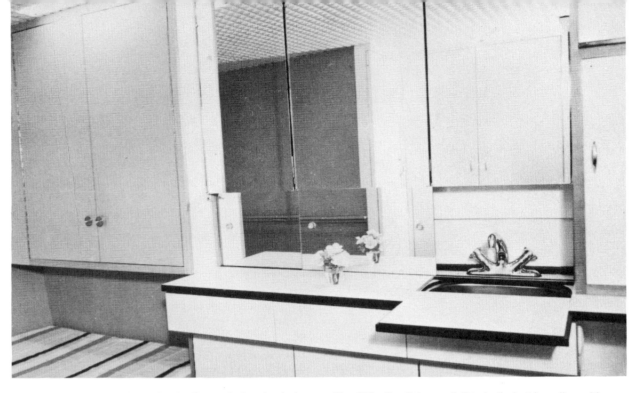

Fig. 168 Aft double cabin in Λl, the first yacht interior design by David Hicks, is elegantly simple with clever use of mirrors concealed lighting, ventilation, toilet units, and textured insulated deckhead.

Fig. 169 Small but well fitted all-electric galley with eye-level oven, separate hob unit, sink and louvred metal doors concealing cupboards and refrigerator.

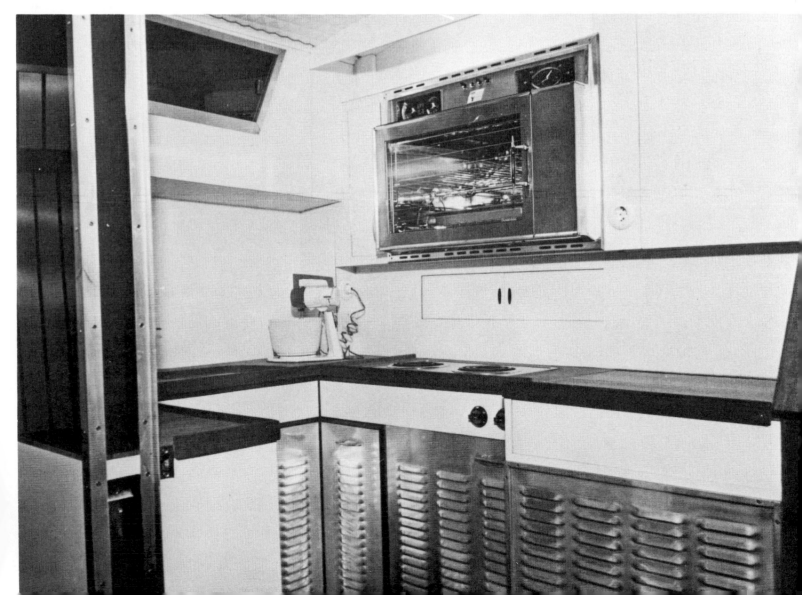

If the yacht is a sports fishing yacht then there must be room for the equipment required for each guest and for each fishing chair. If the yacht is a sunbather then there must be room for all six sets of mattresses or deck chairs, both when stowed and when in use.

If the yacht is a cocktail shaker then there must be room for twelve to sit and a cocktail bar for twenty-four. It might be possible to go on citing cases, but the number of people for whom a yacht is arranged cannot really be assessed by counting the beds – with one or two obvious exceptions, of course.

Fashions in the Design of Yachts

The desire not to be unfashionable rather than a desire to be fashionable rules the shapes and layouts of yachts. Yachtsmen are by tradition the most conservative of people, but even a cursory glance at old pictures of yachts will show a much greater difference of aspect and treatment than is accountable for by the march of science. The old-fashioned motor yacht could be, given skilful design, just as seaworthy, just as speedy and just as comfortable, sometimes more so, than the latest launching from many a modern yard. One might build a replica of an old-fashioned vessel in all the splendid improved modern materials and with all the splendid modern adjuncts and fittings, and such a yacht might well outpace, outcomfort and outseakeep anything you like but she would not by any means be a commercial success. The yacht would be unfashionable.

Fashion in this case and perhaps in many others would seem to be dictated by a need to demonstrate by exaggeration that one was not doing the wrong thing. In eighteenth century society where working was a misfortune confined to the lower orders, fashion dictated for the gentleman such elaborations of dress that even a visitor from another planet could see who was a worker and who was not. Now the tables have turned somewhat and it is the non-worker who is the social disaster with the non-creative worker

Fig. 170   The saloon of the 80 ft motor sailer yacht Green Lady *furnished with all the comforts of home.*

fast on his heels. The fashionable garb now indicates that here is a creative worker, and even evening dress has become suitable wear for dashing off a quick sculpture or even knocking out a set of yacht lines.

The same process can be seen with yachts. When there were thousands of small trading vessels scurrying around every coast the yacht had to be strikingly different, although treading the same waters. If you were to think for a month about a finish for a yacht hull which could not possibly let it be confused with a trading vessel, you could not do better than to suggest cemented white enamel. If tonnage regulations governing harbour dues were forcing workaday vessels to adopt blunt ends, why then your yacht must have a long tapering form which is quite unmistakably useless for carrying barrels. All seamen like to decorate their craft, and all yachts are but toys at heart and therefore to be brightly finished and lovingly embellished. A delightful convention has grown up that yachts are finished and kept up to a standard only equalled by drawing-room furniture even in face of the particularly destructive elements of sea and sun. Brasswork which has to be polished every day and woodwork which has to be washed over with drinking water from time to time are employed for their very prettiness; this is perhaps affection rather than fashion. But today when it is unfashionable ashore to be a butterfly it is clearly just as unfashionable afloat. Motor yachts of this decade often have a serious workaday air about them; there is not one which would not convert in an hour to suit a more serious purpose. When the royal yacht *Britannia* is advertised as being really a hospital ship at heart, can one be surprised that many smaller motor yachts have become miniature pilot boats and warships to the eye? The modern craft is entirely practical if you wish to practise seamanship and navigation and electronic position finding, and entirely practical for the working crew of guests to work her. She is often only impractical if your tastes run more to seaside sunbathing and dancing.

Decoration and Finish

A yacht, being a pleasure vessel and a toy, generally requires a slight exaggeration of decoration and finish. Very few yachts are lived on board for

Fig. 171 Traditional grace arrived at without effort in this Royal Toronto Yacht Club ferry boat.

more than a few weeks at a time and a scheme of finish which might be too garish or too dull for a house does not have time to pall. Holiday homes in general show this tendency and the yacht is the holiday home of all time. Yachtsmen do, of course, have as wildly differing ideas on what is the proper way to decorate the insides of their boats as they do on every other subject. One or two generalities however can be seen.

One must realise that the yacht is a self-contained box with ventilation only entering from the top. The yacht has to be kept clean, either by a paid crew at great expense or by her owners who think they are on holiday. In a house a lot of the dust and fluff is swept up at floor level. In a yacht it has to be gathered together and lifted out. In a house most of the furniture is portable and easily ported should anything get spilt but in a yacht spilt milk, for instance, can easily become cryable over. The decoration and finish therefore have above all things to be basically practical. Given that, it can then be as dashing and eye catching as you can stand or as atavistic and restful as you can bear.

First on the list should be non-slip cabin soles.

Fig. 172   The saloon of the Ocean 40 *illustrates another approach to interior design with traditional wood finishes and businesslike RT and navigational instruments in the corner.*

Fig. 173   *The saloon of* Southern Flight.

Fig. 174 The strictly practical non-decorative approach, but still seamanlike.

On one well-known large yacht if the owner's wife should happen to slip on the tiled bathroom floor while the door is open and the yacht rolling, then it is some 25 feet she will fly before landing in her bed. Even in smaller craft a slippery sole makes life on board impractical at sea. In some vessels the whole complement have to cling together in the wheelhouse on passage and only venture below when she is tied up to the dock.

We think that the best non-slip and most handsome cabin sole is teak planking with holly splines. The teak should be treated with a filler to reduce its absorbency of damp and spills. The next best thing is a really good carpet properly secured and stretched. If such a carpet has a foam rubber base the squash down when stood on forms its own tiny leerail, making for great stability.

The finish for furniture is a big subject full of different points of view, and the only observation which we would like to make is that rubbing and kicking surfaces are by far and away better varnish wood finished, that is, the skirtings and ladders and handholds and hatch entries and drawer and locker handles and corners of furniture and bulkheads. Varnish has an astonishing facility for remaining respectable in appearance. It polishes

as it wears and absorbs black marks while you watch.

Next in height order comes upholstery and the most popular upholstery coverings are without doubt either vinyl or similar plastics, or sailcloth. The vinyl on a knitted cloth base, sometimes with a thin sponge-rubber intermediate layer, has all the virtues except through ventilation, and sailcloth makes a better hot weather sitting or sleeping mattress cover. Leather can be treated these days to be almost as good as vinyl in terms of wear and waterproofness and is still without peer for real comfort.

Table tops without doubt are expected to be impervious these days to boiling water, alcohol and scratching. If any such disaster should occur, it is more likely that the host will apologise for his yacht rather than the guest for his clumsiness. Such a finish can be in the form of one of the applied decorative laminates or can be a surface formed on the table itself with any one of a range of super varnishes, polishes or paints. At one time only the galley working surface and the saloon table were expected to be so treated, but now it is only sense to treat all surfaces where a drink, cup of tea or kettle might be placed.

Rising even higher in the cabin we come to

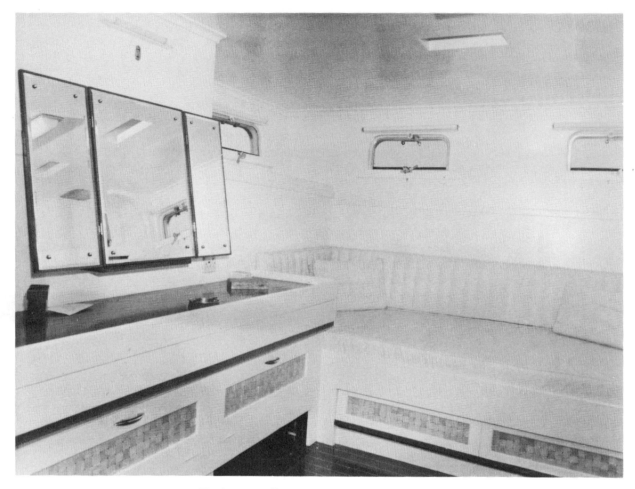

Fig. 175 A simple cabin arrangement. The inset panelling on the drawers and bunk lockers is woven Western red cedar — decorative, ventilating and rot resistant. The mirror conceals an emergency escape hatch. 62 ft motor yacht Giftie.

bulkheads and overheads. Here is great scope for the decorator who should only remember that most yachts are subject to some degree or other of condensation. This in a bad case can take the form of overheads covered with moisture drips which have to run off and somehow find their way, like a little river, right down to the bilges. In a good case the outward effect might be no more than a modest dampness which, however, can sometimes start the dreaded mildew going, perhaps in the ceiling material itself or even in the glue sticking on a vinyl wallcovering. Bulkhead and overhead coverings should also be, as far as possible, of a fire retardant type.

Ventilation into and around the accommodation is important and if ventilation can be worked into a scheme of decoration so much the better.

Many yachts use decorative grills for the panels of lockers and drawer faces and it is a pleasure to see the traditional louvred doors and panels coming back into favour. A yacht without proper ventilation is rarely sweet to live in after only a few months.

In northern climes we seem to like our colour schemes of decoration to be rather soft and overall to be fairly light in aspect. We use a great deal of white paint to brighten up the light which filters in through the windows from leaden skies. In warmer and more exotic parts the colours can be much brighter so as not to look too dull against the sun-illuminated colours of the landscape, but withal a relief for the eyes against the glare is sought by the use of generally darker colours. In one yacht we fitted yellow glass windows throughout and no matter what the weather the owner always woke up to sunshine. It was a great success although he always declared that the sight of a purple sky when he eventually opened the hatches almost drove him back into his bunk.

The Design of Detail

Detail design may be arbitrarily divided into the decorative and the practical although a yacht of its very nature infers the inextricable mingling of the two. However, there can be no doubt that the biggest pressure on the designer of, say, a hatch or skylight is the practical problem of the exclusion of water from its interior.

Hatches, skylights and companion doors represent nicely one of the many chess games which the designer plays with his twin and cunning opponents of wind and water. Another analogy, perhaps even closer, is to the design of medieval castles where the architect had to anticipate, with limited reserves, the most wily and scheming and relentless enemies. The same principles of preliminary reduction to manageable proportions and then brisk management apply.

There are four main approaches to the problem of making hatches and so on watertight when closed. The word watertight in this case does not, of course, refer to total immersion but to the normal heavy wind-blown spray and solid green water.

1. The simple crude approach is to attempt to forbid the entry of water by shutting everything up as tight as possible. This requires a precision-ground surface mating on a precision-ground surface over a gasket as in a cylinder head, or else the use of soft material such as rubber. It is possible to make a watertight hatch in this manner but it is a losing battle, for distortion or dirt will eventually separate the most properly mated surfaces.

2. The safest approach is to make what might pass for a reasonably watertight hatch and then to make provision, even extravagant provision, to channel away the water that will leak through it. This is the style of the double coaming hatch and is worth every centimetre of its extra size.

3. A variation which can be applied on its own, or preferably with double coaming, relies on the

'clever raindrop theory'. This takes into account the laws of probability and chance. If the joint to be made watertight has its two exterior surfaces making an acute angle up into the air then it will take an extremely clever raindrop to land on its point. Even then the weight of the drop will more likely overbalance it away from the actual joint and drain it away down the slope with its surface tension extracting whatever minute particle may have started through.

4. In these days power craft are bulging with power, and there is usually a great deal to spare for the comfort of the crew as well as for propulsion; a very worthwhile cause would be in making hatches weatherproof. A simple and uncomplicated hatch might have air under a slight pressure delivered into the area where the gutter might be. This would blow out of the cracks and effectively stop any wet getting in. The value of such an arrangement would be to make a hatch light and easily moved at sea. Some more permanent arrangement might be required when the yacht was left unattended. Yachtsmen, and indeed seamen in general, must be addicted to the salt drip and a bit of discomfort or else they might long ago have noticed the simple inflatable seal used to close the canopy of a fighter aircraft. There is many a dark night when such a device and even a bicycle pump to inflate it would make the difference between comfort and misery.

In the double coaming style of hatch care must be taken to get rid of the guttered water as fast as possible. If it is left to lie it will either percolate through the structure or be blown to the wrong place by the wind currents. Anyone who has stood in a modern city square knows how architectural design can summon up a whirlwind out of a summer zephyr. The same applies in the hatch gutters and many a baffling drip has been borne to the owner's pillow by the breeze.

The ventilation of a yacht generally operates from aft to forward as a counter eddy to its passage. This means that there is usually a good healthy draught roaring into a companion entrance placed in the rear cabin bulkhead. Every drop of spray therefore passing in the vicinity automatically gets sucked in. If the well-known principles of orifice design are used in reverse this inflow can be sensibly reduced. If the whole entrance is set aft out of the bulkhead to suit this, a reasonable bonus ensues in allowing gutters to be worked down each side to channel the deck-house water away from the door as the yacht rolls.

In general one might sum up the proper approach to the practical design as one of extreme pessimism. Water will come through waterproof joints, condensation will form on every surface, maintenance will be negligible, every construction material will behave abominably and the yacht will either lie millpond-still or be continually at sea in a ferment and milk will get spilt.

CHAPTER 9
Displacement Craft

General

Eventually in such a book as this there comes a time when the dark corridors of opinion ought to be illuminated by the sight of some actual boats, or at least discussion of some genuine floating cases. We would like to talk first about the slower end of the market. Displacement craft are in fact the endearing end of boating, likable either for good honest ways often displayed in a portly form, or for an air of antique élan rather like a horse-drawn gig with large canary coloured wheels.

Displacement craft cover the whole range of sizes. At the small end they can be too tiny to let loose afloat with high-powered machinery, and at the other end they may have to rest as displacement craft because there is just not enough power available to push them up on to the plane. In between, sheer economics may govern the choice, but more often than not the displacement motor boat is built entirely for the virtues of the type and not as an economy measure or as an inferior version of the planing type. The possibility of such a thought indeed may well appear ridiculous to most displacement boat owners who have long considered the planing craft as an inferior article.

Displacement craft have the whole history of mankind's boating behind them and have the whole of big ship technology at their disposal. The former inheritance is often a pity, as it quite drastically inhibits innovation and experiment. The latter, the craft skills and academic research for ships, might be thought appropriate since the speed ranges are comparable, but in fact is of little value. Big ship interests are in economies, in structures which are miserly with materials and in savings of half a knot of fuel oil over week-long voyages. Displacement boats are interested in seagoing among relatively big seas compared with ships, or concentrate on manoeuvrability, durability or perhaps the top end of performance. In a displacement boat it is usually easier, except at maximum speed, to put in a bigger engine to go faster than to refine hull form in the test tank. It is usually easier to increase the scantlings if there are any doubts as to strength rather than to employ a row of stressmen. In fact until quite recently it actually cost more to make a lighter craft, because it took more time in the selection of the wood and the careful workmanship required with the finer scantlings. Now, with machine-type construction there is an increased pressure on the displacement boat designer to reduce the material costs and enough money in production runs to cover the costs of the calculations.

There is no doubt that it is still respectable to travel around at displacement speeds and slightly pushy to run a planing boat. The proper speed at which a gentleman can be seen travelling rises year by year and now is more or less in the fifteen to twenty knot band, more or less independent of size. This pushes many craft into the semi-planing area, a most unfortunate region full of hazards and disappointments for boat owners. We will include them with the displacement group as it seems more polite to consider them as rather overpowered displacement vessels doing rather well for themselves than as planing boats which could not quite make it. As a type they are much favoured by government departments, harbour authorities, etc., possibly perforce with the equipment loads they are expected to hump around. As a result they carry with them a slightly official aura and an air of professional seamanship which masks effectively their awkward position on the speed/power curves.

Small Boats

Small boats battle in a big world. They must show a wide diversity of form to suit the different calls on their services and they have almost to caricature the characteristics of bigger craft. A river boat, for instance, has nothing to do with heavy seas and hogging and sagging from wave top to wave top. It is unlikely to plunge its bow into anything other than the wash of another river craft or into the occasional bore, but it does have a permanent river current to cope with. If it is to make its way upstream with any regularity it must have speed. All this points towards a long, thin, light craft with the old-fashioned electric canoe seeming a delightful example of this type. The true river boatman is as skilled in his craft as any salt-stained seaman, and therefore the problems of step-in stability which plague the unhandy afloat do not apply. The canoe form exploits the efficiency of a long waterline and fine ends, and combines them with the full prismatic form which extends the usable speed range further. For performance you cannot beat the power/weight ratio

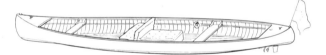

Fig. 176 The electric canoe, the perfect boat for up-river pleasure boating.

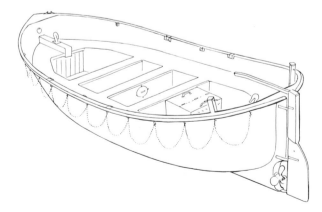

Fig. 177 Safety for no less than sixty-eight souls in open seas is built into the portly form of this 26 ft lifeboat.

and the river canoe is usually a masterpiece of the boatbuilder's art with tiny timbers composed into the lightest possible hull. Electric engines are unfortunately rare these days. Engine noise is reflected back from the river banks to discommode the occupants quite as much as anyone else, unlike open waters. The benefits of a super-quiet running motor are therefore a double blessing for the electric canoe, all wrapped up in a craft which was invariably beautiful and undoubtedly elegant.

Quite the opposite end of boating is shown in the worthy, portly form of the ship's motor lifeboat. These are all heavily controlled by regulations and therefore do not show any characteristics which might ever be thought of as revolutionary. On the other hand, the 26 footer we have shown with just over 9 feet of beam is required, again by regulation, to carry sixty-eight people in rough water and violent conditions. That is, it has to carry no less than six football teams plus a referee or two, or even a full symphony orchestra. Not only that, but it has to be able to carry them, bear them up as it were, should it be swamped, and it is even physically tested to 100 per cent overload. When not required these stout craft have to put up with years of near neglect parked on the sun-decks in weather conditions in which no yacht owner would care to see his pleasure craft. It is not surprising that so many of them turn up in their after lives converted into little family cabin cruisers.

This extraordinary and pleasing type of craft has in its business life to meet official speed requirements of 6 or 4 knots depending on the exact classification, but it is not really interested in speed as can be seen by the heavy, square sternpost immediately forward of the propeller. Its job is just to move its sixty-eight souls a safe distance from the disaster and then to bob around until the rescue team appears. The fuel capacity requirements are for 24 hours under power, say 100 or 150 miles according to type. This covers general marshalling and towing duties around the wreck and short trips into nearby harbours, but is not really a passage-making range in a 3000 mile ocean.

In between these two extreme examples of the small displacement power boat comes a wide range of seagoing launches of which possibly a substantial majority are used for fishing. For this a really good seaworthy little vessel is required

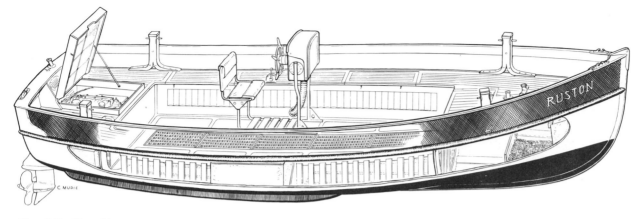

Fig. 178 This 20 ft launch follows the traditional West Country workboat style but with variations to make her more suitable for private pleasure use and for modern construction techniques.

because they work commonly among the fast tides, races and eddies which swirl among the rocks around the edges of the coast in all weathers. They work in fact commonly and normally in the difficult areas of the sea which bigger craft avoid like the plague. We have chosen as our favourite example of the type a little 20 footer which we designed a few years ago. She was built in the West Country and intended very much to follow the local style of craft both in basic shape and in appearance. However, she was also to be built and fitted out in what might be called Solent fashion, not because the domestic commercial brand was in any way inferior, but so that she would appeal more directly to the wealthy immigrants retiring to the west of England after a lifetime further east or north. It was also thought that the local alongshore fishermen already had their own sources of boat construction which were entirely to their satisfaction and that therefore we need not take too sidelong a look at their actual working requirements.

The little launch shows the modest (7 ft 3 in) beam and fine entry of the West Country type together with the gently rounded forefoot under a vertical stem often seen in craft which are hauled up beaches or generally accustomed to taking the ground in a scend of tide. She is intended for light loads in the manner of lobster potting, longlining and sea angling, but also for the occasional picnic. Her deck and well space are uncluttered and usable as far as it is possible, but she can be fitted with a collapsible spray hood forward to give some protection when driving to and from the fishing grounds. All these are fairly

typical. Our so-called improvements lay in the detail of the actual use. The diesel engine with the inboard/outboard drive was thought to be more practical for clearing lines from propellers in a boat which might be fishing solo, and the whole unit generally giving less wear in the typically drying-out harbour moorings. Overall the engine unit was thought to be more suitable for the relatively occasional use of the pleasure craft compared with the day-in-day-out usage of the commercial boat, while at the same time giving a modest improvement in performance to extend her range between tides. Such a boat very often does not get the day-to-day attention of the bread-and-butter boat and therefore we made her completely self-draining both at deck level and in the cockpit. In the same manner, all the lockers were fitted with gutters that would practically

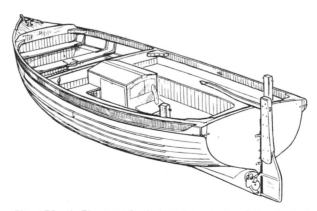

Fig. 179 A Thornycroft designed example of the typical small clincher-built yacht tender of about 15 ft fitted with an inboard engine.

guarantee better than normal watertightness and everything was done to make her as neglectable as any craft which lives in a marina. The fancy steering and control desk is movable so that the boat can be easily rearranged to suit her different occupations as the seasons roll by. Beyond that she had a laid teak deck for appearance and the now customary supply of stainless steel appurtenances.

It would not be right in this section to fail to mention the little launches which were built to be tenders to yachts and which often combined exquisite construction with the practical transport of owner and guests over the most perilous waters in the world — those between the yacht club steps and the yacht herself. To illustrate the type we have chosen a beautiful clincher-built launch which was exhibited at the 1955 London boat show. She was, if memory serves, about fifteen feet long and built by Keith Nelson to a

Fig. 180   This 18 ft GRP launch is the lineal descendant and direct modern equivalent of the 15 ft launch shown in Fig. 179.

Fig. 181   A hull form found to be ideal for its job is maintained in a modern construction. It needs a close look to realise that this traditional looking utility boat is in fact made of GRP.

Thornycroft design, and was one of the first of the now famous range of seagoing workboats which sprang from that partnership.

We were also rather taken with this photograph of the 24 feet 6 inches Bristol Utility boat which at first sight looks a splendid old boat but closer inspection reveals her as a GRP imitation. A third look, however, at the run of the lands and it appears that the moulds were taken off an existing hull. This is how things should be, for a really good boat shape can easily get lost when considered in terms of a five year production cycle rather than as an individual masterpiece.

The Accommodation Cruisers

The displacement hull form is the load carrier of the world but rarely nowadays are boats in, say, the 30 to 50 foot range called upon to lug cargo about except perhaps in the course of a fishing harvest. The size of the cargo carrier has gone onwards and upwards until it is now knocking the million ton mark and even the smallest cargo boats reckon on a few hundred tons at the very least. The knowledge of the full-bodied form in small sizes has largely been inherited by the displacement motor cruising yacht for purposes of accommodation and comfort. This is not to infer that the average motor yacht shows anything approaching the helmet shape of a Middle Ages Hanseatic trader. Far from it, as our first example shows, but it is worth remembering when looking at this style of motor cruiser that the payload is in fact living space for people. The Silver range of cruisers designed by James Bain

Fig. 182   A 36 ft twin screw cruiser built in the 1930s by James Silver to the design of James Bain with a speed of about 8 knots and a range of 250 miles.

and built by Silvers of Rosneath contains in our opinion classics of the type. We show a 36 foot twin screw yacht built nearly forty years ago and which, apart from her speed and chromium plate in place of stainless steel, could be launched today without comment. Her 8 knots still remains the proper economic speed for such a hull though now anything less than 10 or even 12 knots would seem a little slow. The range of about 250· miles is still about right; enough to cross the Channel and back with your guests without exposing them to the general unpleasantness of refuelling. The engines are just aft of amidships with the wheelhouse over, giving short and direct controls. The accommodation lies forward and aft, with the height of the topsides disguised by the paint scheme. The dinghy on passage will be carried on top of the aft coachroof leaving good visibility all round for the helmsman. The only complaint one might offer after all these years is that the accommodation is strictly indoors when under way. Perhaps the weather is getting warmer, but many of the later types of motor yacht have added a small aft cockpit as a kind of open air veranda to the owners' cabin — perhaps as compensation for living over the propellers.

This beautifully simple, uncomplicated and enjoyable kind of respectable marine caravan is becoming rare in new construction. The modern direct equivalent tends to run at 20 knots or more. The greater number of production motor cruisers with accommodation of family size are planing craft, where speed and power are able to replace a fair degree of the seamanship involved in running an 8 knot ship. Those to whom seamanship remains a pleasure for its own sake and not just a question of marine safety appear nowadays to prefer the aggressively seaworthy shape of the fishing or the pilot vessel and a whole range of such craft have been produced since the war.

It is difficult to pick and choose from them as they are on the whole a very attractive bunch of boats. We think, however, that the Francis Jones designed Inchcape type, which is a close relation to the genuine Scottish fishing vessel, illustrates the point well. The fishing vessel and the yacht, of course, only share the same rough sea and have little else in common. A fishing boat is built for heavy use and unconsidered knocks in the fishport as well as for carting a fair amount of gear to and from the fishing grounds. The fishing boat type yacht has a much lighter load to carry

and gets much more considerate treatment all round from her owner. If she were just built with fishing boat scantlings and displacement she would have to be trimmed up with ballast and have to make her way around like a fat man with two overcoats. The proper fishing boat yacht is designed around a somewhat similar appearance and takes in all the good points such as fish hold space for the accommodation and has stout rubbing strakes to deter wouldbe moorers alongside.

It is interesting that Francis Jones himself describes another type, of which *Ketos* is an example, as 'a very successful 45 footer on my favourite pilot boat lines'. *Ketos* has a speed of $9\frac{1}{2}$ knots compared with the $7\frac{1}{2}$ of the Inchcape type on the same overall length. The different

Fig. 183   The Francis Jones Inchcape design translates the seaworthiness of the fishing vessel type into yacht form.

Fig. 184   Ketos, a very successful Francis Jones 45 footer on pilot boat type hull lines and sporting a little steadying sail.

speeds in fact show up clearly in the placing of the stern waves in the illustrations. The pilot boat type in general is much more closely placed to the yacht than the fishing boat in terms of displacement, especially now that in the last ten years pilot boats themselves have improved so much.

Many of the fisherman types and even a few of the pilot boat types are to be seen sporting a little steadying sail. Basically this is to reduce rolling when the craft are stopped or near stopped when fishing or on pilot station, and the sail still has a noticeable steadying effect when a power yacht is steaming along at its cruising speed. It also gives the yacht a nice air of seamanship and adds a grain of comfort to the perennial worry of all those who put to sea with a single engine — engine failure. The logical extension is into the motor sailer and these have developed into the true successors of the cruising yachts, both sail and power, of yesteryear. *Tern III*, in fact, had an engine; Claude Worth's son had a relatively bigger one in his boat, and it seems to us more than likely that a *Tern XXXV* would be a proper motor sailer exuding, as most of them do nowadays, seamanship out of every pore. For a typical example one might consider the Rogger which would not be out of place in anybody's navy, pilot service or fishing fleet, despite her mast and sails and yacht accommodation.

Long and Fine

Laurent Giles is probably better remembered for his outstanding sailing craft designs than for his power yachts, but if he had never designed an ocean racer he would still have become famous for his beautiful motor yachts. He spent the Second World War with the Admiralty where he designed among other craft the ubiquitous MFV. In 1948 he designed the lovely *Woodpecker*, a 70 foot light displacement motor yacht, quite different in every particular from the heavy scantlinged fishing craft but still carrying the same air of elegant workmanlike simplicity. *Woodpecker* has a particularly lovely hull set off with deckworks which are extremely modest by today's standards. Below decks she is laid out, again slightly unusually, with simple accommodation consisting of a large double cabin for the owner and another double cabin in the eyes of the ship for

the guests. The saloon is quite small but just forward of the open bridge is a secondary saloon where the party can sit in comfort and see all round when making a passage in inclement weather. This is a yacht for the knowledgeable owner, as can be seen by the handsome quarters for the crew placed where the owner is often found — immediately over the propellers.

Woodpecker and her later sister *Freelander* are, however, even more interesting craft than their attraction to the eye would suggest. One of the biggest problems the modern boat designer has to cope with is the ever declining displacement as materials improve and scantlings reduce to keep pace with rising costs. *Woodpecker* is an example well ahead of her time in the art of designing a really seaworthy motor yacht with light displacement. At just under 25 tons she compares with the 40 or even 50 tons of contemporary fishing boat type yachts of about the same bulk.

Length without load is comparatively rare among all the pressures of modern boating. Yards are suspicious of length, which is the normal comparison of yacht size and costing. Yacht berths in marinas are graded by length and so, very often, is insurance. All the immediate factors combine to put a basic financial penalty on sheer length, although the improved efficiency of the hull could well pay it back over a few years in terms of fuel bills. Quite apart from the economics there is nothing quite like spare length to give a yacht an air of ease and even opulence. Yachting, for instance, has produced nothing quite so grand as the Camper & Nicholson launches of between the wars. No-one could doubt that here was aristocracy and breeding when one of them hove in sight. There were several variations but basically these were a class of 50 footers with only about 7 feet of beam. These toothpicks of boats did about 20 knots with a single 100 hp engine, but their real superiority in the world came from the lavish use of length with but a single cabin and cockpit for the gentry, a modest driving cockpit for the chauffeur and a long fine foredeck which in fact covered the engine.

Oddly enough the Chesapeake Bay fishing boats are comparatively close relations in hull style. Again the long, fine toothpick form is used for its ability to slice easily through the short high seas which are characteristic of shallow water. For fishing, however, the cabin and the wheelhouse get pushed fairly well up forward in order to leave clear space for a working deck aft. The Chesapeake Bay craft do not achieve the same snobby look about them, but the fine hull form with its sharp entry forward is again particularly attractive.

Some years ago we were commissioned to design a pair of sports fishing boats which might well be considered as somewhere about the upper crust of the fishing world. These were two

62 foot yachts for a pair of distinguished yachtsmen who were champion sports fishermen of the Bay of Biscay. The yachts were built in Spain with dimensions which verged towards the long fine form on which we are so keen. With their 62 feet they had only 14 feet 6 inches beam, relatively a little more than *Woodpecker* but still allowing a very easy hull for the rough waters of the Bay. Incidentally these two boats contain

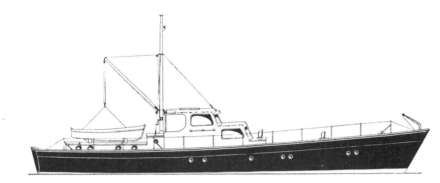

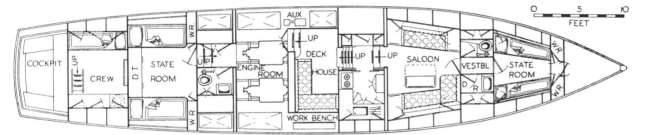

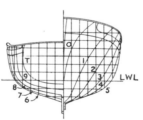

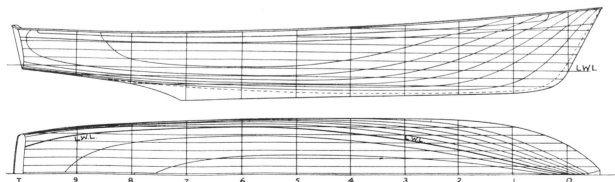

Fig. 185   Plans of the lovely Woodpecker of Poole, *designed by Laurent Giles in 1947.*

Fig. 186 *The sheer arrogance of the pre-war Nicholson yacht tender has never been matched.*

Fig. 187 *The slender hull form of the Chesapeake Bay fishing boat may be descended from the log canoe and is ideal for the short steep seas of sheltered and shallow waters.*

Fig. 188   Meche III, *one of a pair of sports fishing yachts for the Bay of Biscay.*

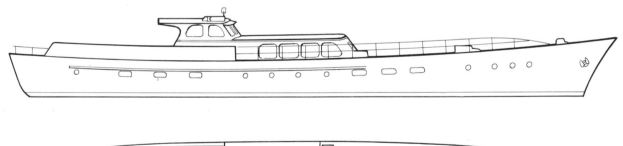

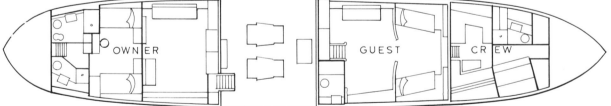

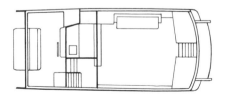

Fig. 189 Rodi's Island III, *a yacht built in the grand manner.*

some of the finest joinerwork we have ever seen.

Finally, when talking about the long thin fine yacht it is impossible to ignore *Rodi's Island III*, designed by de Vooght and built in Holland in 1960. Her proportions of about 18 feet 6 inches beam to 101 feet in overall length are not unusual for her size but she was built in the same grand manner as *Woodpecker*, with tiny deckworks for her length. The accommodation was also laid out grandly with but one suite for the owner and one for his guests, making a total complement for the craft of four plus two crew. This prodigal use of length, however, could not last and when she was sold into the Mediterranean her striking appearance was perforce changed to suit the more conventional requirements of hot weather living and an owner who cherished his friends in some numbers.

Specialised Craft

In a book especially directed to the many aspects of power yachting we may show a slightly unreasonable tendency to veer off into the more obscure kinds of workboats. It is not just that there are so many innately attractive craft to be found in the commercial end of the waterfront, but because the specialised vessel is often knocking on other boundaries of naval architecture. The genuine pleasure craft has a fairly circumscribed specification of requirements — load, range, speed and even appearance. The majority in fact even run to a kind of family resemblance. It is all too easy to accept the current range of power yachts as the only possible ones. A good look at a few commercial craft is educational and shows that in a great many areas in yacht design we are a great distance from the slippery slope where parameters start to get unsafe.

The commercial tugboat, for instance, carries a payload of power not pleasure, comfort is a factor only of commercial necessity and appearance a more or less happy accident. The vessel we have chosen to illustrate this department is a 71 foot steel tug designed by Derek Cove of Vancouver. First note that enormous, by yacht standards fantastic, propelling device under the stern. A con-

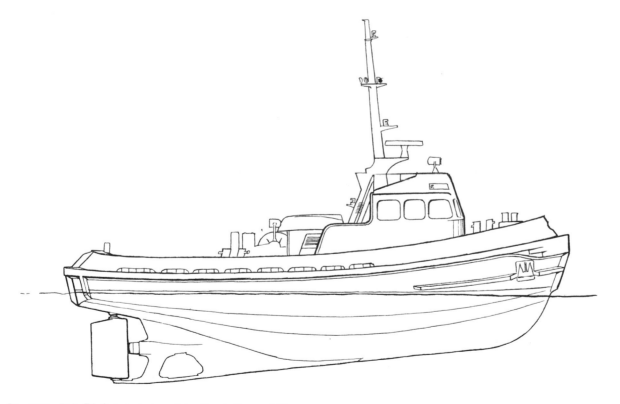

Fig. 190 This 71 ft tug designed by Derek Cove of Vancouver is the same size as many yachts but with a relatively enormous displacement and gigantic nozzle propulsion unit.

trollable pitch propeller surrounded by a steering nozzle nine feet in diameter is necessary for her daily work. The nozzle incidentally increases the propeller thrust in the situation where the craft is moving slowly itself but is required to maintain a high bollard pull. The nozzle itself is used in place of a rudder for steering and gives the extremely fine control of the direction of thrust required for towing. Next consider the engine, placed forward immediately under the semi-funnel with its 1440 bhp, enough to give a 70 foot yacht of normal displacement a speed of 30 or even 40 knots. The rest of the hull is effectively filled with tanks for 12,000 gallons of fuel, 8 tons of water ballast, two 30 kilowatt generating sets and a tiny toilet compartment and oilskin locker. The crew, who do not live on board, inhabit the modest wheel-house which is in effect half galley and half work-ing area where the destiny of leviathans may be decided. With such power pushing so much weight on so short an overall length the wave making will be very heavy when such a hull reaches its normal maximum speed. The wave making in fact will be so heavy that the sea will effectively be cleared from the centrebody. With

this prime stability area out of action the ends of the tug have to be kept full, particularly the stern, to leave her with adequate stability.

Some of the older motor yachts get pleasantly ribbed by the modern yachtsmen because they were planned with all the undesirable elements, crew, galley and engines, pushed right up into the bows as far as possible from the owners' quarters. We now know much better that engines go in amidships or even aft as a matter of course. We also know that the galley has to be on the upper deck or you will not get a chef — amateur or professional — and that the crew will only tolerate normal human living conditions. However, the 107 foot stern trawler, also designed by Derek Cove, gives a little food for thought in terms of layout. In this case all the crew and machinery are once again pushed right up forward, for pure commercial convenience of course, but in a kind of craft which values above everything else its seaworthiness. The whole of the forepeak of the hull from the funnel forward is engine space. The whole of the forecastle is crew accommodation, and the upper deck accommodates the wheel-house and the captain. The extreme forward posi-

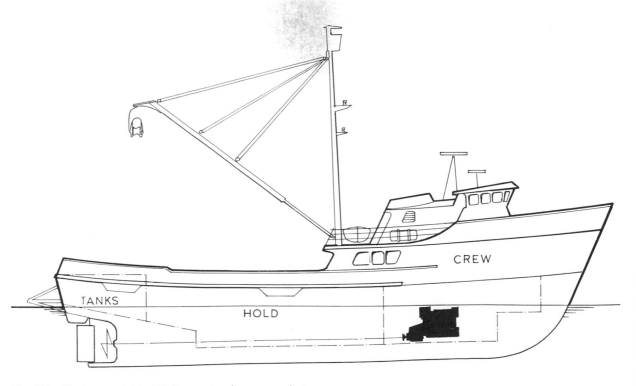

Fig. 191 The layout of this 107 ft stern trawler goes against many of the accepted precepts of yacht design without apparent effect on her seaworthiness.

Fig. 192 *This large and powerful vessel is a skiff for seine netting and is launched over the stern of her parent ship.*

Fig. 193 *Another of our favourite vessels, a Spanish steam tunnyman, now becoming a rarity.*

tion of the wheelhouse is interesting. In practical terms it is an excellent situation for it rides high and dry, forward of the main spray coming on board. The motion will be worse than the normal after position of most yachts but it cannot be too bad. If it actually affected the efficiency of the vessel at sea it would only last as long as it took to muster the gang with cutting equipment and welding torches. Another feature which strikes against many long-held views on seaworthiness in yachts is the siting of the fuel and water tanks at the transom to balance the engine weights. The centrebody is, of course, the hold area for the 300 tons or so of herring catch but when she is on her way to the fishing grounds the weights on board are well spread out in a manner which many yacht designers would declare heretical.

A ship like this stern trawler usually carries on board a skiff to tow the seine net round into the giant circle in which it operates. This skiff is another fascinating boat for anyone who might be given to thinking that clear water is essential for the operation of a propeller of any kind of efficiency. In order to avoid fouling the nets the seine skiff is fitted with giant fins underneath with

a large propeller and rudder tucked away in the middle. Incidentally, the skiff is kept on a kind of launching ramp over the stern of the mother ship — perhaps pointing an easier way of launching the yacht tender than all the fidget with davits and cranes.

Another of our favourite power boats is the North Spanish steam tunnyman. Or at least they were when they still used steam but now of course they are virtually all converted to diesel. Eminently seaworthy, for they work well out into the Bay of Biscay in all weather, the Spanish steam tunnyman is an elegant double ender with extremely fine waterline endings underneath high flaring bows and sterns which finish in an extremely sausage shaped deckline. Apart from the sheer beauty of the hull form they have a quite incredible capacity to move through the water without disturbing it. The fine waterline forward eases the waves apart without setting up much of a bow wave and the fine lines aft restore the parted waters together scarcely troubled by their excursion around what is after all a good commercial seagoing hull. It is a fashion in yachts at the present time to put up with heavy wave making at moderate speeds. In our crowded yacht

Fig. 194 *A 44 ft steel built RNLI lifeboat at 13 knots in rough going.*

harbours wave making is as anti-social as running a generator all night. It is tolerated because it is usual and thought to be necessary, but perhaps the hydrocarbon shortage will turn a spotlight on low-speed efficiency and we shall see yachts based on the steam tunnyman on all sides.

This section would not be complete without a reference to the RNLI type of lifeboat. Scarcely a commercial craft, it occupies a singular position in the world of boats. Lifeboats demonstrate the results of a single-minded approach to practical quality unequalled in any other field. For the amateur or professional crews engaged in lifesaving in rough water nothing is too good in terms of fittings and equipment and quite enormous care is taken over the quality of all parts of the hull, engines and equipment. The boats are very well looked after and show a distinctly brave face to the world with their traditional bright red, white and blue colouring and polished metalwork. Lifeboats built to these standards are properly expensive and this coupled with a conservative outlook kept many lifesaving craft rather at the back end of the advances in boat design over the last few decades. We have therefore chosen the 44 foot lifeboat class which originated with the United States Coast Guards and which was taken up by our own RNLI somewhere around 1964. These boats effectively marked a more open thinking on rescue craft and especially the introduction of a reasonably vital ingredient in rescue — speed. Older lifeboats no longer actually carried the traditional bow and stern buoyancy chambers but they all looked a bit as if they might. The 44 footers presented a reasonably normal profile to the world and still held full 180° self-righting. With their 40 foot waterline length a maximum speed of about 9 knots would be normal but these boats sported a chine aft and a flat afterbody and with about 400 bhp of diesel engines ran right up into the semi-planing range with speeds of 13 knots. Other points of interest include the high position given to the helmsman and the use of a foam plastics filled case on the wheelhouse roof as part of the self-righting buoyancy.

Multihulls

The multihull boat is something of a recurring phenomenon in boating. Every hundred years or so it seems to come winging down on the scene from some distant hill to be hailed by devotees as a seagoing revolution and generally the greatest thing since bootlaces were invented. For all we know the catamaran was probably the second boat to be invented, followed by the trimaran and then rafts. Certainly the early powerboat experimenters thought a lot of them, especially where the paddle wheels could be popped in between the hulls. The latest coming stems from the re-introduction of multihulled sailing craft in the fifties. For sailing craft the multihull offers a high power/weight ratio (giving performance) without the cost and inconvenience of a ballast keel and, compared with the single hull, great stability (giving gracious living). For power hulls the multihull configuration has a great deal to offer. First among these, of course, is the different kind of living where the principal accommodation is high and central and the deck space is phenomenal. Next comes the shape of the hulls which have, almost perforce, to be long and fine and particularly efficient at the difficult speed ranges, and this is often coupled with shallow draft.

In sailing craft there is some balance of costing against the ballast keel but generally speaking the multihull form cannot escape the basic fact of life that two hulls or three must cost more than one. Volume for volume, weight for weight, workmanship for workmanship, the sums are inexorable, the cheapest way to go to sea is in a single hull. Many an unfortunate boatbuilder has tried to buck this truism in recent years, leaving in the wake an erroneous background impression that the multihull represents the cheap end of boating. They have, in fact, more to offer in boating for their extra cost than the single hull and should properly be considered at the carriage end of the market.

The principal virtue of the multihull form for power boats lies in its usable stable deck area and this makes it invaluable wherever a working platform is required among the wonders of the deep. Fishermen, divers and marine archaeologists, for instance, make increasing use of the powered multihull, with the power yachtsman some way behind in exploiting the possibilities. The problem has partly been in the weight of accommodation which at deck level can often be clearly seen to be unreasonable if considered allocated hull by hull. Athwartships stability is taken care of by coupling up the hulls sideways

Fig. 195   The power workboat catamaran Currahntiki *just before launching, with the important semi-submersible forms just visible at the foot of the port bow.*

Fig. 196   Although this looks at first glance like a dock full of boats and at second glance like the 'don't put all your eggs in one basket' school of design, it does represent a logical answer to the problems of motor powered multihulls.

Fig. 197   Green Lady is not, strictly speaking, a trimaran but a twin tunnel hull.

but this does nothing for the pitching moment. Many multihulls suffer from quick pitching and the companion effect — heavy thumping in the tunnel. Heavy knuckles in the forebody are often used to reduce pitching, and nacelle-like protusions are used under the joining wings to muffle the slam. Both these are palliatives, more or less effective depending, for instance, on the actual conditions and the actual fore and aft metacentric height. A real answer which may transform power yachting is the work now going on with semi-submersible forms. The first application of this to multihulls that we know about is in a catamaran general service craft working out of Newhaven, called *Currahntiki*. Designed by J. H. Shillitoe, she has a more or less conventional form except for a kind of turbot-shaped swelling at the foot of each bow. Everything else about her seems to add up to a hard-riding craft. She is steel and stoutly built at that, and she is short and has a high superstructure with a heavy steel mast gantry over it. The semi-submersibles, however, are reported as carrying her extremely steadily through the worst conditions. The horizontal plane effect of the form is considerable when under way, in addition to the pure distribution of buoyancy, and we understand that considerable care is necessary to get the proportions right.

Now to lighter things, a quick look at another favourite vessel, the American catamaran *Ridgeley Warfield*. It is possible to offer ribald comments about her as a one-boat fleet but she does demonstrate another answer to the problems of multihulls in rough water. Here the two fine and elegant hulls forward of the deckhouse act much as stabilisers dipping and thrusting into seas well forward of the main body of the craft. Their buoyancy will already be steadying and lifting when the bridge deck is lining up for what would have been a good slam.

Two hulls mean that unless some special arrangements are made for the machinery this has to be spread between the hulls with consequently poor access and high cost. There is a great deal to be said for the triple hull form where a normal engine room and systems can be established in the relatively large centrebody with the wing hulls more or less devoted to stability and safety buoyancy. The only power yacht of this form with which we are familiar is *Green Lady*. Because the hull structure is continuous she is not strictly a trimaran or even perhaps a multihull — technically

Fig. 198 *The Giles designed 48 ft* Ravahine, *another beautiful powerboat hull, designed to operate at speeds up to 20 knots.*

Fig. 199 *A boat which would be recognised all over the world as a Peter Thornycroft design, this 34 footer was moulded by Tylers and finished by Keith Nelson.*

she is a twin tunnel hull but any passing fish would be hard put to it to see the difference. Her 80 feet are arranged with, practically speaking, all the accommodation in the deckhouse and all the machinery, systems, fuel and so on in the centre hull. One of her surprising abilities is her excellent steering. Despite the theory of steering it is impossible altogether to rid the mind of the feeling that a boat with no less than three long straight and parallel keels ought to be one which is 'not readily turned from her course'. In fact she turns in two or three boat's lengths with quite modest helm on. It may be that the pressure build-up at the tunnel entrances effectively moves the centre of lateral pressure forward so as actually to enhance the steering. *Green Lady*, we think, shows off admirably the prime virtues of the multihull power boat. The deck areas are vast by comparison with a single hulled yacht of similar length and the accommodation is all upstairs rather than down.

Semi-planing Yachts

As times and possibilities change, designers have to accustom themselves to operating in different performance areas. Now that light construction is almost obligatory due to material costs and the supply of high-powered engines outstrips in cost attractiveness the heavy traditional motors, yachts have got faster. One of the current skills of the yacht designer is in pushing respectable and comfortable craft to perform, generally very well, in the awkward range of performance — semi-planing. Here the yacht is running up to the hump in the resistance curve beyond which true planing occurs. For the designer it is an area of performance full of problems. Resistance, and therefore performance, can be heavily affected by a number of features which would have only a modest effect in other parts of the speed range. Trim is, as often as not, at a maximum and propeller blade loading can become a problem with the attendant tendency to cavitation and so on. A yacht designed to operate in this speed range has, however, enough endearing characteristics to make all the difficulties acceptable. One which is not designed for this range but just happens to perform there through overpowering a displacement hull or underpowering a planing hull may well, on the other hand, turn out to be a pure pain in the neck.

In semi-planing boats there is no doubt that we admire, as much as any other boat, the 48 foot day cruiser *Ravahine*, designed by Laurent Giles. She cruises at 17 knots and has a maximum of just over 20, placing her bang in the range. As a pure displacement boat she would run up to 10 knots and if she were a proper planing boat she would be seen at 24 knots or over. *Ravahine* is designed, slightly unusually, with a hard chine forward and a round bilge aft — a reversal of normal practice. She is, however, essentially a round bilge hull form with the forward chine acting purely as a spray shedder. *Ravahine* is another boat in the grand manner with a large cockpit area for fishing, a very large engine room for her twin Foden diesels and a forward cockpit leading to a modest forward cabin, toilet, etc. She is uncommonly similar to an admiral's barge in many ways and looks appropriately powerful and impressive when under way.

One of the great advantages of the semi-planing boat in its usual form is the ability to slow down comfortably in rough water. High speed when it is appropriate and comfortable is therefore added to the normal virtues of a good all round sea boat. Currently there is no better exponent of this art than Peter Thornycroft, whose commercial power boats built by Keith Nelson and others are recognised worldwide. These fine high-bowed craft are of round bilge form with a very tight turn to the after bilges and a flat afterbody. Examples of the type have entered in many powerboat races and without any remarkable top speeds to be competitive in flat water wait for the rough stuff to slow down the top-speed boys. The Thornycroft boats are essentially seamanlike and designed for efficient operation in the semi-planing band. They can be driven up to full planing speeds with, we imagine, some deterioration in efficiency compared with chine hulls, but always with that essential ingredient of the open water workboat of being able to operate in all conditions and at a wide range of speeds to suit those conditions. Such an authenticated hull form is in great demand for yacht use, especially for owners to whom seaworthiness is an attraction and seamanship a goal.

The semi-planing boat requires at once a fairly balanced hull form as do all seaworthy craft, a long waterline with as little beam as possible to let her normal displacement speed merge into something faster without too much of a shock, and at the same time a flat efficient afterbody to keep the stern from sucking down at speed. Our own favourite shape for the job is shown by the 30 foot cruiser *Favonia* which we designed a few years ago. She had to be built in plywood which serves to discipline the form into single curvature elements but also emphasises the characteristics. Here we first used a double chine form which we have subsequently developed for a wide range of yachts and workboats of all sizes. The lower chine effectively outlines the area of the bottom on which the planing system will start to build up when she is running fast, and the sharp chine edges to it both make the breakaway of the water more efficient and also limit the spread of skin friction. The upper chine serves to get away from the narrow bottom shape into a fuller form and brings the hull shape which the sea feels in rough water closer to the round bilge it seems to prefer.

Favonia is fitted with two Volvo Penta diesels with outdrives and has a speed of about 15 knots. These units were especially fitted to allow her to take the ground in Bembridge Harbour. To the

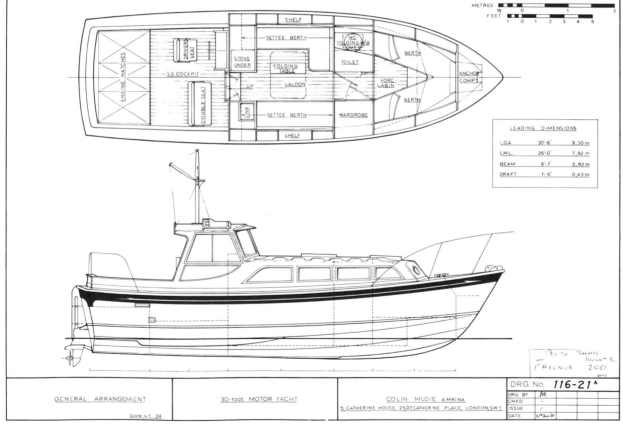

Fig. 200 The plans for Favonia, *a semi-planing 30 footer designed for a speed of 15 knots.*

same end she was fitted with a pair of vertical bilge keels at the aft end of the bottom, right out at the chines. In model testing they appeared to have an effect on trim and resistance and when we had a chance to try *Favonia* without them we were all poised for significant results. It is interesting that there was no measurable difference.

Large Yachts

Many a quite modest yacht looms a little large when the spring fitting-out bills turn up, but a large yacht is a distinct type of vessel in its own right. It is not just that it is more of the small ship rather than the large boat, but that it is run and operated as a ship. In what one might modestly call ordinary-sized yachts the owner is the executive captain of all he surveys. Professional crewmen in ordinary yachts vary extensively in

role but generally the command of the yacht and the responsibility lie fair and square with the owner. In a large yacht there is a professional captain in charge who takes his orders from the owner but who remains responsible in practice and in law in the same manner as does the captain of a million ton tanker for the actions of the vessel.

This basic difference casts a wholly different light on the scene. The yacht is now expressly arranged for the social pleasure of life afloat rather than as a vehicle for the owner to practise his own seamanship or to exercise his screwdriver and spannermanship among the mechanical parts. To many of us this would seem a loss rather than a gain when looked at in an abstract kind of way, but its attractions seem much more obvious when you are upside down in a heaving bilge changing filters.

The problem in selecting a few large yachts to

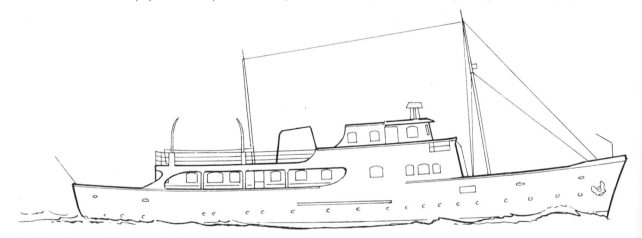

Fig. 201 Maureen Mhor *was designed by G. L. Watson and built by Yarrow's in 1961.*

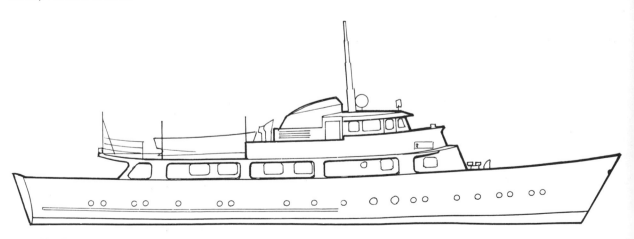

Fig. 202 The Giles designed Aetea.

illustrate their virtues is that each and every one is the result of a great deal of care and experience and is quite different from the next. We have chosen the 105 foot *Maureen Mhor* as our first example. She was designed by G. L. Watson and built by Yarrow's in 1961. *Maureen Mhor* exemplifies to us the virtues of the small ship type of yacht designed to cruise far and wide with great efficiency and reliability. Her home port is Inverness and she must have visited every port in the Western Isles as well as voyaging much further afield. You can almost guarantee that in any visit to a Scottish anchorage *Maureen Mhor* will appear for an overnight stop. You can certainly guarantee that you will see smart seamanship for she is run to a high standard. The really interesting thing is that she is the choice of a most experienced owner and the tool of an equally experienced crew which, coupled with her successful years in service, rate her more than a passing glance. Fashions come and go, and probably if she were to be built this year she would appear with a little more dash in her styling, but this should not stop the appreciation of just how well the little ship type works out in practice. *Maureen Mhor* is of almost classical proportions, with 21 foot of beam to her 97 foot waterline length, and her twin Gardner diesels each of 200 hp which give her a speed of the order of 12 knots.

Another yacht of almost similar dimensions, again showing what can be done with a small ship, is *Aetea*, designed by Laurent Giles and built in 1964. She is set off by a handsome funnel on top of what are really quite modest deckworks to make a balanced and powerful looking yacht. *Aetea* is unusual in that the accommodation is arranged for two families and is complete with playroom. The whole of the main deckhouse is used for saloons – main, dining and smoking. The galley, untypically, is relegated down into the hull quite well forward. *Aetea* is designed for a speed of 12 knots, again with Gardner engines. This is quite a modest and economical speed and does not really require the transom stern which is normally associated with the need to keep the aft end powerful in faster craft.

Next on our list is one such faster yacht. She is the 90 foot motor yacht *Valvanera III*, which we designed a few years ago for a Spanish owner. *Valvanera* has a speed of 20 knots and for this increase in speed over the two yachts mentioned above she needs two 800 hp Cummins diesels, four times the power. Twenty knots is well into the awkward speed range for such a craft and one where the issue between hard chine and round bilge form is not easy to resolve. Our solution is a compromise form but essentially *Valvanera* is one of the new generation of larger yachts whose antecedents, shape and other characteristics have come upwards rather than down, carried on

Fig. 203   Valvanera III, *designed for a speed of 20 knots.*

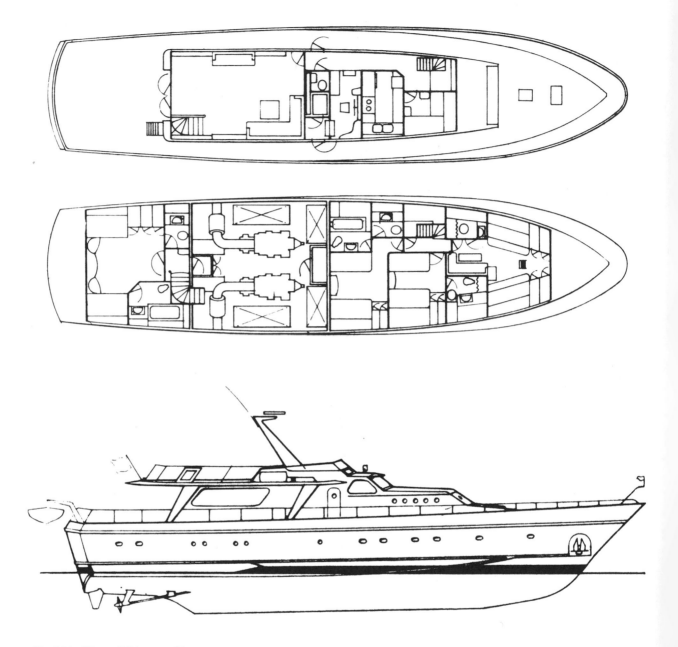

Fig. 204 Plans of Valvanera III.

a wave of high-powered lightweight diesel engines. Her range is comparatively short, 500 miles or so in place of the 1500 miles to be expected in the slower yachts. However, with her capacity to get over the ground a yacht like *Valvanera* can be operated differently, spending, if it is desired, every night in harbour while still making 200 or 300 miles a day if necessary. With the extensive insulation it is doubtful if her powerful engines are any more intrusive to life on board and her general operating speed sets up the beginnings of planing with its great blessing of reduced rolling. In general accommodation and comfort systems there is little to choose between the two types of yacht. Where the pinch begins to show is the positive interest in keeping weights on board to the minimum that goes with a yacht of performance. Such things as tenders and dinghies are generally much less lavish in a yacht like *Valvanera*. It is interesting also that in appearance *Valvanera* gets away without a funnel more easily than would a slower yacht.

CHAPTER 10
Planing Craft

General

It always seems a shame to divide boats up into planing and non-planing types. There is a certain feeling that it is somewhat derogatory to one group or the other and that in an ideal world the poor things should be able to get on with the work they were built for without stigma. Nevertheless the division at the present time at least is very real and not altogether to do with the performance of the various craft when mixed with water and fuel. The displacement craft stems largely from a moderate to low technology level. The boats are built and delivered to their owners who, by and large, have the knowledge and know-how to look after the structure and machinery themselves or to have them looked after to their orders. In terms of outside control by any registration authorities a satisfactory rate of inspection might for instance be annually. The planing boat, however, is or ought to be running at a higher technical level with very much reduced but more tightly controlled safety factors. At the very least she should be taken at the technological level of the modern motor car, with similar rates of inspection and maintenance. Only the reduced hazard levels really allow a good quality planing boat to get away with less rigorous levels of technical control than a light aeroplane. Perhaps we exaggerate, certainly many fast planing boats seem to get away with less maintenance than the dog in some boating families.

Planing boats come in all sizes, shapes and types — like other boats. Their shapes depend heavily on the duty they are built for and as much as with other boats can be downright unsuitable and even unsafe if used in the wrong context. A big feature in their form is the amount of power with which they are blessed. Marginally insufficient power and the boat will have to be long and thin to have any hope of reaching through semi-planing to a little bit of the promised land. Enough power to go planing but with nothing to spare condemns a boat to the short and fat form, while the real aristocrats of the performance world can spend some of the top speed potential on comfort in rough water with hull forms of great elegance and not all that dissimilar to the front end of a whaleboat, the classical ideal of the seaman.

Planing boat hull forms are highly developed over an extraordinarily limited range of shape. Thousands of forms of very much the same shape have been tested high and low in the test tanks and the subsequent craft have had their performances minutely scrutinised on trials over the measured distance. The amount of actual development testing is minimal almost to the point of disgrace. Yachtsmen, some perhaps more than others, retain some feeling for the romantic mysteries of life and believe that there is magic to be had for the finding, and that undiscovered genius lurks in the attic somewhere ready to produce the necessary breakthrough. Not for them the cold comfort of research and development, and certainly not with their carefully saved spending money. The established builders are therefore too busy building them conventional and tried craft. This leaves research and development to the designers with their spare time and own pockets, and to individuals with particular interests. Both the hydrofoil and the hovercraft for instance are essentially in the boating business on the technology of another industry. Both types have a great deal to offer, but they appear from a background of research and development costs which leave the boating industry not only green with envy but distinctly uneasy. It is not possible to be certain that the hydrofoils and hovercraft are by any means the right way ahead for fast boats. We have a modest feeling that the planing boat, researched and developed to the same extent, might also be hailed as the latest modern miracle.

The range of sizes for planing boats is still expanding and in both directions. Planing boats are getting smaller, probably spanning the size gulf which always existed between the water ski and the runabout. The supply of ever more powerful lightweight engines allows bigger boats to take off every day. Planing boats are also spreading. Once they were mostly pleasure, racing or military craft. Now fishermen see the virtue of speed in terms of money, and like to spend as little unproductive time as possible commuting to and from their fishing grounds. They can also see the commercial sense in being able to change to another fishing ground in a hurry when the weather starts to break. Hospital craft, fire boats, crew boats, ferries — it is extraordinary how speed in itself is necessary and valuable to our ordinary everyday lives.

The ability to plane, however, is not a universal specific for all aspects of life afloat. In 1947 Mr J. W. Thornycroft, a member of the great fast boat designing family, was moved to comment in *RINA Transactions*:

> 'Between 1934 and 1938, owing to the great showmanship and extensive publicity on the part of a firm, newcomers to the small boat-building industry, officials and responsible naval officers were mesmerised into being persuaded that a "V" bottom of hard chine type of hull was something new (in fact a new invention) which made obsolescent all former designs of round bilge hulls. It was even suggested that destroyers, cruisers and the *Queen Mary* should adopt a "V" bottom hard chine form and be driven on the surface of the water rather than through it.'

Nowadays one can still see the same mesmerism at work and it is not so long since the deep vee hull was hailed as the answer to all problems, and it is possible now to see another such panacea, the spray rail, strapped round the most unlikely hulls to the probable detriment of their qualities.

Small Planing Craft

The only criterion for the size of planing surfaces themselves is whether they will carry the required loads. Indeed, quite portly gentlemen have been seen planing on the balls of their feet in skilful displays of the water skier's art. It is even quite likely that some high-powered outboard engines could steam along happily on their cavitation plates without benefit of boat at all if they could be set off fast enough. In fact the limiting factor when considering the smallness of boats is stability, a factor brought into prominence by the relatively undue size of the human frame when used with small boats. The average fairly chunky planing form compares reasonably with the average round bilged boat as far as stability at rest is concerned, and when under way in straight lines the planing action builds up the stability even further. The danger point is in turning, when the centrifugal forces on the crew sitting relatively high have to be balanced by a nicely gauged banking action.

Our smallest planing boat is a 10 footer we designed some years ago for a sporting Irish client. She was very much a bluff-bowed dinghy above water but with quite a modern vee form underneath set off with two heavy vertical chine rubbers which served both as bilge keels and as fences for the planing surface. For interest we did a full polar static stability analysis of the little boat and found on paper what we suppose everybody knows from practice — that the danger areas in dinghy stability are the transom corners. All our dinghy designs since have these raised as high as we can make them and we are certain that we have reduced the inundation rate accordingly.

With its enormous beam of five feet, the little 10 footer proved to be a very pleasant boat and it turned in a speed of 25 mph with an 18 hp outboard engine. It is also an excellent boat for practising slaloms through the deserted moorings on a sunny winter morning. We have always thought that a simple boat like this would provide inexpensive but interesting racing comparable to club racing of sailing dinghies. Offshore powerboat races in their present style are comparable to international events for sailing boats, and none the worse for that except that the background of local evening and weekend racing that the sailing-boat man gets is almost entirely missing in power boats. There is no reason why powerboat racing, in comparatively open water, should not be as simple and as popular as dinghy sailing. A single committee boat would do, with the races taking up circular courses round it. Races might last, say, twenty minutes and there might be six of them in one session. This difference from sailing boat practice would mean that any minor mishap, possibly mechanical, would not ruin an evening's endeavour or a season's points.

We once designed a small inexpensive race boat suitable for amateur construction with this kind of racing also in mind. The prototype came out with an inboard/outboard installation, which was a pity for it took away the basic idea of inex-

Fig. 205 Our 10 ft general purpose dinghy designed for planing performance with outboards of up to 20 hp.

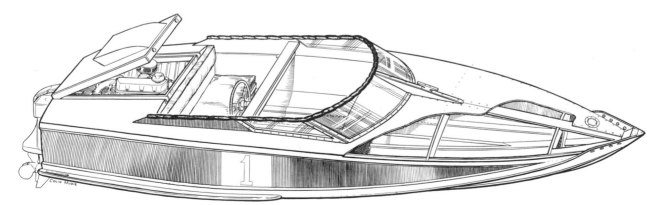

Fig. 206 Prototype of a small inexpensive power boat intended for club racing.

Fig. 207 Hi-Foil — Peter Nott demonstrates the little hydro-foil he designed.

Fig. 208 The arrangement of planing foils on the Hi-Foil.

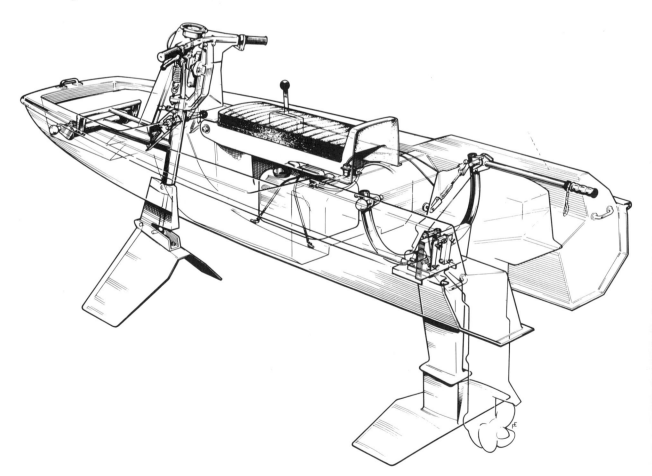

pensive racing with low horsepower outboard engines. We have always slightly regretted not following up this kind of boat but it takes a great deal of campaigning to change the face of racing.

Another of our favourite very small boats is the tiny hydrofoil designed by Peter Nott and called the *Hi-Foil*. Less than 9 feet in length, she is the nearest thing to a bicycle that we have ever driven over water. The little boat is powered by an outboard engine and rides at speeds of 30 mph on a simple and elegant foil system. There is just enough skill required to drive her up on to the foils and keep her there to make life really interesting and boastful. If you do not get it right she just plops down on to a conventional planing hull all ready to be coaxed up again. The whole standard of skill is carefully gauged to make hi-foiling an extremely addictive activity. Unfortunately, however, foils are expensive, cumbersome and to a degree vulnerable; they are also alarming if you are driving among bathers.

Little fast boats are essentially fun boats and will not normally be used for tough seafaring. Their venue is along the pleasure beaches and among the unskilled holidaymakers, which means that the future would seem to be with the waterjets. Sand is the perennial problem, but the attractions of driving among bathers and off and on beaches without worrying about propellers and rudders seem to be overwhelmingly in favour of the waterjet-driven scooter boat.

The Rectangular Boat

The very first planing form patented in 1872 by the Reverend Ramus (a Sussex clergyman interested in speed at sea) was a rectangular two stepped, almost flat-bottomed, hull, and it is likely that in terms of pure planing efficiency there has not been much real improvement. The Reverend Ramus's model made the point simply and clearly that there was no virtue in a sharp bow in plan view if you were not intending to cut the waves with it. The rectangular form is essentially a planing shape, if we ignore such things as rafts which are also able to get away without clipping the waters.

The first of the modern-style rectangular boats was probably the Hickman sea sledge, which was more or less a normal boat form split down the centre and reversed. The exterior faces of the hull

were practically vertical plates and the hull between a sort of tapered tunnel which swallowed the bow wave and rode on it; in general it seems to have been very successful. Unfortunately so was the patent which protected it and development was almost stopped. There was a flurry of sea sledge activity when the form came out of patent a few years ago, but by then it had been practically superseded by the Boston Whaler type designed by Ray Hunt.

The Boston Whaler has been one of the most successful innovations in power boats this century, only equalled by the same designer's work on the deep vee form. In the Whaler hull the basic rectangular boat was sophisticated with a central bow and two minor bows at the edges which finished in small steps. The success of the form was both in an attractive shape and in good performance. The stability at rest was outstanding, making for a very useful everyday boat for anything from fishing to ferries. The performance under way at speed was good and the hull form showed a capability for smooth running over any height of wave which could be massacred inside the tunnel area. From the Boston Whaler sprang a worldwide plethora of copies and minor

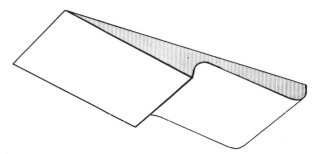

Fig. 209 The Reverend Charles Ramus's original planing form.

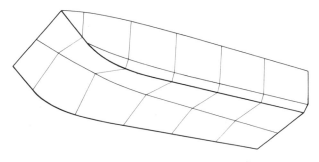

Fig. 210 The Hickman Sea Sledge inverted hull form.

Fig. 211 *One of the most successful innovative powerboat forms of this century.*

Fig. 212 *Rotork 12 metre Sea Truck in use as a workboat in Singapore with twin 188 hp inboard petrol engines and a speed of over 30 knots. It can carry 5 tons.*

innovations leaving the whole concept of the rectangular boat with a new reputation for seaworthiness and general performance.

The most rectangular boat must be Jeremy Fry's Sea Truck. This comes in 8 and 12 metre sizes in the form of a small landing craft normally fitted with a let-down bow which serves as an entry ramp off the beach. The hull form is very much along the style of an enormous water ski — dead flat with a turned-up nose — but sophisticated with a scheme of bottom runners which at speed trap air to reduce skin friction. Nothing could be simpler and more efficient and the Sea Trucks plane around carrying loads which would be instant death to the performance of, say, deep vee hulls. The flat form would not be acceptable in a very small boat because of the instability at rest and on turning. The Sea Truck is big enough to reduce these problems right out of sight.

The main feature in the degree of different hull forms to be seen in the rectangular boats is probably related to the sea duty required of them.

The hungry hollow bow is an excellent form for any wave height it can actually swallow (as a rough guide) but begins to feel it in bigger seas. The advantages, however, both of the rafting stability and usable deck space would seem to be as attractive for fishing as anything else. We once designed a 27 foot fast fishing boat in GRP foam sandwich construction. The basic hull was heavily armoured in wood not only to take the knocks of a rough commercial life but also to bring her appearance into line. It was thought that a bold sheer would also help to get her accepted among a conservative industry and we like to think that the boat finished up looking as if she would not be out of place in any fishing harbour. All this partly concealed a basically rectangular hull of so-called cathedral form. She differed from the runabout versions of this form in the care we took with the buoyancy distribution both athwartships and fore and aft to make her motion comfortable in a seaway when stopped and when running fast. This gave her an

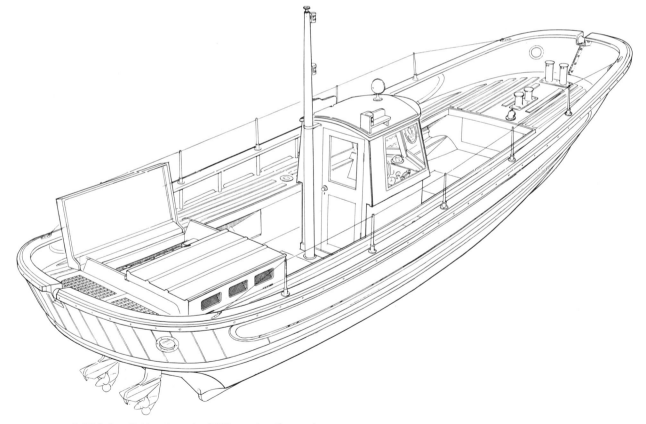

Fig. 213 A 27 ft fast fishing boat for GRP construction and Mediterranean use.

especially deep and gothic form of cathedral. Another point which may be of interest is that she was fitted with twin inboard/outboard engines. These were thought desirable both for performance and for quick access to the propellers to clear fouled lines, etc. However, there were at the time and place doubts about the regularity of servicing and the quality of on-board maintenance. The engines were therefore arranged to be podded in unit form so that they could be removed and replaced in minutes. This meant that fishing would not be held up for engine trouble and also that the machinery would be maintained in a proper workshop ashore.

Another rectangular planing boat is the catamaran form but this is almost exclusively used for raceboats and we would prefer to discuss it under that banner.

Planing Cruisers

The planing cruising boat is the staple product of the modern boatbuilding industry, covering some 70 per cent of all craft built. There are so many of them about that you can hardly see them. If you actually look for them you may be surprised how many can be found in any harbour and even more surprised how many of them there are up the creeks and along the canals. On any nice day there are dozens of them carrying family parties across the water but without the impact on the eye that the sails of even a dinghy make in the sun.

By and large they are excellent boats. It is possible to complain about the engine installations in some and the size of the cleats or navigation lights in another, and so on, but all told they represent a really healthy breed of pleasure craft. They are not generally the property of dyed-in-the-wool seamanship fanatics with bad cases of sodium chloride addiction. Such gentlemen are often fairly noisy and even forthright in their opinions of 'gin palaces' and 'motor boxes' as they prepare to put to sea with all their prejudices showing. They fail to realise that the planing cruiser was not ever intended for their kind of boating or their kind of seamanship. The planing cruiser is built for a wider range of marine pleasures and very much intended to take the relatively unskilled boat owners around in as much safety and comfort as possible. Such an owner rarely puts to sea in bad weather, but the majority of boats are in fact good sea boats if caught out in it. The interiors and cockpits are arranged with a heavy emphasis on life on board at anchor and in the marina rather than when passage making. This, too, is a different approach but justified by speed. Very few have occasion, with planing speeds, to spend more than a few hours at sea in a day and, truth to tell, offshore passage making out of sight of land in a fast boat is rarely a pleasure. The longest three hours we know are those between Cowes and Cherbourg (about 70 miles) or from the east end of Cape Cod canal to a welcoming port on the Maine coast. Night passages are rare and therefore the full seagoing sleeping equipment of leeguards and so on is not required. In a planing boat which can choose to travel by day only an idiot would prefer to run at high speed at night where any debris in the water would be impossible to see. Speed is not only a sensible part of seamanship it is to a certain extent a satisfactory substitute for some of it.

There are so many planing cruisers to choose from that we thought we would be invidious and so chose one of our own first. This is the Shetland 536, which as its name implies is 5·36 metres in length, or about 17 feet 7 inches, and which we designed for Shetland Boats to replace an earlier model on which they had built their fortunes. Our terms of reference outlined in detail the interesting and desirable characteristics of a small planing cruiser for mass production and for mass purchasing. First it had to be extremely flexible in the amount of outboard power that could safely be fastened on the transom — anything, in fact, from a single tiny outboard which would not exceed the four knot limit on canal cruising to twin giants which would take her around at show-off speed and pull water skiers up with ease. Next she had to be stable when stood on. Many of her owners would be first-time buyers with first-time boating families who might be discouraged from buying if the boat gave heavily under their feet when first they stepped on board. She had, of course, to be comfortable when running in rough water and interestingly enough she had to be quiet; the noise of the sea on the hull can be as alarming at times as the movement itself. Space in the cabin had to be ample for what was possible — sitting, sleeping and so on — without straining for what was not really possible like full headroom. She had to be self-buoyant if ever swamped, not because it was anticipated she would be but because it was a reasonable safety factor and a good sales point. Last but not least the 536 had to be arranged to suit quite rigorous production requirements.

Her gullwing type hull does a great deal for the seafaring qualities required and also allowed us to reverse the true working chine curve up forward to keep it as close to the waterline as possible. This is where the spray is shed. The surface slick starts at the spray root and slides up the bow, very often actually travelling forward. The combined forward direction and accelerated (doubled) velocity means that it will feather off a rising chine at the bow to make a wet running boat. The obvious cure is to stop the chine rising and keep it as close to the horizontal as possible.

Other boats of our design where we put a great deal of work into the chine area of the hull include the Maclan 22 and its sister the Maclan 25. These are fast cruising boats nicely fitted out inside, and powered with single or twin outdrive engines giving speeds between 22 and 30 knots. In order to encompass the required accommodation the upper parts of the hull had to be fairly full in form and our problem was to relate this with a good soft running bottom without losing too much in the deepness of the vee. We were also concerned that this would be used quite often as an open water boat and that therefore good sea kindly running would be required at all speeds. The solution took the form of a double chine in the shape of a scallop where the normal chine would be. This reduces the impact beam of the bottom and takes the corner out of the sectional displacement curves. The upper chine enters the water close to the transom so that a quick increase in well swung-out buoyancy is available to reduce rolling when loads step on board at the dock.

Ray Hunt's basic type hull with its constant section deep vee form was instantly accepted when it first appeared and has since passed not only into legend but into the stock-in-trade of a great many builders and designers. The purest line of descent lies probably with the Bertram Boat Company of Miami (Dick Bertram himself and his famous racing Moppies figuring somewhere

Fig. 214   One of a range of modern GRP production boats, this unsinkable Shetland 536 is filled up to deck level with discrete celled polyurethane foam — for safety, insulation and sound absorption.

Fig. 215 Bertram 31 Express cruiser.

Fig. 216 Huntsman 31 — twin cabin version with centre cockpit. Designed by Alan Burnard and developed from the Fairey Huntsman 28 and Swordsman 33.

in the form book, of course). From a range of boats, we have selected the 31 foot Express cruiser as the Bertram boat which seems most representative. It is interesting to compare her with the Fairey 31 foot Huntsman designed by Alan Burnard and which shows a true European development of the theme. Both are rough water bred and both spring from stables with a great deal of racing experience. The Bertrams pop across to the Bahamas and the Gulf Stream and the Faireys work the rough waters around the British coast and across the Channel. The Bertram is in every way a bigger boat with an enormous beam of over 11 feet and generally a more upright and worthy appearance. The Huntsman has only 9 feet 8 inches beam and a fine bow and sleek profile. The comparison of accommodation may not be fair but, where the Bertram is a two and

occasional four sleeper, the Huntsman 31 has found a market for a boat with two separate sleeping cabins at the expense of a great deal of open air cockpit sunshine space.

The Italian designers are probably the boldest of us all in trying out the possibilities of new shapes. Italian yachts often show a light hearted extravagance which puts us all to shame. Not for them the seriousness of life reflected off the grey waters of the North Sea or the Atlantic. Every line in a British yacht will be there for some serious purpose to do with the sea, although often arranged and composed to a handsome appearance. The Mediterranean yacht would seem very often to have a superstructure to suit the mood of the moment and not be in the least ashamed of decoration and embellishment. The Italian designer Franco Harrauer is always in the forefront of

Fig. 217 Franco Harrauer's Tiger Shark design, showing the logical modern approach to sports fishing.

this approach and we show a picture of his Tiger Shark design as an example of his work. The bow, you will see, is logically split into two components to allow a solid spear-fishing platform extension of the deck. The flying bridge is also as designed and decorated as any superb Italian car and gives a similar impression of high performance whether the yacht is under way or not.

Among this generally jollier approach we have watched, almost with dismay, a trend led by Baglietto as far as we can see from this distance, towards yachts with the full introverted, protected and aggressive styling which one normally associated with the military. Perhaps the sun has to be shut out, perhaps it is a desire for privacy when moored in crowded yacht harbours, but it may just be an anticipation of the cataclysm, and that we suppose is what worries.

Large Planing Craft

Planing is a youthful sporting way of getting around and large yachts tend to belong to elderly financiers. Add to that the cost of such power for private use and it is easy to see why the really big

planing yacht is something of a rare animal. There are physical problems too, even more than those of transporting the gold between one vault and the next. The biggest lightweight diesels which are available in what you might label as the ordinary cooking brands run up to a maximum of about 1200–1300 bhp. If you install three or even four of these you will only just get a 90 or 100 foot yacht up into true planing. There are more exotic diesels such as the Napier Deltics which will give you over 3000 bhp at a usable power/weight ratio with eighteen turbocharged cylinders in three banks of six. By now, as an owner, you are committed to a full naval type specification of engineers' maintenance and overhaul — and probably accountants as well. Petrol engines are more or less out for big yachts. Apart from the feeling of danger, the big petrol engines have been completely superseded by jet engines in the aircraft builders' interests. Nowadays if you want your big yacht to fly you are committed to flying it by jets, because there are just not the petrol engines about.

Jet engines are in principle natural units for yachts. Their small size and high performance equate very well with the yacht payload of pleasure space. The large quantities of fuel required

Fig. 218 Mercury, *gas turbine yacht with fast patrol boat antecedents, designed by Peter Du Cane and built by Vospers in 1960.*

Fig. 219 HMS Brave Borderer — *familiar to all at the early* Daily Express Cowes/Torquay *races as starting boat and guard ship. Designed and built by Vospers.*

can be tucked away easily enough in the modern hull constructions. Furthermore, the quality of the fuel itself is, we understand, not too critical and this fits to a hair the description of the stuff that comes out of the pipe in many yachting harbours which shall be nameless. Jets, however, are basically designed for other industries and other technologies and it is natural to expect that there will be teething troubles and disappointments in their application to yachts.

Top of the list in big fast yachts must be *Mercury*, a really gallant attempt at high-speed pleasure boating *par excellence.* Mr Stavros Niarchos, a great patron of our industry, required a yacht with a cruising speed of 50 knots. Where else should he go for such a vessel but to Vospers

and to Commander Peter Du Cane? And what else should it be based upon other than their successful *Brave* Class fast patrol boats fitted with three Bristol Proteus 1250 marine gas turbines each producing 3500 bhp at 11000 rpm? In addition, at full blast each jet outlet in the transom produced an additional 500 lb or so of jet thrust as bonus. *Mercury* was built at 102 feet in overall length with similar machinery and, like the *Braves*, even with gas turbines for the auxiliary charging plants, making her the first all-jet yacht. The hull form is also similar to the *Braves*, which use the traditional shape developed by Vospers with a full deck line forward and a flat body aft. The foot of the transom is in fact a straight line, apparently to allow a single trim flap to be fitted

Fig. 220 G. A. Trenta, *originally named* GA-40, *was designed by Vospers and built in 1962 at Varazze by Cantiere Baglietto.*

across the hull. *Mercury* is built of laminated timber covered with glass fibre laminate.

Perhaps in terms of the development of boatbuilding *Mercury* is not all that significant. Judging only by the follow-up orders she may not have been all that successful but if she is in any way a folly she is a folly in the grandest manner because there is nothing mean about *Mercury*.

It may be interesting and only fair to mention the *G.A. Trenta*, a 90 foot motor yacht designed by Vospers for Giovanni Agnelli at much about the same time as *Mercury*. Dr Agnelli asked for a maximum speed of getting on for 40 knots and a cruising speed of 30, bringing her nicely into the planing speed range. She was fitted with three Fiat diesels (what else!) each of twelve cylinders and giving 1350 bhp each. She again follows the traditional Vosper hull form, and it is slightly chastening to hear that such experienced designers first considered the Hunt deep vee form for her but abandoned the idea because they preferred their own form for the top speed efficiency.

The designs for both *Mercury* and *G.A. Trenta* were run in wind tunnels, not only to check on the aerodynamic drag but also to see that the draughts in the open or closed control bridges

and round the decks would not make them unbearable. It is quite an off-putting thought that both these craft will never put to sea in less than 30 knots of self-induced wind (moderate gale) and that *Mercury* at full belt is experiencing heavy gale force winds.

Special Planing Craft

It often takes commercial necessity to prick some of the pomp of both yachting and high performance engineering. We are all more or less brought up to think well of a high polish and fine craftsmanship. Scientists have brainwashed the lot of us into reverence for the exactness of life where six places of decimals are in themselves better than two. An opinion based on calculations is accepted before one based on experience and anyone who views computer outpourings as 'rubbish in, rubbish out' is considered a heretic. Every now and then one comes across a rebel to put things back a little into perspective. An aeroplane flying along upside down for instance must cast some doubt on the sheer exactness required in the sections of wings. For our purpose the planing boat is put into some relief by the abalone boats working out of Santa Barbara on the Californian coast. The abalone is, as no doubt everyone knows, a large shellfish (7 inches across to be legal), which has to be prised off the rocks in deep water with a tyre lever. It is fished by skin divers and the whole affair is very much one of muscles and of toughness. Some of the abalone fishermen treasure their reputations for toughness and stick it in everyone's eye by liberally coating their boats with tar. The boats themselves look a bit like ex-government craft but are thus very heavily disguised. Flat out for the kelp beds where the abalone grow, the rough tar fleet make a sight for red eyes as they pound along at good planing speeds casting a fairly awesome snook at the stainless steel and varnish yachting jobs out for mere pleasure.

The crew boat is one particular type of well established commercial design which fills power yacht designers with envy. Fine big boats with powerful engines to carry comparatively small loads to and from the oil rigs, crew boats are concerned one hundred per cent with reliability and speed. Space is there to be used lavishly for machinery layouts and for accommodation, and simplicity is actually appreciated. The result of such a specification is usually a very handsome boat. We were impressed with a 65 foot version built by the American Lafco Company of Lafayette in aluminium which was chock-a-block with clever detail in the construction and fit-out. Typical perhaps is the Lafco method of achieving the exact and proper running trim. The aluminium bottom plating extends aft of the transom and on trials is attacked from deck level with an enormous spanner-like tool. The extension flap of plating is just twisted up or down like a proper adjustable transom flap until perfection is achieved. The spanner is then removed and the boat delivered to her owners. The 65 footer is powered by twin GM 12V–71 engines giving about 500 hp each, and all this to deliver about thirty-eight people to work. Crew boats generally back up to the rig so

Fig. 221 Most fast planing boats are highly finished and smooth. This is one of the abalone fishing fleet working out of Santa Barbara on the Californian coast. These rough and tough and tarred-all-over boats plane out to their fishing grounds at over 20 knots.

Fig. 222   A 65 ft crew boat by Lafco of America. Note the big engine room vents amidships and the handy grab rails on the forward face of the deckhouse.

Fig. 223   The 100 ft Jaguar crew boat at 25 knots. Built in Louisiana, USA, in aluminium by Breaux's Bay Craft, she carries sixty-one passengers and three crew.

Fig. 224 Dabchick. *An estate service launch based on our standard 21 ft hull, she is of cold moulded wood construction and has a speed of over 40 knots.*

Fig. 225a, b *Two further versions of standard multi-strake hulls. Below left, a GRP raceboat built by Tolcraft and, below right, a wooden hull by Workboats.*

that crew and baggage can be lifted off by some crane-hoisted pallets. They all therefore sport a steering position looking aft in addition to the normal position in the wheelhouse and the after deck is kept flat and low to avoid hang-ups.

Another impressive crew boat which took our eyes is the 100 foot *Jaguar*, one of a type built by Breaux's Bay Craft of Loreauville, Louisiana. This large and comfortable vessel cruises at about 22 knots and has a maximum speed of about 25 knots with her twin GM 12V–149 engines delivering 800 bhp each. She carries sixty-one people plus a bit of cargo. This is quite an impressive performance compared with power yachts; it is partly due to her aluminium construction, of course, but also reflects the omission of an extra 20 tons or so of insulation and furnishings, tenders and deckworks, which a yacht of her size would require to be considered as normally fitted out.

At the other end of commerce there is

Dabchick, a 21 foot fast estate launch we designed for use on a Scottish loch. *Dabchick* is employed in taking shooting parties and equipment up and down the length of the loch in all weathers. High speed meant that she could get in twice the amount of work when she was afloat and reduced the number of times when she had to be launched out of her boathouse or towed on land to her working location. *Dabchick* is designed therefore for a speed of 40 knots and is powered by twin 125 hp Mercury outboard engines. Also, because Scottish mist might hamper her operation, she is fitted with radar, which makes a brave sight on her small dimensions. *Dabchick* is arranged with low bulwarks around a flush deck so that she can accommodate such loads as dead stags or extra persons, and she also sports a small sit-in type deckhouse which provides cover for the ladies in the party when it rains and also a secure stowage for the guns. It was decided that the rough stony edges to

Scottish lochs would not suit a GRP hull without maintenance and repair facilities within a hundred miles. *Dabchick* therefore was built with a cold moulded wood bottom and a generally wood construction throughout.

Raceboats

Racing fast boats in open water is surprisingly exciting. Passage making in boats of even an equivalent performance can be a bit dull but competition somehow transforms the situation. It is like distilled sailboat ocean racing. Driving a fast raceboat is steering up, round or through every

Fig. 226 Bow view of a modern raceboat for comparison with an old-fashioned runabout. Difference is not very marked although the aft bodies are quite different.

Fig. 227 Bow view of an old-fashioned runabout for comparison with a modern raceboat.

wave in quick time balancing out at the same time the questions of breaking the hull, breaking the engines, breaking the crew and using up fuel against an involved tactical game with other boats. Six hours of it and you are as involved with the sea and as tired out as if you had been round Fastnet Rock twice without a watch below.

The modern raceboats are not really fast in terms of any evolutionary graph of powerboat speed development. In the 1930s boats of similar power were circuit racing in comparatively open water at a hundred miles an hour. It is difficult to see at first, other than in terms of sport, what the current breed as produced by the modern rule requirements is achieving. One might mention seakeeping ability in rough water, but it is doubtful if the latest boats are very much of an improvement on the Thornycroft coastal motor boats of the First World War. Their true value to boating is really much more penetrating. The offshore racing power boat has put reliability into the whole range of everyday planing cruisers.

It is an indisputable fact, often forgotten in the heat of preparation for a race, that the first qualification for winning a prize is actually to finish that race. A fast power boat driven hard in rough water behaves in an outright ridiculous manner which would never be tolerated except in the name of sport. All this leaping, banging and slamming is worse than for any other vehicle known to man. It could easily be stopped if anyone wanted to — we have had a prototype with a suspension system for years. However, it makes for very good sport, not only in testing the physical stamina of the crew but in providing extremely testing conditions to sort out the engine installation. If it were not for some such sieve to catch the really skilful driving and the really careful preparation one might just as well run the races in flat water or indeed in the test tank or on the computer. In which case we could all stay at home warm, dry and unimpacted.

In the early days of the current series a great many boats put to sea to have a sporting go and to see how they fared. A great many 'hit logs' and gave up racing but quite quickly a fashionable form emerged which has developed as years have gone on. The very first requirement, quickly understood, was for the softest possible ride to keep the machinery in one piece. Here the Hunt hull first established something of an ascendancy, and indeed the winner of the first Cowes/Torquay

Fig. 228 Dick Bertram's 36 ft Brave Moppie, *which in 1965 took the world diesel record at 57·7 mph and won the Cowes/Torquay and the Miami/Key West races.*

race was of this form. The characteristics were a long keel and a short bow overhang coupled to the deep vee hull. More worrying perhaps was the very wide flat foredeck which must have been a liability at aerodynamic speeds. Such a forward deck would give a lot of lift and give the hull a tendency to jump bow-up in a seaway and then at the high angle of attack the deck would stall, as it were, and the hull be dropped back on to the sea quite suddenly. The early Moppies tended to have the crew right aft where they would have an easier ride but only making this aspect of the aerodynamics a little worse. Our favourite of the Moppies is *Brave Moppie*, Dick Bertram's famous 1965 boat which won the Cowes/Torquay after taking the world water speed record for diesel boats at 57·7 mph. These diesels are unusual for flat-out raceboats, which normally go in for petrol engines. The power/weight ratio of the petrol engine is better and highly tuned engines are in reasonable supply. *Brave Moppie* had a pair of GM 6.71 diesels which in normal guise deliver about 275 bhp each; we do not know what the actual horsepower output was in racing tune. These engines were installed right aft (to give them the softer ride the crew had been getting in earlier boats) and drove twin props through vee drives. The crew rode immediately forward of the engine room, getting on for halfway up the boat.

The aerodynamic lift area of the foredeck was greatly reduced but any balancing lift from the after deck must have been spoiled by the crew sticking up from their cockpit like sore thumbs immediately in front.

The two *Tramontanas* are next on our list. Both were designed by Peter Du Cane and both are extremely interesting raceboats. *Tramontana I*, it will be remembered, massacred the second Cowes/Torquay race with no less than 2308 horsepower of Isotta Fraschini petrol engines. She was 42 feet in length with an above water profile a bit like the Moppies with a long waterline and short bow. Other than that she was quite different, with the traditional, highly efficient Vosper hull form running from a deep sharp vee forward to nearly flat sections at the transom. The drivers sat in comfort strapped into seats inside a proper wheelhouse. This mighty vessel was so superior that she promptly precipitated a change in the rules which effectively and sadly banned her from racing for ever. Her owner, Dick Wilkins, got Vospers and Peter Du Cane to build him a very pretty boat to the new rules and to the reduced engine capacity regulations. *Tramontana II* was fitted with four Jaguar engines and had her share of success. Her hull form, however, adopted the constant vee form of the Americans, although not so pronounced, on a hull which still showed

Fig. 229 Tramontana, *winner of the 1962, the second Cowes/Torquay race.*

Fig. 230 *Below.   Despite her race number, this is* Tramontana II.

the wide shoulders and narrowish transom of the traditional Vosper form. It is obvious that great attention was given in *Tramontana II* to the aerodynamic value of the deck and deckworks. Notice also how such an experienced designer again puts his crew under cover, realising before many others that it is the crew quite as much as the machinery that gets the boat to the finishing line.

The chief influence in the shape of the modern raceboat must be that of Renato Levi. His fine-formed 'Delta' boats quite demolished the widely held view that offshore powerboat racing required rather serious-looking short-ended large craft. Whereas designers up until that point had been trying to stop the boats jumping out of the sea, even to the point of fitting ballast tanks, 'Sonny' Levi produced a type of hull which performed extremely well over a whole range of attitudes. It may not be fair to say that they did not care whether they were in the water or out but they certainly gave the impression of making the best of the latter. A raceboat in fact goes faster out of the water clear of skin friction and the Levi Delta to a certain extent re-invented porpoising as a means of getting down the course faster. The very deep vee hull with a plethora of spray rails did not vary very much in efficiency in immersion and greatly ironed out the sudden variations in bottom pressure which damaged the flatter craft. The long thin form also ironed out the resistance variations of a plunging boat which may in a few yards have to cope with anything between the heavy drag of semi-planing and the freedom of flying. Aerodynamically the form was excellent. The long needle nose had very little aerodynamic lift which if it developed at all was concentrated aft over the machinery weight giving level flying if anything.

To represent the type we have picked *Barbarina* whose beautiful gently curving form looks more like the front half of a Baltic racing sailing boat than the home of around about 1600 horsepower for use in rough water. The four engines are spread in pairs forward and aft of the cockpit and all this packed as far aft as possible, in fact where the buoyancy of such a hull is at rest and the planing surface at speed. On moorings there looks as little of her as a river skiff but the

hull is deep and under the foredeck there is space for two bunks, toilet compartment with shower, and chart table. The four engines drive four propellers, a fact worth mentioning for the impressive view they give from aft when out on the dock rather than for any intrinsic worth of such a complicated installation.

The only criticism we would have of the Delta form is our perennial obsession with balance. The lovely long needle-nosed boats run with perhaps the front half of their length out of the water and with nothing behind. The damping effect of such an unbalanced pendulum in a seaway is probably excellent but we have a feeling that such an effect can be achieved as easily from reduced motion in the first place. In our own sally into offshore raceboat design with Anthony Needell we drew a hull form for the *News of the World* with the hull projecting aft of the transom or the running step of the transom moved forward up the hull, depending on your point of view. We also took a great deal of care with the aerodynamic form of the deck even to the point of a grill on the foredeck to stop suction (or lift) building up when the bow was tossed up by the sea action. She was, possibly as a result of all this, a very steady running boat and we always felt that

Fig. 231 The rear view of 'Sonny' Levi's sleek and slender Delta, Barbarina, *is impressive. She is a four engined (1600 hp) fast commuter capable of nearly 60 knots.*

Fig. 232 News of the World *running in rough water at over 40 knots. The bustle stern can just be seen and it is noticeable how level she is 'flying'.*

Fig. 233 American Eagle — *one of Don Aronow's famous Cigarette Series.*

this approach had been justified by her performance. *News of the World* was designed to accommodate four diesels coupled together to drive twin shafts and this perhaps as much as anything else is responsible for our obsession with simplicity as a factor in winning races.

No discussion of raceboats would even begin to be representative without the names of Jim Wynne, Don Shead and Don Aronow appearing. All three have designed outstanding race-winning boats and have driven their own boats to win races themselves. Between them they have moulded the divergent forms of the early years into a fairly unified line of approach with boats which are graceful, light, strong, and unmistakably fast, offshore raceboats. They have shown that it is not necessarily the big boats that win in rough weather, an early view, and again and again that

the fast boat which streaks away at the beginning of the race is very often the fast boat which streaks back home first. In fact, that speed is not incompatible with reliability. To represent this current breed of raceboats we could not do other than select a Cigarette. These boats have been dominant for a few years now and are primarily interesting for their full centre-of-the-road approach to shape, due perhaps to an increased interest in the brake horsepower to be got out of the engines and propellers inside the rules. To be honest we find them perhaps a bit alike and even slightly dull, reminiscent perhaps of the power boats of fifty years ago. Soon the stepped hull will be back running in open water and the next cycle of progress will begin — possibly in conjunction with the jet engines now coming in for raceboats.

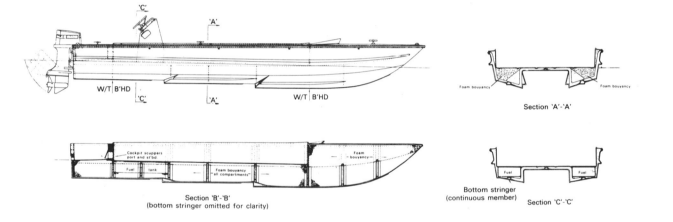

Fig. 234   The aluminium hulled Fairey Interceptor.

Catamarans

The planing catamaran is a curious craft especially in its current vogue for raceboats. At the moment it is sweeping the board in the small classes and extending upwards in size at quite a good rate of progress. Rule number one in a competitive life is that you cannot beat the power/weight ratio if you are comparing like with like. The catamaran can never hope to compete in structural weights with the single hull and so the attraction must lie in some other aspect. The clue comes when you are bounding along in your 1000 hp boat at 60 knots or so with a crew of three. You look up and what do you see but an aeroplane of the same general dimensions, rather more crew on board, with its 200 hp engine throttled right back so as not to pass you too quickly for the photographs. Everybody is really quite well aware that every fast power boat would an aeroplane be if the rule makers would let it. The artificial requirements imposed on maritime sport include the need for all power thrust to be in the water, no wings and a payload of accom-

modation and equipment. The catamaran has been allowed, thank goodness, to get away with a wing between its two better halves, disguised as a necessary structural bridge. The wing picks up a substantial ground effect to the general betterment of performance. The lift effect is proportional to size and speed in the normal way and this can be seen by the general dominance of the catamaran among the smaller and faster raceboats. A little more peering down Nelson's telescope with a blind eye by the rule makers and we might see something really interesting develop. A genuine flying fish of a boat perhaps with the pilot skimming from wave top to wave top picking up propulsion from a quick burst of power while passing through chosen billows. This flight of fancy has been possible since at least 1909 when Rudyard Kipling concocted a mock advertisement for the bat boats of the future including one with 'triple set of Hofman vans giving maximum lifting surface of 5327 sq. ft.' 'Tarpon,' it went on, 'has been lifted and held seven feet for two miles between touch and touch.'

But to return to the present. The classical

Fig. 235   One of Norman Fletcher's racing catamarans.

Fig. 236 *12 metre catamaran sports fisherman* Stephano III, *designed by Franco Harrauer.*

catamaran of the current circuits is the brainchild of the Molinaris — father Angelo and son Renato. The early versions looked a bit like a Levi or a Shead hull split down the centre, reversed and separated by a bit of wing with a chord which matched their length. The later developments have principally been concerned with the wing which has been shortened into more efficient proportions. The leading edge has been pulled back leaving the hulls sticking forward in the so-called 'pickle fork' configuration. This also has the effect of bringing the centre of wing lift further back under the weights of the driver and engine thereby reducing the tendency to flip over at speed. A great deal of it is, or ought to be, based on the research into seaplanes in the 1930s which, incidentally, set down all the possibilities for deep vee hulls and even spray rails in great detail.

The next stage in planing catamarans must be in the development of the stepped hull again and in fact this is what Fairey Marine have achieved with their aluminium hull Interceptor boat. This 25 footer travels at a speed of over 40 knots powered by twin 135 hp engines. She is a full multi-step form with side vented steps.

The planing cruising or accommodation catamaran is a rare animal for much the same reasons that make the displacement equivalent rare. The double form is expensive, the engine room is split and the complications bump up the costs. The only justification is for a specialised use, and Franco Harrauer has made one as an interesting fast sports fisherman. She is the *Stephano III* of 38 feet length with 18 feet beam, powered by twin 100 bhp diesel engines. Her speed of 15 to 18 knots is only just verging on full planing and obviously this is more a matter of owner's requirements than that she could not be powered up to a faster speed. In that length she has quite remarkable accommodation with no less than four double cabins and two single cabins in the hulls. They are rather small but adequate for a fishing party making its way out to the day's sport. For the actual sport there is an admirably large after deck, an upper bridge control position and, of course, the beam across the hulls forward must make a first-rate spear fishing platform.

CHAPTER 11
Engines and Installations

General

In the bad old days of the last century marine prisoners were often incarcerated in hulks. A power boat with a poor engine installation is likely to produce something of the same situation. If one, properly, ignores the kind of old-fashioned unpropelled houseboat that is no more than a barge, then any marine craft without her means of propulsion is a disaster. Her crew are but prisoners on board waiting only to be allowed to pay a substantial fine for release by salvage or shipwreck. It used to be said that it was a good investment to buy the best engine that one could afford. Now that nearly all engines are quite reli-

able the wisest investment is more properly in getting the very best installation.

Like so many things in a boat, a really good engine installation depends a great deal more on the integrity and knowledge of the mechanics who fit it up than on the intention of the designer or the builder. For some years recently we have had the opportunity to inspect a number of engine installations in small standard cruisers. In practically every case it was possible to see that the manufacturer had started out with the best of intentions. The installation equipment was of good quality and not stinted, space and access were adequate, ventilation, controls, etc. all allowed for. In a high proportion, however, the

Fig. 237   Belt and braces. If choosing the propulsion method is difficult you could have alternatives like this — paddle wheel or propeller.

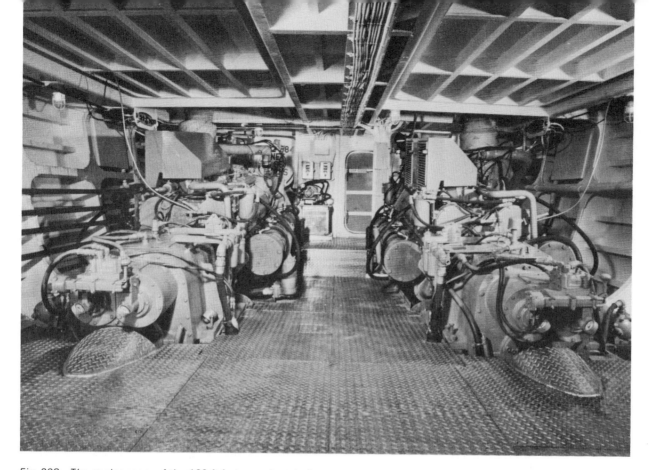

Fig. 238 *The engine room of the 100 ft fast crew boat built by Breaux's Bay Craft, fitted with twin GM 12V-149 engines with 2 : 1 reduction gearboxes. Note the ample space which can be allowed in a commercial craft where reliability and therefore maintenance are extremely important.*

whole intention was spoilt because some detail was stupid. In one boat the 'make and break' of the electrical system was placed exactly an inch away from the carburettor. In another the electrical leads were draped across an unprotected exhaust pipe flange. Often pipes touched each other so that the knocking of vibration would eventually harden and make them brittle. All are important points for the security of the yacht and its occupants and all are points which are as expensive to do wrong as to do right.

The sticks-and-string yachtsman takes great pride and pleasure in the tiddly appearance of spars, sails and rigging. It is odd how often the power yachtsman appears to feel nothing but shame for his propulsion. The engine and all its works are not for public view and the lifting of most engine hatches is an occasion of some embarrassment, like dirty linen being searched by the Customs. Even engine manufacturers promote this atmosphere by supplying their large and expensive products crudely painted by any industrial standards, never mind those of yachting. This sets the standard for the engine space, which

quickly degenerates into a roughly finished compartment of machinery very susceptible to oily dirt and very unattractive to keep clean.

Why engine manufacturers have not tumbled to the fact that a super finish on their engines, like those they show at exhibitions, would be so worthwhile for yachts that yacht owners would actually pay for it, we do not know. First, of course, is in the advantage to the engine. No fitter would dare tread all over enamel and chrome, cracking flanges and flattening pipes, where now they treat most engines with the contempt their crude finish deserves. Second, the installation of a lovely shining machine is always done more carefully than one which is apparently of little value to its makers. Third, the owner would then take pride in engine, installation and engine room. Maintenance becomes more attractive, oil leaks and so forth are picked up at once and the owner's friends taken to see the engines as well as the more upholstered areas of the craft.

An engine room, arranged and used with care, need never be dirty or smelly, it is only neglect that brings on these conditions. In fact the best power seaman we knew (a Scandinavian, in case anyone wonders) had his yacht arranged so that the normal access to his cabin was through the engine room. The latter had varnished woodwork and enamelled bulkheads like any other compartment in the vessel and the engines were kept in the state of cleanliness that is normal to all other parts of a yacht. The owner and his wife could walk through in evening dress without even a thought about a smudge of oil. It is unfortunate that so many engine rooms are hidden away for so many good reasons. Nice machinery working well ought to be as attractive a sight to the power yachtsman as a genoa jib pulling well to the sailor. At first thought the aesthetic differences might seem to be too far apart, but think how attractive is a fire engine with its gleaming machinery.

Machinery noise is basically thought to be unattractive and great steps are taken to reduce the sound penetrating from the engines to the living compartments. The accepted limit of reasonable noise is that conversation can be carried on in a normal voice. All noise on the same decibel reading, however, is not equally objectionable. The hum of a power station turbine is well known to be of great help in inducing concentration. The background noise of pumps and generators imparts a peculiar and comforting ambience to life on board a big ship. The intermittent thump of a single cylinder fishing boat engine brings with it a tremendous feeling of reliability (oddly enough, for one usually prefers to be reminded of more chances than one). The unhappy roar of an ill-tuned engine is disquieting, and some diesels make a thoroughly irritating noise no matter how they are silenced. Perhaps as engine makers become civilised they will begin to give some positive thought to the impression their engines make on the world outside their test beds.

Choice of Power Unit

Anyone choosing a power unit or units for a new yacht is faced at every boat show with apparently endless ranges of glistening and obviously technically superb models. Weighing up the advantage of one against another would seem to be a matter for close estimation by experts involving as much calculation as for an airliner. In practice one finds very few problems in arriving at the correct

answer and rarely is there even a close finish between rivals to consider. The factors of choice are quite clear and logical and might be put in the following order:

1. The engine must have the right power output
2. The weight must be within certain limits depending on the type of craft
3. The engine must have a reputation for reliability
4. The relative cost of the engine must be appropriate
5. There must be maintenance facilities and a full supply of spares in the normal cruising ground
6. (Should there still be more than one choice left) comes the question of the best fuel consumption or the most convenient configuration.

The order of importance does depend on individual cases and the factors can be reversed for dramatic effect, e.g., 'Reject all engines with a reputation for being unreliable'.

Of all these points, reliability and a proper range of service stations under your lee are undoubtedly the most important for all but racing craft.

First cost sounds important but as the power unit is only a part of the total cost of a new boat it is, say, only half as important as if it were being purchased by itself. Fuel consumption also sounds important but again it is generally covered by fitting tanks to the new yacht of sufficient capacity for the range required from the craft. The extra cost of fuel is also masked for the yacht user by, sometimes, the happy anticipation of the pleasures of the deep to be enjoyed on the subsequent passage. Engine noise ought perhaps to be on the list but this again ought to be covered by the designer in the design of the engine space environs, but noise always costs money in its suppression.

Petrol engines of any power these days are almost without exception converted automotive engines. The conversion covers principally the replacement of all non-marine grade light alloy castings with marine grade, fitting a proper marine cooling system, altering or replacing the sump so that the lubrication system will function at the normal engine attitude afloat, which is at up to 15° slope, rather than the normal horizontal posture found in cars, fitting a new or altered exhaust manifold to suit the new exhaust system, and tuning the engine generally to be suitable for long stretches of continuous running rather than the variable conditions met on the road.

In addition, precautions should be taken against the damper life of a marine engine by a bit more protection around the plug leads, etc. The petrol engine is normally quiet running and free from vibration. The power output curve is often quite steep near the top and the engine needs very good attention if the manufacturer's output is to be maintained through the season. Better, if possible, to reckon on a normal maximum of say 75 per cent of the brochure output and surprise yourself on occasions.

Petrol fuel is a fire risk but that risk ought to be seen against years of appallingly poor installations in inferior craft. The petrol engine is cheap and is often used in a cheap and dangerous installation. A properly installed petrol engine in a properly equipped and maintained yacht is probably as safe as any other installation.

Petrol is expensive fuel in many parts of the world and it is possible to run a low compression relatively inefficient petrol engine even less efficiently on paraffin. The engine is started by petrol and run until there is enough heat generated in the exhaust manifold to warm the paraffin vapouriser fitted to it. The fuels are swopped over and the engine chugs along quite cheaply. Before stopping, the fuels are swopped back again so that the engine is ready to start with petrol through its works next time.

The famous Kelvin petrol/paraffin engine is still to be seen about in some older boats. This involves real first principle marine motoring in its handling. First, each cylinder is fitted with a priming cock. A liberal dose of petrol all round and when the engine is cranked you are at least rewarded with an explosion or two if any spark is about. The instructions on procedure when (not if) the engine should seize up are also eminently practical. They take the following lines: 'Open priming cock and insert iron bar. Tap smartly with hammer provided.'

The diesel engine is intrinsically more expensive and noisier than the petrol engine and perhaps less amenable to the amateur engineer. They have the happy characteristic that when they stop for an un-obvious reason the yachtsman can only try bleeding the fuel for air bubbles before giving up and relaxing.

Fig. 239   If only engines, once installed, could stay as smart as this. Cummins V8-300-M diesel.

Fig. 240   Miss Embassy's Rolls-Royce Gnome free spool gas turbine engine has a power output of over 1000 hp at 2500 rpm.

Diesel fuel is relatively cheap compared with petrol in most parts of the world and the sickly smell can normally be so vented away as to be negligible. Diesel fuel does not catch fire with anything like the same ease as petrol and therefore is to be preferred for the carefree craft. However, once burning it is equally dangerous and, for instance, fuel spillage in the bilges should be avoided. Diesel engines normally have a fairly flat topped power graph and the output is more reliable. However, most fast running diesels tend to get a bit stressed at full power. If they can normally be used at cruising revolutions they will last for years and years.

The gas turbine is an absolute natural power unit for small craft. It is small and reliable and will burn any old fuel you give it except sticks or coal. The problems of gearing the output down to shaft revolutions, coping with the red-hot high-thrust exhaust and carrying enough fuel for its insatiable appetite will soon be solved. It may also soon be practicable to carry a spare engine in the locker in case one should eventually wear out when you are not expecting it. We are all used to the particular high-pitched whine of an aircraft gas tur-

bine and perhaps have even come to think of it as denoting modernity and reliability. The disadvantages, apart from not yet being sufficiently developed for small boats, lie in the low power output at low revolutions making, for instance, for poor acceleration. Paraffin, the normal fuel, can be less volatile than petrol but probably remains as a slightly greater fire risk than diesel fuel.

The Wankel rotary engine also shows great promise for marine use but its future afloat will depend on its development in other contexts. Boating as an industry can rarely provide a market sufficient to cover first development costs.

The shining exception is in outboards where a pure marine line of advance has been followed, and continues to be followed, producing a very sophisticated standard of engineering. The outboard engine increases in power every year and, in terms of power and weight, already challenges the inboard petrol engine. The prime advantage of the outboard is that it is a completely engineered single unit propulsion outfit of relatively light weight. The whole unit is removed and taken to the workshop for maintenance and this is both a strength and weakness depending on the

Fig. 241   The De Havilland Ghost jet engine in John Cobb's Crusader *drove her at over 200 mph with a 5000 lb thrust.*

nearness of the dealer. The outboard engine gives a hull clear for all its length on the one hand and on the other concentrates the engine weight right at one end of the craft. We should also mention that fuel consumption is usually greater in the outboard motor than in equivalent inboards. The facility of easy access to the propeller for its maintenance is extremely valuable. Quite apart from the emergency clearance of weed or rope it is easy to forget what an important part this rather insignificant bit of twisted sculpture plays in the performance of the yacht. Many yachtsmen are apparently unable to make the mental connection between the cherished and expensive engine at one end of the prop shaft and the nicked and blunted prop at the other. The daily reminder and inspection of the propeller is one of the side benefits of the outboard engine and also of the inboard/outboard type of installation. The latter is immensely popular and it can only be for two of the same reasons as the outboard. The installation is extremely simple in most cases, the clear bottom allows use in shallow and drying out waters, and the propeller can be wound up into sight for inspection. The big disadvantage is in the complexity of that part of the unit which is mounted outside the hull. In boats of any size the unit often has to be mounted with its basic centre part awash which must, theoretically, be unreasonable for any bit of machinery. The unit is also a little vulnerable to passing disasters but proper protection, both practical and by insurance, can cover this.

Choice of Installation

One of the engineer's arts is to pick the very greatest simplicity for his machinery. Complication may be and nearly always is justified, but the introduction of any complication ought to be after a good rearguard battle for simplicity.

The most simple installation, and that which should be considered first, is a single engine with direct drive to an underhull propeller. Standard engine, standard gearbox, with fixed mountings, driving a single direct coupled shaft running through a standard stern tube to a propeller supported by a single bracket, is about as simple as most would want to go. The major disadvantages which usually drive people on to more complexity are the extra skill required in boat handling and

the basic insecurity of having only one driving force on board. So the next step is to double up the installation and to fit two such sets side by side. So far so good, and one might reckon that beyond this point the designer gets driven by matters which are probably outside the ideal concept. The pressures of cabin space or engine odour can mean vee drives. A particular brand of vibrating engine can mean flexible mountings. An odd shaft line can mean intermediate shafts. A particular and not easily obtainable power requirement or cruising speed can mean three or four engines with various convolutions of connections between them to the propellers either singly or in groups.

The trouble with flexible mountings is that every connection to the engine including the shaft has to have a flexible link to match the maximum amount of movement to be expected from the engine. This movement includes not only the amount the motor will wobble about on its own account, but also the movement due to the rolling or pounding of the vessel in adverse, even emergency, conditions.

In hard running racing boats this might mean as much as the equivalent of seven times the engine weight bouncing on the mountings giving perhaps seven times the movement to the top of the engine. A single flexible coupling is sometimes seen installed between the shaft and engine but this is intended to reduce vibration from the propeller rather than as a complement to flexible engine mounts. Two such couplings are necessary to absorb engine movement relative to a shaft which is supposed to and should, advisedly, stay straight.

Vee drives, however convenient, absorb power between engine and propeller. Rumour has it that it might be as much as 5 per cent but reputable figures seem hard to come by and we may be doing them an injustice. That part of the boat which lies over the propellers is often made fairly hideous by their noise and vibration. To reverse the drive shafts through vee drives and put the engines themselves in this area would seem to be a logical and rough justice. Also, if the general weight distribution will allow, the aft position for engines often works out most conveniently for the accommodation. The engine and all its works and smells can be firmly bulkheaded away and the cabins arranged on one level.

Transfer drives are essentially another form of

Fig. 242   Twin Detroit diesel 6-71X engines each of 550 hp. This vee drive installation was shock tested in sea trials to over 25 g.

vee drive with a second input connection to allow two engines to drive a single shaft in tandem. This is often seen on raceboats looking for the higher efficiency of a single propeller but unable to find a single engine of the right power. Another use is on bigger vessels where, for instance, two diesels are coupled to each shaft either for engine selection reasons or to allow more economical cruising when one engine on each shaft can be shut down. Whatever the purpose of it all the complications multiply. Ideally the engines should drive the vee drive with only an isolating clutch so that the ahead and astern gearbox can be placed separately on the output side of the vee box. If the standard engine gearboxes are used then the coupling and interlinking of the engine and gear controls can be elaborate. It is also worth mentioning that when two engines are coupled in tandem they have to find their own mutual speed but one will be working at full power for that speed and the other taking life easy. A quadruple tandem coupled installation is what is meant by complicated.

The outdrive installation is dead simple and very suitable for smaller boats. The only modifica-

tions which are normal to the standard pattern are in the use of extra length propeller struts to lift the transom unit, with all its problems, above water, and in the use of an extension shaft to allow the engine to be placed further forward and possibly lower than the transom unit. Although this latter sounds a useful feature in practice the connecting shaft runs high through the space, getting in the way of everything one might have used it for. The whole situation for inboard/outboards seems to be just waiting for the services of a good electrical or hydraulic engineer. The days of passing power around with large whirling shafts were in the last century, and there are better places for engines than balanced on the transom.

The hydraulic drive is of course not unknown and from time to time various attempts are made, with varying success, to introduce rather low powered, modest efficiency units. By and large, they do not look convincing. An exception is the Hydrodrive unit which is designed to take quite high horsepower and the relative efficiency has been pushed up by the use of variable pitch propellers. The combination of hydraulic drive and propeller pitch control make very good sense

Fig. 243 *The advantages of an outdrive installation are obvious to the eye, but they do look a little vulnerable when seen out of water.*

Fig. 244 Uno-Embassy *has two 600 hp 8 litre cast iron V8 Kiekhaefer Aeromarine petrol engines close coupled at the extreme aft end of the boat. One might be tempted to pass a quick teapot over those sixteen waiting cups.*

Fig. 245   The CRM petrol engines in Tramontana.

Fig. 246   Aft installation of twin 120 hp OMC petrol engines with outdrives in this 23 ft cruising boat leaves all the forward space for rest and recreation.

and results in a single propeller carrying strut per unit under the hull. The way must also be clear for making the whole thing retractable at some future date.

Variable pitch propellers are, from the designer's point of view, very, very desirable. In theory the pitch can be adjusted to suit the load and the engine run at its ideal speed. The reverse gearbox is also theoretically no longer required since the blades can be put into reverse pitch. In practice most of these benefits do occur but the speed of operation remains the problem which, together with cost, tends to take it out of the small craft field. In some variable pitch installations the pitch cannot be changed under way, or rather while the propeller is actually rotating. The two principal methods of operation are mechanical and hydraulic. In the former it is usual for the propeller shaft to be a hollow tube with a small second shaft inside it. This second shaft slides up and down the propeller shaft and the lower end prods the blades round to the right angle. The difficulty comes in controlling the upper end of the shafts, resulting in some fancy machinery. The hydraulic operation is sometimes achieved in the same way down the whole length of the tail shaft, but would seem to be better done down the P bracket. Variable pitch installations, especially in smaller craft, tend to keep the normal engine

Fig. 247   Dowty-Hamilton jet turbine unit powered by Ford Zephyr marinised engine.

Fig. 248   These large river passenger boats in the USA claimed to be the original jet boats. They show a hull form evolved when rough water did not need to be considered. With their water jet drives they can navigate in very shallow water.

Fig. 249 *The jet drives and exhausts of the passenger river boats shown in Fig. 248.*

reverse gearbox for speed of operation. Any internal mechanism of course increases the dimensions of the propeller boss to what appears an ungainly size but this seems to be more than compensated by the overall efficiency.

The water jet units are very attractive for their clean underwater style. It is clearly advantageous if propellers and rudders and struts and brackets can all be removed from the bottom of the hull. It also feels good to have the propulsion unit inboard where there is a chance of putting it right should it go wrong. The water jet unit therefore should, we feel, be more popular than it has actually proved. The unit is essentially a tunnel with the propeller in it with one end open to the sea in the bottom of the boat and the other arranged as a controlled direction water jet orifice. It is rather vulnerable to sandy water and not quite as efficient as the more normal installation but probably owes its lack of universal success in boating applications to the normal financial reasons.

The Drive to the Sea

The shaft, to a power boat, is as important as the mast to a sail boat. It is fitted through the largest unprotected hole in the hull to project, with all its important appurtenances, in the maximum vulnerable position between the hull and rocky seabed. Its appearance outside the hull is often

in the position of maximum electrochemical corrosion activity. In addition in some installations the angle and placing of the shaft can have important effects on the attitude of the hull under way and the efficiency of the propeller.

The simplest installation is where the shaft runs for the greater part of its length inside the hull or structure emerging only through a gland and bearing to carry the propeller, probably in an aperture installation. Such a shaft is usually carried, in way of the hull, in a tube fitted with a gland at one end and two bearings. The gland for convenience is usually at the inboard end but some yachts are to be found with outboard glands as well. The shaft dimensions are determined only by the torque loading from the propeller possibly modified slightly to suit the bearing spacing. With the shaft virtually concealed from the sea the only problems to be expected are bearing wear after a long and healthy life.

Unfortunately aperture installations are rarely found in modern yachts which largely prefer a twin installation and are looking for high efficiency from their power units. This installation usually takes the form of a long shaft log through the modest rake of quarter or bottom lines with the shaft supported by one or more brackets. Shaft, brackets and rudders all build up a substantial appendage drag which can mount up to at least 10 per cent of the hull resistance itself. It then becomes of reasonable importance to fit the smallest diameter of shaft. The limit is reached either when the best quality material is fully used for the engine torque or when the support of the thinner shaft requires an additional outside hull bracket.

Slow speed boats can afford the additional resistance of an A bracket just ahead of the propeller for the big increase in strength which it gives. The relatively slow turning propeller suffers less behind an A bracket than the fast turning propeller of most fast boats. For these there is no real alternative to the single-legged P bracket. The faster the boat the more care is required with the brackets to reduce resistance and interference with the propeller. It is usual to give these a substantial rake down to the propeller boss to achieve the maximum clearance to the blade tips.

Propellers work the better for being deep in the water and the worse for being heavily angled. The key to the balance of the situation lies in the

Fig. 250 Sopwith's Telstar *at speed in rough water in the 1968 Cowes/Torquay race, showing clearly the reason for extending the propeller and rudder well aft of the boat. She is still getting propulsion and is still slightly under control when flying at least two feet clear of the sea.* (Motor Boat & Yachting *photograph.*)

clearance from the hull required by the blade tips. If these are too close the propeller can produce heavy vibration and noise, both inefficient and unpleasant. The normal allowance is of the order of 18 per cent to 20 per cent of the diameter of the propeller. The blades will fling out centrifugally any small rubbish which gets drawn into their compass and it is usual to protect the hull immediately over the tips with a metal plate which can often conveniently be carried back over the top of the rudder area.

A relatively new fashion for power boats is in the use of so called zip struts for the propeller and shaft. In this case the normal P bracket is placed aft of the propeller and carries on its trailing edge the rudder. This reduces drag at the expense of the vulnerability of the propeller. However, this does not seem to have proved a problem for raceboats and probably would not for cruising boats. The zip strut allows very good fastening which can, if required, be taken right up the transom for strength. Like practically everything else it does add some complication in that it has to have a method of disassembly for changing propellers.

It is probably an intermediate development to running the drive to the props down the strut, and a pitch control could also be incorporated.

Shaft bearings are almost universally of the water lubricated rubber type nowadays. The usual type has a fluted rubber tube bonded to a bronze tube which is press fitted into shaft logs and brackets and kept there with one or two retaining screws. A variation on this theme has a flat fluted rubber sheet of carefully cut dimensions which is just rolled up and dropped into a machined recess in the housing. Replacement is then only a matter of withdrawing the shaft and slipping in some fresh bearings.

There are various stern tube assemblies about and some in current use are, in our opinion, downright dangerous. These have a metal fitting to the hull with a rubber hose connection to the gland. This allows them to be used to cover a reasonable difference of installation angle, which is of course most convenient. If, however, the gland should run hot or dry and seize up, the very next thing that must happen is that the rubber will tear off its mountings and the sea will be free to come in through a large hole. Other 'universal' shaft logs use some form of metal ball connection and these of course are much stronger. Although the shaft log which can accommodate a change of shaft angle is attractive in concept there is no doubt that a simple log made exactly to suit the boat is better. It seems such an important part of the installation as to deserve proper consideration.

The tube usually incorporates the bearing which is followed, going up the shaft, with a lantern ring arrangement in way of a water connection from the main engine system. This ensures that there is a good supply of water at the bearing, cooling the gland and flushing out the tube. The gland is usually a normal industrial type of packing gland with two or three rings of packing and a screw-threaded or flange-bolted pressure ring. It is often thought healthy that the stern glands should dribble greasy water into the ship when running but this is debatable. If there can be any argument about this then the best answer must be to stop it. This in turn is apt to lead to anxious owners groping down in the engine space to see if the stern glands are getting warmer than they should. However, an inexpensive remote reading thermometer does the job better.

Shafts, of course, should be straight but it is extraordinary how many are not. Shafts therefore should be as straight as possible with some thought given to the possible movement of hull and disturbance of shaft which will inevitably occur in some conditions. Good clearances should be allowed off any projection or housing which occurs midway between bearings. It is also an old dodge that shafts should be made with the same taper to propeller and to coupling so that they can be end for ended when worn in way of bearings.

Fuel Supply

Fuel for boats comes in a wide degree of purity depending upon the port and the supplier. The principal contaminant is water, usually due to condensation forming in the storage tanks, but a measure of rust and general dirt is not unknown. Some of the rougher engines used by fishermen seem to work on almost any grade of diet, but the automotive-derived marine engines normally found in power boats are a great deal more sensitive. Dirty fuel attacks the running of the vessel

at two of the points where the seaman is most vulnerable. Starting from cold and continuous running in rough conditions can become difficult. The problem is therefore of the first importance in the fuel installation, after safety.

In addition to shore-derived pollution, fuels can breed their own problems inside the vessel. Petrol in the presence of copper or brass can form a thick gum sufficient to block supply pipes or disable a carburettor and the tiny naphthanic acid content of the fuel for diesel engines will attack zinc and therefore galvanised steel plate or fittings.

The first contact of fuel with the vessel is at the fuel tank fillers. In small craft these may just be a screw cap with a pin vent hole on the tank itself but it is preferable, if the boat be big enough, to fit some kind of on-deck fuelling point so that spillage cannot drip down into the bilges. Spillage on deck, although not so dangerous, is tiresome and not 'for pleasure', and fuel fillers are sometimes seen placed in the topsides themselves or right aft on the transom where any spillage goes directly overboard. These solutions sometimes make any refuelling from shipboard carried cans difficult and the best arrangement is undoubtedly to have a fuel filling box. This is basically a fuel-tight area where spillage is contained and all the fuelling accessories like funnels and rags can be stored. Ideally it should have a piped drain with a cock to allow spillage to be drained to the sea (or into a can) at the right time rather than in the marina. Above all the fuel filler must be heavily electrically bonded to the sea. The first effect of a metal fuel hose nozzle touching the filler must be to earth it. Otherwise any modest difference in the basic static electrical potentials of yacht and nozzle can result in a spark and even the most modest spark in this context can be, in fact is likely to be, the beginning of a disaster. This is such an important part of power boating safety as to be worth every owner's time to check the earthing situation personally before he fills another tank.

Fuel fillers, on another plane of disaster, should also be clearly identified. The word FUEL cast into the deck plate is the very least requirement to avert the hoary joke of filling the fuel tanks with water. Better by far to have PETROL, GASOLINE, PARAFFIN, KEROSENE or DIESEL written big and, in an ideal world, the required grade and identifications would also be given close beside the filler. What may be a few hours delay to land transport can be a lifeboat job afloat.

The filler pipe connections should always be as large as possible and a yacht of any size should have connections to cope with the pressure fuelling common at most commercial installations. The pipes from filler to tank should maintain the same size as the connection all the way to the tank and be run as straight as possible. With pressure fuelling this is as important as big tank vents, for a blowback can, in an instant, change your enamelled jewel of a gentleman's yacht into a stinking slum. In petrol tanks of more than a few gallons capacity the fuel filler pipe should be continued inside the tank down to within a few inches of the bottom to reduce splashing with its heavy and dangerous fumes.

Fuel tanks come in various guises. Often, such is the pressure on the social volume of a yacht, they have to be fitted into such odd shaped spaces as are left over. The best that can be said for this is that it quite often works out all right. The fuel load is an important weight and variable at that. The best position for tanks is as much a matter for the hull architect as it is for the engineer in a well planned vessel.

Most modern craft are built with some form of continuous skin such as metal or GRP. This brings with it an increasing tendency to make tanks as integral parts of the hull, even the hull structure. A volume of the right size is compartmented off with the ship's skin itself forming one of the tank walls. It is often then impossible to fit proper sumps and so on but these minor disadvantages are well outweighed by the simplicity and low cost and the excellent use of hull space. Big ships often use their double bottom construction as fuel tanks but for yachts, especially high-speed power boats, such a flat form of tank is to be avoided. The distortion of the skin with the movement of the vessel can, especially with full tanks, build up an instantaneous hydraulic pressure enough, so we are told, to split tanks or rupture the attachments. It is quite common for tank interiors to be GRP finished even if the yacht herself is not. Some new craft occasionally suffer from a shedding of the glass fibre strands which may not have been sufficiently covered with resin. Just for this possibility these tanks should have filtering arrangements in the supply line to take care of it.

Rubber or flexible skinned fuel tanks have a great deal to be said for them. They make use of nearly as much hull volume as an integral tank but yet are separate and removable. The same hull compartment can be used but without the full treatment necessary to make it fuelproof, thus reducing the extra expense always to be expected where one item is replaced by two. The modest elasticity of the skin allows a flexible fuel tank to absorb impact better and the simplicity of installation allows them to be used to provide additional fuel capacity. Apart from any other use they are ideal for temporary passage tanks.

It may seem a bit obvious to say that fuel tanks should always be big enough but in practice they very rarely are. Apart from being the subject of a companion truism to the one that every yacht should always be a foot bigger, the actual usable proportion of the tank volume is not always appreciated. It varies, of course, from installation to installation but it is rarely possible to use the bottom 5 per cent of fuel for certain in a moving boat, and rarely possible to fill a tank to within 5 per cent of the top. In addition the fuel supply line to the engines should be taken out clear of the bottom of the tank to make proper allowance for water and sludge. It would be a particularly well-designed tank which had a working capacity within 10 per cent of its actual capacity. In addition the tank itself will contain baffles and pipes and odds and ends like capacity gauges, etc., so that the actual capacity can be 5 per cent less than the outside dimensions.

Fuel tanks usually contain baffles, partly for simple structural reasons but also to ease the ferment within. The inside of a tank of a boat in rough water is like a maelstrom, a quite exceptional sight. The fuel swills and roars around with the situation getting worse and worse as the fuel tide drops in the tank. The best value of a sump in this situation is to provide a small area of comparative calm where a continuous supply of fuel can be drawn off for the engine. It is easy to see that every drop of rust and gum and water will be mixed up with the fuel in rough conditions and extravagant means of filtering them are required before they get to the engine. In a diesel engine installation air is as big a hazard in the fuel line as anything. If the tanks are at all inclined to be shallow in style in a diesel installation then a small settling or service tank should be arranged in the fuel line. This is kept full by pump and gives matters a few minutes to calm down and air bubbles to escape before getting down to business.

A new approach, which might provide easier conditions for fuel afloat, is to foam a porous plastic into the tank. This at the expense of about 10 per cent of the volume provides a universal baffle. Fuel can move about, but slowly. Fuel supply is not affected in that it percolates down to the supply point amply fast enough. It just cannot move freely enough to need further control in bad sea conditions.

The best intentioned of fuel tanks will eventually contain some water. In some ports a reasonable dose is supplied with the fuel, mostly from condensation in the metal tanks in which it is stored rather than from any avaricious impulse. Then the tanks of the craft themselves will suffer from condensation at some time. If the tank can be left in peace for a few hours then the water will find its own level at the bottom clear underneath the fuel. Should there be a convenient cock at the very foot of the tank the water can be drawn off. In other installations the water is pumped out through an internal pipe reaching down into the tank. This ought to be a routine maintenance job and in some climates and some ports should be done daily. The gums and solids are however really only cleaned out by getting into the tank with cleaning devices. In a big yacht this can mean a man climbing down a manhole into a tank, and in a small tank no more than inserting an arm up to the elbow. The access hatch is therefore suitably called a manhole and should preferably be placed on top of the tank where there will be the least strain on its fuel-tight capabilities.

Fuel tank vents are often miserable little pipes wending their twisting way from the tank to the open air. Their principal problems occur during fuelling and inadequate vent pipes are often the cause of a blowback. They should be approximately a third of the diameter of the filler pipe and spring from the furthest part of the tank top from the filler entry. It is usual to lead them directly with only upward curves to a swan neck outlet tucked away somewhere convenient on deck. The swan neck outlet being cut diagonally so that the gauze with which it is covered should not cut down the free area.

Some diesels wash and cool their fuel pumps with the fuel itself. Five times the fuel required for the cylinders is drawn from the tank and the excess returned to it. The warm fuel should pre-

ferably be put into the tank at the opposite end to the supply so that it will have the maximum cooling before its next circulation. In special cases, perhaps where tank capacity is small or the tank exposed to engine room heat, it may be necessary to fit fuel coolers. Here the fuel supply line before reaching the engine fuel pump is water jacketed from the engine cooling system.

The power seaman has to have a reasonable idea of the fuel in his tanks at all times and especially in rough conditions. By knowledge of capacity and consumption it is possible to work in a kind of Dead Reckoning style but, like on-deck navigation there is nothing, absolutely nothing in the world, like an absolute fix. The simplest fuel fix is a sight of the fuel itself and in some craft with translucent GRP tanks this is now possible. Some tanks are fitted with transparent manholes for the same reason. The mechanical capacity meters normally work on the position of a float hinging from the tank side or top, on the end of a long thin arm. This has obvious possibilities of failure in the rough fuel conditions which can occur in offshore tanks but in general is surprisingly reliable. The hydrostatic pressure gauges have much less vulnerable moving parts but the old-fashioned standbys of sight gauges or dipsticks are still common and effective. Sight gauges ought to be made in a more modern manner and then might be very popular. Those which are available today are obvious leftovers from the early days of the industrial revolution with curly brass cocks and thick dull glass. Dipsticks are sometimes difficult to use in a boat dashing around in rough water. A word of warning should also be given that the dipstick arrangements in a fuel tank should include a guide tube for the stick together with a raised block or platform to take its impact. Many people seem to feel that they are not getting full value for their measure unless they dash the sounding rod into the tank like a javelin and hear it stop with a good hearty bang. In addition tanks fitted with dipsticks should be fitted on top with a specific area where the stick can be rested for dripping while being read. One common arrangement is an oversize cap, leaving a ledge inside around the hole on which to rest the stick.

Tanks full of fuel can be as heavy as the main engines and, if separate metal tanks are used, need to be mounted on structural bearers of the same quality. Tanks are sometimes bolted direct to the bearers through angle bars welded to their sides but are more commonly held down with metal straps. These run over the tank surfaces, over felt to reduce chafe and drumming, and are through-bolted to the ship's structure often with some kind of tensioning arrangement. Separate tanks should be fitted over drip trays extending completely underneath them so that any fuel drips from anywhere about the tank are collected and allowed to run to a point convenient for mopping up. This is often omitted nowadays and the drip trays confined to small ones placed under sumps and control cocks.

The supply of fuel from the tank must be as fail safe as possible. The trouble really begins in deciding which is the right safety to go for. If the fuel supply cock is placed at the bottom of the tank and a fault should develop in the line the whole contents of the tank will gush forth. If, however, the supply line is taken up inside the tank to emerge, with its supply cock, on top a break in the fuel line should only mean the loss of that in the pipe itself unless a siphon should start. The latter is obviously the safer arrangement and is commonly used for petrol engines. However, air getting into a diesel fuel line is such a menace that it is often thought better to take the short route from the tank bottom rather than risk a possible air entry at the top of a long system. The relative position of tank and engine also comes into the picture. It is better for the engine fuel pump if it is saved work through the fuel arriving by gravity or from a similar level. This carries with it the risk of fuel flood which might stop the engine at a tiresome moment and be dangerous in its own right among hot manifolds and so on. On the other hand fuel which has to be lifted up to the engine puts more strain on the pump and inevitably tends to lead to fuel loss when there is trouble with pump or pipe — again more than likely to be at a tiresome moment. The intermediate tank arrangement where a small service tank is used as a gravity feed is undoubtedly the best but, as is often the case, the best costs more and is only better on rare occasions.

In time of trouble or when leaving the boat to herself for a time it is common sense to turn off the fuel at the tank. The classification societies, with every justification, require that the cut-off cock be operable from on deck, usually by means of an extended spindle from the cock itself. Whether you go to this length or not it makes

extremely good sense to avoid having to kneel in an oily rolling bilge to cut off the fuel whether at sea or on your way to the yacht club ball.

The usual measure of the pipe size for the supply lines to an engine is the size of the connection which the engine maker provides on his machinery. This should be regarded as the irreducible minimum rather than the maximum, and it is often beneficial and never a disadvantage to fit larger fuel lines with perhaps the final flexible connection to the engine of pipe to the engine maker's ideas. In fuel systems where two engines can be fed from one tank it is necessary to remember to use fuel piping big enough for their mutual supply at full power.

Engine makers rarely take too much cognizance of what goes on around their product when installed in a boat's engine space. A sump to suit an angled installation, exhaust manifolds exiting to the gearbox end of the engine and the units placed high to save them from a fate worse than death in the bilges are apparently about the extent of the marine engine makers' interest in the environment of their product. On the subject in hand most engines come supplied with a lubricating oil filter and a fuel filter. The former is fine but the latter is usually quite inadequate except for canal cruising in the care of pernickety old ladies. A marine engine, and we had maybe better add 'in our opinion', needs to have outsize fuel filters, partly for the heavy duty which they will have after a year or two if not sooner and partly because it is unseamanlike to play about with the reliability of the prime mover. In addition it is, still in our opinion, imperative that some form of duplex or dual filters be fitted so that a new clean filter can be brought into play in place of a dirty one at a moment's notice. Cleaning filters at sea is good seamanship if you prefer to do it there as a regular routine maintenance, but it is the result of bad basic seamanship if it becomes imperative in moments of stress.

There are many schools of thought on engine fuel systems and arrangements but the simplest and possibly the best is the one tank one engine system. Emergency cross connections must be provided and they will also take care of tank levelling or any other manoeuvre. Normally, however, each engine is supplied by its own tank and, if diesel, returns fuel to its own tank. Other tanks are used to supply these basic engine tanks. The advantage of simplicity also gives reliability in that, for instance, dirty fuel problems should be isolated and when one engine coughs to a stop there is no immediate prospect of the other doing the same.

The Supply of Air

To many of our engineer friends fresh air is a phenomenon to be enjoyed briefly at the end of a long watch amid the ambience of hot oil, hot lagging and hot paint common to engine rooms of bigger yachts. Air is one of the important ingredients of propulsion and only its being on free issue from the heavens reduces it from proper consideration. If air were rather rarer, like the liquid oxygen on board a space rocket, it would arrive at the combustion chambers through a properly engineered flow path neatly metered and filtered. As a basic ingredient in the ship's progress and as a principal engine space and machinery cooling medium, the air supply deserves full status among the engine systems.

In seagoing craft the air envelope from which

supplies are drawn is often nastily and terribly wet. Rain, wind, sea spray, blown spume, spindrift and even the condensed moisture of fog all crop up in those conditions where the power mariner is particularly relying on the reliability of his power plant. A certain degree of moisture does, of course, make an engine run the sweeter (remember the water bombs used to try to get car engine air damper?). The problem therefore is simply one of baffling or filtering out the solid water down to drip size, which is no more than a normal marine ventilation exercise. The principles of water trap ventilation are reasonably well known.

What may come as a surprise is the quantity of air an engine needs. Some manufacturers may even tell you, though a remarkable number still leave it to the intuition of the installation engineer. A good rough guide is to install vents of twice the size of the engine air intake to cope with the engine's combustion requirements alone. Another measure of the air vent area required by diesels is to allow one square inch for every two engine horsepower for natural ventilation and for every three hp with power ventilation. Water trap vents can well be

Fig. 251   The large air scoop mounted above the engines in Uno-Embassy *is an idea borrowed from Grand Prix racing cars.* Uno-Embassy *won her first race four days after her launching.*

Fig. 252 *The smokestack or funnel is often the centrepiece of the decorative scheme.*

properly isolated it makes good sense to use the power fans to blow air in and to let it come out under its own volition. The slight pressure increase in the compartment is good for the main engine air supply and also for reducing spray through hatches and so on. However, if the compartment is part of the accommodation of the yacht then a pressure increase in the engine space tends to blow engine room air, and smell, out through every hatch, crack or other opening. Here it is better to make the power fans into suckers at the hot end of the circuit thereby lowering pressure inside the engine room and making the air flow in through hatch cracks rather than out. The engine intakes then need special treatment if the engine is not to suffer and a special air supply should be trunked from the fresh air, directly and independently, to the vicinity of the engine inlets.

Fig. 253 *This funnel is almost modern art and also carries the radar scanner.*

bigger to allow for the poor air flow past the baffles. The reason for the large vent size is that the engine maker has carefully, possibly even scientifically, designed the interior of his air inlets while the vent trunking is not likely to be so well arranged and will also have great areas of skin friction to reduce the air flow.

The great majority of engines are primarily cooled by water but the engine space as a whole relies on a circulation of air. The degree of circulation depends on the outside climate and the heat efficiency of the machinery inside the engine space. A rough guide, however, is to aim for a complete change of engine room air every two minutes. This is easily calculated and allowed for but almost inevitably requires some power driven fan installation. The normal natural ventilation of a ship's compartment is from aft to forward and therefore the logical circulation for power driven air would be to help rather than hinder this movement. The cold air should be trunked right down to the bottom of the aft bilges and the hot air collected from the top of the forward overheads, giving the best circulation in the compartment. Ideally the arrangement should be duplicated port and starboard so that every corner of the engine space is touched with a cooling draught.

A very good argument develops as to whether to blow or suck. If the engine compartment is

Fig. 254 An extremely practical approach with the smoke-stacks serving as pillars for the canopy.

Fig. 255 Tucked away among all the other things on the deckhouse roof you may just see the main engine exhaust as a tiny pipe with a wisp of smoke.

Fig. 256 The simple approach giving local heating to the helmsman and an inexpensive funnel cap to keep out the rain.

The pressure changes by either system are really quite modest and as the engine is a powerful sucker in its own right the effect on it is only a matter of modest degree. The effect on engine smell about the yacht on the other hand is dramatic. This counsel of perfection, however, can only apply to yachts working in reasonably temperate climates. Hot air, as opposed to warm air, gets a bit thin for fan blades to grab. In hot climates the only way of effectively cooling the engine room is to pump in the slightly cooler air from the outside.

Every now and then at monotonous intervals one hears the story of another yacht whose running efficiency was dramatically improved one day by the opening of the engine hatches. It is such an old story that it is a wonder that every yacht owner has not tried opening the engine hatches just to see if he has been starving his engines, and such an old story that any yacht builder who falls into the trap of inadequate ventilation should feel extremely foolish.

It is by now routine for every power yacht owner to run his fans for a few minutes to clear his engine space bilges of any fumes which may have built up from fuel drips, etc. before making

Fig. 257 *The funnel of a Monterey fish boat. Well protected by the bridge coamings and making a handy ashtray.*

Fig. 258 *This well-protected engine air inlet trunk has, oddly enough, the stub end of the main engine exhaust sticking out of the top. The normal eddy currents of air about the deck would seem certain to recirculate a fair proportion of the exhaust down again into the engine room.*

sparks with his starter motor commutator. In addition it is worth running fans to cool off the engine space after the motors have stopped. The stopping of the engines also stops the water cooling circulation and the hot machinery can only dissipate its therms into the surrounding air. One day an engine maker will make full provision for the practical use of yacht engines by installing a water circulation pump which can operate independently of the engine. It should not be necessary to mention that engine room fans must be of sparkproof type and that air trunks should be lined with a sound absorbent. Many a carefully insulated room pours forth noise through the unguarded vents and the engine gets the blame for being noisy.

For safety there should also be good and simple provision for stopping the air supply, for nothing spreads fire so fast as a good forced draught. Not only must there be means for stopping power fans but preferably also some positive method of shutting off the natural ventilation. With modern fire extinguishing systems the need physically to cut off the oxygen supply to a conflagration is much reduced but if it can be arranged it is one more nail in the nightmare.

Lubricating Oil Systems

The lubricating oil system of most marine engines is simplicity itself. The oil is held in the sump at the bottom of the engine, picked up by pump and circulated to all required parts and allowed to drain back to the sump. A pressure relief valve to control the maximum oil pressure and a filter are built into the circuit and occasionally also some form of oil cooler. In fast running engines or those of exceptional power it becomes more difficult and more important to maintain an oil film at the principal bearings. This requires oil at higher pressure but if anything a lower temperature. Lubricating oil is then kept in a separate tank outside the engine and a complete piped circulating system used inside it. This so-called dry sump lubrication allows really extensive oil coolers to be fitted or at least provides a big enough reservoir of oil to make sure that it enters the engine at a reasonable temperature. These external oil tanks are usually made of stainless steel and among their other virtues greatly simplify an oil change.

Most wet sump engines are provided with a

little hand-operated sump pump with which the engine oil can be extracted into a loose container. Fresh oil is poured in at some convenient point on top of the engine and that is the whole operation. It is obviously a dockside or dockyard job but the yacht will remain the more pleasant if there is room for the oilcan to reach the filler conveniently and an easy connection for the hose or place for the can at the pump outlet spigot.

Two-stroke petrol engines involve a system which makes use of the engine sump as part of the combustion cycle and therefore they generally have to imbibe their oil mixed with the fuel. Two-stroke diesels are different and work with a sump full of oil like other engines.

It is always preferable to take along some spare lubricating oil so that the engine may be topped up as required. Commonly this is to be found in the form of a rusty drum or can loose on the engine room floor. It really is worth fitting a special tank. Not only will it be fastened down out of harm's way but it can be fitted with a proper draw-off cock to allow the owner to top up his motors without wrestling with an intractable, oily and dirty drum. Such an oil tank should have means for easy filling and it might well be best in most cases to give it an on-deck filler. On bigger yachts the amount of oil carried can increase until it is usual to carry a complete oil change for all engines in yachts with, say, more than 2000 or 3000 miles range. Such vessels are then committed to a waste oil tank to pump the old oil into, but this degree of complication will seem nothing compared with the multiplication of the other systems which will have found their way on board.

Last but not at all least is the possible fire risk from some lubricating oils. High flash point oils are available and are well worth while when a cracked oil pipe can spray your engine room with a near atomised mixture ready to be ignited by, say, a hot exhaust manifold flange.

The Supply of Cool

Marine engines are not exotic, and yachts are surrounded by air down to one level with water below that, both commodities being free. It is therefore no surprise that the cooling systems for yacht engines rely on either air or water.

Air cooling is less common than it perhaps deserves to be. It is simple and cheap and has that prime virtue for the mariner of not requiring holes in the hull below the water. A less fortunate aspect is the low calorific value of air compared with water so that a rather large supply is required. Large air inlets and outlets and sizable trunkings are required compared with water pipes. Also, unless a funnel is fitted the warm air from the engine is normally discharged into the turbulent layers around the craft and so gets around the vessel. Another factor in the against column is the absence of a water jacket around the engine so losing a very good noise blanket. Air cooled engines are invariably noisier than their water cooled equivalent. This is not a matter of exhaust silencing but of the basic noise from within the engine, composed of the cylinder firing bangs, the rumble of bearings and so on.

An old friend pointed out to us recently that a very successful combination could be made of air and water cooled engines; for instance, an air cooled generator coupled with water cooled main engines with the generator air circulation being used, in effect, as the air supply for the main water cooled engines.

Water cooled engine systems divide themselves into two types — those which rely solely on salt water and those which use salt water to cool a separate fresh water supply which is the one actually circulated around the engine. Boats which normally float solely on good fresh water have not got the same problems, but many lakes and rivers are only nominally fresh and the same arrangement of a separate fresh water system then applies. Salt water itself is a reasonably corrosive fluid especially when run hot through aluminium castings. Equally as bad is the way that engine heat evaporates off the water leaving caked salt deposits behind which, after a period, seriously affect the engine cooling flow. Simple salt water cooling systems are therefore normally used only for those engines which began their design life as marine engines and are used in temperate climates. Such engines are made with large cooling passages and a great deal of cast iron. Fresh water cooling is almost universal for the automotive-derived engines.

All salt water systems and some combined systems start with a shipside (bottom) seacock and strainer. The outside hull fitting is often given scoop form to direct the water straight into the seacock under pressure. In most modern vessels there is ample positive pressure on the exterior of the hull in the midships body for the water supply. Only if the intakes are in the after body of a slow speed hull with rising buttock lines will there be likely to be any negative pressure to need boosting by scoop faced inlets. In fact there is very little justification for an exterior grill at all, for the convenience of being able to poke a stick clean through the seacock should it ever get bunged up with mud or weed is more important.

The seacocks themselves are usually joined directly to the strainer housing for the same reason. Seacocks, like every major control item in the engine space, must be reasonably easy of access. Lever cocks must fall into their normal position, which for a motor boat is open. It is convenient if the top of the seacock can extend above sea level so that it may be taken off for inspection without risk of an engulfment but, with the seacock handy, this is not essential. The strainer inside it should be matched to the normal duty of the boat and it is not overdoing things to carry two or three different sets to suit differing environments. In the open sea the strainer is guarding against fairly large lumps of matter — seaweed and such — and the strainer apertures can be as big as a quarter of an inch with advantage. With river use, however, there are all manner of fine strands and matter about and a fine mesh screen is necessary. Whichever is in use, the free area of the strainers ought to be at least twelve times the area of the engine water inlet pipe.

Seamen have a natural dislike of holes in their craft — a phobia which will possibly decline with the increasing use of one-piece hulls. It is therefore both sense and good superstition to keep every pipe which is open to the sea strong and solid as long as it is below the waterline. Salt water supply pipes are therefore usually made of solid copper to where they rise clear above the waterline and are close to the engine intake, and then are connected with flexible pipe to reduce the vibration hardening of the copper.

The salt water is pumped by an engine driven pump around a heat exchanger for a fresh water system or around the engine itself for a salt water system and then driven off to its final destiny which, more than likely, is to be injected into the exhaust and stern tube. The pump is just an ordinary pump with little to say about it except that it is surprising how few boats carry a spare impeller for what is quite an important item.

Other fresh water circulation systems do not require a pumped supply of cold salt water, for what is all around the engine room but cold salt water? The fresh water pipes themselves are taken out of the hull and run alongside the keel for so-called keel cooling and back again direct to the engine. Another variation in metal ships is to use the hull plating itself as the heat exchanger wall and to circulate the fresh water over a large area of the inside of the skin which, of course, is washed and cooled by the broad ocean outside. This is called skin cooling. Both these systems are so delightfully simple that their modest snags must be exposed in order to explain why they are not universally used. Keel cooling pipes are a little vulnerable and make cosy nesting homes for barnacles as well as adding to the hull resistance. Skin cooling has hydraulic problems, putting great pressures on the joints when a small movement occurs in the hull panel, and with the fouling of the ship's bottom the cooling becomes a little variable in effect.

Of the water flow around the engine there is little to be said, for this is the manufacturer's problem and usually reasonably well arranged. The thermostatic valves recirculate a proportion of the cooling water to keep the engine running at the planned temperature with surprising accuracy. The only real complaint is that for the great majority of marine engines it is necessary just after starting and before it warms up to look over the side or feel all over the pipes to discover whether the water is circulating properly. A simple gadget on the engine itself with a signal at the helmsman's position would remove another of the irritating minor chores which beset the conscientious owner of a power yacht.

Exhaust Systems

Once upon a time, when power boats were young and full of steam, the exhaust system was not just a discreet jettisoning of obnoxious effluvia but a major aesthetic exercise. The smoke stacks were not hidden or subjects of apology but stuck up straight and looked everyone boldly in the eye. Smoke stacks were a symbol of power and glory. The more there were and the bigger they came the better, for the more powerful and the faster the vessel. Alas for the good old days, for things are not what they were. We are convinced that at one Cowes regatta we saw a hatch open on top of the funnel of the royal yacht *Britannia*, and that a seaman appeared, silhouetted against the setting sun, who promptly dragged down into his funnel all the bunting with which she was dressed overall. It might have been a little-known naval mutiny by the black gang, promptly hushed up, but who could view a funnel in the same light after that? In fact modern funnels usually appear to be trying to disguise themselves as something better. Many have become mutated wheelhouses, others little more than faired excrescences while some of the more ambitious would do better service as a logotype symbol for an amusement park. Funnels have more to do with the naval architecture and the aesthetic architecture of the craft these days than any real connection with exhaust. This emerges privately from a puny stub pipe which might stick out of the hull anywhere as easily as it might from the funnel.

Unfortunately there are few steam power boats about these days and therefore the subject of marine exhausts refers almost exclusively to internal combustion engines. These exhausts come in two main types: the dry exhaust where the fumes are discharged directly to atmosphere and the wet exhaust where water is mixed in to cool and silence the mixture before its ejection from the hull. The latter is by far the more common type for

Fig. 259 This stark, lonely, exhaust outlet and silencer represents the basic needs of its fisherman owner.

all power boats between tiny launches and those big enough to sport working funnels.

The dry exhaust is hot for its whole length and therefore requires extensive insulation or water jacketing if it is to be reasonably safe and comfortable to have on board. The tail pipe in a dry system has very little silencing property so it also becomes essential that a silencer, probably of expansion box type, be fitted. The pipe should be steel and therefore, for its length, the system is heavy. Little launches fitted with tiny engines sometimes use a dry exhaust run to a transom outlet, but for anything bigger the hot exhaust unless sufficiently cooled will be an embarrassment in company and a funnel type outlet essential. This sounds as if we reluctantly arrived at such a solution. Far from it, for the shortest and best way to get rid of exhaust is to take it straight up and out of the engine space. The short pipe and natural heat rise reduce back pressure, the pipes do not have to be run through difficult parts of the accommodation and the system is practically accident proof. Perhaps even more attractive for yachts is the possibility of the exhaust discharge point being clear above the disturbed air envelope around the moving vessel. Not until you experience a high funnel exhaust outlet is it possible to realise how much exhaust is carried along around a yacht with a shipside or transom outlet. In one yacht the exhaust clearance by funnel was so successful that the owner complained that he could now smell everything else.

A dry exhaust line has to be carefully insulated, especially from wood and anything else which is vulnerable to heat. The bottom connection to the engine manifold has to be made with a flexible joint if the dry line is solid pipe and, if possible, a little downward loop should be arranged with a small drain pipe to collect and disperse any rain or condensation. The drain can conveniently always be left open if it is elbowed into the main pipe with the elbow pointing with the gas flow. Rain should be kept out of the line to reduce rusting and such, and this in practice requires some kind of cap to be fitted over the end of the tail pipe. It is rarely convenient to bend this tail pipe to a horizontal or to swan neck it because of the complications resulting from a wind blowing from some other direction than ahead. The normal solution is to hinge a little flap on to the straight-up end. This is blown open by the exhaust but closes of its own weight when the engine is not running. This little cap should be considered with great care as it is undoubtedly one of the most annoying noises afloat to hear the cap 'bouncing' metal on metal to chatter and ring when the engine is running slowly. It is, with carefully tuned metals, even more annoying than a sailboat halliard frapping on a metal mast, because it keeps time with the engine.

The principal advantages of a wet exhaust system lie in the cool pipelines and simple silencing which it produces. Great care has to be taken, very great care in fact, that there is no possibility of the water getting back to the engine. Also, as water pump failures are not unknown, the pipe

Fig. 260 Two smart smokestacks reducing windage to a minimum. The thin tail pipes are generally speaking placed well away from a casual clutch by an unstable crew which might bend them.

run ought to be capable of being run dry for, say, a quarter of an hour without resulting in a further disaster pouring poisonous fumes into the interior of the yacht. Even if the engine has a warning system you might be passing through the pierheads when it goes off and wish to travel a little further before stopping.

There are many variations on the wet exhaust theme. In some the engine manufacturer provides water injection elbows to be mounted direct off his manifolds, or something similar is made up by the installation engineers. Others have water injection silencers further down the line, even in some raceboats right next to the shipside outlet. Obviously the closer to the engine the less the need for hot pipes to be insulated. The water, once injected, has to be given a clear downward path to the sea if it is not to accumulate and perhaps flood back into the engine and disaster. The slope from injection to outlet must be quite positive, say of the order of 3° minimum plus the maximum trim which the boat is likely to reach when running. Six degrees might be taken as the normal maximum but it is possible to see craft proceeding along at a disgraceful 10° of trim. If the exhaust line is in any way vulnerable to water getting back to the engine, and even if it is not, it makes sense to fit a hinged flap over the transom outlet to act as a flap valve in strong following sea conditions.

The transom is the preferred outlet for the exhaust of most boats, probably because it is the most sociable place for the smell and splutter when in harbour and because it is felt that the fumes are left behind when the yacht is running. It is undoubtedly a nuisance in most boats to have to drag exhaust piping right through the accommodation from the engine room to the transom and the arrangement of the declivity for drainage gets more and more difficult as it gets longer. There comes at some point a good case for a side exhaust. With a single engine this can even be arranged with outlets port and starboard off a common pipe so that it never comes out to windward. With twin engines, as long as the outlets are well cowled and well above water, the results are not too anti-social. Of course if any outlet is in any measure immersed in the sea the exhaust will kick up the sea into a nasty spray and that is the more obnoxious when it happens at a side outlet than right aft. Provision has to be made in the slope of side exhaust for rolling and as this might be as much as 15° the run down ought to be a good 20°. Quite a common installation these days is to combine the side exhaust with a long exterior tunnel running right aft to the transom. This gets an awkward installation out of the after accommodation and the exhaust tunnels can form a decorative feature for the hull. Being on the outside they are vulnerable to damage but again, being on the outside, it does not matter too much.

Underwater exhausts are regarded rather suspiciously and yet, if properly designed, are perfectly acceptable. We have heard of two reasons which might make their use unacceptable in some circumstances. The more serious is that the underwater drumming from such a system frightens away game fish and therefore should not be used in a yacht with ever a thought of sports fishing. The second reason lies in the discomfiture of one owner who found that the exhaust, trapped under the hull, rose still hot and fumy through his lavatory outlets to the embarrassment of himself and his guests. The normally quoted bogy, however, is that of back pressure but we have found it to be negligible provided a pressure relief pipe is fitted in the system. This takes the form of a miniature exhaust run from the main line clear above the outlet and taken

Fig. 261   The simplest possible engine and rudder controls allow this Chesapeake Bay fishing boat to earn its living and contrast sharply with the elaborate control desks of modern pleasure craft.

to a small shipside outlet. Any significant back-pressure build-up, as might be when reversing, is lost through this small pipe.

All wet exhaust outlets are through-hull fittings and like all such should be fitted with seacocks if the yacht is to be used away from the canal bank. The exhaust pipes are usually large and the seacocks also large, heavy and expensive and it is tempting to risk their absence. A broken exhaust line could easily sink the ship and if by any chance a seacock is not fitted it only makes sense to carry on board some large wooden bungs already shaped for some hero to thump up the orifices in time of need.

Engines vibrate even if they are on fixed mountings and allowance has to be made for this in the arrangements of the exhaust line just as in every other engine connection. With a dry exhaust and an engine of any size there is little alternative to fitting a short length of expensive exhaust bellows direct to the engine manifold to take up the movement. On small engines it will probably be possible to use a length of the flexible steel spiral wound tubing often seen in car and industrial installations. This does not last very long but is cheap and easy to replace. On wet exhausts it is often convenient to use solid pipe to the water injection elbow or silencer with these mounted on the engine and effectively vibrating with it. The flexible portion can then be introduced in the water cooled pipe with greater ease and cheapness. There are quite a few manufacturers of exhaust hose suitable for these water injected exhausts and this is simple to install as well as allowing the necessary flexibility in the changeover from engine to hull mounting.

Water injection, by cooling the hot gas, has a very similar effect to an expansion chamber silencer and often water injection is used on its own as the sole silencing for an installation. If like us you prefer a boat to run fast and quietly it is worth installing a second silencer or a specialist water injection silencer. Anything must help to deaden the noise but silencing is a specialist job and it is far better to get the engine and silencer maker's recommendation not only as to best silencer but also as to its exact place in the exhaust line. It is also worth remembering the strong corrosive properties of hot salt water when injected into the exhaust line. The various neoprene and other plastics silencers will probably stand up better against this corrosion than a steel silencer unless

Fig. 262 The rather stark but no doubt effective exhaust outlets of La Belle Simone.

Controls and Instruments

Controls and instruments connected to power are what modern life is all about. The survival of the fittest has less and less validity nowadays, muscle power and physical size are becoming an embarrassment, and all because man has power and can control it with the help of instruments. A yacht is essentially part of the secret Walter Mitty life of her owner and her control position is its focal point. The 'command' of smooth running machinery is a universal specific for life's cares, and the choice and placing of the command tools is as important psychologically as it is practically. Poor fishing power boats are often equipped with not much more than two stiff wires with loops on the end sticking out of the engine box and are adequately controlled for their delicate work. Many a yachtsman spends hundreds of pounds on instruments and controls of really dubious practical value and gets every penny's worth of it in pleasure.

Whatever the approach, instruments and controls have one overriding requirement — they must

be reliable. Better by far to stick to the bent wires than to install a shiny instrument or control on which you cannot rely. Which having been said, we must admit that instruments and controls are at the present time generally of good quality. Most cases of failure seem to be due to inept installation, inept maintenance or inept use.

The principal controls cover speed and gear with sub-controls which might, for instance, cover the choke of a petrol engine or the stopping of a diesel. As sophistication advances there is a tendency for interconnection to occur. Already the most popular control levers combine gear and speed so that there is no possibility of inadvertent gear changing when the engine is running fast, with the consequent embarrassment and chagrin of expensive noises from the gearbox. Such sequences of operation are extremely simple to arrange when compared with many of the complications normally fitted on board a modern vessel. Electric controls are already in use for outboard engines and are far from being a gimmick, rather are they a harbinger of the future. Electric, or rather electronic, controls are widely used in industry where delicate control is required of large and expensive power. Apart from the obvious advantages of the simplicity of physical connection between engine and controls, it is possible to fit electronic units with sequence circuits to take care of almost any kind of engine misuse. The electronic circuit is developing under such intensive research, takes so little power to operate and has the most modest amount of nuts-and-bolts type engineering in its make-up, that it is an absolute natural for power boats.

At the moment, however, mechanical control is almost universal. By far the most common relies on the Bowden cable and its variations. A cable, double coiled to keep it stable in torsion and length, is used moving lengthwise inside a flexible tube, usually of coiled metal covered in plastics. The control movement is applied between an end connection on the cable and another on the tube and the movement repeated at the engine end. A surprisingly large thrust can be conveyed by this simple means — as much as 1000 lb for a heavyweight cable on a straight run reducing to perhaps half this if the run is full of relatively tight bends. Such cables require at least 15 inches of radius for their tightest bends, with small cables reducing this figure down to the order of 8 inches. This installation radius is normally the biggest problem in arranging a cable route. Perhaps the next biggest problem is in making sure that cables are reasonably clear of any hot, or possibly hot, part of the engine. A cable, covered as is normal with vinyl, melts into an immovable lump if ill-treated with excess heat. Cable installations are more vulnerable to wear and misuse than some other types but are cheap and readily replaced. They can also be combined with other systems and, for instance, the control head can be fitted with interlocked electric switches to prevent starting the engine when in gear or without safety fans running.

In any arrangement where the engine and control station are reasonably close to each other and well placed it is possible to use a simple wire or chain arrangement to connect the two. The corners are fitted with sheaves and some foolproof method of maintaining tension is worked in. At its simplest and roughest an iron chain can be led in a manner similar to chain-operated steering gear. At its most complex a system of sheave boxes connected by pipes carrying the cable wires can build an installation of great neatness and efficiency.

A similar set of circumstances covers the use of direct lever controls and variations which transfer the motion through a series of bell cranks and levers. The principal problem is to keep the weight of metal to be moved in the operation of the control down to a minimum and also to reduce the friction in the components. Unless the installation is simple it calls for extremely high quality engineering, both for the weight of operation and for the delicacy of the control itself.

Hydraulic controls approach the convenience of cable operated controls in that only a small pair of pipes has to connect the one to the other. In fact when the pipe bends can be so much smaller than the cable bends the advantage lies with the hydraulic which possibly also has an edge with the increased delicacy and accuracy of control. The disadvantage being in the introduction of another system in the ship and the rather low operating power which can be transmitted by the size of equipment usually fitted in yachts. It is usual in installations requiring a relatively high thrust, such as mechanical gearboxes, to use the hydraulic control on the bridge to operate a slave cylinder mounted on the engine which in turn operates a final electric control. This might be thought to be taking two bites at one cherry.

The choice of type of control does of course depend on the exact circumstances of the vessel herself. The most convincing reasons for the use of one kind of equipment are often completely overwhelmed by the practical possibilities. To refer again to the impoverished fisherman operating his boats with wire rods, it is likely that the best reasons for another kind of installation could be advanced, to be trumped in the last resort by the depth of his pocket. In round terms, however, the cable type of control is satisfactory for almost every installation but might well be replaced with a more solid arrangement where usage is high, maintenance low and the connections direct. The crude lever and bell crank is very good value where fineness of control is not required but heavy loading is — such as with some of the more antique mechanical gearboxes. Conversely the finely engineered lever and bell crank system can give very fine control with a modicum of power in it.

The placing of the controls is largely governed by the convenience of the helmsman who is the modern master of the engines. Speed and gear controls must be placed so that they can be operated with one hand while the other holds the wheel, or at least with both hands while the wheel is held steady with boot or tummy. This places the controls within a quite circumscribed area. In most yachts it is also convenient that the controls be accessible for operation by another person. The helmsman might have to concentrate really hard on the direction in which he is driving.

Dual station controls only require the interlinking of twin sets of cables or whatever system is being used. Usually the only penalties are in a slightly heavier control operation and the possibility of two minds with quite different thoughts attached to the same engine. Although these are both control problems the latter is more a matter for the master than for the installation engineer. It is possible to obtain controls with station disengagement in case you fear a touch of mutiny.

The other end of the control situation is the return of information on the effect of the controlling. On the one hand you can look out of the window or over the dodger and see the sea going past which gives, in effect, good information on the boat state. Information on the engine state is however generally conveyed through instruments. The principal bit of knowledge that all is well in the prime mover is given by the oil pressure. A good oil pressure infers that all is well with the mechanical parts of the engine, a moderate pressure infers that important parts, principally the bearings, are wearing out and an absence of oil pressure announces the impending seizing-up of the motor — a disaster slightly worse than dismasting is to a sail boat.

The next most important instrument is, in our opinion, the water temperature gauge which, in the modern engine, replaces the quick thrust of palm against cylinder block of the good old days. This gauge, placed in various parts of the system according to the engine maker's ideas, gives information that the cooling system is or is not working in its own right or is or is not coping with some situation inside the engine. It operates more as a warning than does the oil pressure gauge, and a fluctuation in its reading indicates more a situation to be watched than, necessarily, impending disaster.

Nearly every new engine seen nowadays is electrically started and therefore the vessel is dependent on the electricity in reserve for life should the engine stop or be stopped. For the power seaman the third most important piece of knowledge from his engines is that they are busy poking electricity into the batteries in a satisfactory way. The engine ammeter is usually so connected to the battery circuits that it shows charge

and discharge rates referring to the battery rather than to the engine charging circuit alone. So important is the electricity in an electrically starting vessel that we would put the voltmeter or battery state meter in the same category as those already mentioned.

In rather a section by itself is the tachometer or engine revolution meter. It is not strictly anywhere near as essential as those gauges already mentioned, for the engine speed, propeller speed and boat speed are all so related as to be readily appreciated by looking over the side and to be gauged by the position of the speed control. However, there is no denying the satisfaction of exactness and most engine manufacturers include a tachometer in their standard instruments. These come in two distinct types. The mechanical one is operated by a thick metal-bound cable carrying a twirling shaft all the way from some convenient spot on the engine to the main control panel where an instrument full of spinning wheels and counterweights does its stuff and indicates the engine speed. The second type uses the engine connection to drive a tiny electric motor which then transmits current to an accurate ammeter which is calibrated in engine speed rather than in amperes. In addition it is possible to run an engine speed meter off the spark plug static in a petrol engine. All types of revolution counters work with reasonable accuracy but raceboat drivers seem to be particularly keen on the direct action cable type on the grounds that it is usually still operating at the end of the race.

The next range of instrumentation implies a close interest in the correct functioning of your engine, either because you are looking for every ounce of power or because it represents a substantial financial investment. Whether gearbox oil pressure comes into this list or not depends on its oil linkage with the main engine. However, tidying up the main information by taking the water temperature at both ends of the system and the oil temperature is usual, together with such items as fuel pressure. Outside this some valuable information lies in the engine room temperature and even pressure, and the presence of a remote-reading stern tube temperature gauge saves many a pair of greasy fingertips. Special cases have special requirements but any vessel with a complete set of informers on these lines for both engines, together with the basic ship and navigational information displays, can look any airline pilot squarely in the eye.

Engine Attachments

Engines and motors are produced in such prodigious quantities these days that it often seems easier to fit a separate power unit for each mechanical task than to attempt any kind of combined system. This often leads to the ludicrous situation where a tiny electric pump is seen working its little self to death to cope with some emergency while the main engine, perhaps a thousand times more powerful, sits silent. If the vessel should suffer an inundation the owner and his crew may also be seen pumping and bailing for dear life while their expensive and powerful machinery idles. Plainly it makes sense to have some provision for making other use of the main power supply apart from simple propulsion.

Most engines are in fact fitted or fittable with a power take-off, usually no more than a vee belt pulley stuck on to the nether end of the crankshaft or to some other conveniently rotating shaft in the works. The engine is not designed to deliver anything like its full output in this manner and the power actually removable from the power take-off is limited by the manufacturer to some figure of the order of 10 per cent of the maximum. This power comes directly off that available to drive the boat along and whereas it can be used continuously the loss of say 30 hp from the top end performance of a 300 hp motor is more than even the most equable owner will usually stand. The power take-off is therefore most often used for intermittent loads and is ideal for running a high capacity bilge pump, a sizable generating set for quick battery charging or a refrigerator pump for a deep freeze system equipped with holdover plates. A clutch can be fitted, usually on the auxiliary equipment, so that putting it into operation is simple, even possibly by remote control. At worst, fitting a pulley belt in place is not too much to do if the ship is sinking.

The engine is also available for use in other directions. One of the simplest and fundamentally worthwhile connections which can be made to it is to use the sea water circulation system as an emergency bilge pump. The normal bilge lines, or a special emergency set, are taken to a three-way cock on the inlet side of the sea water circulation pump. Instead of pumping the sea around the engine and overboard this will then pump the bilge water around the engine and then overboard. A 500 hp diesel for instance has a salt water pump capacity of 100 gallons a minute. Such a system is not used except for the occasional emergency to avoid oil and bilge waste clogging up the system. Also, many engines have neoprene impellers in their salt water pumps which deteriorate badly if exposed to oil for any length of time.

Another thought-provoking contrast of marine life is to see the owner of an expensive engine, which is busy turning the fuel he has bought into heat energy, standing only a few feet away from it and shivering with cold. It was often remarked how the crew of a vessel with air cooled engines would cluster on the small after deck — entirely explained the moment it was realised that it was in this area that the hot air was discharged. It would seem a modest thing to do to blow air past some part of the exhaust system and trunk it to the crew in any vessel which puts to sea in the cold.

Such a system with rather more elaboration is often used to heat the hot department of the ship's domestic water supply. The exhaust gases are taken through a waste-heat boiler on their way to atmosphere and a fair proportion of their heat extracted for re-use. The beauty of such systems is that they do not affect the performance or the fuel consumption of the engine. Something for nothing, at last, provided that you have forgotten the installation costs.

The Arrangement of Engine Space

Any detached observer gifted with the power to contemplate all yacht engine rooms as a whole would probably remark first of all that they revealed the amazing adaptability of the human frame — how it can twist and contract and stretch to avoid hot surfaces, and squeeze through narrow gaps in whirling machinery and lie head first to spanner away effectively at something important in the bilge. No-one would pretend that there was anything ideal in sight but the plain truth is that most yacht engine rooms are too tightly packed. It makes sense and even logic, for the payload of a yacht is the amount of owner's and guest accommodation not the machinery space. Such tight juxtaposition of machinery can be and normally is made to operate with great success but requires something of the chess game in the installation design. Maintenance has to be played in the mind several moves ahead and the consequences of minor disasters should be kept under control.

The tidiness of the installation engineer is one of the biggest factors. Some will produce an engine room with a feeling of space and grace just because every item is neatly and discreetly placed. Another fitting the same equipment without mental planning will finish up with a fair imitation of one of those old-fashioned American Wild West locomotives which were built inside out with guts blatantly displayed, apparently as a totem to impress the Indians.

Every part must as far as possible be removable for maintenance with the minimum of disturbance to the other equipment. Equipment is often seen parked nicely in place but with the ordinary removal of its cover involving a major disturbance to all about it. The various parts of the engine which have to be unbolted for some degree of inspection or maintenance are often difficult to appreciate. Engine manufacturers are sometimes also lax in providing this information and the removal of what looks from the outside to be a simple cover plate may involve withdrawing several feet of odds and ends fastened to its interior.

The older and larger marine engines are open to major maintenance in position, but most are far better for being removed completely for stripping. This is a major operation but there should be a path provided up through the ship for removal. Several large bolted hatches in the overheads are normal but, sad to say, it is not all that unusual for the removal of an engine to involve the use of saw and cutter. It seems undignified to handle an engine other than in its natural plane and

provision is usually allowed for the engine to emerge from the ship still horizontal as it was on its beds. However, there is no real reason why the engine cannot be hauled out end first provided the attachments are secure enough. It is also not uncommon to have to unbolt the gearbox and other units to reduce its overall dimensions.

Certain paths of access to important equipment must be planned into the tightly packed machinery space. Apart from engine fitted items like spark plugs, injectors, fuel pumps, starters and so on, reasonable access must be allowed to the stern glands, fuel tank cut-offs and filters, and to the pumps.

Any vessel with any pretensions to seaworthiness carries some spare parts for the machinery and the tools to fit them. When they are required they are usually required with some urgency and should not need looking for. In our opinion it is worth making space for a tool and spares box no matter how crowded the engine compartment. It would be nice to have a work bench in a bigger yacht and a proper tool rack but this reflects more the style in which maintenance and repair work is done in port rather than at sea (except in the biggest vessels) and therefore is of secondary importance.

Engine spaces are best painted white or another very light colour. Not only does this show every drop of oil dripping from where it should not be coming but reflects the lighting of the engine space into all the darker and concealed corners. Engine rooms are rarely lit with natural light, more is the pity, but commonly make do with armoured bulkhead lights and a wander lamp. (Why the lights have to be armoured we do not know, for it is years and years since we have seen one in danger.)

CHAPTER 12
Electrics Afloat

General

Electrical installations have been practicable afloat for as long as they have been ashore. Boats are much damper than houses and therefore the standard of installation and insulation has to be very much better. It is to the misunderstanding of this basic point that the years of electrical problems afloat have been due. In fact it used to be said, bitterly, that the electric wiring was usually done by the yard sweeper when he was not engaged in painting the topsides. Electrics were

not thought natural for boats, poor installations gave trouble, battery capacity was too small and worst of all the voltage used was usually too low. In a poor installation it is true that the lower the voltage the safer the whole mess, but a low voltage lacks the pressure necessary to push its way along wires with the result that voltage drop affects every fitting more than a few feet from the batteries. The system is then relegated to minor duties like cabin lighting, and gas or liquid fuel is brought on board for cooking, main lighting and heating.

Fig. 263   Control bridge of the 53 ft motor yacht Inquisitor *is superbly fitted with electronic equipment. The well-ordered arrangement of the panels is partnered by equally disciplined looms of cables behind the scenes. Thirty-six indicator lights in two deckhead panels show the state of the systems and dials in front of the driver are grouped, as in aircraft, for quick and easy recognition.*

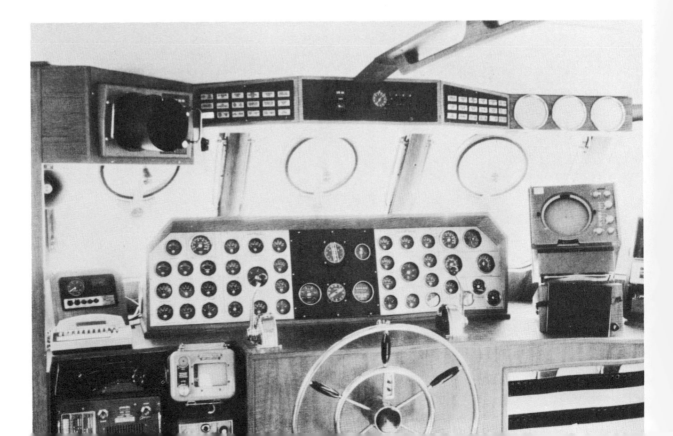

In a proper installation electricity will do most things conveniently and easily but with two major problems: the simplest method of providing enough juice is to carry enough batteries, but these are heavy; the alternative is to have a separate electricity generating engine to supply the current when required, but the great majority of these are noisy. The larger the vessel the less these problems are in proportion. The weight of large batteries can be carried without embarrassment or the generator can be silenced and sound absorbed to an acceptable degree. Marina living has become part of the answer for the smaller yacht where a shore supply connection can give the craft her electricity supply when she is lying in company and the generator noise has only to be controlled and planned for when she is cruising. The very small yacht can also have a domestic electric system in addition to that which is required by the engines in the form of a portable battery to be taken ashore for charging when it runs low.

The electrics required by the engines are the most important by a very large degree. The life of the yacht depends on starting the motors and no domestic consumption should be allowed to interfere with this necessary function. It is therefore usual practice to provide a complete bank of batteries for the engines and another bank for the domestic system. If a generator is carried which is able to provide charge for the main engine battery then the safety factor is partly covered if only the generator starting battery is separate from the main system. The little battery starts the little engine which pops the poundage into the big batteries which start the big engines like any well brought up fairy story.

The largest voltage commonly seen on yachts is either 240 volts A.C. or 110 volts A.C., which are the equivalent mains voltages to be found ashore. Such power is usually supplied by a separate generating engine. At 2 volts a cell it would take a very large bank of batteries to supply direct current of this power, never mind turning it into alternating current. This is why the most common installations use a comparatively low voltage direct current as a basis. Twenty-four volt is probably the most common, with some 32 volt installations stemming from the aircraft industry and some 12 and 6 volt installations stemming from the car industry.

The Source of Electricity

In most houses electricity is something rather remote which appears like magic at the command of a switch. The how and wherefore of its origin is of no real concern, neither is there much need to take any interest in the dull details of its standard and quality. On board a boat, however, every amp has to be manufactured and processed on the spot except when moored to a dock with a shore supply plugged in.

It is also possible to use a natural source for the electricity supply, such as a wind operated generator or a solar battery charger as used in space exploration which converts light directly into electricity. These offer the additional satisfaction of a 'free' supply. However, in general the basic power source, like everything else in a power boat, is an engine of some kind. Electricity is then manufactured from power taken either from the main engine or from one or more separate auxiliary engines. Nearly every marine engine carries

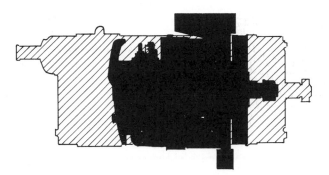

Fig. 264 Alternator, shown black, compared with dynamo of similar output.

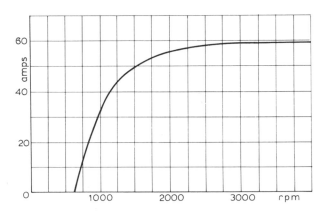

Fig. 265 Typical alternator output curve.

a permanently fastened small capacity generator planned by the engine manufacturer to take care of the charging of those batteries necessary to run the engine starter. An engine power take-off can also be used to run, by belt drive, a somewhat larger generator, whereas the auxiliary engine is usually coupled permanently to its generator as a set.

Until comparatively recently the majority of small generators were dynamos but nowadays an alternator is becoming more commonly fitted. Both are of about the same efficiency and both basically produce alternating current which has to be rectified to give a direct current supply. The basic difference is that the rectification is done mechanically in the dynamo by means of a commutator and brushes, while the alternator uses diodes (a kind of electrical valve) to do the same job. The alternator has therefore fewer moving parts for the same output or, conversely and more usually, gives a greater output for the same size. It is also more flexible than the dynamo in that it can be used over a much wider speed range and the output can be largely independent of engine speed. An additional useful feature, for what it is worth, is that it can be turned in either direction equally efficiently.

The electricity, once produced, has to be cut and parcelled to size. The generator output varies with the speed of rotation and therefore the pressure and supply have to be controlled by a voltage regulator and a cut-out. The latter operates to cut the circuit to the batteries when the generator is producing less than the charging voltage. If this did not happen the current would be reversed and the batteries would supply current to the generator instead. The voltage required to charge a battery is some 10 to 30 per cent above its nominal voltage. The main engines of a vessel are, of course, run at speeds to suit the navigation rather than the electrical attachments and are therefore considered as variable speed drives for their generators. These are then normally fitted with some form of automatic voltage regulation usually taking the same form as that used on motor cars. A vibrating contact regulator of this form also incorporates the cut-out. The voltage in fact in most boat installations does not need to be too precise but should more exactness be required it is usual to fit a carbon pile regulator. The auxiliary generator engines on the other hand are run entirely to suit the electrical department

and are therefore run at constant speed. In large vessels with engineers on duty this allows hand operated voltage regulation to be fitted. By this means the engineer can match the voltage output to the exact requirements of the state of charge of the batteries, making for a generally higher efficiency. Smaller craft, however, still fit automatic regulation although, with the constant speed background, this can be set up to give a more efficient charging service to the batteries.

With a generator on each main engine, often two and occasionally more, in addition to any auxiliary outfits, most power boats have several generators on board. If these are alternators they can be arranged singly or together to charge a single bank of batteries but dynamos, without the diodes, must never be used together as high and dangerous circulating currents can be set up between them. In practice it is best to arrange charging on a solitary basis. A large battery capacity can be split into banks for charging and changeover switches can be arranged for their independent selection.

Capacities of generator and batteries are usually considered on a daily basis. What is taken from the batteries in a normal working twenty-four hours ought to be replaced in the same period. Hence the normal daily operating time for the generator has to be sufficient to produce more electricity than is used in the same period, making another factor to be considered in the choice of generating equipment.

It is not always properly appreciated that batteries are relatively delicate devices despite their massive appearance. The use of the wrong size of generator for charging can, if not wreck the batteries, seriously affect their life and efficiency. The direct relationship between battery and generator varies with types and installations but, for instance, a change in battery type or capacity may

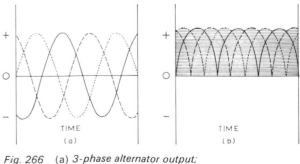

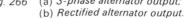

Fig. 266 (a) *3-phase alternator output;*
(b) *Rectified alternator output.*

well require a change in generator size. The main engine driven generators must also be considered at their rating at the normal main engine speed rather than the nominal rating of the unit which refers to the output at maximum. As the battery capacity itself is, or ought to be, directly related to the overall electric installation for the vessel it can be seen that the planning of the whole installation is a matter of some expertise and deserves more careful consideration than has been common in the past.

Storage

It is always necessary to store electricity somewhere on board a modern vessel. At its simplest this need be no more than a flashlamp battery so that the owner can see where to swing his hand when starting the engine into life. Most craft have batteries to start the engines and nearly all of new construction also have an extensive electrical layout which requires a big storage background. The flashlamp battery is an irreversible store which consumes its anodes in giving current but the main batteries are based on a reversible process. They operate on a charge—discharge cycle which can be repeated right through the life of the battery.

Marine batteries come in two principal types — the lead acid and the nickel alkali, also known as the nickel iron. Lead acid is more common, looking at power boats as a whole, because it is initially cheaper and lighter. The nickel alkali does have better operating characteristics for life afloat and lasts very much longer than the lead acid. In fact the cost of storing electricity taken over, say, a ten year period is about the same whichever battery type you choose.

A battery consists of a number of independent cells connected together in series to produce the required voltage. The capacity depends on the size of each cell unit. Each lead acid cell has a nominal voltage of two volts and therefore, for example, a 24 volt lead acid battery will consist of twelve separate cells. Nickel alkali cells have a nominal voltage of about 1·3 volts. Battery capacity is measured in ampere hours and as this can vary extensively with the rate of discharge it is usually given for the current which can be supplied over a declared and standardised time such as 10 or 20 hours. For instance, a 60 ampere-hour battery on a 10 hour rate will give 6 amps for 10 hours. The faster the discharge the lower the battery rating will be. The voltage output during the discharge period will vary. A battery on charge will have a voltage as high as 2·5 volts per cell. A voltage close to the nominal two will be maintained for the first three-quarters of the discharge and then will drop off badly. The standard minimum voltage at the end of the rated discharge period is 1·8 volts per cell.

The lead acid cell consists basically of two plates of lead type material immersed in dilute sulphuric acid; the negative plate being a lead sponge and the positive a plate of lead peroxide. During discharge both take the sulphate out of the acid to form lead sulphate on both plates. During charge this situation is reversed and is accompanied by a certain amount of decomposition of the water diluting the acid, oxygen assembling at the positive plate and hydrogen at the negative plate. These gases do in fact accumulate in explosive proportions at the surface of the liquid. With each cell properly ventilated this mixture escapes to atmosphere where, given good ventilation, it is quickly diluted and dissipated. It is therefore essential that batteries are given very good ventilation during charging. Smoking in the battery compartment, with the possibility of hot ash or fragments of glowing match dropping into the cells, is at the very least, foolhardy. The neglect of this care or of proper ventilation has been the prime cause of quite a few disasters and the suspected cause of many which are put down to unknown causes.

Lead acid batteries are best when set up with some kind of constant charge—discharge cycle. If they are left neglected in an uncharged state the accumulation of lead sulphate on the plates can physically twist them out of shape and gravely affect the performance of the battery. The speed of the chemical action is, as usual, affected by heat and if the batteries are stored in a warm spot in the vessel or the vessel herself normally operates in a high ambient temperature the strength of the sulphuric acid electrolyte should be adjusted. Heat also helps to evaporate the water content from the electrolyte and batteries in a hot situation should have their distilled water topping-up parade at much more frequent intervals. At the other end of the scale the lead acid battery can freeze and burst if exposed to extremely low temperature in an uncharged or low charge state.

There are two principal kinds of nickel alkali batteries of which the more common afloat is the nickel cadmium. The positive plate consists of nickel hydrate with some form of graphite cladding to improve the electrical conduction. The negative plate is cadmium oxide with iron oxide. Both plates consist of perforated steel into which the active material is forced under high pressure. These are then immersed in a solution of potassium hydroxide. The nickel hydrate is highly oxidised when the cell is charged at the expense of the cadmium oxide which is reduced to pure cadmium. On discharge the process is reversed, with the electrolyte functioning only as a conductor and therefore suffering no charge revealing change in specific gravity as occurs for lead acid cells. The electrolyte is diluted with distilled water and, as with the lead acid battery, this is broken down during charging to give off oxygen and hydrogen.

The second kind of nickel alkali battery has plates formed in the same way but with the positive packed with flakes of pure nickel among the nickel hydrate and the negative with an activated iron stuffing. This makes for a battery capable of taking outstandingly fast charging rates although the discharge rate is best suited for small loads. It is therefore principally used where batteries are taken ashore for quick charging and used on board for lighting loads. Alternatively these batteries are to be found on large craft with substantial home generating sets where charging can be done swiftly without too much upset to crew or neighbours.

The choice of battery type is determined by weight, cost and space, related to the situation of the particular vessel. The choice of battery capacity is concerned simply with the amount of electricity which will be used in a normal operating day. At very least the batteries should have capacity to cover this on the understanding that they are recharged daily. If charging cannot be arranged on a daily basis then the battery capacity has to be doubled or trebled to suit the expected style of life on board. Most engine manufacturers recommend a size of starting battery for their engines and this is usually slightly generous so as to allow some quarter of its capacity to be available for ship or domestic electrics. This is rarely enough for any except the smallest vessels and the extra capacity required must be added to that specified for the engine, requiring either a bigger generator on the engine or some form of additional charging.

The aging of batteries reduces their effective capacity and it is a curious fact that the electrical load fitted to the vessel will only increase and never decrease during its life. It is therefore worth being a little generous, say a 10 per cent overestimate, of battery capacity.

Batteries are great heavy things, often in total as heavy as the main engines and potentially as dangerous. Their location and the construction of their bearers and so on deserve almost as much consideration as the main engines. They have to be mounted so that no convolution or shock to the vessel will disturb them. The battery compartment should be well ventilated and in this connection it is possible to wire in an automatic electric fan to run whenever charge is being put into the batteries. It would seem unnecessary to point out that fans used to remove hydrogen from the battery compartment must be of the sparkproof type for a quiet life. Switches, relays or anything else that makes sparks should also be located well away from the batteries. Lead acid batteries should be mounted on acid proof trays — it is no longer necessary to use lead lined trays for there are a number of acid resistant compounds available. The maximum acid spillage which a reasonable man might expect at one time is for one cell to split, and therefore the depth of tray should be enough to contain this amount with the ship rolling to her natural rhythm. It is worth taking this trouble as acid is a devastating contribution to an intricate installation. Good access to the batteries is also desirable so that topping-up is simple, easy and regular, the tops of course kept free from dirt and the connections clean.

Distribution

The majority of direct current installations in the 6 to 32 volt range distribute the electricity produced by the generators through the batteries. If a separate auxiliary generating set is part of the installation it is not unusual to fit a changeover switch so that the full lighting and domestic load can be carried direct by the set. This is often convenient to ensure that the engine starting batteries are not run flat by accident and also to allow the batteries to receive charge from the engine generators. We prefer in the interests of reliability to fit two or three banks of batteries each capable of the full starting or domestic load. In a twin engined vessel each of two banks is basically charged by its own engine to which it also supplies starting current. Domestic lighting is taken from only one bank at a time leaving the other full, ready and willing to start up the engines in the morning. If an auxiliary charging set is fitted this can be arranged either to supply one bank at a time as an alternative to the main engine generator, or to supply its own third bank. All the banks of batteries are made interchangeable by means of switching. In addition the generator should have its own little battery for its own starting if that is the way it is made. At the very least some form of emergency cross connection has to be available so that battery power can reach any engine.

The lower the operating voltage the more important it becomes to keep the distribution wires as short as possible to reduce voltage drop. A few volts off 240 are not really significant but the same number off six would really reduce the efficiency of the system. The generators, the batteries and the engine starters and any other heavy user of electricity should be placed physically as well as electrically close to each other. Big fat cables help to reduce voltage drop but they are heavy and expensive and even bulky.

Many engine direct current circuits work with one pole, usually the negative, earthed, and therefore it is convenient for yachts with engines so equipped to follow suit for the whole ship's system. The various items of equipment on board are earthed direct to the engine or to a main earth plate by means of copper braiding rather than to the nearest shipside fitting. This latter is sometimes seen but not for too long as they are apt to suffer undue electrolytic corrosion. In the earthed return systems it is vital that every item of equipment is earthed on the same pole. A most modest error in this respect can set electrolytic corrosion currents to snapping their teeth about some vital bit of ship. In fact with the increased amount of electrics on board a small failure in the insulated part of such a system due to poor installation or to wear can set up a brisk corrosion situation. Earthed return systems are therefore being generally superseded by insulated return systems.

In a vessel with electrics of any consequence

it is usual to fit a main distribution board close among the engine, generator and battery circle. On it are placed the bus bars – heavy copper or brass bars with heavy mechanically fitted or brazed terminals to act as a main gathering and connecting point for the principal circuits. The name bus is short for omnibus (for all). There has to be a positive and negative bus bar for each bank of batteries but the negative can be common to all if that is the earthed side of the system. The main distribution board will also normally carry the battery cut-off links and switches and changeover switches and also possibly any hand operated generator controls. The distribution boards should also carry an ammeter, voltmeter and battery charge meter in addition to those which may be fitted for the helmsman if these are not mounted, as is sometimes more convenient, on an auxiliary distribution board arranged for the minor circuits. Most lighting and general circuits are arranged as two wire ring main or looped in systems. The ring main system is a great loop attached at both ends to the bus bars and therefore fed from both ends. Light and other fittings are wired either singly or in convenient groups direct to the main at the nearest point. With the other system, groups of fittings are wired into comparatively short loops run from one bus bar to the other and therefore fed from one end only. The various items have to be grouped conveniently into circuits. They have first of all to be convenient geographically so that the circuit involves the shortest possible run of wire to cut voltage drop. Then they have to be convenient arithmetically so that each group adds up to a total current suitable for the distribution wiring and the protective fuses or circuit breakers to be used. Third, and sometimes forgotten, is that the result of a circuit failure should not be too inconvenient. It is plainly absurd, even if neat, to put all the navigation lights, for instance, into one circuit. If the current fails they all go out leaving your vessel completely unlit in the dark. Similarly there will be more confusion if all the lights go out at one end of your craft than if half the lights go out through her length.

The distribution wiring has to be of good quality and of ample size for the current requirements. Stranded tinned copper is generally taken to be best. Rubber used to be the best insulation and armoured lead sheathed rubber insulated cables were the classic recommendation for the successful electrical installation. Nowadays suitable plastics sheathed cables are an acceptable substitute and, being less prone to perishing, are probably better all round. Wiring cables must be properly supported everywhere so that there is no possibility of their chafing through or otherwise getting damaged. In a wooden vessel brass straps or saddles can be used extensively. Conduits or wiring trays are normal in metal and GRP vessels, and the modern plastics conduit box with a closure or lid is ideal. Distribution wiring is best concealed in all the domestic areas of a vessel so that it is not inadvertently damaged by abrasion and all junctions must be made with terminal type junction boxes. Standards at sea have to be higher than those in a house and there is no getting away from this if you want to be safe and reliable.

Combinations

A great many modern vessels take advantage of the necessity for putting a separate generating set on board to fit a high voltage alternating current second system. The supply from this system comes direct from the generator without benefit of battery and is the same as that normally used for the domestic supply ashore, either 60 cycle 110 volt or 50 cycle 240 volt. Battery charging,

probably the origin of the need for the generator, is taken care of by fitting a converter/transformer to produce the low voltage direct current for this job. In the meantime the vessel can enjoy some of the comforts of home at production line prices instead of using specially made equipment. Cooking, water heating, air conditioning, refrigeration, vacuum cleaners, dish washers and electric drills can all now be installed and run off the generating set. At the same time all the normal lights and small fans and lesser navigation equipment will run as usual off the low voltage, probably 24 volt, system. A further advantage is that the whole installation both high and low will function directly from the shore supply line at the dock.

A small generator of as little as 2·5 kilowatts will, used with a little discretion, run a couple of hot plates, charge the batteries and run the hot water system, and provide good service for a boat up to say 35 feet in length. The size of craft fitted with this high voltage type of installation is creeping down, and now it is not unreasonable to find it on board craft as small as around 20 feet. The upper size is not limited and the use of alternating current can extend to air conditioning, deep freezing, television and even electric blankets.

Most units are arranged with 'on-demand' starting which fires the generator engine starter whenever an A.C. equipment switch is turned on. The motor then runs away all by itself for as long as its product is required and switches itself off as the last A.C. switch is turned off. All machinery inevitably makes some noise when running and even with the modern highly sound-absorbed equipment one is conscious to some degree or other that the generator is in action. This is inevitable until the yacht is big enough to carry enough batteries to turn the tables. The direct current battery output can then be transformed and put through a converter to make the high voltage alternating current. The generator can be switched off for periods, maybe at night, and any supply taken over by the silent running batteries. Most equipment run off A.C. batteries is used almost exclusively in waking hours and only such items as refrigerators and air conditioning need to operate during the night when people are especially sensitive to noise. It is therefore common to exclude the refrigerator especially from the high-powered system and to arrange for it to

Fig. 267 Even the galley in a small yacht (this is a 32 ft motor boat) can be fitted with such refinements as electric cooking and hot and cold running water.

Fig. 268 The larger motor yacht can run to more complex electric installations for the galley, including separate hob and oven, power points, refrigeration, etc. This is Romantica, *built by Thornycroft and designed by Fred Parker.*

be run off the lower powered, and silent, system.

In bigger vessels the high-powered system can be extended further into three-phase operation. This means that in round terms three separate series of alternating impulses are taken off the generator during each revolution and passed around the system. Where high power is required, as it might be for an anchor windlass, all three phases are taken to it, whereas for ordinary loads only one phase is wired along. The light loads have to be spread among the three phases to provide a balanced load for the generator and the whole system is a touch complicated to compensate for the increased efficiency of operation.

Protection and Fittings

It cannot be said too often that the best protection against electrical disaster anywhere and especially afloat is to have first-rate equipment intelligently installed. The majority of dangerous situations stemming from the electrical department are due to some tiny sparks charring away at the neighbouring woodwork or inflammable GRP, tiny bit by tiny bit until a nice area of tinder has been built up ready to burst into flames. Sparks are usually the prime movers of the many major explosions due to leakages of fuel, gas or hydrogen fumes. Although not the prime cause of such disaster the absence of the spark might well have saved the day. Switches, relays and similar equipment are known to produce sparks and a certain amount of caution should be exercised in their placing on board. What is difficult to anticipate however is some weak point in a poor installation where there may be a bad connection or a cable placed where it can chafe through to expose the live metal. Hence the need for proper junction boxes and well-protected cables afloat.

When a wire is forced by some electrical mishap inside the system to carry too large a current, the resistance in the wire becomes extreme. The energy thus lost can only turn to heat and the wire becomes warm. Carried to a high degree of overload the wire can actually become glowing hot and the most uncomfortable shipmate. The principal protection against such overload currents is, of course, to fit fuses or circuit breakers. The former rely on the heating action of an overload to heat a short length of metal wire or pack of powder with a very low melting point. It melts before the current builds up to a dangerous degree and cuts the circuit. The circuit breaker is a more sophisticated device and especially convenient for boats. Any extra current passing through a circuit breaker warms up a bimetallic strip which, like a good old-fashioned mousetrap, trips a large spring which throws the switch open. This is backed up by an electromagnetic release which gives instant protection against a heavy overload. A fuse has to be physically replaced, often a tiresome job on a dark and windy night on the rolling main, when the right spare has to be found and inserted carefully into a narrow spot, probably by torchlight. The circuit breaker on the other hand is, to all outward appearance, only a rather clumsy looking switch which works normally when all is well but springs out and refuses to return to the 'on' position until the trouble in the circuit itself has been put right. A momentary overload current is therefore only a momentary problem and anything more serious has to be looked into. There is no chance, and no temptation, to proceed at peril with a wire nail stuck in where the fuse ought to be.

Circuit breakers or fuses must be fitted

in every circuit. Direct current circuits require single pole protection on the unearthed side, usually the positive. Alternating circuits are best fitted with double pole circuit breakers. Circuit breakers, as a requirement, must cover not only the small ship and domestic equipment but also and especially radios, anchor windlasses, large fans and so on. Circuit breakers are neat enough to be left visible in the accommodation of a yacht or even on the main control panel and may be used directly as the control switches for their respective circuits. Fuses need a little protection and are usually boxed away tidily but must still be capable of good access under trying conditions. Incidentally, wood is such a pleasing material that it is tempting to make distribution and fusebox covers of it. Both wood and metal should be avoided, the one gets either wet or can catch fire and the other requires insulation. Boards and their covers should be made of one of the new high di-electric insulating materials such as are many of the new plastics.

Switches have to be able to carry the full amount of current which is ever likely to come their way, as a point of safety and this when added up can be surprisingly high. They are all given ratings to indicate the safe limits of their duties and also the type of current for which they are designed. A switch designed for alternating current use for instance will not survive too long if used for the more onerous direct current. The deadly marine environment quickly corrodes steel and grows verdigris on brass and copper. Marine switches take account of this by not using the former metal at all and having some kind of sliding scraping action of the contacts to make sure that the verdigris is rubbed off on every connection. Household fittings work admirably on board for trials and for a few months afterwards but if you are looking for more than one season of reliability in your installation they should be avoided.

The majority of the switches and light fittings generally available for low-powered D.C. systems appears to come from the coach and bus industry. Apart from their appearance which, being mainly of 1930s' styling, may be unfashionable at any given time, they were never intended to put to sea and have helped to give electricity its erstwhile bad name afloat in small craft. Nowadays there are some specially designed fittings for yachts and small craft on the market of increasingly good construction. However, there would seem to be a largely untapped market for a manufacturer to produce specially designed and elegant yacht fittings. Too often the electric fittings designed for yachts turn a blind eye to the beauty of their surroundings and are content to look like simple engineering of the worst kind.

One of the great enemies of the marine electric fitting is condensation and for fittings both below and above decks there is a fine argument raging as to whether they should be made watertight or not. The opponents of watertightness, in which camp we lie, maintain that it is anyway largely impossible to achieve and acts as often as not to prevent the water which has leaked or condensed inside from draining out again. If the basic wire to bulb connection is reasonably insulated from caked salt then there is, we maintain, no longer an argument for making deck or navigation lights watertight, not to mention fittings on less exposed service, but the water must be able to get out more easily than it can get in.

Fluorescent fittings are basically attractive for small craft because of their modest electrical consumption but somehow they are not as attractive to live with as ordinary bulbs with shades or covers. Perhaps as a world of sun worshippers we are all used to a good yellow content in our light. Oil lights with a high degree of yellow are generally thought more pleasant than electric filament lamps and fluorescents have even less yellow in their output. Some produce substantial radio interference in their operation and this point has to be watched in installation on board craft relying on radio equipment.

Where electrically operated equipment, such as power winches, fans or compressor operated refrigerators, requires the operation of electric motors it is often forgotten that the initial starting current required to get the motor turning can be two or three times the operating current, requiring the whole circuit and equipment to be heavier than might have been supposed.

In selecting fittings the case for using dry batteries should not be overlooked for some of the lesser and occasional loads, such as cabin lighting. They are simple and self contained without the need for circuits and protection. With the need to carry spare batteries they are probably not lighter overall but at least the dead weight can be thrown away when it has delivered up its current.

Screening and Suppression

Every violent movement of electricity — a spark, a surge of current in a cable, or a stop or start of a circuit such as occurs when a switch is thrown — appears to have the unfortunate facility of broadcasting its own radio waves. These cause interference with any equipment on board which is supposed to operate within the regular radio frequencies, such as the radio receiver and the radio telephone. In addition they play havoc with a great deal of the electronic equipment nowadays packed into yachts for their navigation, such as the depth finder and the speedometer log. It is also unfortunate that the interference occurs over a wide range of wavelengths and that the means of suppression only normally covers a small waveband. The choice of method of suppression and the detailed equipment is therefore one requiring skill and experience.

Stray radio waves get about the place by two different methods, conduction and radiation. The former travels along the circuit paths to introduce itself to radio and other equipment while the latter is broadcast to be picked up and re-radiated by anything metal which gets in its path. The two basic defences are to shield all wires to prevent the initial radiation and to provide circuit defences against the conducted currents. This takes the form of capacitors to provide more attractive alternative paths (which all lead to earth) or inductors to produce a high resistance to the passage of the tiny stray currents. A screened cable is no more than a wire with a further cover of wire mesh outside the normal insulated cover. Radio waves have some difficulty in getting out or in through such defences. The high frequency current oscillations that occur in the ignition system of a petrol engine can be effectively reduced by fitting resistors in the leads and combined with a fully screened harness this is fairly efficient in covering this department.

In fact all the metal parts of the yacht's equipment should be bonded together with a good thick copper braid and connected to a single common earthing plate on the hull surface. This reduces and almost eliminates the variations in electrostatic between various parts and the broadcast interference that occurs when static is disturbed or rubbed up the wrong way.

Sparking at commutator brushes in revolving equipment and in switches and so on is best dealt with by fitting suppressors as close as possible to the offender, to which the connection should be made in screened cable for the aforesaid reasons.

Suppression is like vibration in its insidious acceptance and every effort should be made to eliminate it during the first trials of the ship or of new equipment. As with vibration it is too easy to get used to a basically inefficient and correctable set-up. It is no real advantage when you have just missed the essential navigation beacon for the third time to know that the bilges are still being pumped out or that Fred is shaving in his cabin.

CHAPTER 13
Systems Wet

General

In these enlightened days the hull of a power boat is confidently expected to do its stuff safely and efficiently in the ordinary conditions for which it is sold. The engine is also generally reliable and its failure a happening of some drama, quite removed from pinpricks of irritation. The various systems which together turn the yacht from a furniture showroom into a maritime home come into a different category. They affect life at sea or in harbour to a degree beyond their cost or dimensions and in a negative sense. Simply not to have running fresh water on board is nothing, but to have a fresh water system which does not run fresh water every time fresh water is required is unbearably irritating. Many a first-class yacht has been sold down the river with a quite unfair reputation because some miserable system irritated her owner beyond reasonable endurance.

Yachting occasionally goes through periods where escape from civilisation appears to be the grand object. To leave the sophistications of the city and battle with the elemental sea equipped as if for the monastic cell is certainly one form of yachting — everyone to his or her pleasures. We are, it would seem to us, just emerging from such a phase and reverting as fast as money will let us to the more hedonistic pleasures afloat which originally gave yachting its bad name. The word yacht has always been synonymous with *grande luxe* rather than with the monastic life, and luxury needs a generous supply of reliability from the systems that support it.

The bracing air that makes life afloat so attractive has another quality — that of being highly destructive to the majority of fittings and equipment used for life ashore. It is possible to carry ordinary household fittings on board a boat and to fit them up to work as well as they do ashore. Then the sea air with all the associated conditions of condensation and so on get to work and a few weeks later the situation is quite different. Marine fittings still have to be specially made although the increased use of plastics for almost everything must be narrowing the gap. Another basic difference which is not always appreciated is that most installations ashore are static where marine installations are on the move. A fast power boat can thump along experiencing 5 or 6g decelerations every few minutes. This means that every component of fittings afloat has to be looked at from the aspect of fierce movement and shock. Neither aircraft nor motor cars experience anything like marine movement and there is no getting away from the need to manufacture or select special equipment for boats.

Each system must furthermore be accessible and amenable for maintenance and control. This does not just mean that wires and pipes can be reached by taking up floor boards but that they can be understood readily by strangers. Some power boats are lucky enough to have their owner or captain standing by them as each installation is installed but most maintenance and repair is carried out by people who are likely to have only the most modest acquaintance with the vessel. Too often they will spend more time in tracing the system and worrying rather than in actual repair. The crew on board, the owner and his guests perhaps, must also be able to take control of each system if necessary. They need to have quick access to a basic understanding of the system and the effect of each control movement. Pipes for instance should be painted with a standard colour code, wires also and with identification at junctions and entries. Cocks and switches should have identification tallies which actually say what each position should do to the system. It is also elementary that the normal working position should be indicated and that all switches in the normal position would point the same way. Lever valves should be set up so that any vibration will tend to help the handle to hang down in the normal or safe position. Valves which should only be operated in an emergency or after some other sequence of operation should have some form of safety lock. This need not be more than a light string tie which is enough to give even the most casual valve turner pause to consider what he is about.

Very few yachts are built to give their owners the pleasures of working on greasy machinery and therefore the various safety devices employed against overloads and such ought to be capable of simple resetting. The circuit breaker is, for instance, one of the greatest contributions to hedonism — at least compared with mending fuses in a hot lurching engine room. They have the ideal characteristic of immediate indication whether the problem is too large to handle or too small to bother about. Peace of mind is another of the design aims of yachting machinery.

Fresh Water

There would seem to be two distinct schools of thought about the fresh water requirements for small boats. One owner will tell his guests that 'this is a boat not a so-and-so house and therefore you must use very little water'. Such an owner will even go to the trouble of making the supply arrangements positively difficult so as to discourage the use of fresh water for any but the most essential purposes. The next owner will say that although this is a boat he does not see why he should abandon the most minimal of comforts just because he is luxury yachting. There are therefore widely differing views about the amount of water which tanks must provide for small craft. In fact the only common ground is the well-known nautical jingle — 'a gallon a day per man and another for each woman because she wastes it'. Because it is a jingle and well known it has an inbuilt air of a knowledgeable pronouncement and is commonly used as a rule for capacity.

In fact your washing and bathing yachtsman

Fig. 269   This beer barrel gives a running water system at negligible cost.

Fig. 270   Every galley has running fresh water these days.

probably requires as much as five gallons a day in a temperate climate and could use twice that in the tropics. The happily dirty or cleverly clean yachtsman on the other hand can arrange his daily ablutions in a half-pint glass of water, and might find a quarter gallon a day ample for his needs. Water capacity should be judged in relation to the style of the vessel rather than to any arbitrary human intake figures.

The tankage required must also bear relation to the normal geographical environment. A Solent boat working from marina to marina might be happier with little more than overnight water capacity and a tiny bit more speed, while the ocean cruising yacht really does not care if it is ten or twelve days on passage as long as there is ample water on board to allow the choice of the best port for refilling.

Tales of antiquity are full of seamen waxing quite lyrical over finds of 'limpid sweet water' on desert islands and also of them waxing quite wroth over the green, living liquid they commonly found in their shipboard breakers. Nowadays few sailing yachtsmen and certainly even fewer power boat seamen have to rely on their own water supplies long enough for growing things to get a start. Still, it is important that the water supply does remain palatable or at least some of the pleasure of boating is removed. The ability to choose your fresh water retailer is therefore important and affects the tank capacity. There are thousands of miles of coast where the local product which oozes from the tank is to say the least distinctly unattractive. (Patrick Ellam once solved this problem in a typically brilliant way by embarking only sparkling mineral water. Stored in sealed tanks this kept extraordinarily well and every drink of it was exhilarating — and therapeutic — while washing and shaving became an adventure.)

Nowadays water tanks rarely corrode and it is also rare for a tank to become contaminated. The need for multiple tanks to cope with such problems is therefore in the decline. However, it is still known for a fresh water tank to be inadvertently filled with fuel, and long distance power boats are advised to fit more than one tank.

Water tanks are best placed in the middle part of the vessel so that her trim is not materially affected by their being full or empty. In a planing hull there is a good case for getting them a bit forward. The boat with light empty tanks will have an excess of power to push it over its hump on to the plane but when they are full it will appreciate the more level trim at the critical speed. Water tanks are traditionally kept low, often under the cabin sole, in order that their weight will add rather than detract from stability. However, the modern fat planing hull generally suffers from an excess of stability, giving her a sharp awkward roll on moorings, and benefits from the tank being placed high. In fact a tank high on the galley bulkhead can give an impressive running water supply to the sink from a faucet set straight into the tank bottom.

Fresh water tanks are generally in these days made from stainless steel or glass fibre reinforced plastics. Monel is as good, if not better, but is not such a normal boatyard material. Tinned copper used to be highly thought of, and galvanised steel washed with cement inside was another common material.

As materials improve and installation standards rise the need for maintenance in depth is retreating in boats as in everything else. Time was when every sensible owner required separate tanks which could be removed from his vessel both for maintenance and replacement. With GRP construction and welded metal constructions the attractions of bulkheading off an area of construction bounded on the bottom by the actual skin of the boat are high. The tank area will not be as convenient but will certainly be bigger and very much cheaper.

In the early days of GRP water tanks the most horrible tales of terrible taste and exotic growths were common. These stories in fact were true and due to incomplete curing of the resin. Curing now is ensured in any responsible construction by either passing hot steam through the tank for some hours or by giving the tank special heat-lamp treatment. Resin, being an organic material, makes a desirable environment for any potential growths in water during the period when it is curing and giving off the monomer. Should you find your tank thus afflicted a good washing out and the temporary addition of iodine to the water followed by another good washing out should make a permanent cure.

Even if your tanks are built in — rather, especially if your tanks are built in — it is essential to be able to get complete access to their interiors. One day or other dirt will accumulate or get in somehow and they must be cleaned. Manholes should be big enough to allow some poor soul to insert either part or all of his person in the cause of hygiene. Like all tanks afloat, baffles must be fitted to reduce surge, and fillers and vents should be as large as possible for the occasional high-pressure connection. Also there must be some method of knowing how much water is actually inside. In the long run a sounding rod is the surest answer but remote reading instrumentation is relatively cheap and reasonably reliable. In these days of plastics one of the simplest and most effective answers as with fuel tanks is just to fit a transparent manhole cover so that you can actually see what is within. It has the bonus advantage that you can also see the state of the water and everything else inside the tank.

Looking at the boating life objectively it does seem odd that one can go raving mad short of water when surrounded with water on every hand and a boatload of power underfoot. The water still which uses engine heat to convert salt water to fresh is therefore a logical, if expensive, fitment to any power craft. Essentially the system uses a vacuum pump to reduce the pressure inside the still until the relative water boiling temperature falls below that of the engine circulating water which is fed to it. The vapour is then separated off and condensed to give some gallons of fresh water every hour. The still water, if passed through a purifier, can, as a bonus, be used for topping-up the batteries. These water stills would seem to work well if installed to the very letter of the instructions. A tiny variation, however, can be the unidentifiable cause of poor results.

While on the subject of obtaining fresh water from salt it is worth noting the silver nitrate method which uses chemistry to extract the sodium chloride. It is extremely expensive and produces the most awful tasting water suitable only for desperate survival. The conversion kit is usually got up in rubber or plastic bags and a reasonable proportion of the foul taste can be avoided if the conversion is done in glass. The sun stills which are often included in survival kits produce a modest amount of water only if allowed to float quiet and still. Both systems are nonetheless of great lifesaving value and every seaman steaming more than a few miles from his dock should be aware of them.

Water is usually pressure-fed to the individual outlets throughout the vessel. Some simple, and a great number of old-fashioned, vessels use hand pumps but pressure systems are themselves so simple, especially with a reasonable electrical installation, that they have become a normal feature. The simplest pressure system employs good old gravity. A service tank on the cabin top is filled up daily by pump from the main tanks and the cabin supply is drawn direct from it. This has an obvious advantage in giving some direct control on the quantity of water used daily but involves one more rather uninteresting daily chore. On a small installation it is possible to pressurise the water tank by means of an air pump, hand or foot operated. The electrical systems however work on the use of an electric water pump which draws from the tank and pumps up the supply side to a positive pressure. A pressure switch controls the pump. Turning on a tap lets the stored pressure drop, and the pressure-operated switch turns on the motor to pump water along the line. When the tap is turned off the build-up of pressure in the line trips the switch and stops the motor. The better systems usually incorporate some form of intermediate tank, either of elastic rubber or incorporating some other kind of pressure stabiliser to make the operation smoother. There is also another system where the taps themselves incorporate switches to operate the pumps but these have largely been superseded by more sophisticated systems.

The pipe runs in a vessel's pressure water systems have to be passed through her with as much care as a good household plumber uses ashore. That is to say, rather more than is often used by many yards who think of running water as something a little disgraceful. Pipe runs have to be planned to avoid air locks and run to avoid pressure hammering. Copper pipes are traditional for this kind of installation but are often nowadays replaced by plastics — a welcome improvement. The armoured polyethylene pipe and the solid ABS pipe are not only lighter and stronger but much more amenable to the unskilled plumber. In fact if the owner happens to have a hobby interest in plumbing he can have many happy hours with plastics piping introducing yet another facet of the vessel for pleasure.

Waste Systems

It is tempting to start such a section along the lines of 'What goes up must come down' or one of the other laws of nature which are daily being upset. However you approach it, the subject is not one of the most elegant aspects of yachting and the less the pleasure-bent yachtsman has to do with his waste systems the more secure is his pleasure. It is therefore essential, as far as anything other than staying afloat is essential in a boat, that the waste systems are not only foolproof but also idiotproof and moronproof. The natural key to reliability is simplicity and it is worth recalling that one member of the great Herreshoff family of designers is reputed to have surveyed the whole field of marine plumbing and come down heavily in favour of the cedar bucket. Although we can understand this search for simplicity we think that he was perhaps a little hard on the greater number of marine lavatories. These are on the whole extremely reliable and reasonably sanitary. In fact one might say they are usually very sanitary inside and, until recently, very unsanitary outside with their complex maze of pipes and valves and pumps draped all around.

For a boat, the obvious system of waste disposal, though not the most popular system in these pollution-conscious days, is to cast it overboard or, with more discretion, to pump it into that great outdoor tank which is all around. In small craft, wash basins and sinks are usually placed well above waterline and the drains need only to be connected to a shipside outlet. Opinion is divided as to whether outlets should be above or below waterline but our preference is for the latter. The merry tinkle of drains does not disturb the quiet of your anchorage, neither does the organ music of wind whistling up the pipe. On the other hand the underwater outlet type of installation needs more than a rubber bung stopper in the basin, or the most modest roll of your vessel will blow it out and lose you that very last drop of hot water.

A plumbing problem is not a disaster in itself but if it occurs below waterline in a pipe connected to the sea it can quickly escalate. For this reason it is essential to fit all shipside outlets below or close to the waterline with seacocks. If your vessel is already built without seacocks then you should get a nice set of softwood bungs made up until seacocks can be fitted. For the same reason it is usual to make all interior piping below water level of rigid pipe to reduce the prospect of a disaster creeping up when you are asleep or otherwise not keeping an eye on the

bilges. Plastics piping melts very quickly, for instance, in the presence of even a small fire. If this is below waterline the immediate effect is beneficial in putting the fire out but the long-term disaster of sinking from the water flow is at least equally embarrassing. Above waterline the flexible plastics piping is very good value for waste drains. Although it may appear to be adding complication, all pipe drains should be made up in several sections, not as a single length of pipe. It is much easier to extract and clear a short length of blocked pipe than a long one.

The great majority of marine toilets are fitted in under water level locations and therefore they are as a rule designed and installed for that purpose. Similarly the inlet and outlet seacocks must be fitted below waterline and it is always quoted that the inlet should be forward of and below the outlet — another of the great maritime truisms which should be ignored if you are keeping your yacht in a marina berth or on a fore and aft mooring. Here the craft is moored up tight irrespective of the tidal stream and therefore it is possible for her to sit in a current flowing bow-wards. Modern vessels therefore should have the inlets and outlets placed if possible on opposite sides of the keel. Also, such is the march of science, outlets must be arranged to be well clear of such items as the underwater log impeller. All seacocks must have very good accessibility and the outlet pipe must be looped up a clear couple of feet above the

Fig. 271 Simple WC and folding wash basin in a 32 ft fast motor yacht.

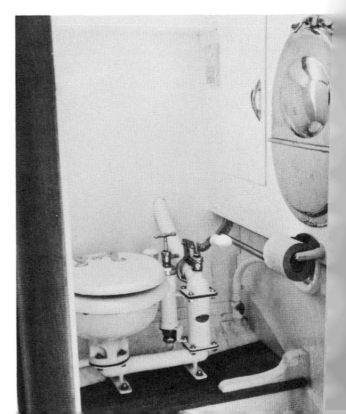

Fig. 272 Twin wash basin installation in the luxury motor yacht Romantica.

waterline to prevent reverse flooding. The top of the loop ought to have a small vent to act as a siphon break but this is too rarely fitted.

When washbasins and so on are fitted in larger craft their drains come too close to the waterline for safety, as do shower outlets in nearly all craft. It then becomes necessary to pump the waste overboard. This is commonly done with a simple hand or electric pump at each unit. However, in a craft of any size the number of pumps and the equivalent numbers of holes in the shipsides for their outlets can mount up and it becomes convenient to drain by gravity to one or more communal tanks and use a common pumping system.

The waste tank ought to be located as close as possible to those units making principal use of it so that the pipe runs are short and the waste water tempted to make a fast passage. The size of tank or tanks can be quite small if fitted with an automatic bilge pump of big enough capacity to deal with any likely simultaneous inundation. If a hand pump or mechanical pump has to be operated then the tank should be rather bigger and have capacity enough for say two days to allow for one day being forgotten. A little com-

plication can make the whole much less likely to be an embarrassment. We prefer to put a smallish waste tank for each group of fittings. Each tank is fitted with its own automatic electric bilge pump but in addition has a larger diameter pipe connection near the top of the tank to the next tank thus connecting the whole set of tanks in series. If one pump fails the tank overflows into the next tank where another pump is waiting and so on down the line. A final hand pump connection completes the chain.

The open sea makes a very good sewer but closer to home things are not so pleasant. Quite a significant number of authorities already forbid what they call 'the discharge of human wastes into surface water'. It does not take much of a crystal ball to foresee that this kind of regulation will soon be universal and we might then all get more clean water for swimming.

Basically such regulations mean that the waste tank, instead of being a gathering ground for shower and basin water taking the same old journey to the sea, becomes a sewage container, part of what is called no less than a 'toilet waste retention system'. The contents of the tanks are only discharged in the open sea or are sucked out by a municipal dockside system at regular intervals. Only the oddest vessels spend all their time at sea and therefore every craft will have to reckon on a dockside discharge system in future. This is no job to linger over and therefore the strongest possible suction, possibly as much as 15 lb per sq. inch will be applied to the hull connection. The pipes and tanks should therefore not only be smooth inside and easy to evacuate but extremely strong.

A straightforward holding tank system requires all the usual non-return traps for contents and smells to be fitted. Vent pipes have to be large to cope with the municipal service and at the same time have to be placed well outside the accommodation and reasonably far away from any hull access openings. An ordinary marine toilet can be used with the normal pump discharging into the tank rather than into the sea. More sophisticated vessels can set up a pressurised salt water flush system similar to those in the households ashore. Such tanks ought to be emptied every other day but there are chemical additives which can be sent down to the tank to break down the sewage and make it reasonable for the discharge periods to be extended to a matter of weeks.

Ordinary water pumps cannot cope with the curious consistency of sewage and therefore a mascerating pump has to be used for those occasions where a seagoing yacht makes her own discharge into the ocean.

As the regulations proliferate we can expect to see all manner of clever waste disposal systems coming on the market. There are, for instance, at this moment many clever electric and hand operated flush toilets which manage to look elegant and ordinary on the outside but which have tucked inside them small individual tanks and treatment outfits. We have also heard of a toilet system incorporating an electric incinerator. The mind boggles a little perhaps at such a development but there is no doubt that the strict anti-pollution laws in most harbours are here for good. We have even heard tell of a marina-inspired system where each docked craft is fitted with a long pipe extension to the waste outlets. Each vessel then pumps her sewage clear out beyond the marina entrance. The only embarrassment then is presumably for those peasants who cannot afford a berth in the marina.

Perhaps more essential than on any other domestic tank, the waste tank should have some positive indication of contents level. It is no matter in which to be caught out when off for a day or week of pleasure boating.

Pumping and Other Salt Water Systems

The pumping of salt water from inside a craft back to its proper place outside is the basic salt water system for any vessel. Pumping is one of the larger dramas of boating and 'All hands to the pumps' one of the more stirring calls of the sea. Triumphant life or exhausted death, issues well beyond pleasure boating are decided at the pumps, or used to be when ships were built of a thousand planks and easily wracked from their designed integrity.

One of the best bits of advice which could be given to the prospective purchaser of the power boat of a few years ago was to check the bilge pump. If it was well placed, with good access and perhaps a little natty seat to use while operating it, reject the boat out of hand. Look rather for a craft with cobwebs on a neglected pump.

The modern boat with its one-piece hull is extremely unlikely to develop the kind of leak where desperate hand pumping is required to keep her afloat. Two separate degrees of pumping requirements are evident. First is a comparatively modest pump to keep drips from stern glands and oilskins and perhaps some rainwater, from accumulating in the bilges. Second is a large capacity pump installed in the hope of being able to cope with an inundation type of disaster. A hole pierced in the hull or a stern gland tearing out or a salt water pipe fracture are all major disasters with the craft in imminent danger of foundering. If the hole can be plugged, even partially, then a good capacity power driven pump taking power from the main engine may save the day. 'May' is the operative word for although it would be a stupid mariner who put to sea without a big capacity disaster pump the present pattern of marine problems shows that leaks are not the problems they once were. It is natural to want to try to save your precious boat when the water starts to pour in as well as being equally natural to want to avoid a raft trip. But if the choice, foolishly enough, lay between a high capacity bilge pump and the liferaft there can be no doubt that the latter is probably the better choice for a first-rate modern vessel. To have to make such a choice would indeed be foolish, for windshields can still shatter and a great deal of water come on board in a very short time.

The first part of a bilge system involves getting the bilge water to the pump suctions. Clear drainage to the lowest part of the bilges has to be arranged from every part of the vessel, even the most unlikely. Condensation as well as domestic drips must be able to trickle freely on the ever downward path to the pump strainer boxes. Waterways must be cut through structure, crannies must be filled and some parts may even need pipe drains to ensure that no little rock pools or cascades are left to promote damp and decay. Bilges are often compartmentalised for convenience and it is common to separate the engine room bilges from the rest to prevent oil spreading through the vessel. The whole drainage to the bilges and also the suction points have to be considered not only for the boat at rest but also at the normal trim at speed. For the latter it is not necessary to get every drop out, but it must be possible to reduce any water in the bilges well below the point where it can splash or swill to embarrassment or be any appreciable weight on board.

The simplest and most efficient way of getting a lot of water out of a small boat is to whoosh it out with a bailer or bucket. This quickly becomes impractical when the topsides are high and the bilges low and impossible as soon as the vessel is decked. In the past all manner of traditional methods of lifting water for irrigating fields have been used afloat for the reverse purpose. The Archimedean screw turned by a crew at capstan bars, and the chain pump which used a large number of small buckets on a continuous chain loop propelled by multi-man crank handles, are no longer found afloat even among the most romantic craft. The large diameter short stroke topless plunger pump was a great favourite for smaller commercial craft until some forty years ago, and it is still listed in some of the more conservative chandlers' catalogues. It was a simple and powerful pump looking like a bucket set flush into the deck and spilling out floods of water to drain away over the planking. The more sophisticated plunger totally contained in a fine brass case makes a pump which can be accommodated more neatly in cockpit or below. The centrifugal and rotary pumps are more suitable for operation by machinery and therefore have become more common with the installation of engines afloat and, especially suited to electric motors, are increasingly found with more elaborate electrical

installations. The semi-rotary pump is really only rotary in that it was essentially a plunger pump bent into a circular form. At one time it was the ubiquitous appliance for official craft but, seemingly not keeping up with the times, has now largely disappeared. Its place would appear to have been taken by the diaphragm pump which is almost universally used for all hand bilge pumps. Apart from general attractiveness as design products, the modern diaphragm pumps have a quite prodigious capacity for bilge flotsam and pump away passing old socks and kipper bones as happily as pure spring water.

If all that accumulated in bilges was water then the bilge pumper's job would be much simpler. When a boat is built or fitted out all manner of quite sizable offcuts of wood, metal, wire, foam plastics and so on get lodged behind the joinerwork despite the most rigorous cleaning, all ready to fall off and bung up the bilge pumps in the first tumble of sea. It is not unknown for all the labels on the tin cans to get soaked off by passing bilge water and, in fact, he who expects the unexpected in his bilge will not be far off.

The suction end of each bilge line is therefore protected by a flat strainer box. The size of mesh or holes depends largely on the type of pump but as a rough guide the total clear area of the box should not be less than three times the cross-section area of the pump inlet suction pipe. The strainer box will inevitably get clogged from time to time and therefore the tail pipe to it should be made of flexible hose so that it can easily be lifted clear for cleaning.

Strong piping is required on the suction side of bilge pump lines for it is quite extraordinary the vacuum which a determined pumper can produce when balked with a blocked strainer box. Also when choosing bilge line piping it is as well to remember that all manner of noxious and corrosive fluids get into bilges in addition to water. Strong detergent, petrol and oil can be reckoned among the more common.

There is only one criterion for the size of a hand operated bilge pump and that is that it should be as large as one man can handle; anything smaller might appear to be taking a chance which may not be justified when viewed on some cold, wet disastrous night. This is commonly thought to be a pump of about 12 gallons a minute capacity. In the same line of thought it is sensible to keep hand operated bilge pump lines

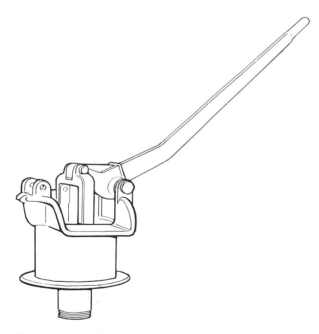

Fig. 273 The mighty Davey Deluge pump with its ten inch barrel throwing over a gallon at every stroke.

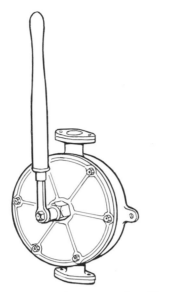

Fig. 274 The pump which has meant a lot of hard work to a lot of people — the classic semi-rotary.

as short as possible (to reduce skin friction drag in the pipes) and to keep the lift of water in the line to the minimum to reduce the fatigue of the operator. It is also best if hand pumps can be worked from on deck or reasonably close to the main companion.

Although they should never be considered as the principal bilge pump it is common to find electric bilge pumps, often with automatic control, fitted to even quite small craft. The automatic control usually takes the form of a float switch where rising bilge water lifts the float and trips a linkage to the switch and so on. These are reasonably reliable in a hard service but their reliability is not yet enough to make them suitable to work unsupervised. The electrical connections must all be made clear above any normal level of bilge water and the motors should be sealed units. The principal control switches will probably be placed at the helmsman's position but there should be a local over-ride switch close to the pump so that it can be switched to work no matter what the automatics are saying. For the reverse case the electric bilge pump must be of a type which will run dry for a considerable period of time — perhaps twenty minutes. Most of the rubber and some of the plastic impellers are ruined after only a couple of minutes of dry running. It is good practice therefore also to arrange matters so that you can tell if the pump is working with water or not. This may require no more than the shipside outlet to be about 12 inches above

water level so that the happy noise of splashing can be heard. Alternatively a transparent section of pipe in the outlet line will also show if water is passing. The outlet line from an electric automatic pump ought to loop up to the underside of the deck before going down to the shipside outlet which, of course, should be fitted with a seacock.

The size at which a boat becomes big enough to require a mechanical bilge pump is arguable but a sensible basis would perhaps refer it to the capacity of the pump which can be driven from the power take-off of the main engine. This should be significantly higher than can be handled by a hand pump. It might also be thought unreasonable to pump out more than, say, two compartments by hand and should the craft have further subdivisions a mechanical pump becomes a necessity. One authority gives a rough guide for pump capacity of about 10 gallons a minute per compartment against the 6 foot head which comes naturally with standing headroom. The number and size of pumps is also such an easy matter for the various safety authorities to latch on to that there is in fact little difficulty in sorting out what should be fitted to your vessel.

The engine driven bilge pump is usually belt driven with a simple clutch which can either be operated on the spot or by cable control. The great majority are self priming and there would seem little justification in modern circumstances for fitting anything else. Such a pump would normally suck from a valve chest to which the individual compartment suctions would run in order to allow each compartment to be pumped in turn. The outlet from the pump would rise to the loop above water level and discharge through a shipside seacock in the normal way. The same pump can also be used to run a deckwash system. One of the valve chest connections is taken to a shipside seacock to provide the clean salt water and the discharge is diverted similarly from over the side to a deck hose. With a large capacity pump the system can be set up to operate a fire hose in addition to the deckwash and anchor chain wash.

In a bilge system of any complexity care must be taken to see that all the control cocks are not only very easy of access but very clearly marked. If the ship starts to fill or to flame it is unreasonable to expect clear thought and cool action from those on board. In addition the piping systems should be of good size — at least an inch inside diameter — and be arranged in short lengths so that sections can be easily removed for clearing if they become blocked. It is also worth ensuring that the pipe connections used are such as to allow a length of flexible hose to be installed past a blockage in an emergency.

Salt water is also sometimes called on to eke out the fresh water in such applications as washing dishes, and for this a simple hand pump drawing direct from the sea is nearly always used. In larger vessels salt water can be used for lavatory flushing and, for this arrangement, is the same as for pressure fresh water except that the great self-filling sea around replaces the tank. Both header tank or automatic electric systems can be used but with checking to see that the pressure supplied is ample, more than ample, for the requirements of the sanitary fireclay. Lack of attention to this kind of detail is apt to put people off yachting.

Hot Water Systems

In many craft, especially in the tropics, the strange sight of a crew member standing in the cockpit putting on his or her oilskins preparatory to going below can be seen. This you can be sure has nothing to do with water coming through the deck seams (which in fact is a desirable built-in feature of some hot weather craft), but rather the cook preparing to go below to boil a kettle. Oilskins are very good protection against boiling water which is perhaps one of the most unrecognised dangers in any craft moving in deep waters. Water at boiling point is usually only required for cooking the ingredients of tea, coffee or cocoa. All else about the ship can be more than adequately dealt with with water at the same temperature as comes from the household taps ashore. If your marine style of life includes washing, shaving, dish washing, clothes washing, bathing or showers then a domestic hot water system should be considered, both for the convenience and luxury of it and also for the safety of not boiling any more water in kettles than is essential.

Before taking leave of the humble kettle, however, one type of hot water system deserves notice for very small craft fitted with showers. The kettleful of hot water is poured into the shower tray and diluted with cold until the toes approve and are prepared to step in. A small pump, hand or electric, then pumps the temperate water to the shower head and recirculates it as long as required before, at the turn of a cock, pumping it all away over the side.

For bigger craft the decision has to be made whether to install a common system supplying warm water to a number of outlets or whether to fit an individual water heater at each outlet. The latter has an immediate attraction of combining both simplicity and multiplicity. The failure of one heater does not condemn the whole vessel to cold water and there is no system of pipes to install and to give trouble with air locks, reverse flow and knocking. The individual water heaters are almost invariably the smaller domestic units used ashore or for trailer caravans. The gas geyser is perfectly reasonable run off propane or butane bottled gas always provided the installation is good and the user not too bone-headed. In other words the bottled gas geyser reflects and extends all the traditional arguments for and against gas installations in general. The ventilation of the water heater is important and often neglected. The electric water heater for this application more usually takes the form of a small storage tank with an automatic temperature controlled immersion heater, in fact a miniature version of the main system installation. Where, in a lightweight vessel, it does not make too much sense to keep two gallons of warm water on the bulkhead over each washbasin, it is possible to use instant water-heating units although these have something of a reputation for requiring the most careful installation. Individual electric units take a fair bit of electric capacity to run and the choice of heaters may well be governed by the engine room output.

If you take running hot water as a serious part of yachting then there is no doubt that a full blown system is best. It requires even more care in its design than a household system because of the way a boat will heel and pitch and it requires at least as skilful installation. In our experience it is not a thing to ask of a builder who might be doing it for the first time.

The basic heating units are electric, gas or oil-fired, or the heat may be taken off the back of the galley stove however that may be fired. Electric units take the familiar household form of an insulated tank of good capacity fitted with an immersion heater and thermostat control. The electricity usually being of 110 or 240 volt A.C. supplied by the auxiliary generating set. One useful variation takes into account the relatively mean quantities of electricity generally available for domestic use in power vessels. In this, the heating tank is divided into two compartments connected by relatively small holes. The hot water congregates in the upper chamber by convection, providing a half tankful in relatively short order, while the cold supply and the heating element and so on are in the lower compartment which takes longer to heat. The second half of the tank is therefore providing only a back-up capacity of hot water for those relatively few occasions when a full tankful of water is required.

Gas installations in boats are best kept short and therefore the gas-fired water heating boiler is, despite its efficiency, not all that common. There can be little doubt that the oil-fired boiler is probably the best system for a cold weather boat where radiators are required as well as basins and baths. The oil burners have the great advantage over the electric generator of being almost noiseless. The fuel supply can come from the main tanks of a diesel yacht and the whole system can be automatic. There are various proprietary methods of getting the diesel to burn, all involving some kind of pumping and spraying arrangements to get the diesel in a fine spray mixed with air, when it is readily combustible. The heat is passed to the tank water through a heat exchanger.

There are other sources of heat in a power boat and it always seems a pity to see waste heat pouring out of the exhaust pipes and galley funnel while you may be washing in icy cold water. There are many thrifty schemes available therefore which extract part of this waste heat and the most convenient use for it is to heat domestic water. Both engine exhausts and galley stoves can be fitted with waste heat boilers. For the former this may involve little more than a jacket around part of the hot exhaust through which fresh water is circulated. Most of the larger coal, solid fuel, or oil-fired cooking stoves incorporate a water heater as part of the combustion chamber surround. It is possible to get by with just a waste heat system for domestic heating, provided it is large enough and very well insulated to reduce the rate of cooling when no waste heat is available. The best use is as a back-up system to

conserve electricity or fuel but it has a basic disadvantage of needing some kind of circulation thermostat in the system if the possibility of overheating is to be avoided. Overheating, even to boiling point, should not be an embarrassment as far as the installation detail is concerned but water temperature over, say, 70° C will cause furring inside the circulation pipes. Complete blockage is a not unknown consequence.

Hot water systems come in two main types: circulating and direct. In the latter the water heater is either installed as part of the pressure line or the heater and storage tank are so placed as to give gravity waterfeed to the outlets. The water supply line then leads through the vessel with branch outlets to each supply position. The main line is made of bigger diameter pipe than is really required and is insulated and thus forms a kind of long, thin storage tank extension. The large diameter also serves as a modest insurance against the supply to the last point in the line actually drying up when the others are in use. This is a simple and direct system but has the disadvantage that the water in the pipes cools off to cold if it is not used and renewed thus wasting heat as well as giving annoying delays, and wasting water, before the supply turns hot at the basin.

The circulating system uses the natural tendency for hot water to rise and cold to fall to induce a circulation of water in a pipe looping from the storage tank all round the vessel and back to the tank. Water from the top of the tank where it is hottest is piped off in a smooth and ever-downward sloping tube which eventually returns the, by now cooler, water to the bottom of the tank. At various points around the circuit hot water is drawn off to give a supply or put through a minor branch circulation to a radiator or other heater.

If, as is not unusual in such an awkward house as a yacht, the necessary downward path with a minimum of 2° pitch cannot be achieved, it is possible to fit a circulating pump to blast through the difficulties. However the natural circulation, once achieved, is very much preferable.

Where a reasonable number of radiators are to be fitted in a vessel where they may not always be in use these should be arranged in a separate circuit so that the rust and such which might accumulate during their lay-off periods does not get passed around to the guest and galley washbasins. The radiator system can be separated from the main direct system by fitting a heating coil for it in the storage tank.

The size of water heating equipment required can be calculated by adding up the maximum use to which it will be put. This probably amounts to a situation where every member of the crew is having a good hot bath or wash before going ashore on a freezing cold night. The amount of washing water is readily estimated but the heat required to warm the interior of the vessel is more difficult. There are published tables giving the heat transmission of GRP, wood or metal and their insulations to set against the required interior temperature and the expected exterior temperatures. The heat transmission of radiators is basic information supplied by the makers and the two can be balanced. Like almost everything else in life afloat a good excess of heat supplied over losses expected is sensible and 15 per cent need not be too modest.

CHAPTER 14
Systems Dry

General

The word 'dry' in relation to any of the systems fitted to a boat is enough to bring a hollow laugh from any passing salt-stained mariner. The problem with most dry systems is to get them dry enough to operate. From the first, any such arrangement must be contemplated as if it were to be continually damp and whatever the prime purpose of the system it will probably have to include some kind of drying or water shedding before it gets down to the real work. Not only do most boats live out of doors with water all round and rain above, but they are often so arranged that the condensation flows free behind the panelling. In addition to this basic soaking in fresh water the craft will probably be given from time to time a real old dousing with salt water. Most of the salt will be washed off with fresh either from hose or rain; all that is except that which has penetrated into the nooks and crannies of the pipes and wires of the various systems. Salt never refuses to absorb any dampness that might be in a high humidity day atmosphere, and thus ensures that the word dry in relation to systems is largely relative.

The basic awful warning having been made, one hastens to say that it refers to the detail design of the installation and points the essential difference between systems afloat and those on shore. With the proper attention to detail required by the rather indifferent environmental conditions the basic systems can be run dry enough. The owner and his guests will also, or should also, have their pleasures unmixed with the doubtful blessing of dampness below.

Systems often require machinery for their operation. Nothing is more annoying than a high-pitched popping of somebody else's generating plant on a quiet evening. On the other hand the quiet hum of a distant electric motor is somehow soothing and gives the vessel a comforting feeling of being alive. The selection of systems machinery is almost always on the basis of efficiency but you should also take into account the effect of the machinery noise on your carefully planned and expensively attained marine environment. Noise is a comparatively unexplored area of luxury except for the understanding that the less there is the less likely it is to annoy. Sound insulation is becoming better understood and most modern vessels are a great improvement on previous craft all the way back to steam.

Ventilation

Ventilation comes in various sizes to suit both climate and people and it is the latter who require the greatest range. What is a well ventilated craft to some will have others stuffing socks up the vents and battening down the hatches for comfort. A snug cabin to another will have visitors in the first throes of oxygen deprivation after five minutes. It is just not possible to lay down any universally acceptable quantitive assessment as to the ventilation requirements of vessels. The only common factor is that whatever the amount the circulation must be thorough. Ventilation may be difficult to define but lack of it is both obvious and deleterious. In vessels made of rottable materials such as wood, a drying draught must wash around every piece of the structure or else decay will ensue. In craft constructed of more modern materials the lack of air flow will not harm the structure to anything like the same degree but still air grows stale.

In the good old days before marinas were invented most of the better vessels lay afloat on swinging moorings. For at least half the day they had a chance to lie wind rode, bow to the wind. Under way, such are the vectors of wind and progress, the wind also came normally from ahead for at least a proportion of the day. Thus the designer could rely on a basic natural ventilation set up with the wind coming in over the bow. As long as boats are built with high pointed bows and flat transoms the passing wind will be diverted up over the boat and return as an eddy at the after end, thus making the natural ventilation flow inside the craft run from aft to forward. Incidentally this is why an apparently protected cockpit door will pour spray into the cabin.

Craft which tied up alongside docks for their normal moorings were either the craft of the extraordinarily rich with a full crew to fan the ventilation air around personally if necessary, or else they belonged to those who had to save the cost of a mooring. Such craft had probably started on their last decay and nobody thought the worse of their ventilation for that. Docked craft get the ventilating wind from forward only by meteorological whim, and then possibly only by arrangement with the harbourmaster, and so the natural ventilation scheme may not do its stuff.

The marina or dock moored craft has to be considered for winds blowing all round the compass and the prevailing wind may blow as surely from aft as it might from sideways.

Ventilation involves a throughput of air, not just a stirring around of an air filling in a cabin by fanning it. One of the best arguments is whether it is preferable to push outside air into the boat and let it find its way out again, or to suck the inside air out and let the outside air come in where it can. The former involves a slight increase of internal pressure in the boat and the latter a slight decrease. The criterion probably depends on the craft and its service and might vary from compartment to compartment. There are a great many devices inside most boats producing smell and even dangerous fumes which must be sucked away fast. To feed air into a compartment with a smell will only spread it right through the vessel. On the other hand a slightly pressurised interior is a defence against spray. An outgoing current of air will tend to carry water droplets away with it in a surprisingly effective manner. The draughts inside such a boat will all be from warm inside to cold outside, the right arrangement for comfort in cold climates. So for dangerously fitted and smelly craft operating in the tropics a suction system is

essential, whereas a Spartan pure vessel in the Arctic would be better off with a pressure system. Other craft lie somewhere between but probably, with safety more important than human comfort or rotting structure, the suction system will be chosen.

The amount of flammable vapour which can cause an explosion is frighteningly small; for instance, it has been quoted that a teacupful of petrol produces enough vapour to blow up a 50 foot vessel. Those areas therefore where the flammables or explodables can collect deserve special ventilation. The object is to achieve a quick displacement of the contaminated air and to ensure this both inlet and outlet ventilation must be planned rather than left to chance. It is not taking too much trouble to trunk both to the required spot or area. Exhaust fans must, of course, be of the sparkproof variety unless you like playing Russian roulette with a full magazine.

Most yachts, unfortunately, spend the greater part of their lives unused. The basic venting system must therefore be arranged for a closed ship. It is easy enough to open windows and hatches when people are on board but nothing is more off-putting than the awful smell of stale bilges and dry rot as the hatch opens. Basically all that is required is a little ventilation to every part of the craft to keep even the most gentle breeze flooding around while she is shut up. This can be achieved as long as there is access for the air both in and out of every part with the same double access standards for the whole hull as well. If your vessel is on a swinging mooring then a directional type of vent such as a cowl can be used. If, however, you cannot guarantee the winds of heaven being properly orientated then it is best to use vents which can act as either inlet or outlet depending on which way the wind is blowing. You can rely on the general eddies around the boat to set up ventilating runs if the access holes are there. Cowl vents are probably a mistake for any vessel without a permanent crew to twist them into the right direction. It is worse than useless to set up any venting system which is likely to be in opposition to any natural flow.

For the hull the basic ventilation access should be at the very forward end of the bow and at the transom corners. If possible the deckworks should have a similar arrangement with vents also arranged at the top outboard corners of bulkheads and any other parts which might become backwaters of dead air with a through draught running from bow to stern. The furniture also must be properly ventilated. Linings should have vent slits or grills at the corners and air access should be arranged into and out of every locker, drawer and compartment. It sounds a great deal of work but need not involve more than leaving a slit in the linings or using a grill face to a locker. In fact once the principle is established it is a great deal easier to achieve perfect ventilation than it is to get perfectly fitting joinerwork. Galley lockers particularly require good ventilation and it is a good idea to make the galley facings in a bolt-on manner so that complete cleaning can be easily achieved. A single rotting potato out of sight requires more than ordinary ventilation to remain sweet-smelling.

The modern GRP vessel often has elaborate and waterproof inner linings as part of the accommodation fit-out and this offers great opportunity to establish vent trunks. It is possible to arrange the whole requirement of basic venting including watertraps in the thickness of the lining in this manner leaving special deck vent fittings for special applications. The inlet openings can be protected and concealed in the arrangement of deck mouldings or they can be used to form part of the basic decoration like the radiator grill of a car. Similarly, goosenecked vent fittings can be incorporated in shipside bulwarks.

Hatches and skylights can also provide a source of ventilation even when closed. It is — bold words — perfectly possible to make a really watertight hatch or skylight which allows a little minimal ventilation. The standard watertrap vent box principle is well known and is applied in various forms to manufactured vents of varying degrees of effectiveness and beauty.

Ventilation for crew comfort can be divided into medical and social. The former is to allow sufficient fresh air for the requirements of the crew in such a manner that the draughts are directed away from the backs of necks both sleeping and awake. Under the social ventilation heading might be placed the lavatory extractor fan which in small and not well-insulated craft can with advantage be a little noisy. Galley ventilation is important but in a boat of any size it is well worth considering whether a smell absorbent of the activated charcoal type should be fitted. Wind-tunnel tests have shown that a boat is encircled in a turbulent air envelope to a considerable height and that any presentable galley vent outlet will only transfer the galley odours from inside to circulate about the deck.

The amount of fresh air required in running a boat may be arguable but there are some standards for ventilation which are accepted on the principle that if you want less you can stuff up the openings. The standards are calculated on the time it takes to replace completely the volume of air inside each compartment. Engine rooms should have a change of air every two minutes and so should lavatories. Galleys and saloons should change every five minutes and sleeping cabins somewhere about seven minutes. Bilges, apart from explosive vapour areas, will remain sweet with a change every hour but even a change of air twice a day will do. Air can be supplied or extracted by power fans which will have a manufacturer's known rating. Trunking can considerably reduce the air flow and if any length of trunking is involved it might require a doubling of the fan rating. Natural wind-blown air is usually assumed to be approaching at about a hundred feet a minute and to this should also be added any ducting losses.

In any warm water vessel and for some cold and temperate vessels provision should be made for fitting insect screens. Some of the quietest and most beautiful anchorages are infested with minute flying monsters and a fine mesh screen will be the only defence. Windows are quite commonly fitted with such defences but provision should be made in the normal basic vent system to fit screens on the outboard openings. It is also good policy to have vent openings fitted in any case with louvres or coarse mesh to prevent larger vermin wandering in.

Another point in considering air flows is to ensure that the engine, galley stove and anything else which might flare into flames should be out of the direct draughts. A liberal and well-intentioned supply of air is all that a tiny flame needs to make itself into a furnace.

Condensation

It is a toss-up whether this paragraph belongs more in the wet systems department rather than in among the dry. However, as the intention of a discussion on condensation is perfect dryness we thought it might as well be included here.

Sea air has every possibility of being humid on its own account and the interiors of yachts often accommodate a great many more moisture producing appliances than the average house. Take the crew or guests, for instance. The average adult breathes out something getting on for three ounces of water in a night's sleep, or you might rate it at six people to the pint. During the day they can do a great deal better than that and then there are kettles boiling and hot showers, not to mention the pint or two given off by the normal galley arrangements in the course of an hour of cooking. It is easy to see that we must start looking at the problems of condensation from a yacht interior which may be full of air at a high degree of humidity. The interior temperature during an evening might be for comfort say 70° F. The chill night air has only to cool the yacht's side down to half that (admittedly a very cold night) for three-quarters of the water vapour in the air to be precipitated perforce on the cold surface.

Condensation therefore occurs principally in badly ventilated boats where there has not been sufficient air change going on to take off the excess humidity generated inside the craft herself. It also occurs badly on inadequately insulated surfaces just because they are cold. Condensation is a genuine killer of yachting pleasure. It causes fungus, destroys protective finishes and attracts dirt, all of which 'ain't yachting'. A very small improvement in ventilation is often sufficient to make a considerable difference. There is likewise little excuse for lack of insulation these days when foam plastics and such can be added for very little weight penalty. Burning a heater on board your yacht during the winter lay-up will be worse than useless unless it is, say, an electric device which does not add to the water vapour. It is much better to go in for really Arctic blizzards of ventilation.

Air Conditioning

The human body mechanism is a marvellous device for coping with a very wide range of atmospheric conditions. This is, however, quite different from the state of actually feeling comfortable, a situation which for most people occurs over an extremely limited range of such conditions. Bodily comfort in a yacht is entirely to do with the occupants and therefore it is the human heat engine which should be assessed rather than any other factor — a point often forgotten in the onrush of technology and a normal background of mechanical devices.

The human machine is essentially an internal combustion engine burning food for fuel in addition to what it receives from the sun and other sources. In order to keep that machine at an equable temperature the excess heat has to be lost. In proper conditions about 25 per cent is lost by conduction and convection, 43 per cent by radiation, 30 per cent by evaporation and as little as 2 per cent by breathing. The radiation and evaporation are a surprisingly high proportion of the whole and the Victorian ladies who were reputed to 'glow' in the heat, since sweating and perspiring were for the lower orders, were not kidding. In high temperatures evaporation becomes the biggest factor, in cold weather it is conduction and convection which count.

Since the cooling of the body depends partly on evaporation, both temperature and humidity are important as also is the velocity of the air movement over the body surface areas. An inter-related range of these factors can produce the same feeling of comfort and these are called thermo-equivalent conditions. Most people find comfort in a temperature range from about 68° to 71° F in a relative humidity range of 40 to 65 per cent, and most air conditioning systems set out to produce results in this region.

True air conditioning refers to a fairly complete control of the atmospheric conditions inside the yacht. It should take into account temperature, humidity, air motion and cleanliness, and might be combined with the removal of bacteria and smells and the injection of beneficial elements, as might be ionisation. It is extremely rare for a yacht to have the full air conditioning treatment in this manner. In yachts it usually has to be little more than temperature control combined with a fan driven air circulation and possibly a modest dust filter. In most yachting areas of the world the temperature problem is one of too much rather than too little heat and therefore the main emphasis is on air cooling.

The cooling system is essentially the same as for refrigerators and consists of two main types, compression and absorption. The former compresses a gas such as freon, thereby making it hot. The heat is removed by water cooling and the gas is then allowed to expand, thus becoming very cold. In the absorption system the compressor is replaced with a generator where refrigerant ammonia is first absorbed and then driven off with the application of heat. The low temperature is then distributed, either directly into an air stream blown past coolant coils or by means of a heat exchanger and an indirect coolant like brine circulated past compartment outlet fans. Heating is achieved by passing the air over a surface heater, usually at the compartment outlet. Humidification, if required, is achieved by some form of air washer using a recirculated water spray. Air cleaning is done by water washing or, more normally in yachts, the use of some replaceable or cleanable air filters in the system. Air conditioned air may then be mixed in a chamber to the required conditions dialled down for it or may just blow directly out of the machine.

Air conditioning is controlled essentially by thermostats which may be placed in the individual compartments. A full system would also incorporate automatic temperature and humidity control devices and a clock system to allow programmed operation.

The amount of air conditioning required is assessed by a reasonably simple sum which takes into account the insulation values of the yacht sides and overheads, bulkheads, etc. added to the other sources of heat in the yacht. These can be divided into two main components for the air conditioning load. The first is the sensible heat made from the actual transfer through the compartment boundaries, the radiation heat from the sun, the heat given out by the occupants, heat which infiltrates with outside air, and the heat given off by any appliances and so on. The other is the latent heat of the water vapour in the air and includes the moisture given off by people as well as that which is involved in the air supply and so on.

In practice air conditioning arrives on board the yacht by two different basic approaches. One is to install a central unit, possibly in the engine room, which distributes air conditioned air to each compartment via ducting. The other is to install a quite separate unit in each cabin. It is also possible, as we mentioned before, to distribute cooled brine from the central unit to provide the cooling for a cabin fan unit. The central unit is most efficient and less noisy but involves insulated ducting to carry the cooled air all round the yacht, taking up what might otherwise be valuable accommodation space. The cabin units provide less sophisticated air conditioning but are more immediately controllable by the occupants. A further advantage is that a faulty unit can be disconnected and replaced in a few minutes. There is no overwhelming advantage one way or the other and the choice ought to depend very much on the type of use required of the yacht and where she will be based.

Cabin units tend to use exclusively recirculated air but the more sophisticated sets prefer a measure of fresh air, up to say a quarter of the mixture, and it is not uncommon to allow for 15 cubic feet of that fresh air per person per minute.

Heat Insulation

Most yachts are warm weather butterflies and therefore when talking about heat insulation one is generally concerned with keeping the outside heat out rather than the inside heat in. However, the latter should not be overlooked. It would seem likely that some form of hypothermia may well be involved in the mindless state which some cold weather yachtsmen get into, especially when mixed with a little seasickness. One reads far too often of yachts being driven on and on to their doom by cockpit-bound cold and wet zombies, when a spell below in a warm insulated cabin would have restored their wits in no time. Incidentally many a yacht owner will never believe it but it is now medically established that sleeping in a cold cabin lowers the resistance to life's little ailments.

Heat travels by conduction, convection and radiation. In general metals are excellent heat conductors, liquids less so and gases make the poorest conductors and therefore the best insulators. Air is an excellent insulator but sadly only while it is perfectly still. As soon as it is in motion it carries heat along by convection and also allows radiation to pass easily, and the entire insulation qualities disappear. Of the metals, copper is an excellent conductor with a k value $\left(\frac{\text{btu}}{\text{hour ft} \,^\circ\text{F}}\right)$ of 220, where aluminium has a figure about 115 and steel 28. These can be compared with wood at about 0·1 and a figure of approximately 0·025 for the normal insulating materials such as cork, glass fibre matting, polyurethane foam or fibre insulation boards.

Thermal insulation is measured in terms of its U value which refers to the number of British thermal units lost by one square foot of the material over an hour, with a one degree Fahrenheit difference between each side. The better the insulation, therefore, the lower the U value. These values are well documented and it is possible to make a reasonable estimation of the value of any insulation scheme for a yacht. A normal wooden hull without special provision will have a U figure of about 0·35, and even a modest amount of insulation on the topside and overhead would reduce that figure to a half or even a third. Insulation depends both on the U value of the structure, etc. and also on the thickness of the still air film around it. Not unnaturally in a yacht exposed to wind, the still air film on the inside may remain unchanged but that on the exterior will get thinner the more the wind blows thereby reducing the insulation and promoting heat loss from the hull.

Insulating a yacht against heat is practically impossible without proper ventilation. Most of the heat comes into the yacht through the upper part of the hull, topsides, decks, etc. Inside the hull the warm air rises to the undersides of the same areas and it is necessary by some ventilation scheme to get rid of that internal warm air, replacing it by cool.

In hot climates the relative value of radiation transfer and conduction and convection are different from cold climates. In cold climates one tries to get as much radiated warmth into the craft through large windows and then to retain it through good insulation and double glazing and so on. In hot climates one tries hard to keep out the radiant heat. In fact if anyone were foolish enough to fit double glazing in a tropical yacht she would be impossible to live in. Glass gives very little resistance to radiation but the four insulating boundary layers of air of double glazing make an excellent barrier to the heat getting out. Glass in any case is undesirable in tropical countries. When sunlight passes through it the wavelengths are increased, leading to a positive increase in the infra red or heat rays.

In hot weather vessels it may be best just to leave the windows open but this may not be possible owing to the flying midget monsters that abound. Fly screens alone might be best but for greatest heat reduction the glass windows should be very well shaded, either by deeply recessing the portholes, or by keeping windows under shady canopies or if nothing else by using louvre screens, on the outside of the glass of course.

Still air being such an excellent and inexpensive insulator the principle of most insulating materials is the so-called high void with the greater part of them composed of air spaces with the air stopped from movement by being trapped in solid matter. Mineral wool is made by melting some kind of rock type material and then spinning it up like candy floss. Glass wool is produced in much the same way and both are sold in convenient slabs. In use these, together with the foam plastics slabs and other proprietary insulations like corrugated asbestos, can be stuck straight into the structure between the beams and frames. There is little point in insulating the frames whose actual thickness, front to back, is quite a useful insulation on its own. Comparatively recently a squirted foam plastics process has been used for yacht insulation. This appears to be convenient and quite as good as the rest, but it does look a bit disturbing before the panelling goes up in an immaculately built vessel like a yacht. Wood, incidentally, has a cellular structure full of enclosed air spaces, providing very good insulation properties. A wood with a thin cellular structure and large air spaces, a light wood in other words, will be a better insulator than a heavy one. One inch of western red cedar is, for instance, noted in the architect's handbooks as having a thermal insulation equal to a five inch brick, or nine inches of concrete.

The actual temperatures taken for the U figures depend on the surface temperature of the materials. This not the same as the air temperature but is always a great deal higher. For instance, on a 65° F day a white paint surface might have a surface temperature of about 80° F, a polished metallic surface perhaps a few degrees higher and a matt black surface might be as high as 110° F. It is misleading actually to touch the surfaces to try and check their temperatures. A black wooden surface might feel quite cool because the touching hand quickly absorbs the excess heat. The cooler metal surface on the other hand might well feel hotter because the excellent conductivity of the metal brings along reinforcements as fast, or in fact faster, than the hand can absorb them.

Radiation heat is best reflected back to whence it came and this can be achieved by a polished surface. A layer of aluminium foil in the insulation can achieve respectable results but unfortunately not for long as the aluminium polish fades and grows dull. However, it is such a simple thing to install it is worth doing if only for the first season.

Noise Insulation

The actual materials used for sound insulation and for heat insulation look very much the same when in place and are often confused. At least they are often assumed to be equally valid for both jobs. Unfortunately this can be far from true and both functions have to be considered separately. Even where, in some cases, the materials may be identical the method of employment may be quite different.

Sound is a periodic disturbance in the air which in its path becomes alternately denser and rarer. The eardrums pick this up and vibrate with the same frequency to pass the message on to the brain. Sound requires a medium for its distribution and cannot, for instance, travel through a vacuum. Its speed varies with the medium. For example, in air it is approximately 1100 feet per second, in sea water getting on for 5000 feet per second and a metal such as iron will let sound pass at 16000 feet per second. Sound energy is measured in decibels on a logarithmic scale. This gives fairly misleading figures at times should the logarithmic aspect of the scale be forgotten, which it tends to be. A noise of 30 decibels when halved will give a figure of 27 and if halved again the decibels only come down to 24. We think the whole scale should be inverted because that is what noise in fact feels like. A single decibel's worth extra at the top end of our scale would qualify for a round hundred extra points at the very least. Perhaps a sort of Beaufort scale would be a better guide. We can all recognise easily enough the flat calm equivalent of noise, to be followed perhaps by the 'zephyrs can just be heard' for force 1 and so on through the scale right up to force 17 noises where 'whole mouths are in violent motion but no extra noise can be distinguished'.

Noise travels in two methods as far as insulation is concerned. First is airborne noise and second is noise carried through solid material, which is called impact noise. Noise can also be reflected from appropriate surfaces. When sound is produced continuously in a compartment it is reflected back repeatedly from bulkheads, ship-side, furniture, etc. with the result that the intensity of sound in the compartment can build up to a higher level than it would in the open air. In fact unless the compartment is very well insulated the whole yacht may qualify as the compartment in question and often does. If the source of the noise is stopped the sound will take an appreciable time longer to die away. It is rare for yachts to sport echoes but these are only another consequence of the same effect. Reverberation of this kind is reduced by sound absorbents which are not necessarily sound insulation. They will reduce the general level of sound but not affect the actual noise, from an engine for instance when you are standing beside it in the engine room.

Sound is normally absorbed in two principal styles. First is the use of porous materials into which the sound penetrates for its energy to be dissipated to heat. Second is the use of a panel type membrane which picks up the vibration itself and loses it in harmonic movement. The first is particularly suitable for high frequency noise and the second for low. The two types are often combined with porous absorbent panels mounted, for instance, on battens to suit some particular noise frequency range. Yachts, especially in engine rooms, have problems with the porous materials, which tend to suck up oil fumes, thus both spoiling the material and causing a fire hazard. It is usual therefore to fit the perforated tile sound absorber over a glass or mineral wool pad, the latter tucked up in a plastic bag or otherwise protected from the fumes. It is possible to vary the effectiveness of the tiles to suit different noise ranges by variations of hole size and spacing in the face tiles, but it is difficult to get any figures from the machinery makers to which to match them.

For the greater compartment involved – the accommodation outside the engine space – it is still sensible to fit sound absorbents. These can be in the more acceptable form of carpets, curtains and soft furnishings which all have good sound absorbent properties. In fact there is nothing that sets a yacht off quite so well as a really good carpet, especially if it is on top of a lead thread and rubber underlay. The boat will be immediately quieter both for machinery and for sea noise and even the crew will actually be less noisy about the yacht for it is unnatural and unproductive to stamp about and shout on top of a good carpet.

That is about as far as most yachts go in terms of sound control but it is really only just starting the job. Airborne noise, for instance, gets funnelled about the yacht along trunking and control ducts, a situation which is not difficult to remedy. Most of the noise, however, is so-called impact transmitted sound and that is much more difficult to cope with, especially inside a boat built of excellent sound transmission materials. The only thing to do is to insulate the transmitting faces completely, either in the compartment where the noise originates or in the compartment in which you do not want to hear it. This means a system of false faces of insulating material attached with non-conducting fasteners, because even a single metal nail or screw through the insulation into the structure will ruin the effect. A fact which it is very difficult to convince a boatyard about. The provision of an insulated engine room is probably something of a pipe dream with so many systems leading in and out. It is possible, however, to insulate such tiresome noise makers as generators and water pumps without too much difficulty.

Fortunately yachts are getting bigger and the pressure on interior space is relaxing. There may be space available soon for full sound protection in place of the half effective insulation which is all we can manage in the space we are allowed at the moment.

Fire Prevention

Of all the dangers to craft afloat perhaps fire is the most potentially devastating. Man has an instinctive fear of flame and a boat is a terrifyingly small environment in which to battle with it. Boats are also inevitably built with a great deal of combustible material and are largely powered by dangerous fuels. The danger of even a tiny flare-up extending into a complete and comprehensive disaster is always very real indeed. Fire prevention is as much a state of mind of designer and crew as is seamanship and in truth equally easy although very much less practised.

It is astonishing to us how often the first principles, even down to nursery school level, are ignored. We once saw a boat where the make and break of the electrical system was mounted so as to be physically underneath the float chamber of a carburettor. Her owner obviously thought that we were unduly excitable and alarmist about his future. Another boat had a neat device for stopping the gas bottle from falling about — someone had wired it to the exhaust pipe! Both these vessels belonged to seamen of the tarry breeches calibre who would never put to sea without anchors and a steadying sail but both were quite prepared to blame the Almighty if anything mechanical went wrong.

Even if the machinery is laid out and completed for reasonably efficient normal fire prevention it is extraordinary how many, perhaps 75 per cent, are vulnerable to a minor mishap. Plastic fuel lines and glass bowled fuel filters are the rule rather than the exception, but it would only take a lick of flame from a minor fire to let the fuel loose and turn it into a full-blooded disaster.

The first line of defence is obviously in the materials with which the boat is built. Most woods are extremely resistant to fire, especially dense woods like teak or iroko. All timbers in large size also prove difficult to get really burning, as anyone who has burnt a log will know. Very often the surface finishes are the things which actually start burning and spread the flame. Two methods are used for fireproofing wood: the first is to clad it with metal or special paint which will exclude air from the wood itself; the second is to impregnate the wood with a chemical which when warmed gives off a gas which will mix with the flammable gases given off by the wood itself and make them non-combustible.

The fire risk with GRP construction is much the same as with wood construction and a small improvement can be made by coating the surface with fire-retardant resin. There are various processes of which the most promising is perhaps one where the action of heat forms a protective skin which gives off gases and generally protects the main GRP structure from the flame. It is not possible to use fire-retardant resins at the present time for the whole structure since the characteristics, particularly weathering, are wrong and so it is a question of applying protection either in specified areas or over the whole inside of the moulding. Other plastics vary heavily in their flammability but in general those you use on board boats should not be worse than wood. Most in fact come under the self-extinguishing category which need continued flame to keep them burning. On the other hand the meltable plastics, acrylics and nylons for instance, can be very hazardous in a fire situation by dripping hotly and spreading the fire. They are also extremely dangerous if they drip onto people.

Of all the causes of fire afloat, petrol is currently on the top of most lists especially in hot climates. This is both fair and unfair, for the danger relates more to the installation and maintenance to be found on board some yachts than to any intrinsic dangers with the fuel. After all, we travel in the same climates in petrol driven motor cars and aeroplanes and would be downright astonished if the one next door blew up. One motor cruiser we know suffered a fuel pipe blockage in rough waters off the mouth of the Clyde. The South African engineer brought us back safely to Gourock by sitting astride the engine splashing petrol into (and around) the open float chamber at regular intervals as the boat rolled. He was also smoking at the time, perhaps to give us all complete confidence in his skill. The opposite end of this horror story is the fact that as little as a teacup of petrol in a warm bilge plus a minute spark and a whole boat will blow up. Petrol really must be treated with respect, even with extravagant formality.

The basic engineering of the installation must be good, of course, and fuel tanks should have readily accessible cut-off cocks if only to promote good habits. The fuel lines must siphon back into the tank in case of a leak rather than into the bilges — all these are first principles. The real danger is from petrol vapour and all drips from carburettors ought to be straight into flameproof trays. Petrol vapour is heavier than air and will therefore drain to the lowest point. All spaces where petrol vapour could accumulate ought to have excellent and sparkproof ventilation and this includes tanks. Incidentally, the tank vents should not, as in one craft, be situated close outside the opening galley window with the cooking stove close inside.

Diesel oil is generally regarded as a much safer fuel than petrol but once it is alight it is more difficult to extinguish. Diesel is designed to ignite in the cylinders in spray form, and it is possible to get a small leak in a pressure line which will produce just such a spray in the engine space all ready to light off anything hot enough in the vicinity. The mere use of diesel is no excuse for poor firemanship in the engine room. We were shocked after one disaster to discover, as perhaps we ought to have known, that the lubricating oil used in a diesel engine may have a much lower flash point than the fuel itself. It is possible, we understand, to get high flash point lubricating oil but how often is it offered or even indicated by the engine manufacturers?

Cooking gas is another favourite explosive on board boats. It is well understood to be dangerous and usually gets treated with proper care. Everyone understands that it is heavier than air and that elaborate self-draining precautions are necessary in normal use and that bilges especially need to be watched. There are in fact quite well organised regulations and recommendations from all manner of officials on the subject which allow for most things except the occasional idiot. As dangerous in many ways but scarcely given the same concern is the hydrogen given off by batteries during charging. Many apparently unexplained explosions may be due to hydrogen which, being lighter than air, accumulates in overheads waiting for as likely a spark as that which fires off the petrol or gas explosions. Once the danger is realised it is easily dealt with by some form of gas collecting canopy over the battery bank with a direct run to a deck vent immediately above. For special precautions with large battery banks it is possible to fit an electrical (sparkproof) extractor fan switched on by the charging circuits so that it is always in operation while hydrogen is forming. Incidentally, a valid fire precaution is an accessible battery cut-off switch in case of fire. Even a small fire can damage electrical wiring and installations which may set up an arcing situation which means that the combustion is self-igniting and only a complete cessation of the electricity supply will stop it.

In the bad old days electric wiring was thought to be unmixable with sea water and yachts. In fact quite sensible people preferred to put to sea with paraffin and matches rather than take any electrics with them, which shows the sort of reputation it had. Things are different now and any well-found yacht is replete with wiring and electrical apparatus. The installation may be excellent technically but it ought also to be checked to see that minor problems will not lead to arcing, sparking and flame. The degree of such attention falling somewhere between that given to hotels and that given to aircraft.

In the accommodation furnishings and so on a normal degree of attention is required to see that what can be fireproofed is, and what cannot be is limited. All that the designer can do really to defend the boat against a fool with cigarettes and matches is to avoid flammable foam upholstery and to make sure that there are no little cracks where a glowing cigarette may roll away out of sight. It is not that the risks of this kind of fire are any greater than they are ashore, it is just that the consequences can be much more difficult to cope with. You cannot rush out into the garden, nor is it as easy to reach the fire brigade.

Once you have fire on board what can you do about it? The first action, after getting the people out, is to cut off the air supply by shutting doors and windows and so on. Many commercial craft are required to fit shut-off flaps to all engine room and galley vents, an excellent arrangement which ought to be used more widely in yachts. Next you apply yourself to the fire extinguishers, unless of course there is an automatic system.

Fire comes in three main types and the treatment for each can be different. The type A fire refers to wood, paper, textiles and so on, and for this kind of blaze water is as good as anything. A special fire hose or deck wash hose can be used, or even buckets of water will help. The type B fire refers to flammable liquids and this type of blaze is best dealt with by smothering. Type C refers to electrical fires and the important factor in tackling them is that the extinguishant should be non-conducting. Water will not do at all and any electrically conducting material thrown at an electrical fire will only spread the problem and give the operator a nasty shock for his trouble.

The type B fires are extinguished by a reasonably wide range of materials. The simplest is an asbestos blanket which is quite the best way of dealing with small fires especially galley flare-ups. The dry powder extinguishers spray out a specially processed bicarbonate of soda (plus a few other ingredients) to lay a thin blanket of non-toxic and non-abrasive material. The air foams are best where there is a risk of re-ignition because of the thickness of the blanketing material. Carbon dioxide is best where it is essential that the extinguishing agent should not damage or leave a residue. For the electrical fires the powder or carbon dioxide are best.

BCF is becoming increasingly used afloat after its introduction in the aircraft industry. It works by providing an atmosphere capable of extinguishing flame and is good for a wide range of fires, covering all three types. BCF boils at about $-4°$ C and emerges as a combination of gas and evaporating droplets. It has a small toxic risk and is not currently approved for use in manned spaces.

Soda acid, carbon tetrachloride, chemical foam, methyl bromide and chlorobromomethane should not be used in boats. In some countries they are actually forbidden as they can be dangerous to people in confined spaces or can attack the materials of which the boat is built causing an equal, if opposite, disaster.

Some extinguishers are rated as non-toxic but this should not be regarded as a white card to swan around below decks during a fire because, these days, all fires can produce dangerous residues.

CHAPTER 15
Edge of Performance

General

In most things there seems to be a relatively easily attained level of performance. In intrinsic terms this performance may be altogether good enough. Fortunately we are nearly all nasty competitive creatures and if we cannot compete with our neighbours we will compete with ourselves. It is this competitive element in life which gives it an edge and also a need for an edge to the performance of boats. It is but human nature always to try to do things as well as possible and better than last time and we should not feel guilty about it. To write about the edge of performance is almost certainly to be out of date in detail but the principles remain true. First among these is this necessary feeling of having done one's best. To know that you have tried to do everything to make your boat go faster is halfway to its actually travelling faster. To know that you have done

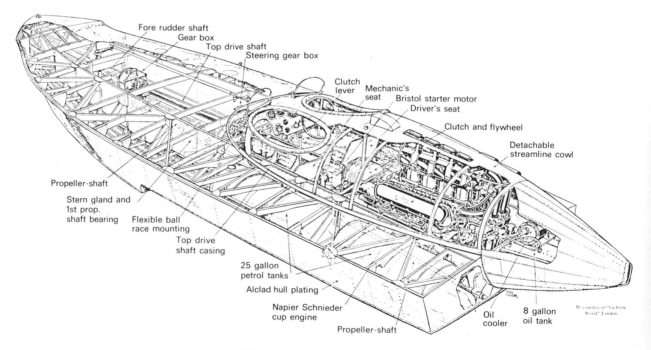

Fore rudder shaft
Gear box
Top drive shaft
Steering gear box
Clutch lever
Mechanic's seat
Bristol starter motor
Driver's seat
Clutch and flywheel
Detachable streamline cowl
Propeller-shaft
Stern gland and 1st prop. shaft bearing
Flexible ball race mounting
Top drive shaft casing
25 gallon petrol tanks
Alclad hull plating
Napier Schnieder cup engine
Propeller-shaft
Oil cooler
8 gallon oil tank

Fig. 275 Miss Britain III. *She had a single 1375 hp super-charged Napier Lion engine giving a propeller speed of approximately 9000 rpm. She is 24 ft 6 in long with an 8 ft beam. In 1933 she set a new world salt water speed record for single engined boats of 100·132 mph. (Max Millar sectional drawing showing layout and construction: courtesy* Yachting World.*)*

Fig. 276 Propellers, trim tabs, rudder and that shiny hull all contribute to the edge of performance — and having a trolley and pit like these to use must encourage care and attention.

everything to design the boat better than last time can raise the tiny inspiration that actually improves it. You cannot beat the mental approach to performance.

In moments of frankness merchant seamen will tell you, 'Never, never ever put to sea on a maiden voyage.' Trials will show up most problems in a new boat but they are carried out in a false atmosphere where the tenseness lies in assessing the boat. Get her out on the sort of voyage she is meant for and the attentions of the crew are on their jobs, not on the boat. This is when the stray wood shaving, for instance, gets shaken out of the linings and, not noticed, makes for a vital part. This is when the experts are all ashore, not standing ready to brush the errant shaving out of its danger heading, and things begin to go wrong. The chances of a raceboat completing its first race are statistically quite small unless it has been at least once around the full course beforehand. The gallant last ditch approach to performance, with the boat in the water the night before, is one of the most expensive ways of wasting money afloat and that is saying something.

An object lesson is always valuable and when we think of an edge in performance we like to go and see Scott Paine's *Miss Britain III* in the Maritime Museum at Greenwich. Her performance in the 1930s still puts us all to shame and she is a masterpiece of careful detail, reflecting the hours and hours of careful trials and development which went into her performance.

Power

Power is the prime element in performance for without it there is nothing but a raft. Producing more power than the next chap is a good start to beating him down the course. In owners' and designers' terms producing more power comes from the detail design of the installation, and the tuning and care for the machinery. Every engine tuner and every raceboat driver, and indeed every designer, has his own ideas on what makes for extra power when the outfit is fired up and running. Any diligent listener would soon become confused and bemused because in general views on power are contrary. It seems that it is as important to have strong views on engine tuning and installations as to know what they might actually be.

The engine or engines are often given expensive factory tuning without proper regard for the environment in which they are going to operate and delicate work at the bench may be quite overwhelmed by something crummy in the engine room. Not enough attention is given, to our minds, to the choice of fuels and lubricating oils, to engine air inlet temperatures and pressures, and even to the composition of the air the engine will have to work in during the race. Exhaust back pressures are usually considered but often in a somewhat cursory manner. Even the water pump is using available power and the careful design of the water inlet and piping might make a worthwhile marginal improvement.

Next consider the losses between the engine and the propellers. It is often thought enough that the bearings and glands are kept cool when running by a good supply of cooling water. The heat the coolant is running off again is energy which ought to be applied to the propulsion. A single-minded approach not only to getting the engine to produce the maximum power but also to reduce the losses which must be subtracted from it is important.

Then you come to the propellers. Once, long years ago, when we first started power boating we thought that propellers were an exact science. Painful experience has taught us that even if it is, it is much more often practised as an art and often

very badly at that. Once we rarely had anything but admiration for the beautiful bronze artefacts that arrived at the yard, usually a few hours before launching. Often we had a long stern chase to find out what had gone wrong with the performance estimates and were astonished to find that as often as not the propellers could properly be blamed. Of course, there were other reasons, like overweight boats and under powered engines but the propellers were often downright crude. Of one supposed pair of propellers, one of them turned out to have as much as two inches difference in pitch between its three blades; the other was something similar but adding up to a different average. Several times we have been shown propellers which were as much as twice their proper weight (but each of the pair a different weight) with thick ugly blades better shaped for stirring rice puddings than for high performance motor yachts.

Now we approach new propellers with narrowed eyes and an intense interest in their vital measurements including blade area. In general the art has been improving over the last few years but still it seems that, after perhaps hours of careful propeller design, the final casting may well be attacked by an artist with a grindstone subject to off days and temperament.

Would also that some manufacturer would set up a lending library of propellers so that a range of them could be tried in short time during trials leading to an order for the final set. Too often, in

Fig. 277 There is no reason why trim tabs have to be the untidy appendages often seen. This Chris Craft shows a very neat housed installation.

large yachts, such are deliveries, the propellers have to be specified and ordered months before the final extras are added to her. In raceboats you cannot be sure of the efficiency of the propellers until you have tried several.

Weight

There is a rumour about that Uffa Fox kept a steam roller outside his drawing office window to remind him of the proper place of weight in the world — namely ashore. The rumour, we can say, is untrue, but Uffa was the genius of modern small boat design and even rumours based on his known views on the subject deserve respectful consideration. From the first this one rings true, as any swimmer with lead weights in his pockets will agree (if he has time). When looked at from this angle it may seem odd that there is a considerable school of thought which equates weight with seaworthiness. When a small vessel is labelled a 'good sea boat', in inverted commas, the mind brings up immediately a picture of a stout beamy short ended craft of immense scantlings sitting deeply in the water. Generations of such good sea boats have been trundling about the oceans accumulating massive evidence apparently concluding that weight is of itself a factor in seaworthiness. This is of course looking at the whole situation through a looking glass like Alice. First in fact came the heavy boats — heavy because of the weight of cargo and stores they had to carry for such voyages and heavy again because of the weight of wood construction necessary to carry those cargoes and stores in addition to the omni-

present rot. The centuries of development have made the heavy boat comfortable at sea rather than shown that they are of themselves the archetype of seaworthiness. A quick look at the canvas boats of Tristan and such superb rough water boats as the Deal galleys or the Admiralty whalers rounds off this point of view in a satisfactory manner from the historical aspect. A glance round any anchorage will confirm it. For instance, we were recently struck by the contrast between a beautifully shaped heavy boat and a rather ugly light boat of about the same size. The beautiful boat ground its way painfully through the sea while the ugly one danced. One battled with its environment as an obvious extension of the solid land whereas the other responded and belonged. Light weight boats must be considered as a new line afloat, only recently even possible thanks to the new materials, and not as merely lighter versions of heavy boats.

Weight, on its own and without regard for its dynamic effects, is not too important for heavy craft. These commonly run in a fairly low speed range where skin friction costs as much as wave making. A few pounds extra here or there are modest as a percentage of the overall weight and their effect on speed even more cut back by the speed range. For light craft, however, weight becomes of great importance and, given a good hull form to start with, quite the biggest factor in performance. In fact given the reasonable hull shape the power/weight ratio is perhaps as much as 95 per cent of the total factor affecting the performance. This projects weight into the top bracket of importance for performance.

Such a bald statement is of course too large

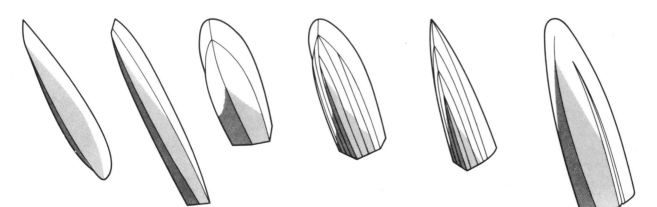

Fig. 278 In all these performance hull forms weight is still the major factor.

and comprehensive. It is possible somehow to save weight in practically every component and one quickly arrives at a cost/weight/save basis of choice and a cut-off point determined by the depth of the owner's pocket and the cost effectiveness of each item. Life being what it is these two points rarely come within striking distance of each other.

Weights in a raceboat are so important that it is worth considering a certain amount of breakage. Structural weights should be considered, as in aircraft, in terms of their importance against disaster and for a raceboat this might range between losing the boat and losing the race. If a piece of structure does not affect anything in that range then its safety factor can be reduced to unity.

The Appendages

It is becoming fashionable to clutter up the bottom of boats with all manner of bumps and obstructions. Sometimes they improve performance, too often they do not. Hours of labour to reduce hull drag, and indeed hours of labour to buy more powerful engines, even hours of labour

Fig. 279 Tank testing for optimum spray rail position. The tank spray can be much more alarming than real life spray — see Fig. 280.

to clean the hull and polish the propellers, can be negated in an instant by the casual bolting on of some of the detritus of technology. There is no reason why transducer heads for electronics, earth plates, valve outlets, sacrificial anodes and propeller bracket palms, should not be flush with the hull surfaces these days. Some shaft outlet glands are finished with great nuts and bolts, usually bang in the water flow of the propellers, as if the engineer had entered for a competition in modern sculpture.

Spray rails became fashionable in the wake of the Hunt deep vee and were, and in fact are, to be seen strapped around many hulls which would be faster and drier running without them. Spray rails have two strictly limited functions. In the forebody they act principally as spray shedders. From the spray root a surface slick of pressurised water rides up the hull in an equal and opposite direction to the pressure at the spray root itself. This is usually thin water, transparent and difficult to see, and often travels up the hull in a forward pointing direction. The spray rails stop this surface slick, break it up and return it to the sea surface. Or they should. In some cases they can actually accelerate the rising water to spray it high and wide ready to be caught by the wind and carried directly at the helmsman. You can recognise this effect because it feels like being under a shower rather than at the wrong end of a bucket of water.

The other function of spray rails is to define the planing surface and give it efficient edges. This is usually done by the chines proper and the spray rails are only required where the chine cannot do the job. In the deep vee hull this may mean that they have to run full length fore and aft. In craft which operate at a wide range of speeds the amount the hull rises from the water will vary and this can be another excuse for spray rails to be fitted to define different ranges of planing surface. A spray rail which runs under water is likely to be a positive loss in all directions. It is just possible that in some cases they may drag a little air under the hull with them but this modest drop of air lubrication is unlikely to compensate for the extra surface drag.

The size of section of spray rail also needs a little care. It just is not good enough to screw on the same section as a neighbouring boat. The exact size can alter the efficiency of the whole hull.

Fig. 280 One of the boats built to the tank-tested design, shown in Fig. 279, in action.

Fig. 281 Where is the spray coming from? This picture shows the spray-generating properties of spray rails. The thin unbroken layer of water is riding up the hull from the forefoot to be distributed and broken off by the rail into a big feather spray.

Fig. 282　*Blunt ended rudder and carefully faired struts and chocks in a fast power boat. More fairing still would be worth while.*

Fig. 283　*Spray rails working well and a nice level ride. This 19 ft Italian built* Mastiff *cruised 1587 miles round Italy in 100 hours running time.*

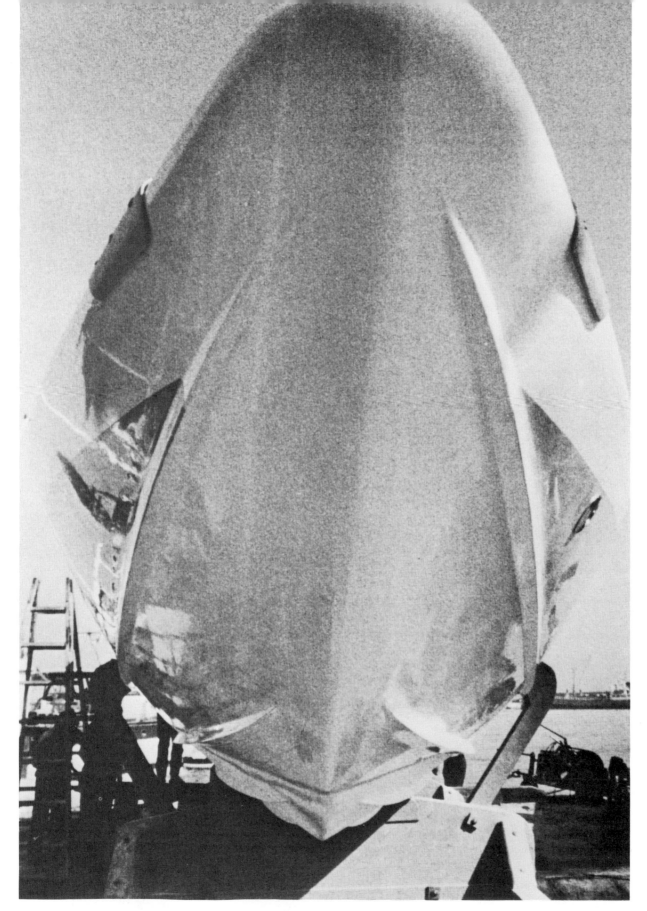

Fig. 284   The super efficient spray rails of a fast Levi hull.

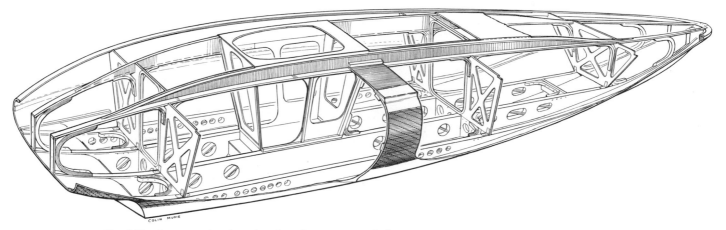

Fig. 285 Cutaway drawing showing the structure of the
News of the World *power boat.*

Fig. 286 These spray rails are obviously doing an excellent
job but it can be seen that they are largely being used for
structural rather than hydrodynamic purposes.

The Structural Engine

After the power/weight ratio and waterline length
the next most important factor in top performance
is the structure. It is an aspect of design we have
been working on for some years. As far as we can
estimate it involves about two per cent of performance — quite a respectable race winning margin. It could be applied to any vehicle, car, plane,
bicycle, with a power limitation and a real interest
in every ounce of speed.

We started by considering a group of the
remaining mysteries of performance in boats.
These generally take the line of questions: Why
do new wooden boats go better than old wooden
boats? It cannot be due, as so often reported,
to the extra weight from soakage, for the same
weight can be carried in the new boat in ballast
and she will still go faster. Why does replacing
the garboards often transform the performance of
an old sailing boat? Why do racing sailing boats
go better with very tight fore and aft rigging? The

straight sail luff is slightly aerodynamically worse than one which sags and the sailmaker can cut his cloth to any shape. Why did the traditional American wooden craft go better than boats built to the same shape in the European manner? Why do some boatbuilders build better competition boats to the same displacements than others? And why do some boats out of a bunch of production craft, apparently identical, perform differently to the rest? One can go on: Why does a boat with a young crew go better than one with elderly gentlemen on board? And come to it — why does not crew weight affect performance as much as dead weight? It is possible to query some of these questions but not the general mass of them nor the direction in which they point.

The answers all seem to us to be in the energy losses in the structure, skin and components of the craft. All boats move in bending or in twisting

if only to a tiny degree when moving in water. If the movements were recorded and the boat taken ashore and physically distorted to reproduce the same movements quite a lot of energy would be involved. It is normal practice when testing materials to record the energy used in, say, bending a specimen and then the energy returned as it straightens. This forms the so-called hysteresis loop for that material, the loop representing the amount of energy lost in the cycle. The same effect of course happens with the complete boat. In terms of energy-in/movement/energy-out, the hull acts as an engine and it is the efficiency of that engine in which we are very much interested. The lost energy, one way or the other, must come from power which might have been applied to propulsion or to some other worthwhile cause.

To go back to our questions. Most of the answers to them lie in the question of movement

Fig. 287 The little Missel *prototype with its suspension system for the bottom is driven here by the late Ralph Loosemore.*

or of tune. New wooden boats, if you were to unscrew the planking, would spring apart, whereas in old boats the planks and timbers have over the years succumbed to their curved form. The new boat is therefore in a pre-stressed state with a considerably reduced movement and much smaller loop in the hysteresis curve. The pre-stressing or tuning is also affected strongly by the rigging, or by new planks, and of course by the materials of construction. The crew question relates more to the hysteresis loops of young limbs compared with old and the relative movement energy each absorbs or returns to the hull.

Of course, this is where the real problems start. Our first research was into the actual planking and framing materials used for boats and we found to our delight that we got surprisingly large variations of results from apparently similar samples of different woods and different combinations of woods. About that time we designed a structure for the *News of the World* raceboat based on our ideas on structural energy conservation and incorporated the results of the materials research. The *News of the World* showed an unexpected edge of performance which was very encouraging. We have gone on gently from there, but with some care, for the amount of energy returned is one thing but how fast it comes back is another and where it returns is yet another.

The rate of return appears to be related to the efficiency of the structure. A quick whip back into shape and even beyond, leaves less time for energy to be absorbed and appears to be generally desirable. However, in the time involved it is possible for the initial impact, say, of wave energy to be returned so fast that the return occurs during the impact period, effectively doubling the pressure loading on the skin. This was confirmed by NASA research into the impact of spacecraft on the sea surface at the end of their missions.

In the same manner it is no use the energy imparted to the hull as it shoulders its way into a sea being returned to the bows for this will only increase the resistance. Ideally the energy should be gathered by the centre structure and returned aft, adding to the propulsion.

The principle is sound and the results effective but there are large areas of 'don't know' still to be investigated. Once the idea is accepted you can see energy being dissipated on every hand in most boats. A locker door binding gently in its frame with hull movement is wasting energy which must come from somewhere. So is the dinghy rocking gently in its chocks, so is the engine room hatch of a racing power boat nodding in its soft rubber chocking, and so is the crew strapped into his upholstery. The crew, however, has his own internal combustion engine which allows him to return it and even to over-

Fig. 288   Fletcher Arrowshaft 25 ft Class III offshore power boat showing high efficiency at speed.

Fig. 289 Starflite III, *holder of the world outboard speed record in 1960 at 122 mph. A single-minded approach to flat water performance.*

compensate. Perhaps, perhaps, it might even be possible to put positive power into the structural hull and cut its resistance. Perhaps that is how dolphins work.

You may say that if the structural engine energy is any appreciable factor then it would have shown up in the resistance and powering calcula-tions long before now. The answer is that there is plenty of room for it and a dozen more like it under the general heading of wave making drag. There is even room for it under skin friction. In fact, there are many inexact areas of boat per-formance where anything up to five per cent of performance may be concealed.

CHAPTER 16
The Past and the Future

How Far Back Do We Go?

If you wanted to go right back to the very earliest of powered boats you might find yourself considering the quinqueremes and other many oared vessels of the centuries just before the birth of Christ. Not strictly in the mechanically propelled category, yet these vessels with the rhythmic power of their multiple oars and the menace of their metal-sheathed rams must have had an appearance of mechanical ferocity far in advance of their time. The 'arms race' of the third century BC had a peculiarly apt meaning, for when one side built many-oared quinqueremes, or fives, the opposition built sixes and sevens, and so on through sixteens, eighteens, twenties and thirties, until Ptolemy IV trumped them all with a forty — four hundred feet long, fifty feet in beam and with an estimated four thousand oarsmen. Whether or not this was actually built and how it was rowed is conjectural. How the oars were arranged in these vessels has been exhaustively discussed and as yet there is still little evidence to support any one theory. It seems highly unlikely that there were, for instance, forty horizontal layers of oars in Ptolemy's boat. Perhaps there were forty diagonal groups a side with five oars to a bank and an average of ten men to an oar, or perhaps the forty denoted the number of men who rowed a group of oars of a number so far undetermined. Probably the greatest difficulty was in finding enough experienced oarsmen and keeping them in step. Perhaps somewhere there is an ancient carving which will explain it all and we will once again be left amazing at how clever were our ancestors.

It is difficult to discover exactly how fast these high powered boats were and their sprint speed

Fig. 290 The Viking ship was essentially a power boat designed for minimum resistance when the power supply was muscle. The construction was also the ancestor of a whole family of building methods only just dying out. This is the Oseberg ship preserved in a cathedral atmosphere near Oslo.

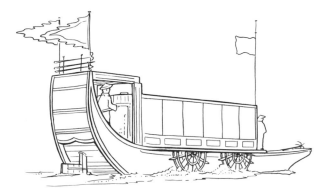

Fig. 291 *The Chinese were early users of paddle wheels. This sixteenth century vessel was powered by a man-operated treadmill.*

Fig. 292 *Leonardo da Vinci had thoughts on paddle wheel propulsion. Note the reversing mechanism operated by canting the main driving wheel over to the other cogwheel.*

must have been a carefully calculated, reserved maximum and a national secret. However, a $7\frac{1}{2}$ knot sprint speed is given for a 170-oared trireme.

The use of applied manpower to propel boats against wind and tide was considered in various ways other than the traditional oared propulsion. Paddle wheels were another form of drive power and numerous experiments with man powered paddle wheels paved the way for later adaption to mechanisation after the development of the marine steam engine. Paddle wheels were used by the Chinese and, as might be expected, Leonardo da Vinci had advanced ideas for paddle wheel propulsion; in the sixteenth century a Spanish paddle wheeler 'powered' by fifty men was reported to have done $3\frac{1}{2}$ knots and, incidentally, gave rise to myths of early steam power because

steam was seen rising from cauldrons of hot water on her decks (bath time or lunch?).

The history of invention is strewn with the names of those said to be the first to try something. Power boating is no exception and the last years of the eighteenth century and the first of the nineteenth are full of stories of marine engine experiment. It was a fertile time for new ideas and particularly for applications and extensions of the work of steam pioneers Newcomen and Watt. The blow by blow history is well documented and looking back it is amazing to see how often this year's new thought turns out to have been tried in practice nearly two hundred years ago. Frequently inventive ingenuity was in advance of technology but experiments with, for instance, such things as jet engines, steam turbines, amphibious craft and multihulls have a very modern sound.

One of the first to anticipate the possibilities of a steamboat was a French doctor, Denis Papin, who at the end of the seventeenth century described how a steam powered piston might be used to drive paddle wheels and who made detailed proposals in London in 1708 to the Royal Society. He tried a man powered paddle wheeler but his advanced ideas for steam propulsion were not put into practice in his lifetime. Another prophetic power boat application was described by Englishman Jonathan Hulls in his 1736 patent for a stern wheel tug driven by a Newcomen 'atmospheric' engine. Who actually was the first to use an engine, rather than man or horse power, to move a boat through water may never precisely be known. There are several claimants between the years 1775 and 1788 and which is given credit somewhat depends on which reference you take and which country you support. It seems most likely that credit should go to one of two Frenchmen, although local jealousies and the subsequent revolution have somewhat obscured the records.

It seems that in 1775 Jacques C. Perier experimented with a small steamboat on the Seine, but since it only had about one horsepower the engine could not push it against the current. Although this may have been the first steamboat, the first successful one was probably that of the Marquis de Jouffroy d'Abbans whose 140 foot *Pyroscaphe* went up the River Saône at Lyons against the current for fifteen minutes in July 1783. This practical demonstration of marine steam power was made with a horizontal double

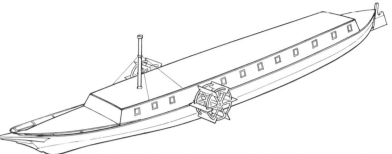

Fig. 293 M. le Marquis de Jouffroy's Pyroscaphe. Drawn from a print in the Science Museum.

acting cylinder over 25 inches in diameter, with a 77 inch stroke and driving two paddle wheels 13 feet in diameter.

During the next few years a great deal of experiment was done on both sides of the Atlantic. In America John Fitch succeeded in driving a steamboat on the Delaware River in 1786 at about three miles an hour. This was an unlikely looking vessel propelled by twelve vertical steam driven oars, rather like a crewless Indian canoe. A year later, in 1787, James Rumsey's steam driven water jet boat was run on the Potomac against the current at about three knots. (Most of these early experimenters made proper note of the fact when their boats actually went against the current.) Meanwhile, in Scotland Patrick Miller, who had for some years been experimenting with man powered paddle wheels in multihull boats, installed a Symington steam engine in a 25 foot double hulled boat, powering two paddle wheels between the hulls. Successful trials at five knots were run in 1788 (with Robert Burns among those on board) and the engine can still be seen in the London Science Museum.

Patent after patent relating to steamboat propulsion was taken out as improvements and variations were put forward in the years that followed. Paddle wheels were the most common method of pushing the water out of the way, but such things as duck foot paddles which closed on the forward stroke and opened out to push aft were also experimented with in Britain and America. In America a patent was taken out for an amphibious vessel, the 30 foot *Orukter Amphibolos*, which made a sixteen mile demonstration journey by land and river in Pennsylvania.

So much experiment in Europe and America was followed by practical success and a number of firsts were claimed in the beginning of the nineteenth century. The *Charlotte Dundas* was the first practical steamboat and tug; she was a stern wheeler and was used experimentally in place of horse drawn boats on the Forth and Clyde Canal in 1802 (though they said that the wash disturbed the canal banks). The first really commercially viable vessel was Robert Fulton's famous *Clermont* (with an English Boulton & Watt engine) which was regularly used as a Hudson River ferry between New York City and Albany in 1807. The first seagoing steamer was the American *Phoenix*, launched in 1808, which voyaged round to New York from Philadelphia and then ran as a packet boat between there and New Jersey.

The screw propeller also made a fairly early appearance on the power scene. A patent was taken out by the American steamboat pioneer John Stevens in 1791 and after various experiments he successfully ran the first screw driven boat *Little Julianna* at Hoboken in 1804 at a mean speed of four miles an hour and even reaching seven to eight miles an hour for a short distance. As she was only just under 25 feet in length this speed shows that she was in fact driven just about as fast as the hull would go. There was inevitably some rivalry between the paddle wheelers and the screw drivers, which later culminated in tugs of war between vessels representing each type tied stern-to-stern — won conclusively every time by the propeller driven boat.

Commercial motives undoubtedly spurred these powerboat pioneers, though it is difficult to believe that some of them did not get a good deal of pleasure boating incidental to their experiments. A print of Mr Patrick Miller and his friends enjoying a first steamboat ride seems to bear this out, it was yachting if ever we saw it.

However, there is little doubt that the early steamboat enthusiasts were regarded with some disdain by the sailing yacht gentlefolk. For a long time, perhaps even still, the word yachting was taken to imply sailing boating and not to include motor boating. A schism still exists and although many people have a foot in each camp there are many more who do not recognise the existence of another camp at all.

The problem faced one of the earliest motor yachtsmen, Mr T. Assheton Smith, who is reputed to have resigned from what is now the Royal Yacht Squadron because they would not recognise steamboats as members' yachts. In a classic resolution in 1827 the Royal Yacht Club as it was then known, resolved:

Fig. 294 Elegant vessels with clipper bows and pretty counters.

'That as a material object of this club is to promote seamanship and the improvement of sailing vessels, to which the application of steam engines is inimical, no vessel propelled by steam shall be admitted into the club, and any member applying a steam engine to his yacht shall be disqualified thereby and cease to be a member.'

Nevertheless Mr Smith went ahead and built the 120 foot paddle yacht *Menai* and several others after her but it was 1844 before the Squadron came to terms with these new pleasure vessels. First they lifted their ban for steam yachts of over 100 hp and in 1853 all restrictions. Could the fact that Squadron member Queen Victoria had the paddle yacht *Victoria and Albert* built in 1843 possibly have influenced the decision?

The practical identification of such pioneers as Mr Smith and the later support of such powerful advocates as the Royal Family and the Squadron gave great impetus to the building of steam yachts and before the end of the nineteenth century by far the greater number of yachts registered over a hundred tons were powered boats. Many were elegant vessels with clipper bows and graceful counters although with a touch of the hybrid about them. With belt and braces caution they kept some canvas to hand and most had tall funnels fighting for distinction between high masts.

The large auxiliary steamer was an ideal pleasure vehicle for extended cruising and many covered thousands of miles using sail when the wind served and steam when it failed. These grand vessels of from 500 to 1000 tons were a unique type which has not really been repeated in the years since. Perhaps the nearest in spirit, although not in size, are the current crop of high powered motor sailers which perform equally well under power or sail.

It was, nevertheless, for many years not unusual to have a yacht described as a motor boat while still sporting a certain amount of mast and sail. The first all aluminium power boat, built in Switzerland in 1892, was one of these and beside her clipper bow and bowsprit had twin masts which quite dwarfed her funnel.

The smaller launches more often had the courage of their owners' convictions and relied solely upon engine power, particularly for river and estuary use. This was a time for delightful little launches powered by gasoline, paraffin or naphtha,

coal or even electricity. Many were used as tenders to larger yachts and others purely for pleasure jaunts. A nice little launch which to our minds epitomises this last kind is the 12 foot *Nina*, built in New York and once named as the tiniest steamer afloat. Her beam was about three feet and her twin three-bladed propellers gave her a speed of about five and half miles an hour. The funnel was movable and could be lowered for bridges and her all-up weight was 215 lb (plus 40 lb of best charcoal). Most delightful of all she

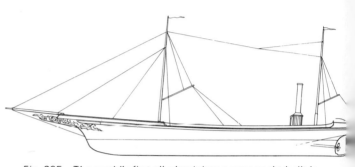

Fig. 295 The world's first all-aluminium power yacht built in Switzerland in 1892 by Von Escher Wyss & Co. 36 ft long by 5 ft 3 in beam, with a 2 hp naphtha engine giving about 5 knots.

Fig. 296 The little steam launch Nina *was a vessel undoubtedly for pleasure.*

Fig. 297 Bramble, another attractive steam launch, was carvel built in teak about 1900 and is still well cared for and in use today.

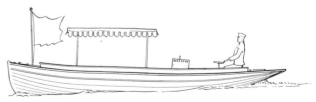

Fig. 298 Gottlieb Daimler's motor launch.

could be steered with the feet, thus leaving the hands free to tend the engine or, doubtless, to wave to passing admirers.

The breed of long slender motor boats in which the engine had obvious pride of place had great appeal and many of them have been kept carefully until the present day, perhaps because their polished brass and canvas canopies recall an age we like to think of as less stressful than our own. A fair number of these veterans, carefully preserved and regularly maintained, turn out for rallies, particularly in the United Kingdom and in America. Even the coal burners are welcomed despite the smoke which is now considered so polluting.

What might be thought the first real motor launch was a little boat with a modest 1½ hp benzine engine which the motor man Gottlieb Daimler tried on a German lake in 1886. In partnership with Steinway, of the piano company, he later produced larger gasoline engines for marine use, showing them at the Chicago World's Fair in 1893. From these small beginnings we now have marine engines running to thousands of horsepower. Although steam engines, particularly in launches, were still popular, by the end of the nineteenth century they were being ousted by the internal combustion engine. Not everyone was prepared to concede that steam engines might have had their day, and in particular Nathanial Herreshoff, that designer of many lovely little launches, took a fair bit of convincing. Only when his new little steam launch *Swiftsure* had been raced and beaten by a 75 horsepowered Panhard engine in a boat called *Vingt-et-un II* was he finally persuaded. There is no doubt that apart from being readily available because of the growth of the motor car industry, the internal combustion engine had obvious advantages compared, for instance, with the coal burners and though the engines themselves were initially no smaller than the steam engines all the adjuncts took less space. As they grew lighter and more compact so steam power disappeared from general use, with the notable exception of the steam turbine.

Power boating history has few tales to compete in *élan* with that of Sir Charles Parsons and his *Turbinia*. She must have shot her way through the sedate Royal Diamond Jubilee review of the Fleet in 1897 at 34½ knots like something from outer space, flaunting her name at her masthead and bow. She was built by Parsons to draw

attention to his revolutionary, patented, turbine engines. She was only one hundred feet long and was powered by three turbines driving three shafts and nine propellers. Her sensational appearance must have made the Victorian Navy feel old-fashioned in one fast run. However, surprisingly perhaps, the ploy was a success and a charitable Navy built the first steam turbined destroyer two years later, powered by Parsons engines similar to *Turbinia*'s. It might have been thought that this would set a fashion for turbine powered yachts since *Turbinia* was similar in size to many of the then current pleasure vessels, but this was not the case. In fact, with one or two exceptions and spasmodic outbursts of interest in, for instance, gas turbines, there has never been a really widespread interest in the turbine as a source of power for marine motoring.

Harmsworth Cup

Racing under power probably began with a steamboat race for a twenty guinea cup put on by the Royal Northern Yacht Club in their August regatta in 1827. The race, which took three hours and began and ended at Rothesay, was won by a Robert Napier steamer, the *Clarence*. It was in its way a portentous event. It was this race which attracted the attention of Mr Assheton Smith to the idea of a steam yacht and to Mr Robert Napier himself. It resulted in Mr Smith's quarrel with the Squadron and his eventual commissioning of Napier to build him the steam yacht *Menai*.

The name Napier is one which occurs in the marine engineering world through the years, and just as that first steam yacht was to influence power yachting for decades so were other bearers of the Napier name, either on bows or in engine rooms, to influence speedboat racing for further decades in the first half of the twentieth century.

Since the early days of the motor car industry, the marinised internal combustion engine has benefited from the research and development and the widespread use of the car. Rivalries on the motor racing tracks were paralleled on the water, and it was not long before international interest in speedboat racing was aroused. The catalyst for this competition was to be a cup offered in 1903 by Sir Alfred Harmsworth. Originally called the Harmsworth Cup (later altered to the British International Trophy) it was open to boats of up

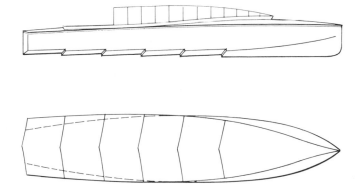

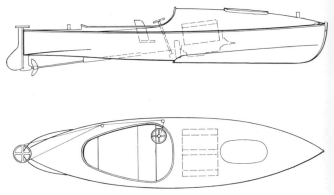

Fig. 299   The 40 ft five stepped hydroplane Maple Leaf IV *brought the Harmsworth Cup back to England in 1912.*

Fig. 300   Thornycroft's First World War coastal motor boats evolved from experience with such racing boats as Miranda IV.

to forty feet in length, driven by a national of the country concerned and with engine power built in that country. It was poetic that the first winner of the cup and of the world water speed record should be Mr S. F. Edge's *Napier I*, at a speed of 19·53 mph. The Harmsworth Cup races, during the years that they were hotly contested, in fact came to stand for the world motor boat speed record. The next year was a really international contest with three French, one American and five British entries, and the winner was the French boat *Tréfle-à-Quatre*, the only time that this race was not won by either a British, American or Canadian boat. The following year the Cup was brought back to England by *Napier II*, but in 1907 it was won by the United States with *Dixie*. It is interesting to see that the winning speed at this time was over thirty miles an hour and that within six years it was well over fifty.

These early years of the British International Trophy were marvellous ones for the development of fast motor boating, and they take in those of the big breakthrough in hull form with the practical application of the hydroplane, which in this context refers to the planing type of hull. The other kind of hydroplane is in a fascinating but rather different world where the hull rises right out of the water while floats, foils or blades attached to the hull keep contact. This foil concept was investigated by, among others, the Wright brothers and also, in a patent application in 1905, by Professor Enrico Forlanini; but their hydroplanes, although in contact with water, ventured more into the aeroplane's ambience.

The hydroplaning boat was no invention of the nineteen hundreds, but, like so many other bright thoughts, had been put forward many years

before. The most practical design was advanced by the Reverend Charles Meade Ramus in 1872 and experimented with by the Admiralty under the supervision of the famous Mr William Froude. Mr Ramus's idea was that the hull should be made of two wedge shaped bodies, one behind the other, which would enable the boat to lift out of the water. His proposal to the Admiralty was for a ship 352 feet long with two planes each of 150 feet in length. The idea came to nothing mainly for lack of engines with suitable power/weight ratios, another case of an inventor being before his time. He did, however, conduct dramatic trials with rocket power, though not, we gather, with a 350 footer.

Successful experiments with hydroplaning and air lubricated hulls were carried on at about the same time in America, France and the United Kingdom and began to make an impression on racing in the six or seven years before the First World War. When in 1910 *Dixie II* of America won the Harmsworth Cup her speed was over thirty-six miles an hour, but one of the challengers, the Duke of Westminster's *Pioneer*, was obviously a very much faster boat with speeds of about forty miles an hour. The Americans recognised this in an admirable memo sent by the Commodore of the Motor Boat Club of America which, announcing to his members that they had retained the Cup, continued,

'The Board desires to call attention to the fact that while the result of the race is a victory for the club, one of the English challengers showed a speed so greatly in excess of that of *Dixie* as to make it evident that in the contest of next year (informal notice of which has already been received) new boats of a speed much higher than that of any American craft must be built for the defence of the cup. This is a matter which should engage the attention of the club and its members at an early date.'

Engage their attention it did, to good effect. Although *Pioneer* was again one of the challengers in 1911, the Americans kept the Cup, with *Dixie IV*, and it was not until 1912 that the five stepped 40 foot hydroplane *Maple Leaf IV* took it back to England. She won it again the next year and there it stayed until after the First World War. Although the Harmsworth Cup races were by no means the only ones during this period before the war, there were regular races in America and Europe including the Gold Cup races, an annual Monaco event, a cross-channel race, and a London/Cowes race, the Harmsworth Cup fulfilled the donor's intention of making it a truly international contest.

When the war began many yachts joined, or were 'pressed' into, the Navy. The raceboats were not in themselves usable, though it was suggested that small fast boats could be used as submarine spotters, but undoubtedly the development work which had been nurtured by racing was valuable for the wartime fleet and in particular for the coastal motor boats, such as those evolved by the Thornycrofts from their work with racing motor boats such as *Miranda IV*.

Maple Leaf IV held the Cup and the world water speed record of over 57 mph from 1913 until 1920 when both were taken over for the next decade by the Americans in the person of Garfield A. Wood in his series of *Miss Americas*. These were built for him by Mr Christopher Columbus Smith's company, later called Chris Craft, and the first *Miss America* was powered by two Liberty 425 aircraft engines in a 27 foot boat. This policy of putting into the boat as much horsepower as he possibly could was one which he pursued with great success throughout his motor boat racing career. He took the world water speed record up to 93 mph in 1929, by which time he was driving *Miss America VII* with 2300 hp.

By the 1930s the British contenders for the Cup had gone in the opposite direction from Gar Wood and were putting smaller, lighter engines in smaller boats. This policy resulted in some very fast vessels but never managed to bring back

the Harmsworth Cup to Britain. It was held by America for 39 years altogether and was won by Gar Wood no less than eight times. It was not until 1959 that the Cup left the USA and then it was only to go north to Canada, won by *Miss Supertest III* in that year and in the two succeeding years. Since then interest has diminished and the Cup itself languishes unfought-for in the custody of the Royal Motor Yacht Club at Poole — which is a pity, because it is an impressive piece of Edwardian silverware with a jolly scene of motor boats chasing each other through a metallic sea.

Record Breaking

For many years water speed record breaking and the Harmsworth Cup races went hand in hand and the current holder of the one usually had the other on his bookshelf too. Sir Henry Segrave broke the sequence in 1930 when he brought the world water speed record up to 98 mph with *Miss England II*. He had already done remarkably well in racing against Gar Wood's 2300 hp *Miss America VII* with his little Fred Cooper designed, Hubert Scott Paine built *Miss England* and her single 930 hp Napier Lion engine. His record breaking *Miss England II* had two Rolls-Royce engines of 1900 hp each but the triumph of the record was marred when she sank and Sir Henry Segrave and one of his mechanics were drowned. Later, the same boat was raised, reconditioned and reached a further record speed of 103 mph with her new driver Mr Kaye Don. He and Gar Wood topped each other's records successively for the next few years until the challenge was taken up by Sir Malcolm Campbell with his *Bluebird*s. His record breaking career on land and water attracted great acclaim in the years before and after the Second World War, and was emulated by his son Donald until his tragic death on Coniston Water in 1967. Their achievements, though no less courageous, were in a very differ-

Fig. 301 One of the most beautiful raceboats, Miss England II, *was 32 ft long and powered with twin Rolls-Royce engines.*

Fig. 302   The three pointer Bluebird *built by Vospers for Sir Malcolm Campbell in 1939.*

ent world from that of the power yachts that people use for pleasure as well as for the serious business of racing. The more recent meetings held annually for boats of different sizes and capacities in order to make record attempts are much more in the spirit of pleasure yachting, although the commercial element of the sport quite properly does take a close interest in the efforts.

Racing

The boats that were developed for racing in the Harmsworth Cup and for record breaking became intensely specialised — and expensive. It was this perhaps as much as anything which finally resulted in the falling-off of interest. The owners

of ordinary, even thought fast, power boats could not enter them for the 35 mile slog around a five mile circuit in an effort to win the best out of three races which was the Harmsworth Cup contest. It is hardly surprising therefore that in the 1950s there should have been a re-invention of the offshore race, followed later, of course, by the re-invention of the offshore racing power boat. In 1956 Red Crise and Sam Griffith rounded up thirty boats for a race from Miami, Florida, to Nassau in the Bahamas, crossing a nicely varied stretch of water. Then in 1961 Sir Max Aitken inspired a British offshore race from Cowes to Torquay for cruising power boats. Few, if any, of these early racers were built specifically for the job, but the whole thing was organised with immense efficiency and care for safety and a stringent system of scrutineering was inaugurated, so that while many were to drop out of the competition in bad weather there has to date never been any serious loss or injury to competitors, though many a boat has suffered sadly.

From these two major races has grown a circuit which can take the *aficionado* round the world in a series of annual races.

The original racers were very much the kind of boat you could take across channel and cruise happily aboard, but inevitably the specialists moved in, paring down accommodation from the luxurious, through the uncomfortable to the downright impossible, until now there are out-and-out racers and cruiser/racers in the larger classes and a wide selection of classifications for the smaller raceboats, depending on dimensions and engine capacities.

The Detachable Engine

No look at the history of power yachting would be complete without inclusion of the outboard motor. No other single method of pushing a vessel through, and sometimes over, the water is quite so widespread. There are thousands of large yachts in the world, but every large yacht usually has at least one outboard powered tender. There are millions of dinghies in the world, and a high percentage of them have an outboard somewhere in the outfit. There are hundreds of raceboats in the world and a majority of them have an outboard engine or engines — some have four, five or even six on the back end with lavish abandon

Fig. 303   A clutch of outboards powering a Magnum 28 race boat.

and keep replacements with the shore party for instant renewal.

By far and away the majority of outboards are now fuelled with petrol, but in the early days there was even a steam driven outboard. It was actually not until 1907 that Cameron Waterman produced the name 'outboard', having successfully set up the manufacture of the Waterman Porto, the first outboard engine to be sold in quantity. In these early years, however, it was as often as not called a detachable engine, which in many ways was a better description.

One of the earliest and most enduring names associated with outboards is that of Ole Evinrude. in 1907 he designed and built an engine which in basic outline has been the standard outboard shape ever since. This engine, with its horizontal cylinder, vertical crankshaft and driveshaft with power direction changing gears in a submerged lower unit, is immediately recognisable as a forebear even of the fat and full powered monsters of today.

The potential of this unit, which could be detached and carried away from the boat at will and serviced away from the water without the need to take the boat as well, was immediately recognised (a friend to whom Evinrude lent his prototype engine returned it with orders and

Fig. 304   Believed to be the first Evinrude outboard.

Fig. 305 *This sterndrive unit was made and marketed by Johnson Motors in 1932 and was intended for adaptation to existing inboard engines. It is said to have worked well but as interest in outboards increased the market for this sterndrive disappeared.*

money for ten more). Developments such as tilting, underwater exhausts, reversing, multiple cylinders, flywheel magnetos, electric starting and, more recently, rotary power, have followed each other over the years.

Weight and noise always were, and to some extent still are, problems, particularly as the horsepower increased to over the hundreds, but the introduction of lightweight alloys, underwater ex-

hausts, vibration elimination, and sound absorbent covers, have all helped. Racing assisted and speeded development, especially of the higher powered outboards, and the Second World War was also indirectly responsible for further research.

Although petrol is usual and has been almost since the beginning of outboard history, diesel and electric units have been introduced from time to time, though these are not and never have been widely used.

The outboard has been applied to almost every use one can think of, both commercially and for pleasure craft, since its beginnings at the turn of the century. Jim Wynne even made an outboard powered Atlantic crossing, in a 22 foot Coronet Explorer in 1958, which would seem to be taking testing to the ultimate. This may have inspired him to turn his attention to the development of the inboard/outboard system, which combines the economy of an inboard engine with some of the versatility and convenience of the outboard. Volvo Penta were pioneers in this field with their Aquamatic units, and we ourselves had a telling demonstration of their practicality in a report on some Caribbean police boats we designed for use with outdrives. The first patrol using the boat had a bumper catch of poachers and smugglers who had not realised that these apparently inboard-engined boats could follow them without damage into the shallows of the mangrove swamps.

Except that these units were required in the specification and were better suited to the size of boat, we might of course have had a similar effect with a jet driven boat. Jet power, like most other things connected with power boats, had been thought of in the seventeenth century but, once again, was one of those inventions that needed the right power unit in the right place and with the right fuel. Its modern development has been largely the inspiration of a New Zealander, Bill Hamilton, who designed his Turbocraft system in the 1950s. A great advantage of the system is the elimination of all the conventional underwater gear and appendages. The only aperture in the bottom of the hull is an intake grid and every other part of the unit is clear above the line of the transom bottom. Apart from its obvious appeal to bathers, water skiers and users of shallow waters, it allows, should you so desire, for spectacular boat jumping — as was once demonstrated for us

Fig. 306   A 20 knot police patrol launch with inboard/out-board units.

Fig. 307   The Fred Cooper designed Dowty Turbocraft jet boat.

by Donald Campbell who drove through the air with the greatest of ease in a flying leap over a causeway between two lakes.

Future

The chance to look into a crystal ball is irresistible. It is impossible not to view the future mainly in the light of what we would like to see, though some of the unpalatable bits seem inevitable.

We are told again and again that the age of leisure is coming and this must mean that power boats, and indeed all yachts, will inevitably have to be easy to look after without too much professional help. Leisure for everybody means high costs per man hour and though the specialists will be needed for the complicated jobs the aim must be to keep these to a minimum and to keep routine maintenance within the capability of the owner, should he prefer and require to do this himself.

In our age of leisure there is likely to be time for not one but a number of hobbies. This means a type of boat owner who has many interests and divides his time between them. He will use his boat, but not all the time. He will like looking after it when he can but will also like to be able to leave it with a fair certainty that it will not corrode, moulder or fall to pieces while he is away. He may be one of a co-operative sharing the initial and running costs, each member of which will want to make full and good use of his time afloat. Or the boat may be chartered and so involve the owner or owners in the increasingly onerous responsibilities laid down by the law for such ventures. This all betokens a particular breed of boat – not less handsome, not less individual, not less likable, but a great deal simpler to use and much less reliant upon day to day yard maintenance and owner overseeing. The designer and builder will make every possible use of every modern convenience and material available ashore and they will continue, as they have done in the past, to inspire new maritime adaptations of some apparently unlikely ones. (Many commercial applications find their way into yachting well before they go into general household use.)

This trend away from the traditional in yachting does not mean that all the 'tiddly bits' of boatwork will disappear; quite the contrary. Just because he has the time and can take pride in how he cares for his boat the owner of the future may well choose to give himself a great deal of trouble and much therapeutic handiwork to do about his boat. The system might well fall into either a 'make work' or a 'no work' category. Our future owner will more than ever be able to select for his boat completely carefree items leaving himself the things he likes doing, whether it is engines, or brightwork, or making model ships out of matchsticks.

If he has not much time or just does not want to do it himself he will be able to have his boat serviced in the same way that he does his car. Marine service stations, for the small boat not necessarily near to the water, will do the 100 hour and 1000 hour servicing with their electronic testing equipment to hand. There is not all that much difference in the consequences of a car breakdown and a boat breakdown. One may happen at 70 mph while the other may happen at sea. Each could have results of various shades of disastrousness, and each 'tool' demands regular care and attention to avoid unnecessary dangers.

In our crystal ball we see a number of aids which will help to make the system idiotproof. We see power pods, as interchangeable as programs in a computer, and traditional engines in capsules for easy removal or transformed with replaceable inserts of parts, instead of the lumps of metal hung round with bits like a Christmas tree one so often sees in the engine space nowadays. In fact, we see every possible item of equipment in the boat sealed and isolated so that it can be replaced as a unit rather than tediously taken to pieces by the yard handyman. We see transistorised electronic controls with sequential circuits to take care of misuse. We see the fuel being sealed in disposable containers which fit into their appropriate tank area, so that the supply is always clean, reliable and there are no foul tanks to see to. We readily foresee the time when no-one will be allowed to empty any kind of pollutant in territorial waters so that every boat will have its own sewage container, with appropriate shoreside disposal. We see the time when no yacht will want to sit and grow weed and barnacles, and so will have its own overcoat (or should it be trousers?) and will wallow cleanly in its personal plastic pool, suitably doctored with anti-fouling fluid.

Inside the boat there will be great use of

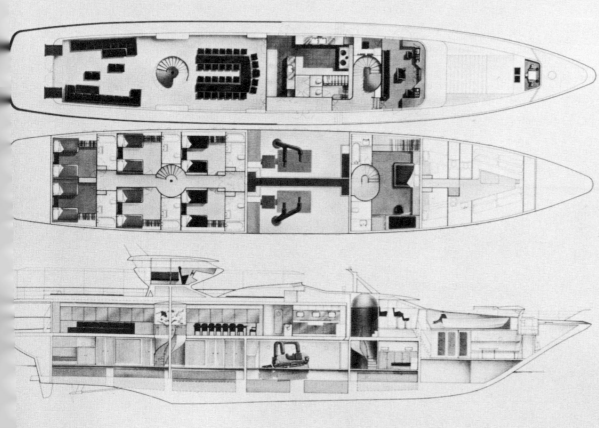

208   Preliminary design studies for a 148 ft hot climate power yacht drawn by us for Souters of Cowes. (Visuals by Arthur
)

washable and replaceable surfaces, fittings and equipment, with many disposable items to make the housekeeping easy for those who prefer to spend their time on other things. Temperature and air condition control will be taken for granted in anything over the size of a runabout, both for the well being of the crew and also to keep the equipment in top operating condition.

In the areas where the boat differs from the shore establishment, that is to say the bits that touch the water, there will also be many changes in the future. For instance, something will have to be done about propellers and the other untidy odds and ends that stick out all over so many modern power boats. The ideal should be a lovely clean underwater form with perhaps only a pair of faired fish fins with internal controls, as stabilisers. Propulsion, if it cannot be done by an energised skin like that of a porpoise or snake or by fin flipping like a fish, ought to be by some kind of water jet. If this is not possible then there might be a retractable hydraulic or electric drive unit, extendable for propulsion and withdrawn to reduce resistance or for maintenance.

Now that electrics are no longer frightening afloat the electric drive might return to favour, especially as some electrical manufacturers show signs of moving with the times (the design of standard electric motors in this country has only varied in detail in fifty years) and now that marinas can provide easily accessible electric power, should regular topping up be advisable. Then of course there are various rocket motors all nicely developed for space use.

As in all aspects of yachting you pick and choose the details you prefer from among the plethora available for each kind of boat. You arrange your boat to suit the kind of life afloat you are looking for. Standards vary enormously, but it is usually true that the unattainable in luxury yachting this year turns up in the more modest vessel the next. We thought it therefore might be interesting to look at some of the items we considered for a design study recently completed for a large and luxurious motor yacht.

It was anticipated, as with all the best pipe dreams, that there will be ample finance to provide life and leisure at sea upon the scale that the owner could command ashore. Engines, therefore, of sufficient power to push her at the

Fig. 309 The Missel *with its suspension system to improve the ride in rough water.*

required speed are specified, as are auxiliary generators, and auxiliaries for the auxiliaries, of ample capacity to provide for any drain when away from a shore supply.

The yacht is to be modern but not exaggerated in style, with perhaps her only departure from the norm an enclosed flying bridge shaped rather like a Fabergé egg. This serves several purposes. It is a private and self-contained area, reached by direct staircase or lift from the owner's suite, where confidential discussion and entertaining may take place. It has an all round view of the deck area (floodlit when required) of the yacht and the surrounding sea and has duplicated handling controls. It will therefore also serve if required as a watch tower, or a docking bridge.

The main bridge is the nerve centre of the yacht and all engine and equipment controls emanate from or are repeated here. It is laid out for a dual purpose, the primary one of course being the command and running of the yacht by her professional crew. It is, however, recognised that a knowledgeable owner and his guests may these days pilot and navigate their own aircraft as well as having close familiarity with all kinds of electronic equipment. So the control and direction of such a delightful plaything as our yacht cannot in fairness be left entirely to her crew. The bridge has comfortable viewing positions for guests and, for the owner, a master command chair complete, Star Trek style, with systems and autopilot controls in the arms. The main displays of radar, speed, depth, etc. are fitted in enlarged overhead screens so that they may be readily seen by everyone. The navigation bay is equipped with all the usual devices plus a programmable table top computer; this enables anyone with the smallest understanding and interest in such arts to plot the course. Over-ride control of all equipment vital to the safety of the yacht remains in the hands of her captain or the owner as appropriate. There are also inbuilt safety factors to avoid damage by the joker who likes to play with the systems control buttons just to see all the pretty lights come up red.

Adjacent to the bridge is the radio room with its contribution to navigation and communications and fitted with everything from document facsimile transmitters to worldwide communications radio, since our owner is not the kind of man ever to be out of touch.

Perhaps the next area of interest, though not

Fig. 310 Hydrofoils at Cowes — but these belong to the Red Funnel ferry. They are still unusual in yachts.

always considered so, is the engine room and its environs. This, as befits the location of the most expensive items of machinery in the whole vessel, is generously spaced and meticulously maintained. It is not, in the proper meaning of the term, unmanned machinery space, but in general it is controlled from a separate observation cabin. The reasons are twofold: the first is that the engine room crew, though they need to keep in close contact with the machinery, do not necessarily want to have to live with it at close quarters all the time, and secondly so that anyone can take more than a passing interest in its complexity and operation. To this end a minor form of *son et lumière* is put in operation, describing by taped sound and indicating lights just what is happening and where and even why. This cunningly encourages a proud interest in their charges on the part of the engineer and his men and educates the passers-by, for interest and amusement, in a little appreciated working area of the ship.

To ease further the operation and care of the systems throughout the yacht we arrange as far as possible for all piping, electrics and other devices, to run through an accessible tunnel. This opens up such jolly possibilities as a crew member being able to clear a blocked drain while madam is still in her bath with neither necessarily being aware of the other.

On deck there is a helicopter landing pad, hydraulic crane for lifting out the boats and a hydraulically operated hatch cover under which they can be stored. The boat compartment shares the yacht's air conditioning system and so they do not suffer from undue weather or temperature variations. There is also a swimming pool on deck for those who do not enjoy the sometimes polluted sea. As an additional feature it may have a translucent bottom so that those in the saloon may view the scene.

The accommodation has all the usual adjuncts

of galley, laundry, deep freeze and so on, plus a medical room with oxygen and other life sustaining items which might be called on in a hurry. Everywhere is air conditioned and can be heated as required. In general, every item of equipment in the yacht has been considered as a replaceable unit if it is at all complex, it being in the long run cheaper to fit a new item than have perhaps unskilled or semi-skilled labour tinkering with it.

There is of course a separate owner's suite and there are guest rooms each with its own bathroom. The crew are equally well accommodated. Every room has its own radio, TV and tape recorder, and there is quadrophonic sound in the saloon and dining room. As an additional diversion there is closed circuit television including a camera with ordinary and infra red lenses fitted under the bow so that the below surface scene can be viewed day or night, and as a side benefit any rocks ahead can be seen in good time.

The saloon is a vast entertainment area which may be opened up with the dining room to make a drawing room 45 feet long. After all, if you have such a pleasure vessel it is only kind to share it.

Aware that the concomitant of such a lifestyle these days is often a job that is demanding and sometimes dangerous, we have also considered

Fig. 311 One factor in the design of boats nowadays is the question and cost of storage when not actually in use. A typical American boat store at Galveston, Texas.

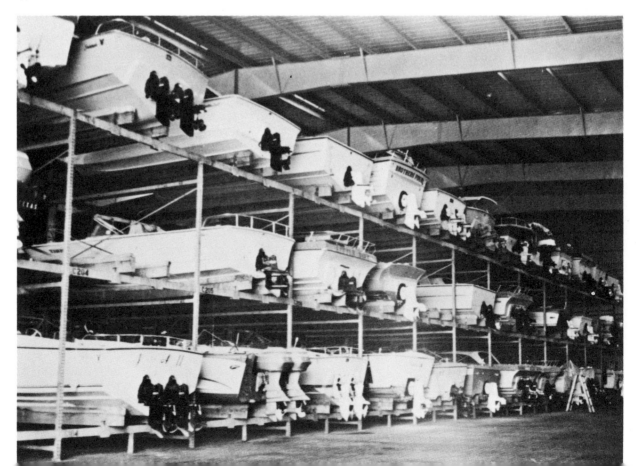

this yacht as a protectable place for confidential meetings or conferences, as well as a place for rest and recreation. A good many of the design considerations therefore serve a dual purpose in these security conscious times, a fact which those who need it appreciate. One Middle Eastern client nodded understandingly when it was pointed out to him that the area marked 'cloaks' just outside his main apartment could easily be relabelled 'and daggers' if he decided to station a guard there.

The Quiet, Soft Ride

Perhaps the two major changes that will come in the future will be in the realms of noise and the provision of a smoother ride. These are the two things which most strongly affect those who power boat. Noise pollution is becoming as acute a topic as water pollution, and it is accepted that nervous resistance decreases as the decibels rise. Therefore we see our boat of the future being silenced both inside and out, so far as it is mechanically and humanly possible. Great atten-

tion will obviously be given to sound absorption, but since the sound waves have to go somewhere even greater attention will be given by manufacturers to producing the quiet power unit, which perhaps brings us back again to the electric drive.

How is the smoother ride to be achieved? We can assume that engine power will grow, and therefore increasing power will be available to compensate for any reduction in planing efficiency necessary to promote the more comfortable ride. To a great extent this is the effect of the deep vee, although it has one or two fringe benefits at some parts of the speed range. Personally we think we have gone if anything too far with the deep vee form and, although we can expect modest improvements in ride along the lines mentioned it seems clear that we need rather more heroic action if we are to do more than nibble at a gigantic problem.

We ourselves have approached the solution from two angles. The first is in arranging some kind of shock-absorbing system in the bottom. At its simplest this has involved the so-called flexible bottom where the internal structure is designed to move with and absorb the shock from an impact

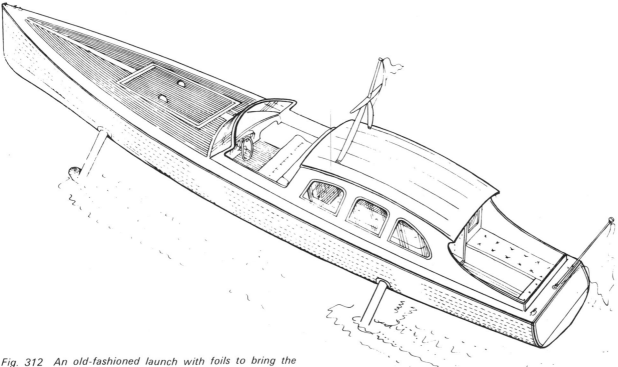

Fig. 312 An old-fashioned launch with foils to bring the performance up to date.

with the sea. This has a certain measure of success and certainly none of the 'flexibles' has ever really had a hard ride. However, the construction of a properly flexible structure is difficult and the result slightly disturbing to the eye. It is odd to watch the bottom heaving as the boat races along — too odd perhaps, and we have only tried this very occasionally. In a way such a construction may provide too great a 'sink' of absorption. The impact energy is frittered away through many different parts of the hull never to be used again. Ideally the energy should be taken and stored, even for a few seconds, and returned to the hull surface when it can be of positive assistance. Thus the hull plunges, the impact is absorbed, the hull pauses and begins to lift again and the impact energy is returned at the right rate and in the right place to lift the craft bodily into her normal trim.

The second approach merely takes the first to a logical conclusion and separates the planing surfaces from the buoyant hull by a shock-absorbing system. This works superbly well. We have a patented prototype called the Missel which has a buoyant hull twelve feet long superimposed on twin planing surfaces which extend forward beyond the hull to give an apparent overall length of fourteen feet and apparent stepped hull form. The surfaces are attached to the hull by means of loose bolts over thick rubber and the principal shock absorbing is accomplished by air bags set between planing surface and hull bottom. These air bags can have the amount of air in them altered quickly by pump and the ride can be soft or hard according to whether the air bags are soft or hard. It really is a stimulating experience to drive such a vessel sitting softly while the bow of the planing bottom thumps away independently. Here is one prophecy then, that soon fast boats used in rough water will incorporate a suspension system greatly to improve the ride, and those without something of the kind will be considered as unsophisticated as carriages without springs.

Perhaps in the same breath we should mention hydrofoils and hovercraft. There is a distressing tendency for engineers and designers to gather into tribes and to have inter-tribal wars. The hydrofoil engineer is a separate specialist from the hovercraft engineer and they are both quite separate from the planing boat engineer. As the marine sociological conditions progress perhaps the barriers will come down, for we have a

suspicion that a dash of hydrofoil and a pinch of hovercraft might improve a great majority of planing boats.

Another factor on which we have done a little work which points to the future is in the aerodynamic design of the hull above water. Fast boats with extensive deck areas are now travelling quite commonly at the speeds at which light aircraft are to be found taking off and flying. It is obvious that considerable forces are generated and that they cannot be ignored as a factor in the performance and ride. In fact a complete small wing fitted right aft makes a great deal of sense in providing an aerodynamic stabiliser. If this were fitted with ailerons it would be a great deal more efficient a trim tab than the metal ones fitted to hulls. Of course, in a 40 knot following wind the whole thing would be useless, but it has such general prospects as to stand a good chance of being a common feature in a few years time.

Surely we will see some determined attempts to produce a real flying fish craft which will flit from wave top to wave top under the control of its pilot, alighting only for another power boost from the obligatory sea propeller. The machinery could be of constant speed type which turned the propeller at the same speed whether travelling light in the air or under heavy acceleration load in the sea. The wear and tear on the engine would be heavy but not at all beyond the wit of man — perhaps some kind of inertial drive might do. The flying would cut down the net resistance and therefore the ultimate fuel bill. Already we are trying to design race boats which spend as little time as possible in the sea, for it is really so much quicker to go by air.

We might also look to marinas to have some influence on the shape of boats of the future. Yacht parking space will almost universally be sold on the basis of overall length and overall beam. The economic vessel will therefore assume a rectangular deck shape. This trend is already well established in America in the form of so-called mobile houseboats. These are now mobile enough, we observe, to win prizes in offshore powerboat races and to cruise enormous distances and, in fact, to assume all the normal functions of a yacht. The rectangular form can be of catamaran or trimaran or gull wing or cathedral or even cheese-grater style, but an outside bet might be made that the sidewall hovercraft could easily

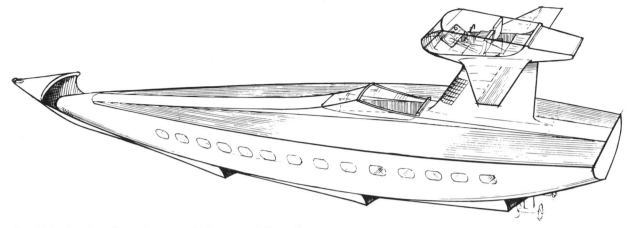

Fig. 313 Another flight of fancy which seems daily to be getting closer.

become a normal yacht form when power becomes just a little cheaper yet.

Perversity and romanticism are not unknown among yacht owners. The more there is a trend towards multiple production plastics, no matter how elegant, some will want to demonstrate their individuality and also perhaps their ability to buy the custom-built article. The hand crafted appearance is more likely to remain among yachts than among, say, cars because a yacht is essentially for pleasure. There is often a strong element of nostalgia and, just as you can now buy a reproduction Model T Ford or a reproduction steamboat, so you may be able to buy reproduc-

tions of other classic power yachts. They may even make the replicas smell of the evocative odours of the past — new varnish, real leather, rope of natural fibre, linseed oil and wet oilskin.

It may take time for a revival of the beautiful craftsmanship and appearance of, say, the launch of the 1920s but it also happens that this launch form is ideal for running a planing surface through the semi-planing speed range. It might not be stretching the imagination too far to think of a future that includes a revival of the old-fashioned gentleman's launch, but complete with retractable hydrofoils to bring the performance right up to date.

Index